HISTORY OF
United States Naval Operations
IN WORLD WAR II

★

V O L U M E   S E V E N

Aleutians, Gilberts and Marshalls
June 1942–April 1944

Rear Admiral Richmond Kelly Turner USN

In the background: Colonel N. D. Harris USMC, Commander J. S. Lewis,
Captain J. H. Doyle

HISTORY OF UNITED STATES NAVAL
OPERATIONS IN WORLD WAR II
VOLUME 7

Aleutians, Gilberts and Marshalls

June 1942 – *April* 1944

SAMUEL ELIOT MORISON

Introduction by
Commodore Commander James C. Shaw, USN

UNIVERSITY OF ILLINOIS PRESS
Urbana and Chicago

First Illinois paperback, 2002
© 1951 by Samuel Eliot Morison; © renewed 1979
by Augustus P. Loring and W. Sidney Felton
Reprinted by arrangement with Little, Brown and Company, Inc.
All rights reserved
Manufactured in the United States of America
P 5 4 3 2 1
∞This book is printed on acid-free paper.

Library of Congress Cataloging-in-Publication Data
Morison, Samuel Eliot, 1887–1976.
History of United States naval operations in World War II /
Samuel Eliot Morison
p. cm.
Originally published: Boston : Little, Brown, 1947–62.
Includes bibliographical references and index.
Contents: v. 1. The Battle of the Atlantic, September 1939–May 1943—v. 2. Op-
erations in North African Waters, October 1942–June 1943—v. 3. The Rising
Sun in the Pacific, 1931–April 1942—v. 4. Coral Sea, Midway and Submarine Ac-
tions, May 1942–August 1942—v. 5. The Struggle for Guadalcanal, August 1942–
February 1943—v. 6. Breaking the Bismarcks Barrier, 22 July 1942–1 May 1944—
v. 7. Aleutians, Gilberts and Marshalls, June 1942–April 1944
ISBN 0-252-06963-3 (v. 1); ISBN 0-252-06972-2 (v. 2); ISBN 0-252-06973-0 (v. 3);
ISBN 0-252-06995-1 (v. 4); ISBN 0-252-06996-x (v. 5); ISBN 0-252-06997-8 (v. 6);
ISBN 0-252-07037-2 (v. 7)
1. World War, 1939–1945—Naval operations, American. I. Title.
D773.M6   2002
940.54'5973—dc21   00-064840

University of Illinois Press
1325 South Oak Street   Champaign, IL 61820-6903
www.press.uillinois.edu

To

The Memory of

HENRY MASTON MULLINNIX

1892–1943

Rear Admiral, United States Navy

Preface

THE PRESENT VOLUME in the *History of United States Naval Operations* picks up the story of the Aleutians campaign in June 1942, where it was broken off in Volume IV. It then describes that mighty sweep of the Pacific Fleet across Micronesia which began with the assault on the Gilbert Islands in November 1943 and included the capture of the Marshalls. Parallel operations in the South and Southwest Pacific have already been covered in Volumes V and VI; Western New Guinea and the Marianas are reserved for Volume VIII.

Except for the gallantly fought Battle of the Komandorski Islands, the tale of this volume is one of amphibious warfare. Both the preparation and the execution of Operations "Galvanic," "Flintlock" and "Catchpole" have been described in detail, so that the reader can understand the anatomy of a major amphibious operation from the first strategic plan to the final Island Secured. These campaigns of 1943–44 were not only important in themselves; they marked a great advance in the art of war; and the assault on Tarawa aroused so much controversy that I felt I must turn it inside out.

In this volume, too, carrier warfare develops new powers; fast carrier strikes complete a revolution in naval warfare that the Japanese began at Pearl Harbor.

Lieutenant (jg) Henry Salomon USNR and I participated in the Gilberts and Marshalls operations and began writing the first drafts of Parts II and III in November of the same year. Mr. Donald R. Martin, who has been on my small staff continuously since February 1943, was with us at Pearl Harbor and there compiled the task organizations, which in this volume have been arranged in a new manner to save space. When the war ended, Parts

II and III were stowed away until additional information, especially from the Japanese side, could be obtained; and such information proved to be so abundant that I rewrote Parts II and III in 1950–51.

In the meantime Commander James C. Shaw had relieved Lieutenant Commander Salomon, and Lieutenant Roger Pineau, one of the Navy's Japanese language scholars, and Mr. Richard S. Pattee, a student of naval history at Harvard University, had joined my staff. Mr. Pattee specialized in submarine operations; Mr. Pineau, in all Japanese aspects. Commander Shaw compiled the first drafts of chapters i, iii and iv; and, out of his ample experience in carrier warfare as gunnery officer of U.S.S. *Bunker Hill,* wrote the Introduction on Fast Carrier Operations. Detached for sea duty in September 1950, he was relieved by Commander Frederic H. White, who supervised the charts, which were drafted by Mr. Charles H. Ward and Miss Isabel J. Gatzenmeier of the Naval War College.

Many officers of the United States Navy, Marine Corps and Army furnished me with information that would otherwise not have been recorded, and in conversation brought out factors and facets which I would not otherwise have known. Among those whose assistance and guidance I wish particularly to acknowledge are: —

The late Mr. James Forrestal, Secretary of the Navy and of Defense, who took me by the hand when this work started, and got me out of Washington, D.C.

Mr. Francis P. Matthews, Secretary of the Navy, who "passed the word" that this series should continue.

Fleet Admiral Chester W. Nimitz, Commander in Chief Pacific Fleet and Pacific Ocean Areas, whose friendly and benevolent attitude provided me with fair winds throughout the Pacific.

Admiral Forrest Sherman, who, as Deputy Chief of Staff for Plans and Operations to Admiral Nimitz, as Deputy Chief of Naval Operations, and as Chief of Naval Operations, has frequently given me valuable advice, information and support.

Admiral Raymond A. Spruance, Commander Fifth Fleet and later President of the Naval War College, who made important suggestions and clarified my views of naval strategy.

Vice Admiral William L. Calhoun, Commander Service Force Pacific Fleet, who himself undertook to indoctrinate me in the rudiments of fleet logistics.

Lieutenant General Robert C. Richardson USA, Commanding General Pacific Ocean Areas, who interpreted the Army point of view in amphibious warfare.

Major General Julian C. Smith USMC, Commanding General 2nd Marine Division, who read the first draft on Tarawa and made valuable corrections and addenda.

Rear Admiral Charles J. Moore, Chief of Staff to Admiral Spruance and previously one of the members of the Joint Chiefs of Staff planning group, who instructed me in the strategy of this series of operations.

Rear Admiral Charles Wellborn, Jr., Deputy C. N. O. for Administration, who ordered mines swept up that obstructed my passage, and enabled me to steam steadily at flank speed.

Rear Admiral Richard W. Bates, Analyst of the Naval War College, who more times than I can remember has given me the "last word" on a disputed point.

Rear Admiral John B. Heffernan, Director of Naval Records and History, who has given me the finest kind of support and encouragement, as well as the benefit of his own wide experience in the Navy.

Captain Ralph C. Parker, Analyst of the Pacific Fleet, whose instructive conversations are memorable for their wit and wisdom.

Captain James M. Steele, Planning Officer on the staff of Admiral Nimitz, who instructed me in the principal steps in planning these operations.

Captain Ernest M. Eller of the Combat Readiness Unit, Pacific Fleet, who received me into the official family at Pearl Harbor and has been a constant source of friendly advice and sound information.

Mr. Robert Sherrod, war correspondent par excellence, who generously gave me the benefit of his experience in the Aleutians and at Tarawa.

Now that the outward passage is ended, and we shall be homeward bound shortly, I wish particularly to thank all the members of my staff, past and present, including Miss Antha E. Card, who began as a Wave and has continued as my civilian secretary. No historian has ever had more able, loyal and devoted assistants and collaborators. They have amply confirmed my decision in 1942 to keep my staff small and expert. Without their help it would have been impossible to have produced seven volumes since the close of World War II.

This volume is dedicated to the memory of Rear Admiral Henry M. Mullinnix, a native of Indiana who graduated from the Naval Academy first in the Class of 1916. He served in destroyer *Balch* of the Queenstown contingent in World War I, and later as engineer officer in other destroyers. In 1923 he completed a postgraduate course in aëronautical engineering at Annapolis and the Massachusetts Institute of Technology, qualified as a naval aviator, and for three years had duty in the engine section of the Bureau of Aeronautics. There he was one of those mainly responsible for developing the air-cooled engine for naval aircraft. In 1927, after helping to fit out carrier *Saratoga*, he served in her successively as assembly and repair officer, assistant air officer and commander of one of her bombing squadrons. During the decade of the 'thirties, he held important positions at the Pensacola and San Diego Naval Air Stations and the Pearl Harbor Air Base; served as navigator and executive officer of seaplane tender *Wright;* as aviation officer on the staff of Commander Battle Force; and as commanding officer of seaplane tender *Albemarle.* Beginning in the "short of war" period of World War II, he commanded Patrol Wing Seven of Catalinas based at Argentia and Iceland, which contributed greatly to the safety of transatlantic convoys. For a year, from March

1942, he was air officer of the Eastern Sea Frontier with immense responsibilities in anti-submarine warfare. Then, following a four-months tour of duty as captain of *Saratoga*, he was promoted to flag rank at the age of fifty-one and given command of an escort carrier division which had the duty of rendering close support to the amphibious forces in Operation "Galvanic."

Admiral Mullinnix, one of the most gifted, widely experienced and beloved of the Navy's "air admirals," lost his life in the torpedoing of escort carrier *Liscome Bay* off Makin on 24 November 1943. He died just as the air arm of the Navy, to which he had devoted the second half of his life, was coming into the fullness of its power and glory.

SAMUEL E. MORISON

Harvard University
February 1951

Contents

List of Illustrations

(All photographs not otherwise described are Official United States Navy)

List of Charts

Abbreviations

Officers' ranks and bluejackets' ratings are those contemporaneous with the event. Officers and men named will be presumed to be of the United States Navy unless it is otherwise stated; officers of the Naval Reserve are designated USNR. Other service abbreviations are USA, United States Army; USCG, United States Coast Guard; USMC, United States Marine Corps; USMCR, Reserve of same.

A.A.F. — United States Army Air Force
AKA — Attack cargo ship; APA — Attack transport; APD — Destroyer-transport
AP — Armor-piercing; HC — High-capacity; HE — High-explosive; all shells.
ATIS — Allied Translator and Interpreter Section
Avgas — Aviation gasoline
BB — Battleship
BLT — Battalion Landing Team
CA — Heavy cruiser; CL — Light cruiser
C.A.P. — Combat air patrol
C.C.S. — Combined Chiefs of Staff
C.I.C. — Combat Information Center
C.N.O. — Chief of Naval Operations
Cominch — Commander in Chief U.S. Fleet; Cincpac-Cincpoa — Commander in Chief Pacific Fleet and Pacific Ocean Areas
C.O. — Commanding Officer
Com — As prefix, means Commander
CTF — Commander Task Force; CTG — Commander Task Group
CV — Aircraft carrier; CVL — Light carrier; CVE — Escort carrier
DD — Destroyer; DE — Destroyer escort; DMS — Destroyer minesweeper
div — As suffix, means Division; Desdiv — Destroyer division
HC, HE — SEE AP
Inter. Jap. Off. — USSBS *Interrogations of Japanese Officials* (1946)
JANAC — Joint Army-Navy Assessment Committee *Japanese Naval and Merchant Ship-Losses World War II* (1947)
J.C.S. — Joint Chiefs of Staff
Jicpoa — Joint Intelligence Center Pacific Ocean Areas

LC — Landing craft; LCI — Landing craft, Infantry; LCM — Landing craft, mechanized; LCT — Landing craft, tank; LCVP — Landing craft, Vehicles and Personnel

LSD — Landing ship, dock; LST — Landing ship, tank; LVT — Landing vehicle tracked (Amphtrac)

N.A.S. — Naval air station; N.O.B. — Naval operating base

O.N.I. — Office of Naval Intelligence

O.T.C. — Officer in Tactical Command

PC — Patrol craft; PT — Motor torpedo boat

RCT — Regimental combat team

SC — Submarine chaser; also Air-search radar; SG — Surface search radar

SCAP — Supreme Command Allied Powers

S.O.P.A. — Senior Officer Present Afloat (or Ashore)

ron — As suffix, means Squadron: Desron — Destroyer squadron

TBS — (Talk Between Ships) — Voice radio

USSBS — United States Strategic Bombing Survey

UDT — Underwater demolition team

VB — Bomber squadron; VF — Fighter squadron; VT — Torpedo-bomber squadron.
M is inserted for Marine Corps Squadron.

WDC — Washington Document Center document; now in National Archives

YMS — Motor minesweeper; YP — Patrol vessel

United States

Aircraft Designations (numeral in parentheses indicates number of engines)

B–17 — Flying Fortress, Army (4) heavy bomber; B–24 — Liberator, Army (4) heavy bomber (called PB4Y by Navy); B–25 — Mitchell, Army (2) medium bomber; B–26 — Marauder, Army (2) medium bomber

C–47 — Skytrain, Army (2) transport; DC–3, Skytrain or Sky-trooper, Army (2) transport

Dumbo — PBY equipped for rescue work

F4F — Wildcat; F4U — Corsair; F6F — Hellcat; Navy (1) fighters

OS₂U — Kingfisher, Navy (1) scout-observation plane

P–38 — Lightning, Army (2); P–39 — Airacobra; P–40 — Warhawk, Army (1) fighters

PBY — Catalina (2) seaplane; PBY–5A — amphibian Catalina; PB4Y — Liberator (4); all Navy.

PV–1 — Ventura, Navy (2) medium bomber

SB₂C — Helldiver; SBD — Dauntless; Navy (1) dive-bombers

SOC — Seagull, Navy (1) scout-observation plane
TBF, TBM — Avenger, Navy (1) torpedo-bomber

Japanese

"Betty" — Mitsubishi Zero–1, Navy (2) high-level or torpedo-bomber
"Emily" — Kawanishi Zero–2, Navy (4) patrol bomber (flying boat)
"Kate" — Nakajima 97–2, Navy (1) high-level or torpedo-bomber
"Mavis" — Kawanishi 97, Navy (4) patrol bomber
"Sally" — Mitsubishi 97, Army (2) medium bomber
"Zeke" — Mitsubishi Zero–3, Navy (1) fighter, called "Zero" in
     1942–43

Introduction

Fast Carrier Operations, 1943–1945

By Commander James C. Shaw usn

BY THE CLOSE of 1942, after the battles of Coral Sea, Midway, Eastern Solomons and Santa Cruz had been fought, both Americans and Japanese expected that carrier *vs.* carrier battles would be repeated. But these flattop duels ceased abruptly with the end of the Guadalcanal campaign, partly because both sides wished to rebuild their depleted carrier strength and train new air groups, but mostly because the first Allied offensives of 1943 in the South and Southwest Pacific could be readily covered by land-based planes. The crucial carrier battles of 1942, with their attendant glory, elation, despair and improvisation, have never been repeated, but the exploits of such fliers as O'Hare, Waldron and McClusky were never dimmed by those of their successors.

The United States Navy's shipbuilding program included 24 large *Essex*-class carriers (27,000 tons) and 9 light carriers of the *Independence* class (11,000 tons) fabricated on cruiser hulls. By the summer of 1943 these ships were joining the Pacific Fleet and their arrival ushered in a new phase of carrier warfare, the hit-and-stay offensive. In the fall of 1943 *Essex*, the new *Yorktown* and *Lexington* and the new light carriers *Belleau Wood, Independence* and *Cowpens* tried their wings against Wake and Marcus Islands. In November *Saratoga, Princeton, Essex, Bunker Hill* and *Independence*, thrusting at Rabaul, withstood a vicious onslaught by all available first-line enemy planes.[1] For the first time in the Pacific war since *Hornet's* strike on Tokyo, United States carriers emerged from an all-out attack without damage.

[1] See Volume VI of this History, pp. 323–36.

This pleasing outcome could have been predicted by anyone who knew the characteristics of the new carriers and their aircraft. Instead of the slow Wildcat (F4F), the speedy Hellcat (F6F) and gull-winged Corsair (F4U)[2] rose to meet Japanese planes which had not been altered since Pearl Harbor. On the decks of carriers and screen alike, anti-aircraft weapons now sprouted in great profusion. Five-inch guns with improved controls, Swedish Bofors (40-mm) replacing the unsatisfactory 1.1-inch, and 20-mm guns with tracking sights increased anti-aircraft efficiency many fold. The carrier superstructures bristled with radar antennae which piped pips into Combat Information Centers, where they were evaluated as friend or foe; and if foe, could be promptly chased by fighters accurately conned from the ships. The plane complement of the big carriers was 90; that of the light carriers, 45; not counting spares.

The development of weapons continued. One of the carrier bomber's disadvantages was limited punch; unlike a ship's gun, it could hit only once. To offset this, planes carried heavier bomb loads and adopted the vicious 5-inch rocket. Fighters were converted into fighter-bombers. Torpedoes, eccentric enough when launched from ships, posed greater problems in planes. The slow speed and low altitude required for torpedo launchings offered an unacceptable hazard to the pilot. By the simple expedient of a drag ring placed on the nose of a torpedo, its falling rate was sufficiently reduced to permit launching at double the speed and at many times the previous altitude. The whole gamut of airborne weapons, excepting the atom bomb, was explored by carrier planes.

Air support of amphibious operations passed from experiment to a fine art. By the time of the Okinawa campaign, carriers shuttled planes to the battle front by timetable, each strike reporting

---

[2] All three types were armed with six .50 caliber machine guns, but the last two carried almost twice as much ammunition as the F4F. The F4F "had an approximate speed of 300 m.p.h.," the F6F and F4U of "more than 400 and 425 m.p.h."; the Helldiver dive-bomber (SB2C) "more than 250" as compared with the SBD's top speed of 230 m.p.h. The TBF increased torpedo-bomber speed from 150 to more than 250 m.p.h. E. J. King *U. S. Navy at War* (1946) p. 215.

to the ground coördinator for target assignment. The Marine Corps, after persistent pleas to be allowed to furnish some of its own ground support, was allotted space on carrier decks for Marine Air Arm planes.

Within each carrier Mother Necessity prompted swift development. More guns, better radar, and faster fire-control solutions were provided to fight Japanese resistance which stiffened as the war moved closer to the home islands. Damage control — the ability to quench fire, halt flooding and patch machinery — an orphan trade in the prewar Navy, so matured that after 1943 only one fast carrier (*Princeton*) was lost, although *Franklin* and *Bunker Hill* suffered grievous damage. Intricate compartmentation, the fog nozzle, fire-fighting schools and the use of screening vessels as fire boats prevented wounded flattops from burning and sinking.

It is easy now to ignore the details of sea warfare in the days of sail. We remember that in 1805 Nelson's fleet of 14 sail pursued Villeneuve's fleet of 28 across the Atlantic and back. Or we remark that the Battle of the Saints was a victory of Rodney's 36 ships of the line over De Grasse's 34. Yet few today can appreciate the quality of seamanship required to keep station with heavy-hulled and high-sided square-riggers, the coördination required to maneuver and fight these ships in confined waters. Perhaps our forebears were at fault for not describing what they took for granted. So we, hoping to have readers a couple of centuries hence, when the airplane carrier of 1945 will be as obsolete as the Seventy-four of 1775, wish to record the technique of operating planes from a carrier. That technique resembles a great work of art in its deceptive simplicity, the result of vast energy and long preparation.

At the top of the carrier organization and of the carrier itself was the captain, a naval officer who had qualified as an aviator many years before. He was responsible for some 2500 souls, 95 to 100 aircraft and 27,000 tons of ship. At sea this officer lived on the narrow bridge, sleeping fitfully in the adjoining emergency cabin. He depended entirely on his subordinates for knowledge of the ship's internal functioning. During a voyage he relied heavily on his second in command, the executive officer, to see that all went well below decks.

At a lower level were the department heads of navigation, air gunnery, communications, engineering, damage control, supply and medicine. "Exec," navigator and air officer were fliers. The others could be line officers or specialists in their own departments. Another key figure, the air group commander, was subordinate to the air officer in matters of shipboard administration but still possessed a great deal of autonomy on board ship. Once aloft, he took complete operational control of his aircraft. When the carrier was in port and his planes were based ashore, he became an administrative commander as well.

Thus, with the exception of the air department, the administrative setup coincided with that of a battleship or cruiser. In the carrier, however, there existed a greater overlap in interests of department heads. Gunnery was intimately tied to the procurement and custody of aircraft ammunition. Communications had a hand in fighter direction, a function of the air department. The first lieutenant (also damage control officer) was responsible for the ship's cleanliness and hull integrity, and gave instructions in these matters to all departments. The engineer officer furnished steam and "juice" (electricity) for the intricate mechanisms of all departments. Supply and medical departments worried not only about food and health but about spare airplane wheels and aviation medicine.[3]

The carrier air group was subdivided into squadrons by type: fighters, scout (dive) bombers and torpedo planes, each captained by a squadron commander. In the early days, the air group commander personally entered the attack. Later, as target coördinator, he circled high over enemy ships and radioed instructions to his fliers regarding what and when to attack.

The passage of time in a carrier was measured not by calendar

---

[3] Doctors qualified as "flight surgeons" wore a distinctive wing insignia, were required to put in flight time and were entitled to flight pay.

but by strikes — so many weeks since we hit Rabaul, so many until we jump Tarawa. At the forward base there would be hectic days of loading ammunition, fuel, food and planes, repairing and testing weapons and machinery. At night there were movies on the hangar deck. Occasionally the crew produced a "Happy Hour" — amateur theatricals and boxing bouts; but the Navy seldom brought the United Service Organizations to the highly advanced bases frequented by carriers. Sometimes liberty was granted. Officers crowded into a Quonset hut where, after purchasing a book of coupons, they could fight their way to the bar and drink bourbon and chlorinated water from wax-paper cups. Enlisted men landed on a beach where they played softball, drank their quota of two beers and wished they had not left the ship. The sailors' favorite recreations were reading mail from home, basketball games on the hangar deck and swimming over the side.

Finally the task force sorties for the strike, ships filing out with the solemn majesty of priests marching to high mass. Once clear, the columns break as if shaken by a giant Neptune, the ships wind in various directions until they are disposed in neat circular task groups. Several days of target practice and mock strikes by the air group follow. The eve of the strike always comes as a surprise. Men ask each other, "Already? So soon?"

Aye, this is it. Through the midwatch the great ship, swathed in darkness, knifes toward the dawn launching position. On the bridge the officer of the deck cons the carrier, issuing occasional low-voiced orders to helmsman or engine room, acknowledging the routine reports of lookouts, quartermaster and radar watch. Despite the proximity of shipmates, each man of the watch finds the silent bridge a solitary station where memories, hopes and fears swarm through his mind. After all, on the morrow it will be each individual aligned against the odds of death; common cause and common peril unite shipmates but the ruthless choices of the dark angel make war a lonely business.

Throughout the vessel other men are awake with their thoughts; engineers, watertenders, radiomen, and gunnery and damage control watches. There are those whose tasks are not routine but peculiar to the character of the "Big Day"; the ordnance men below decks who, stripped to the waist, wrestle bombs and torpedoes from magazines, hoisting them into the bomb racks and torpedo bays; radio engineers who adjust aircraft radios for the last time; mechanics who ready plane engines on which pilots' lives will depend; cooks and bakers who stand before the mammoth ranges and ovens preparing a man's meal for men who will do a man's job. These toilers are mostly too happily occupied to think abstractly. And there are the slumbering hundreds who embrace sleep gratefully as a physical need and a mental release.

Two hours before sunrise a bugler climbs the island ladder and asks the officer of the deck: "Reveille on time, sir?" "On time," is the reply. He keys a few trial notes, pushes down a switch and points the bell of the bugle at a microphone. A strident call pierces the ship, and is followed by a boatswain's mate's imperative "Reveille! Reveille! All hands! Up all bunks!"

Below decks, lights flash on in staterooms and compartments. Men bring minds slowly into focus while stumbling into clothes. Through the head of one sailor runs crazily and insistently the words of a song, "There's gonna be a great day." Another curses softly, unable to find his shoes. A third, entering battle for the first time, spins his brain with the wish that time would do some of that fugiting the ancients talked about. Someone chuckles harshly and says, "Jeez! This is the day we get the big chow!"

A big chow it is. In wardroom and general mess the carrier sailors sit before plates heaped high with thick steaks, fried eggs, fried potatoes, butter-dipped toast, all to be washed down with black coffee. College men hark back to breakfast before a big game, when they ate a similar meal and felt just such mixed emotions.

There is a subtle difference in attitude between a carrier's wardroom and those of other warships. In a cruiser or destroyer, months may pass without a casualty; in a carrier every strike day brings death to someone. Everyone realizes that some of these present are eating their last meal. There are curious, furtive glances from table to table. Then, too, in the flattop there is the certainty that, if the enemy attacks, this ship will be the prime, probably the only target.

Now bugler and boatswain's mate become more demanding. Flight Quarters sounds, followed shortly by General Quarters and the word, "All hands man your battle stations." Scurrying of feet and slamming of bulkhead doors is soon over, and the carrier settles down for her day's doings.

On the flight deck, dark to eyes not yet adjusted, moving figures ghost through the ranks of silent planes. The air officer, perched on the port side of the island, shreds the silence with an announcement over the flight-deck bull horn. The steeds are ready, what of the riders? Gathered in the ready rooms just under the flight deck, pilots listen to last-minute briefings from intelligence officers and squadron commanders — where the enemy is, how he must be met. In coveralls, helmets, parachute harnesses, gun belts and life jackets with oxygen tubes, these flying sailors are no longer the young men who boarded the carrier in the States. Now they are apart, the ultimate link between the citizen at home and the enemy. Of what use is this giant floating aircraft hatchery if they, the pilots, do not deliver the lethal goods? Like the wardroom, the ready-room atmosphere is charged with concealed emotion.

Word floats into the ready-room: "Pilots, man your planes!" Each man grips his navigational chart board, climbs the ladder to the hangar deck, threads his way to where his plane captain — the mechanic charged with upkeep — greets him alongside his own plane. If it be a dive- or torpedo-bomber, the pilot will talk briefly with his crewmen; if a fighter plane, he will fly alone. Once in the cockpit, the plane captain helps him to adjust shoulder straps and leans over his shoulder until the bull horn growls Start Engines! Then a snarl and a sputter as propellers whir, miss, catch and burst into throaty roars. All up and down the after part of the flight deck the blackness is gently torn by exhaust flames flickering like fireflies in a summer garden. The engines settle down to rhythmic pounding while dawn spreads light over the eastern horizon.

On the flag bridge the admiral glances at the latest dispatches, turns to his flag lieutenant and gives an order. Over voice radio the signal rasps out for a turn into the wind to launch aircraft. "Execute the signal!" The carrier heels heavily as the rudder turns hard over. On the yardarm the red and white Fox flag at the dip, meaning that flight operations are imminent, flutters frantically as the speed to windward makes a wind down the deck like a small gale. When the ship is steady on her new course, word goes to the signalmen, "Two-block Fox," and the flag soars to the yard. This is the signal to commence launching, and the captain heads his ship handsomely so that the wind is slightly on the port bow, the best angle for take-off.

The most important man in the ship is now the flight-deck officer, standing abreast the island structure, holding aloft a black-and-white checkered flag. His assistants, the flight-deck chief and the taxi signalmen, gesticulate to the pilots of the leading fighter planes — headshaking, nodding, pointing and beckoning. These signals the pilot obeys in bringing his plane into the take-off spot. The flight-deck officer thrusts his left arm upward and twirls his hand rapidly; the pilot pushes his throttle far forward, racing the engine to a piercing crescendo. The plane quivers and strains at its braked wheels. Suddenly the flight-deck officer points at the pilot, who curtly nods, indicating his readiness to be off. The flight-deck officer glances quickly up the deck, sees all clear, and abruptly brings his flag down. Brakes released, the plane trundles forward, gaining momentum until the tail lifts; then, just short of the bow, the wheels leave the deck. The first plane steers a course slightly to starboard, running lights glowing. Once clear of the formation, it circles in an appointed area awaiting its fellows.

On the carrier another plane maneuvers into "the spot." The flight-deck officer repeats his ballerina motions and the tires hum down the wood. One after another the planes are tossed aloft, fighters first, followed by dive-bombers, and last of all the grossly laden torpedo planes which commence their runs from far aft. Some planes of the outgoing strike are housed in the hangar deck. At intervals an amidships or after elevator descends, swiftly scoops up a plane and rushes it to the flight deck, where it posts off in a hurry.

In short order the deck stands empty; everyone sighs a "Well, that's over," and turns-to on his next job. Planes for the next strike are deftly spotted aft by the blue-shirted, plane-handling crews. Chockmen in purple shirts slide wooden blocks in front of wheels, gasoline crews in bright red jerseys run out hoses to top off gas tanks; ordnance men slip fuzes into bombs and check machine guns. Meanwhile the attack group has formed into huge Vs and winged over the horizon; the combat air patrol has taken station in the zenith, the admiral has altered courses in the desired direction of advance.

It will be a matter of hours before the strike returns, but there are no dull moments. The fighter-direction officer, informed of a suspicious radar contact, vectors out a fighter section. Soon the electric word "Tallyho!" (bogey or bandit [4] sighted) comes in from the fighters, followed by an announcement that the plane sighted is an enemy scout. Regardless of whether or not the fighters nail the snooper, reporting it as "Splashed one bandit," the presence of an enemy plane bodes no good for the task force. The ship's anti-aircraft gunners cast long glances at the sky and make superfluous adjustments to their weapons.

When, later in the morning, radar screens glow with nebular indication of approaching aircraft, fighter-direction officers wait anxiously for identification — friend or foe? [5] It is our strike returning. When they come in view, everyone counts plane noses; yes, some are missing and — look — two falter behind. Trouble over the target. Planes approach the carrier group from a designated bear-

---

[4] Bogey is an unidentified plane; bandit, a plane identified as enemy.
[5] Early in the war there was no radar identification device, and only by knowing when friendly planes were due and from what direction they would come, and by vectoring-out fighters, could one be sure. Later the IFF (Identification, Friend or Foe) made identification more nearly certain, but it was never positive.

ing, sweeping wide to reassure touchy anti-aircraft gunners. "Fox" whips into the air, the carrier slews into the wind, individual planes break ranks like homing ducks and enter the landing circle, the prescribed counter-clockwise route around the formation which will place them in position for consecutive landings. Each must approach from the port quarter.

All eyes on the flight deck shift to the landing-signal officer, who coaches fliers onto the flight deck. The first plane floats lazily into the "groove" astern of the ramp and the landing-signal officer waves two paddles ribboned with yellow strips. He dips one arm to indicate that one wing is low, he holds an arm outstretched to indicate that the pilot is coming in too fast; he raises both arms — the plane is too high for a safe landing. Finally, just as the plane reaches the stern, he gives a quick motion across his throat with one paddle, meaning "Cut the engine!"

The plane hits the deck lightly and rolls forward swiftly. Suddenly, as if a giant invisible hand had reached out, the plane halts; the arresting-gear wire has caught in the dangling tail hook. The plane rears up like a broncho, bounces and squats. Out from the gallery walkways dash two green-helmeted hookmen to disengage the wire. A taxi signalman beckons the pilot; the plane runs forward, perches on an elevator and then disappears below to the hangar deck. A second plane comes in seemingly almost in the slipstream of the first. More and more land on board at remarkably brief intervals. Now one of the cripples, part of his wing fabric in tatters, approaches the groove with wing flaps only partially down. The landing-signal officer guides him watchfully; then, just before the "cut," waves his paddles criss-cross overhead for a "wave-off." The pilot gives her the gun and the plane swoops over the flight deck and off to port for another try. This time he gets on deck, bounces and fails to catch a wire, and piles headlong into an athwartship barrier of head-high steel cables. The wires enfold the fuselage like the tentacles of an octopus and stand it unceremoniously on its nose. Immediately the craft is surrounded by a swarm of men led by asbestos-clad characters who look like old-fashioned teddy bears; these are the fire fighters, known as the "hot papas." Fortunately no flame bursts out, but one of the plane's crew is wounded. Pharmacist's mates and the flight surgeon remove the injured man on a stretcher and take him to sick bay by elevator. A tractor crane appears from below and lifts the damaged plane clear. If badly wrecked, it will be thrown over the side; if not, struck below for repairs.

As the forward flight deck fills with planes, more and more men, like fairy-tale brownies, gather around the craft to refuel and rearm them. When the last incoming plane hits the deck, Army-style jeeps put out from forward of the island, hook onto the tails of planes and tow them aft to be spotted for another strike.[6]

Viewed objectively, the whole scene is one of indescribable confusion; many a battleship sailor on board a carrier for the first time winces at the apparent lack of order. In reality it is efficiency to the highest degree; the seeming merry-go-round is a natural consequence of many different kinds of tasks going forward at once.

When the second strike is lined up on the after section of the flight deck, another launching is pulled off, and so throughout the day as long as the admiral feels that possible profit outweighs the certain risk of remaining in a small area. For, unless the enemy lies to windward, frequent turning into the wind for flight operations holds the carriers to a small patch of ocean. The predicted advance of the ship along any given track might be no more than four knots.

On a strike day the amount of coffee drunk by the ship's company reaches a staggering quarter-ton, twice the normal consumption. It is brought to the highest gun stations in used powder cases; is put into percolators in every nook and cranny below decks. Along with the coffee go huge cartons of fresh doughnuts; and at noon plank-size sandwiches are served at battle stations.

The admiral, the staff Intelligence officer and the air group com-

---

[6] Jeeps were not used on board carriers until 1943. Prior to that the men of the air department (disdainfully called "Airedales" by deck ratings) acted as plane pushers to shove them into position, 8 or 10 men at a time heaving on each plane.

mander put their heads together after the first strike. What happened? The air group commander gives a terse account based on his own observation and those of his flying mates; much of it is conjecture, since aviators attacking in the face of enemy fighters and flak cannot see much of what goes on. Photographs taken on the scene, hastily developed by the ship's photo lab and scanned by trained interpreters, are more valuable than human eyes.

Although possible at any time of day, enemy retaliation would most likely occur after return of the first strike by some of his planes trailing ours home. Then a spine-tingling bugle call — Torpedo Defense — rings out with martial urgency. "Murrrder, Murrrder!" the sailors chant with the bugle as they prepare to fight off enemy aircraft.

Now, like a football team relinquishing the ball on downs, the task group shifts to defensive tactics and formation. Radar grids cease circling and settle on the bearing of the foe, anywhere from 30 to 100 miles distant. The general alarm bangs out its deep, menacing "Bong! bong! bong!" Button up the ship, sailors, put on your tin hats and stand by for a ram! Combat air patrol wings out on courses sent from the carrier. A falling star flares on the far horizon: some plane down in a dogfight. Cruisers and destroyers shoulder closer to lend a hand in anti-aircraft action.

Perhaps C.A.P. knocks down the entire enemy brood; it sometimes happens. But no chances are taken, so that when the silver sheen of a dive-bomber formation clears the clouds, the carrier and defending ships loose a vociferous 5-inch barrage. When the bombers dive, rushing pell-mell down the gun sights, the worried chatter of light guns joins in, followed by the excited protests of heavy machine guns. The sky flowers with black shellbursts, brightens with glistening tracer streams. Enemy planes are hit, burst into flames and splash; others pull out into the "flat" and rush for the far horizon. When surface lookouts report torpedo planes, the carrier, already slithering right and left, begins a fast turnaway to give the "Kates" a long approach while screening vessels fire desperately and voluminously. Bombs bracket the carrier and throw up blobs of soiled sea water. One plumping into the flight deck explodes with a shower of debris. In the excitement nobody in the carrier hears the noise, although many are hurled from their feet. Torpedoes swish parallel to the hull. In two, perhaps three minutes it is all over; the din-filled air is clear, the guns are silent. If the carrier is wounded, the previously idle repair parties — fire fighters, carpenters, ship fitters, electricians — swing into action. They douse fire with lacy spray from fog nozzles and the lather of chemical foam. A hole in the flight deck is quickly covered with a piece of sheet metal. The dead and the wounded are carried below. Then up goes Fox again, and the carrier faces the wind to launch aircraft. Such a carrier is luckier than some; no torpedoes have penetrated her hull, no fire has gutted her hangar deck. Of the eleven fast carriers fighting in the Pacific at the end of 1943, only two went through the war unscathed, but only one was sunk.

At dusk, when the last combat air patrol taxies up the flight deck, even the men serving in the deep caverns of the magazines and firerooms know something of what has happened. In the wardroom and mess halls, men gather to exchange tales. On one such occasion a flier said, "Danger and excitement! I love it!" Everyone laughed briefly. They had food for conversation for a lifetime, but many never enjoyed much of a lifetime. Others did not love that danger and excitement but had to endure it; for, as Admiral Halsey once remarked, the drivers might change but the horses would keep on going right into Tokyo Bay.

PART I

The Recovery of the Western Aleutians

June 1942–August 1943

West Longitude dates, Zone plus 10 time.[1]

For ne'er can sailor salty be
Until he sails the Bering Sea,
And views Alaska's dreary shore
And fills himself with Arctic lore.

Columbus and Balboa too,
With Nelson form a salty crew,
But they are fresh to you and me —
They never sailed the Bering Sea.

So when you boast of fiercest gale,
That ever ocean you did sail,
You can not salty sailor be
Until you cruise the Bering Sea.

— Trident Society *The Book
of Navy Songs.*[2]

[1] The dates and time used by Allied forces. The Japanese used East Longitude dates and Tokyo time, Zone minus 9. Both time zones were widely at variance with local sun time, as the critical meridian of Zone plus 10 is 150° W. For instance, at 0630 "local civil time," sunrise at Kiska would be logged as 0830 by U.S. forces, and as 0330 the following day by Japanese forces. It is not always clear whether data obtained from the Japanese after the war are in their dates or ours; JANAC sometimes lists ship sinkings in one and sometimes in the other. When in doubt I have used both dates, as "23/24 August."

[2] New York, Doubleday, Page and Company, 1926.

CHAPTER I

Nine Months' Arctic Warfare[1]

15 June 1942–18 March 1943

1. *Aleutians Situation*

THE ALEUTIANS theater of the Pacific war might well be called the Theater of Military Frustration. No flag or general officer on either side, with the exception of Rear Admiral McMorris, there won fame or fortune. None of the operations accomplished anything of great importance or had any appreciable effect on the outcome of the war. Sailors, soldiers and aviators alike regarded an assignment to this region of almost perpetual mist and snow as little better than penal servitude. Both sides would have done well to have left the Aleutians to the Aleuts for the course

[1] O.N.I. Combat Narrative *The Aleutians Campaign* (1945); Advance Intelligence Ctr. N. Pacific Report No. 880; War Diaries and Action Reports of participating units, particularly that of Com North Pacific Force. Wesley F. Craven and James L. Cate *Army Air Forces in World War II* Vol. IV *The Pacific, Guadalcanal to Saipan* has an excellent chapter on this campaign. Buaer interviews with Cdr. J. S. Russell 28 Oct. 1942 and Lt. Cdr. P. Foley 8 Jan. 1943. Four Special Staff U.S. Army Hist. Div. translations of reports made for SCAP by Japanese armed forces after the surrender: "The Aleutian Islands Campaign" (No. 851–51), very detailed and documented; "Naval Operations in the Aleutian Area (No. 851–53), which has little on events of this period; "Northern Area Operations" (No. 851–91), the most useful; and "Northern Area Monthly Combat Reports (No. 851–52). USSBS Interrogations: No. 606, Aerographer's Mate W. C. House (the weather man captured on Kiska) "Japanese Second Mobile Force and the Kiska Garrison"; No. 98, Cdr. Kintaro Miura "Aleutian Campaign, Seaplane Operations"; No. 99, Cdr. Nifumi Mukai "Occupation of Kiska, the Kiska Garrison"; No. 100, Capt. Sukemitsu Ito "Japanese Flying Boat Operations in the Aleutians"; No. 101, Capt. Taisuke Ito, and No. 102, Cdr. Shigefusa Hashimoto, "Planning and Operations"; No. 367, Vice Adm. Sentaro Omori "Operations of the 1st Destroyer Squadron"; No. 408, Lt. Col. Kazumi Fujii "Japanese Army Garrisons on Attu and Kiska"; No. 461, Maj. Masuda Shimada, "Deployment of Japanese Army Forces in the Kuriles."

of the war. And that, the Americans would have done — had not Admiral Yamamoto, in his expansive mood of early 1942, directed a carrier raid on Dutch Harbor and taken Attu and Kiska.[2]

These two virtually uninhabited islands were occupied by 1800 Japanese troops on 7 June 1942. Vice Admiral Boshiro Hosogaya, Commander in Chief Northern Area Force, was responsible for their defense. On the other side, Rear Admiral Robert A. Theobald, Commander North Pacific Force, was responsible to Admiral Nimitz for keeping Attu and Kiska pounded down until forces could be spared to recover them.

Japan had no plan to invade Alaska, and American strategists had ruled out invading Japan via this short but rugged route. Japan's object was merely to hold Attu and Kiska, while the American purpose was to prevent any military build-up in these islands, to sever their sea communications with Japan and to destroy their usefulness to the enemy, while awaiting an opportunity to recover them. Yet the high command on neither side would give its local commanders the forces to attain even these limited objectives. The needs of Guadalcanal, Gona-Buna and the Central Solomons pulled everything south. Hosogaya's base at Paramushiro in the Kuriles lay 1200 miles north of Tokyo and 650 miles west of Attu. Ships sailing for Kiska had another 378 miles' steaming through reef-infested waters. Yet a regular service of freighters had to be maintained in order to build up the garrisons at Attu and Kiska, to construct airfields and install defenses.

On the American side Admiral Theobald, who now flew his flag over shore headquarters at Kodiak, felt neglected; but he had at his disposal a sizable cruiser task force commanded by Rear Admiral William W. Smith, a destroyer striking group, six S-class submarines and a flock of Coast Guard cutters and other small craft.[3]

---

[2] See Volume IV of this History, chapter ix, for the Aleutians phase of the Midway campaign.

[3] See Vol. IV 172–74 for task organization in early June 1942. Before the end of the month the naval air arm in this sector was placed under Gen. Butler, and Rear Adm. John W. Reeves relieved Capt. Ralph C. Parker as commander of shore-based naval activities and patrol craft.

Brigadier General William O. Butler USA commanded the XI Army Air Force, an expanding striking group, mostly medium bombers and fighters with a few Flying Forts, but including a useful and growing group of PBYs under Captain L. E. Gehres, based on tender *Gillis*. Major General Simon Bolivar Buckner USA, Army commander of the Alaskan Sector, had only a token garrison, mostly at Fort Morrow on the base of the Alaskan Peninsula.

Distance and weather hampered American operations as they did the Japanese. Fort Glenn, Umnak, 536 miles east of Kiska by air and 660 by sea, was the westernmost American airfield. About 60 miles eastward lay Dutch Harbor, Unalaska, the only American naval and seaplane base in the Aleutians, inadequate at best and damaged in the 4 June raid. Another 155 miles eastward by air or 30 more by sea lay Fort Randall at Cold Bay on the Alaskan Peninsula, with a good Army airfield. Kodiak, the principal advanced military and naval base in Alaska, where Admiral Theobald based his North Pacific Force, is 372 miles east of Cold Bay by air, 505 miles by sea. All supplies for American armed forces had to come from Seattle, and that meant a flight of 1742 miles or a sea voyage of 1957 miles to get reinforcements and matériel up to Umnak.

Any offensive plan by either side was more than likely to be smothered by Alaskan weather, as the season of almost constant fog begins in June. Weather in the Aleutians is always unsettled and often very thick and rough. The hazards of surface and air navigation are greater there than in any other part of the world. Thus, conditions were perfect for a stalemate, and that is what there was for a period of nine months.

In June the Americans staged two bombing offensives against Kiska. The first, on 11–13 June, by Atka-based PBYs and Army bombers from Cold Bay, damaged a destroyer and a "Mavis" or two in the harbor, but cost three Catalinas, and Captain Gehres's tender *Gillis* found Atka too hot to stay. Now the Army Air Force

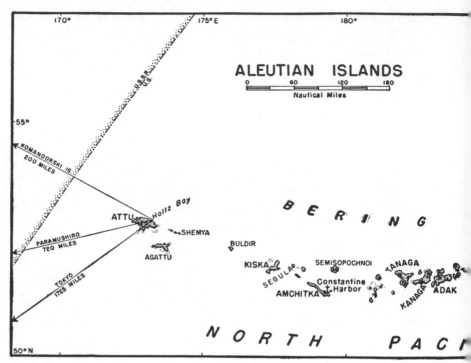

took over. Its first mission, of eight bombers led by Major Russell A. Cone USA, sank transport *Nissan Maru* in Kiska Harbor with a bomb dropped from 15,000 feet. The Japanese at Kiska were not greatly hampered by these raids, but after the transport had been sunk, seaplane tender *Kamikawa Maru* prudently retired to Agattu, 90 miles west. Major Shonen Hozumi on Attu had an easier task than his opposite number at Kiska, since Attu was beyond bombing range of American planes.

On the last day of June Admiral Hosogaya led a formidable task force, containing carriers *Zuikaku, Ryujo, Junyo* and *Zuiho*, from Ominato in northern Honshu, to protect a convoy centered around seaplane carrier *Chiyoda* and transport *Argentina Maru*. The convoy made Kiska 3 July, delivering 1200 men for the garrison — a 100 per cent reinforcement — and six midget submarines. The carriers milled around for a few days hoping to engage American

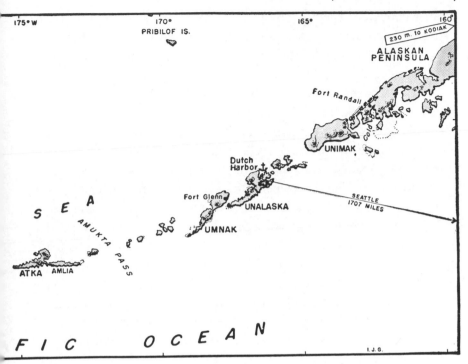

bombers, but thick weather and heavy seas gave them few opportunities. Hosogaya would have been better advised to concentrate on anti-submarine rather than on anti-bomber warfare. On 4 July destroyer *Nenohi*, escorting *Kamikawa Maru* off Agattu, was sunk by submarine *Triton*; and next day destroyers *Shiranuhi* and *Kasumi* were crippled and *Arare* was sunk near Kiska by torpedoes from *Growler*.[4] Ten days later *Grunion* sank two Kiska-based subchasers. *Grunion* was last heard from 30 July when she reported a torpedo attack on an unidentified enemy ship; the circumstances of her loss with all hands are still a mystery, but it is suspected that she was a victim of one of the 200 mines that the Japanese had planted off Kiska.

In August 1942, when the Guadalcanal campaign began, Admiral Nimitz pulled all fleet submarines out of the North Pacific. The

[4] For details of these attacks see Vol. IV 216–19.

S-boats continued their Arctic patrols all summer but were unable to make more than a few nicks in the Paramushiro–Kiska supply line. On the other hand, Japanese submarines accomplished nothing whatsoever in Alaskan waters.

Admiral Yamamoto withdrew the four carriers and other capital ships southward on 7/8 July. This left Hosogaya in command of a skeletonized Northern Area Force. Because of his weakness afloat, he concentrated on creating facilities for land-based bombers to defend the Japanese Aleutians. He decided to build airstrips on Attu and Kiska. The work went on very slowly for lack of construction equipment capable of coping with the spongy muskeg and the underlying frozen volcanic ash. Crews of float-equipped "Zekes" and flying boats, flown in as stopgap defenders, had a miserable time. Out of 24 fighters brought to Kiska in early July, 16 were lost operationally and 6 were destroyed by American bombers; after 60 days only two were usable. The big bombers fared little better. Most of their flights were "weathered out" and the only ship they struck at was seaplane tender *Gillis*, which Captain Gehres had again brought west, this time to Adak. On the morning of 20 July she was attacked from high altitude by three "Mavises" and defended herself gallantly and successfully, sustaining no damage. That episode ended Japanese offensive bombing in the Aleutians campaign. Never, after Yamamoto pulled the carriers out, was Japanese air strength in the Aleutians any obstacle to American air or sea power.

It would have been wiser in the long run to have left the Japanese in Kiska and Attu alone to get frostbite on the muskeg — the Arctic counterpart of that "withering on the vine" so often spoken of elsewhere. But Washington could not let them off so easily. The administration was needled by complaints of American soil being left in Japanese possession. Fears lest Attu and Kiska spearhead an invasion of the Pacific Northwest were being voiced by amateur strategists. In American hands, these two islands would safeguard the route for lend-lease shipping from the West Coast to Vladivostok; and if Russia entered the war against Japan they would be valuable for staging planes to Siberian bases.[5] Even granted that they had a mere nuisance value in Japanese possession, the nuisance should be rubbed out. Admiral King frequently urged Cincpac to "explore and press all possible active measures" against the enemy, and Admiral Nimitz as frequently asked Admiral Theobald to propose something. But Comnorpac felt that he could do little with what he had; he growled at the Army Air Force to cut out inaccurate high-level bombing and come down out of the clouds. Unfortunately the clouds lay snug as a bedspread on the ocean, so if a plane came down it usually splashed.

2. *Bombardment of Kiska, 7 August*

Admiral Theobald was, however, ready to try a naval bombardment of Kiska. On 18 July he hoisted his flag in *Indianapolis* (Captain Morton L. Deyo) at Kodiak, and next day sortied with the entire striking force.[6] The outward passage was uneventful except for the loss of a sailor overboard; although quickly recovered, he was already dead of exposure in frigid waters. On the night of 21 July, as the force approached Kiska in a thick fog, it fueled from tanker *Guadalupe* (Captain H. R. Thurber), without damage. After steaming about next day, hoping the fog would lift, Admiral Theobald postponed the bombardment and retired eastward. He returned on the 27th, groped through a cream-thick fog off Kiska, and again canceled the bombardment. During retirement, upon a 90-degree course change, two of the four destroyer-minesweepers smacked each other, and a third was rammed by destroyer *Monaghan*. All four ships could steam at reduced speed, but there was danger from their working in the heavy seas, and the Admiral did

---

[5] Russian propaganda in 1951 accused the United States of building bases in the western Aleutians in order to attack Russia. The exact contrary is true. A leading motive for all American efforts in the Aleutians was to help Russia.

[6] Cruisers *Louisville, Honolulu, Nashville, St. Louis;* destroyers *Case, Reid, Gridley, McCall, *Monaghan;* destroyer-minesweepers *Lamberton, Elliot, *Long, *Chandler.*   * Damaged in this mission.

not care to risk his force within gunfire distance of Kiska without
a preliminary sweep for mines. Accordingly he retired. It is too
bad that he did not take a chance, because Kiska Harbor at that
time was chock-full of shipping.[7]

Upon returning to Kodiak Admiral Theobald took his flag ashore
for keeps and gave Admiral Smith command of the second Kiska
bombardment mission. Comprising the same ships as the first, less
the four cripples, it sortied 3 August 1942. Catalinas scouted ahead,
searching for holes in the fog, and by noon 7 August "Poco" Smith
had enough fair-weather reports to warrant a close approach to the
island. Navigators plotted a course by dead reckoning, run forward
from celestial fixes two days old, and prayed that unpredictable
currents had not set them too far off. At 1630 approach disposition
was formed, the Admiral bent on 20 knots, and into a fog bank
south of Kiska plunged the ships. An hour and a half later they
emerged into a relatively clear space, and each cruiser hustled two
SOC spotting planes aloft. But before land was sighted the water
shoaled rapidly, fog closed in again and as the navigators could not
figure out where they were the Admiral decided to haul out and try
again. Upon his second approach at 1934, shouts of "Land Ho!"
and cheers were heard from the leading destroyers. The fog had
lifted and there, lo and behold, were the jagged, snowstreaked
mountains of Kiska which few sailors in the task force had ever
seen.

Kiska is a caterpillar-shaped island three to four miles wide, with
a 4000-foot volcano at the northeast head from which the 22-mile-
long body wriggles southwesterly. Halfway down its length Kiska
Harbor bites into the eastern shore and South Head juts out two
miles, nearly joining Little Kiska Island to form the southern arm
of the bay. Most of the Japanese installations were on the northern
and western shores of this harbor. Admiral Theobald's bombardment plan — warmed over from the 27 July fiasco — would have
been considered laughable later in the war, when the old naval
superstition of never exposing ships to shore batteries had been

[7] Three DDs, 2 small minelayers, a tanker, a 10,000-ton transport and 2 freighters.

overcome. Instead of shooting from the harbor mouth within view
of the Japanese installations, he steamed back and forth between
four and six miles south of South Head, over which all his ships
had to shoot by indirect fire, at ranges between 14,500 yards for

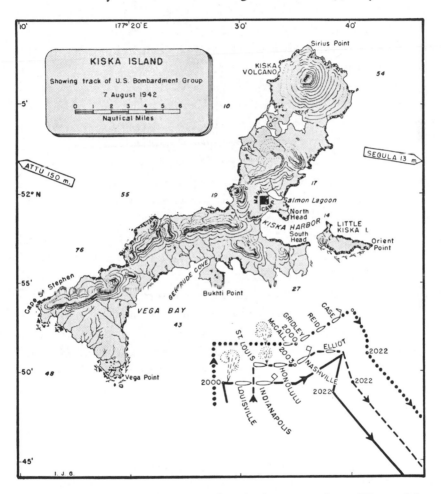

the destroyers and 19,500 yards for the heavy cruisers. That might
have been very well if the cruiser's planes had been able to spot fall
of shot, but a flight of float "Zekes" swarmed at the slow SOCs like
hawks after pigeons, forcing the Americans to duck into clouds,
which defeated their purpose of spotting gunfire. A shore battery

on South Head started chipping paint off *Elliot's* sides with shrapnel from near-misses; a "Zeke" spotting for shore batteries buzzed in and out of the clouds too fast for anti-aircraft gunners to get their sights on him, and dropped a white smoke streamer which helped Japanese guns to get the range and hold it. Another "Zeke" attacked *Case* with bomb and bullets while a "Mavis" tossed bombs through the overcast. After half an hour of this, the heavy cruisers had expended their ammunition allowance, and a submarine periscope was reported. Accordingly, at 2021 August 7, Admiral Smith signaled Cease Firing, turned southeasterly, recovered aircraft and retired. The SOCs were in bad shape from enemy fighter and anti-aircraft fire; one had 167 bullet holes (counting one in the pilot's heel) and two others had over a hundred each; one plane from *Indianapolis* was lost. Those from *St. Louis* could not find their ship but had enough gas to skip eastward along the island chain until they reached Umnak.

The bombardment did score. Captain Taisuke Ito, who had just flown in to inspect defenses, sat in a foxhole and watched the shells "fall like rain." The barracks on the north side of the harbor went up in smoke. Landing barges on the beach were reduced to pulp. A moored "Mavis" was sunk and two others damaged beyond repair, leaving only two which were later withdrawn. *Kano Maru* (8572 tons), a freighter already crippled by a torpedo from *Grunion*, caught fire and became an easy mark for Catalinas which sank her later the same day. But two destroyers, three subchasers and the midget subs were untouched, and only a few men were killed.

3. *Adak and Amchitka*

Before Hosogaya had a chance to think up a counterstrike, Theobald moved again. His object was to establish an airfield within fighter-plane distance of Kiska so that bombers could be escorted all the way there and back. The Army Air Force wanted it on Tanaga Island, 160 miles east of Kiska; Admiral Theobald objected because Tanaga had no anchorage where supplies could be landed, and argued for Adak, 50 miles farther east, where there was an ample all-weather harbor. Both sides appealed to the Joint Chiefs of Staff. These first decided on Tanaga, assuming that no airstrip could be built on Adak in less than four months; but Theobald kept right on hammering until General Marshall and the J.C.S. reversed themselves in his favor.

Fortunate indeed was the choice of Adak. When occupation forces landed, 30 August, they found an almost ready-made airfield, a flooded tidal basin. Army engineers drained and filled it in so that within ten days it was an airstrip. On 14 September the first Kiska-bound fighter-bomber strike flew off from Adak. Already 31 Lightnings and 16 Liberators nested there.

In August the Japanese high command decided to abandon Attu and concentrate on Kiska, as the better "road block" of the two. The garrison was transferred by transports and destroyers in three echelons between 27 August and 16 September. Hosogaya covered this movement with the few combatant ships that Yamamoto had left under his command, but the Americans never caught on. The only contact was made by a submarine, *RO–61*, which entered Nazan Bay, Atka, during a moderate gale on 29 August and slashed open the hull of seaplane tender *Casco* with a torpedo. The tender, with 5 dead and 20 wounded, beached herself safely and later made dry dock in Kodiak, but the submarine did not escape. Next day a Catalina dropped a depth bomb which opened seams in the boat's hull, starting a telltale streamer of oil which destroyer *Reid* (Lieutenant Commander Harry H. McIlhenny) trailed until she made sound contact. Two depth-charge attacks damaged *RO–61* and forced her to the surface where *Reid's* gunners finished her off. *Reid* signaled *Casco*, "Got sub that got you. Have five survivors for proof!" [8]

Autumn sets in early in these northern latitudes. By 1 September

[8] A sister boat, *RO–65*, sank with all hands in Kiska Harbor 3 Nov., "for unexplained cause," according to Japanese records — their euphemism for an operational casualty. The midget subs never saw action in the Aleutians.

it was too late to attempt the recapture of Kiska or Attu; and as the long Arctic night approached it became more and more difficult to sustain a strategy of attrition. On 14, 25 and 28 September and 8 October, bombers and fighters, including some of the Royal Canadian Air Force, mauled Kiska, destroying float planes, strafing bivouacs, damaging two RO-boats and sinking two transports totaling 15,000 tons. On 16 October Army fliers hit and exploded destroyer *Oboro* and damaged destroyer *Hatsuharu* with a bomb on her stern which sent her limping homeward. But the imperative needs of the South Pacific drained the North Pacific of surface and air strength. By the end of October *Honolulu, Louisville* and *St. Louis* had gone south to fight for Guadalcanal, and six 4-stack destroyers had sailed to the West Coast for conversion to fast transports.

Fog screened not only enemy activities; it was responsible for the new Adak strip not being discovered until early October. Even then Adak was subjected only to nuisance raids by small float planes. American submarines, reduced in number, found few targets. The most notable action occurred on 26 October, when *S-31* sank *Keizan Maru* off Paramushiro.[9] Attrition was continued by XI A.A.F. bombers, now expert at hitting anchored ships, although all their skill was insufficient to cope with Aleutian weather. "November blew in with a terrific storm. With 80-knot winds howling and a foot of water on the Adak strip, nothing flew." [10] On 26 November they got *Cheribon Maru* (4016 tons) in Holtz Bay, Attu; next day *Kachosan Maru* (2427 tons) at dock in Attu was "waterlogged and stranded" by the Army fliers. Through most of December this air force was grounded, but it celebrated New Year's Eve by sinking one 3100-ton *Maru* and damaging a second at Kiska.

American occupation of Adak revived Japanese apprehension of an American plan to invade *Dai Nippon* via the Kuriles. Imperial Headquarters caused deserted Attu to be reoccupied before the

[9] See Vol. IV 217–18.
[10] *Army Air Forces in World War II,* IV 371, 373. During the 5 months June–Oct. 1942, the XI A.A.F. lost 72 planes, only 9 of them in combat.

end of October, and sent 1115 more troops into Kiska on 2 December.[11] These troops might otherwise have been committed to Guadalcanal.

Admiral Theobald, observing that a static condition existed, agreed to release cruisers for Guadalcanal, and by 1 December his force comprised only light cruisers *Detroit* and *Raleigh*, four destroyers and a few motor torpedo boats and small craft. The main item on his agenda was the preparation of bases for a forward sweep in the spring. Dull business at best, it was accomplished in spite of darkness, foul weather, spongy or rugged terrain and short supply over the long logistics line. At Adak Seabees and Army engineers worked under floodlight to build quarters for 15,000 men, erect hangars, warehouses, piers, radio stations and dry docks. On Atka an emergency airstrip was constructed for use when Adak was "socked in," and another was planned for Tanaga. At Sand Bay, Great Sitkin Island, a fueling dock, oil tanks and ammunition storage were built at the foot of a smoking volcano. The lack of diversion for men stationed in the Aleutians was more than compensated by the amount of work to be done.[12]

On the other hand, everyone had a good laugh over the unusual logistics supply furnished to a certain high-ranking naval officer. After trying in vain to grow flowers around his shore headquarters in chopped-up muskeg and volcanic ash, he asked Commander Supply Base San Francisco to send him a little fertilizer. That accommodating officer caused a DC–3 to be loaded with manure and dispatched to the Aleutians base. An Army sergeant who opened the door of this plane on its arrival was heard to remark, "Jeez, the war's over! They're sending us horse manure by air mail!"

The war was far from over for scouting Catalinas of Patwing 4. Blow high blow low, thick weather or clear, they had to fly. This

[11] This unit, in 2 transports escorted by 2 light cruisers and 2 destroyers, left Paramushiro 23/24 Nov. with the object of occupying Shemya. Because of the air attacks on Attu of 26–27 Nov., Admiral Hosogaya shifted it to Kiska. ("The Aleutian Islands Campaign" p. 62.)

[12] Data on Aleutians logistics from Rear Adm. Worrall R. Carter.

meant warming up the engines with blowtorches, scraping snow and melting ice off the wings, loading heavy bombs or torpedoes with numbed hands, taking off in the dark, sometimes down-wind with an overloaded plane, and, if the plane were water-based, with frozen spray obscuring the windshield. Aloft in dirty weather radar navigation prevailed, radio aids to airmen in the Aleutians being few and far between. The altimeter, calibrated on barometric pressure, could be very misleading if the plane flew through a weather front where the pressure changed. Any craft forced down into the wild open sea was doomed, and unless rescued promptly the survivors died of exposure. On the flight home there was always the danger of being dashed to bits against a mountain while the plane "hung on the props" over the field, waiting for a hole in the overcast. Once safe ashore, the crew had to help overhaul their Catalina. In the early days of the campaign the PBY ground crews lived a sort of gypsy existence, begging tools, clothes, food and even shelter from the Army or any naval vessel that happened along.

Another outfit which found the Aleutians anything but fun was the motor torpedo boats. The PTs were brought into this area with the notion that under cover of perpetual fog they could easily torpedo enemy ships. Motor Torpedo Boat Division 1 (Lieutenant Clinton McKellar, with *PT–22, –24, –27* and *–28*), recently a part of Midway's defense force, was ferried to Seattle and on 20 August departed under its own power for a 2500-mile voyage through the Alaska Inland Passage and Gulf to Dutch Harbor. There the boats arrived 1 September. Shortly after they pushed on to Adak, where they stood by to repel any possible Japanese landing. When none materialized, they doubled as scout and supply craft for the Army or laid mines. Winter lined the insides of PT hulls with as much as two inches of frost on which the tiny gasoline galley stoves made no impression. Spray and green water, freezing topside, weighed the boats down dangerously. In a squall two collided and all four took refuge in a small cove. For four days they attempted to ride out a gale with indifferent shelter. Anchors dragged and cables parted, three boats dragged ashore, two fetching up on a snowbank. Patrol craft came to help, towlines parted or jerked cleats out of the decks like loose teeth; but three of the four boats were pulled clear.

Destroyer-minesweeper *Wasmuth* (Lieutenant Commander Joseph W. Leverton) was another foul-weather victim. While steaming slow in a gale on 27 December, two of her depth charges shook off and their explosion so close aboard (she was making less than 6 knots) snapped her keel. Tanker *Ramapo* tried in vain to tow the sinking four-stacker, but saved all hands.

Amchitka, a big island with a good harbor 200 miles west of Adak and only 90 east of Kiska, was the next American objective. Aircraft based there could exploit small breaks in the weather, and it would be too bad if the Japanese got there first. Admiral Theobald initiated the move, Admiral Nimitz agreed, and on 21 December 1942 the J.C.S. authorized it to take place a fortnight thence. That ended another bitter controversy, since the Army command had opposed the Amchitka move. Although Theobald was right, as events proved, Admiral Nimitz decided that he was unable to get along with the sister service, and on 4 January 1943 had him relieved by Rear Admiral Thomas C. Kinkaid.[13] At the same time Rear Admiral W. W. Smith was relieved as commander of the cruiser-destroyer strike group by Rear Admiral Charles H. McMorris.[14]

In preparation for the Amchitka landing, the XI A.A.F. made a series of heavy strikes. On 5 January 1943 it sank *Montreal Maru* (6577 tons) at Kiska and *Kotohiro Maru* (6101 tons) off Attu,

[13] A biographical note on Kinkaid will be found in Vol. V 88; one on Theobald in IV 166.

[14] Charles Horatio McMorris, born Alabama 1890; Annapolis 1912 (5th in his class, where his nickname "Soc" was a tribute to his Socratic wisdom); service in battleships; helped fit out *Shaw* and served in her in the Queenstown destroyer force; "exec." of *Meredith*, C.O. *Walke*, 1919. After a tour of shore duty, navigator of *Baltimore*; "exec." of *Burns*; instructor in seamanship, flight tactics and history at Annapolis, 1925–27 and 1930–33 and in the interval commanded destroyers. Navigator *California* 1933–35; senior course at Naval War College; operations officer Hawaiian detachment U.S. Fleet 1939–41; war plans officer Cincpac staff to April 1942; C.O. *San Francisco* May–Nov. 1942. Chief of staff Cincpac June 1943; Commander Fourth Fleet 1946; General Board of the Navy; Commandant 14th Naval District 1948.

each laden with troops and weapons. A small Army garrison commanded by Brigadier General Lloyd E. Jones USA landed on the 12th at Constantine Harbor, Amchitka, from four transports escorted by destroyers, while McMorris's force, *Indianapolis, Raleigh, Detroit* and four destroyers, lent close support. As Amchitka was uninhabited, there was no opposition, but the Aleutian Neptune claimed a destroyer. *Worden* (Lieutenant Commander William G. Pogue) slipped through the surf-lined harbor entrance before dawn to land scouts. On heading out, an unpredictable current swept her onto a pinnacle rock which punctured her hull at an engineroom. *Dewey* tried to tow her clear, but the cable parted and *Worden* drifted helplessly onto a wave-lashed lee shore. When she broached, the skipper ordered Abandon Ship, but it was too cold to save all hands in rough water at 36° Fahrenheit. Fourteen sailors were drowned and *Worden* became a total loss.

When the Americans moved into Amchitka, the Japanese realized that they must either get out of the Aleutians or strengthen their garrisons, finish the airfields and attack the enemy supply line. But any such tactics would put an unbearable strain on shipping, already depleted by the Guadalcanal campaign and United States submarines. Yet they dared not evacuate, lest the Kuriles lie open to American or Russian attack. So Imperial Headquarters on 5 February 1943 decided "to hold the western Aleutians at all costs and to carry out preparations for war" in the Kuriles. Admiral Hosogaya could have benefited by an earlier decision. He knew he had only a month's grace before the American air force at Amchitka, aided by the northing of the sun, would cut his lifeline. Frenzied attempts were made to build an airfield on Kiska, but "unexpected rocks and poor construction materials," as well as "increasingly fierce" air raids, thwarted the efforts of the Japanese engineers, and by 1 April the strip was only half completed. At Attu "conditions were better than on Kiska . . . but it was regrettable to have had no machines such as bull dozers." [15] The strip

[15] "Northern Area Operations" p. 2; "The Aleutian Islands Campaign" pp. 100–01.

at the head of Holtz Bay was not yet ready when the Americans landed on 12 May.

4. *Bombardment of Attu, 18 February*

Admiral Kinkaid now ordered more air strikes and sent McMorris's cruiser-destroyer force to cover the approaches from Japan to Attu and Kiska. On receiving a report from submarine *S-28* of shipping at Attu, "Soc" McMorris approached that island to bombard the shore and fight the ships. Sunrise was actually visible on 18 February; and Attu's icy mountains loomed gaunt and majestic. For once, quartermasters could enter in their logs, "Ceiling and visibility unlimited."

The Admiral, in light cruiser *Richmond*, formed his four destroyers and *Indianapolis* in column. They passed Holtz Bay and Chichagof Harbor to starboard, all eyes searching for ships, but they had all departed; so at 1450 the Americans countermarched to engage enemy shore installations to port. Mountain peaks cast monstrous shadows toward the ocean and the contrasting glare of icefields made the gun pointers squint. At the head of Chichagof Harbor nothing was visible except a vast expanse of snow. Spotting planes reported abandoned trenches and gunpits, but as air photos showed signs of human activity the ships opened fire at five-mile range, making ugly holes in the white, like burns in a blanket. The ships coursed by Holtz Bay, countermarched and closed for a starboard run. But at Holtz Bay the enemy was concealed by snow, and the gunners could only march their salvos up and down, right and left, and hope that they were hitting something. At 1637 McMorris signaled Cease Firing and retired northwestward. According to the Japanese, only slight damage was done by this direct-fire bombardment.[16]

[16] "Naval Operations in the Aleutians Area" p. 39. Casualties 22 or 23 killed, 1 wounded. One building destroyed. Yet on 13/14 Feb., in an air attack, 14 officers and men were killed by a direct hit on a bomb shelter. ("Aleutian Islands Campaign" p. 169.)

McMorris now divided his force for anti-shipping patrol. *Indianapolis, Coghlan* and *Gillespie* under command of Captain Vytlacil maneuvered in loose scouting line about 120 miles southwest of Attu, hoping to pick up something. Shortly after four bells in the evening watch 18 February, an officer on the bridge of *Indianapolis* noticed a lookout in the bow staring intently to starboard. Raising his binoculars, he saw what appeared to be a ship's funnel in the moonlight. It belonged to 3100-ton *Akagane Maru*, with a load of munitions for Attu. *Indianapolis* shaped a course to intercept, challenged, and, upon receiving an answer in Japanese Morse code, opened fire at a range of 6700 yards. Her third 8-inch salvo hit, and the ship burst into flames. Captain Vytlacil wanted her disposed of quickly, so ordered the destroyers to torpedo her. *Coghlan* fired one torpedo which ran hot, straight and normal under the *Maru* but did not explode; another which "prematured" short of the target; a third which passed ten yards astern. It was now *Gillespie's* turn. One torpedo failed to explode, a second frolicked on the surface like a porpoise and missed. *Coghlan* closed range and pumped in several shells but still the wreck floated. She tried one more torpedo which prematured. Now the destroyer sailors knew how the submariners felt about defective weapons.[17] Finally, at 0124 February 19, destroyer gunfire sent the ship down. Two other Japanese army transports which escaped detection by the Americans turned back without discharging their passengers or cargoes.

From air reconnaissance and observations made during the bombardment Admiral Kinkaid inferred that Attu, with no airfield, no coast defense guns and meager anti-aircraft weapons, would be a softer nut to crack than Kiska. As the North Pacific Force had long considered Kiska the prime objective, plans for taking it had reached an advanced stage. But the Admiral and Major General John L. DeWitt USA, commanding ground forces in the Alaskan sector, could get neither the shipping, the supplies nor the men for an operation of the strength that they thought neces-.

[17] For causes of poor torpedo performance see Vol. IV 230–34.

sary. The J.C.S. told them in effect that they could plan and train to their hearts' content, but not try to take Kiska in the near future. So the Admiral, after talking things over with the General and his staff, on 3 March proposed to substitute Attu as the next target. Only a small force would be .required, much of it already on tap in the Aleutians. Admiral Nimitz on 18 March obtained J.C.S. consent and set the date for 7 May, before the foggiest part of the year-round fog season should set in.

While these interesting negotiations progressed, the XI Army Air Force, including its Navy Catalina squadrons, increased the tempo of attrition. The Japanese who were endeavoring to complete airstrips on Attu and Kiska received bomb and bullet doses six or seven times a day in clear weather and sometimes even in bad. After each visit the local commanders begged for more men and better equipment. Admiral Hosogaya had run the blockade once, on 9 March; now he decided to try again, and on 22 March departed Paramushiro in command of two heavy cruisers, two light cruisers, four destroyers and three transports, destination Attu. This move, foreseen by the Americans, precipitated a sea battle in Aleutian waters.

CHAPTER II

The Battle of the Komandorski Islands[1]

26 March 1943 [2]

OFF the Komandorski Islands between lats. 53° and 53°30′ N there took place on 26 March 1943 a naval battle that has no parallel in the Pacific war. A small task group under Rear Admiral Charles H. McMorris fought a retiring action against a Japanese force, under Admiral Hosogaya, of twice its size and fire power; the battle lasted without a break for three and a half hours of daylight; the contestants slugged it out with gunfire at ranges of eight to over twelve miles, without the intrusion of air power or submarines. It was a miniature fleet action of the sort that the Navy, after World War I, had expected to fight in "the next war," with one important difference, that neither side did the other any great hurt.

Admiral McMorris's task group had been cruising on a north-south line west of Attu for several days in order to intercept

[1] Action Reports of CTG 16.6 (Rear Adm. McMorris) and of individual ships; Admiral William S. Pye's Report on the battle, as a result of putting it on the game board at the Naval War College; Cominch Secret Information Bulletin No. 7 "Battle Experience Solomon Islands and Alaskan Areas March 1943"; Buships War Damage Report on *Salt Lake City;* conversations with Rear Adm. McMorris, Cdr. W. S. Bitler and other officers of *Salt Lake,* 7 Nov. 1943. On the Japanese side, a detailed account by Cdr. M. Okumiya in *Inter. Jap. Off.* 399–402, with chart contributed by C.O. of *Tama;* personal narratives by Cdr. K. Miura and Cdr. S. Hashimoto of Admiral Hosogaya's staff on pp. 98–100, 111–15, and by Cdr. T. Kuwahara on pp. 207–08 of same, and the U.S. Army Hist. Div. translations listed in chap. i footnote 1, above; Salomon docs. obtained through SCAP in Tokyo, 1946.
[2] The action took place west of the international date line; but as the North Pacific Force operated on Z plus 10 time, with date as if in long. W, I have followed their practice. Subtract 3 hours to get approximate sun time for the position of this fight. The Japanese used Tokyo time (Z minus 9) and date 27 March.

Japanese reinforcements. He flew his flag in 22-year-old light cruiser *Richmond*, Captain Theodore M. Waldschmidt. Destroyer Squadron 14, Captain Ralph S. Riggs, comprising *Bailey, Coghlan, Dale* and *Monaghan*,[3] acted as screen. A recent and fortunate accession to the group was *Salt Lake City*, Captain Bertram J. Rodgers; "Swayback Maru," as the crew called this thirteen-year-old heavy cruiser because of her pronounced sheer. She had spent six months being repaired after the Battle of Cape Esperance, and with a new crew, almost half of them fresh from boot camp, had just relieved *Indianapolis*. On 11 March, when assigned to the North Pacific Force, she had had but a week of intensive firing practice. Eleven days later she joined McMorris, who had commanded *San Francisco* in the Battle of Cape Esperance and knew what to expect of *Salt Lake*. Although she had never worked with these ships before, she was destined to become their sword, their shield and their buckler in time of trouble.

At 0730 March 26, an hour before sunrise, this task group lay 180 miles due west of Attu and 100 miles south of the nearest Komandorski Island. The ships were strung out in scouting line six miles long, steering N by E. Destroyer *Coghlan* was in the van, flagship *Richmond* next, followed by *Bailey* flying Captain Riggs's pennant, then *Dale. Salt Lake City* steamed next to last in the column, *Monaghan* in the rear. They were making 15 knots and zigzagging. Temperature was just above freezing point. The Arctic day was breaking, light SE airs barely ruffled the surface of a gently heaving sea, and visibility was so good under a 2500-foot overcast that lookouts reported fish broaching many miles away. As one stood on the bridge or forecastle, there was nothing but the swish of a bow wave to break the sweet silence of the sea, so seldom experienced in high-speed naval operations.

The crews had just finished breakfast and were going to dawn general quarters when the van destroyer and the flagship, almost at the same moment, made radar contact on five vessels between

---

[3] Commanded respectively by Lt. Cdr. John C. Atkeson, Cdr. Ben. F. Tompkins, Cdr. Anthony L. Rorschach, Lt. Cdr. Peter H. Horn.

7½ and 12 miles due north. Admiral McMorris promptly ordered his ships to concentrate on *Richmond*. In the dim morning twilight lookouts aloft and radar men at their scopes below vied with each other to make out what manner of ships these were. They appeared to be transports or cargo carriers screened by destroyers and perhaps one light cruiser. As light increased with the coming day, more and more ships were sighted; but, as McMorris later confessed, he still anticipated a "Roman holiday." Gunners saw that ready boxes were filled and gave their pieces a final polish. Prisoners were released from the brig, messmen sliced bread for sandwiches, cooks put coffee on to boil, and all preparations were made for a morning's battle.

A few minutes after 0800 the prospect changed radically and most unpleasantly. First one heavy cruiser and then another was made out, rapidly approaching gunfire range on McMorris's starboard bow; the auxiliaries were now on his port bow. And soon a couple of light cruisers hove into sight.

McMorris had run into Admiral Hosogaya's entire fleet. He was running reinforcements into Attu under escort of every combatant ship at his disposal. Heavy cruiser *Nachi* led a column composed of heavy cruiser *Maya*, light cruiser *Tama*, destroyers *Wakaba* and *Hatsushimo*, light cruiser *Abukuma*,[4] destroyer *Ikazuchi*, two fast and heavily armed 7000-ton converted merchant cruisers, *Asaka Maru* and *Sakito Maru*, which were doubling as transports; destroyer *Inazuma* in the rear. They were on a northerly course approaching a rendezvous with slow freighter *Sanko Maru* which had been sent ahead with one destroyer as escort.

About the same time that the Americans made their first radar contact, the navigating officer of *Asaka Maru* sighted the masts of a ship against the southern horizon 13½ miles distant. Presently more masts appeared. Hosogaya then ordered his force to turn southeastward and engage, while the two *Marus* continued on

---

[4] Flagship of Desron 1, with Rear Adm. Tomokazu Mori in command. These cruisers, completed 1920–21, were slightly smaller than *Richmond*, and carried seven 5.5-inch guns in their main batteries as compared with her ten 6-inch.

their course out of the way. The turn had already begun when the Americans identified them.

They outnumbered the American force more than two to one. *Maya* was longer, heavier and three years newer than *Salt Lake City;* both she and *Nachi* were rated at 35½ knots' speed as against *Salt Lake's* 32¾. And at 0810 *Salt Lake* was still more than three miles behind *Richmond*, endeavoring to catch up. Should McMorris accept battle against these odds? And if he did, how would he fight? Or if he retired, in what direction? He decided on the bold course of trying to catch and sink the transports while his own force was under long-range gunfire, and then to retire at high speed. It was rather a thin hope that Admiral Hosogaya would let him close the transports near enough to damage them; but the Japanese might make a mistake, and even if they did not, the United States bomber patrol flying from Amchitka and Adak, who were promptly notified, might catch the transports.

These were some of the thoughts that passed through the Admiral's mind, and some of the elements in his decision; but the main factor was probably that McMorris wanted a fight badly, and knew that his men felt the same way. Not for nought did his parents name him Horatio! And wisely, as Nelson would have done, he informed Captain Rodgers of *Salt Lake City* that flagship *Richmond* would conform to the movements of the more powerful heavy cruiser.

No spotting planes were launched by the Americans, as McMorris decided to conserve the flagship's against possibly greater need at a later hour, and *Salt Lake's* one available plane had been degassed. *Nachi* launched a spotting plane, possibly two; but owing to poor communications and brisk anti-aircraft fire from the American ships it did the Japanese little good.

At 0840, before the American ships had had time to close into battle order, the enemy opened fire on *Richmond* at 20,000 yards, made a close straddle on the second salvo, and then shifted to *Salt Lake City*. Throughout the action "Swayback Maru" received most of the enemy's attention; he would not waste ammunition on ships whose main batteries could not reach him at extreme ranges. *Salt Lake* commenced return fire with her forward turrets at 0842 and at a range of over 20,000 yards made hits on *Nachi* with her third and fourth salvos, starting a fire that looked serious but was quickly brought under control.

Nevertheless, Hosogaya by changing course and closing range had frustrated the American attempt to get at the transports. McMorris regretfully decided to turn away and forget the auxiliaries for the time being; his chance might come later. So at 0845 he ordered 25 knots' speed and a 40-degree turn to port in order to confuse enemy gunfire. Within three minutes the Japanese had so closed the range that he had to bend on 3 more knots and continue turning until he was retiring in a southwesterly direction with the enemy in hot pursuit on his port quarter.

Nachi now ceased firing because her engineers' carelessness had caused a failure of electric power when the guns were at maximum elevation,[5] but *Maya* was firing steadily with her main battery. A salvo of eight torpedoes, launched by *Nachi* at 0846, failed to score because of the extreme range. Four minutes later she received two 8-inch shell hits.[6] One severed communications on the mainmast and the other exploded on the starboard side of the bridge, killing several men and wounding a score. Two minutes later a third shell exploded in her torpedo tube compartment, creating more casualties. Near-misses drenched the bridge; *Salt Lake* was doing some fancy shooting at a range of almost nine miles.

Flagship *Richmond*, seldom firing at this range, led her by 2000 to 3000 yards. Both ships zigzagged, but *Salt Lake* was making the most abrupt zigs and zags as Captain Rodgers "chased the salvos."[7]

---

[5] According to Cdr. Miura, one of her staff officers (*Inter. Jap. Off.* p. 99), generator steam supply was shifted too early to a boiler that was just getting up steam, and half an hour passed before things were straightened out. The flagship should of course have had all boilers on the line at that time of day in those waters.

[6] Cdr. K. Miura insisted these were 6-inch shells, but he must have been wrong, as *Richmond* was not firing at that time.

[7] This means that when the enemy makes a near-miss one alters course and steers the ship right into the splashes, so that when the enemy corrects his range, on the assumption of his target continuing same speed and course, his corrected salvo will miss.

He chased them to very good purpose, too; as his "exec," Commander Worthington S. Bitler, described it: —

The skipper would ask, "Well, Worthy, which way shall we turn next?" I'd answer, "Your guesses have been perfect so far, Captain. Guess again!" He'd swing right or left, and the spot we would have been in had we gone the other way would be plowed up with ten or fifteen 8-inch shells. The skipper would then look at me with a grin just like a schoolboy that's got away with something in school. "Fooled 'em again, Worthy!" He did so, too; it was uncanny.[8]

Salt Lake now concentrated on *Maya*, which got the range as *Nachi* maneuvered to avoid masking her gunfire. Those who witnessed the action compared these two big cruisers to a pair of graceful fencers, thrusting and parrying for three and a half hours over an ocean dueling ground. Captain Rodgers, as calm as if he were directing peacetime maneuvers, inspired complete confidence; even when his ship went dead in the water, the men on the bridge had no doubt of eventual victory.

The American destroyers did not waste ammunition in long-range firing, and the enemy destroyers, which (with light cruiser *Abukuma*) were ordered to make a torpedo attack, played a cautious game. At about 0902 light cruiser *Tama* was observed to have peeled off from the main formation. She hung on McMorris's starboard quarter, apparently to stay between him and the auxiliaries, and then retired out of sight. *Nachi* and *Maya* with four destroyers now made a wide sweep southward in order to get between McMorris and his Aleutian bases. *Maya*, after launching eight torpedoes which failed to score, at 0910 made her first hit, on *Salt Lake's* starboard plane amidships. Lieutenant Commander Winsor C. Gale and Fireman James F. David were killed; flames burst out but were soon brought under control and the plane was jettisoned.[9] Ten minutes later *Salt Lake* and *Nachi*

---

[8] John Bishop in *Sat. Eve. Post* 5 Feb. 1944 p. 10.

[9] Capt. Rodgers's Report states that the 0910 hit was below waterline and flushed shaft alleys No. 3 and 4; but officers on board *Salt Lake* told the writer that that was a different hit.

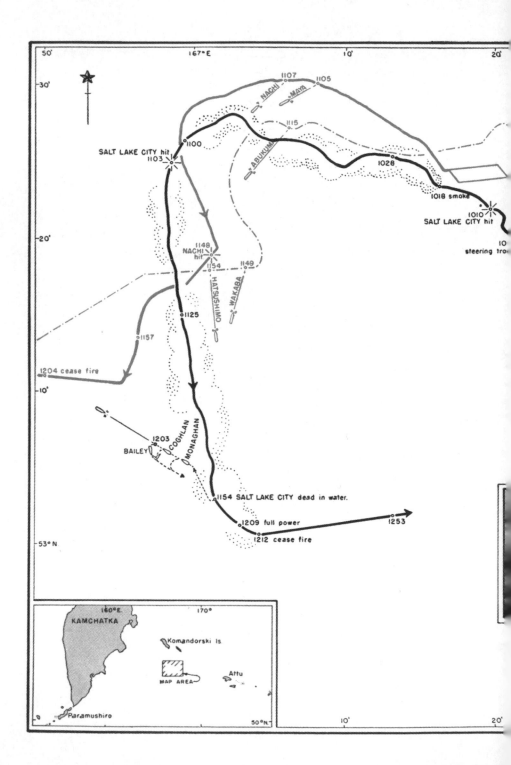

50'   167°E   10'   20'

-30'

SALT LAKE CITY hit
1103

NACHI   1107   1105
              MAYA

1115

1100

ABUKUMA

1028

1018 smoke

1010
SALT LAKE CITY hit

-20'

10
steering tro

1148
NACHI
hit
1154   1149

HATSUSHIMO
WAKABA

1125

1157

1204 cease fire

-10'

1203
BAILEY
COGHLAN
MONAGHAN

1154 SALT LAKE CITY dead in water.

1209 full power   1253

-53°N
1212 cease fire

160°E
KAMCHATKA
170°

Komandorski Is.

MAP AREA
Attu

50°N
10'   20'

Paramushiro

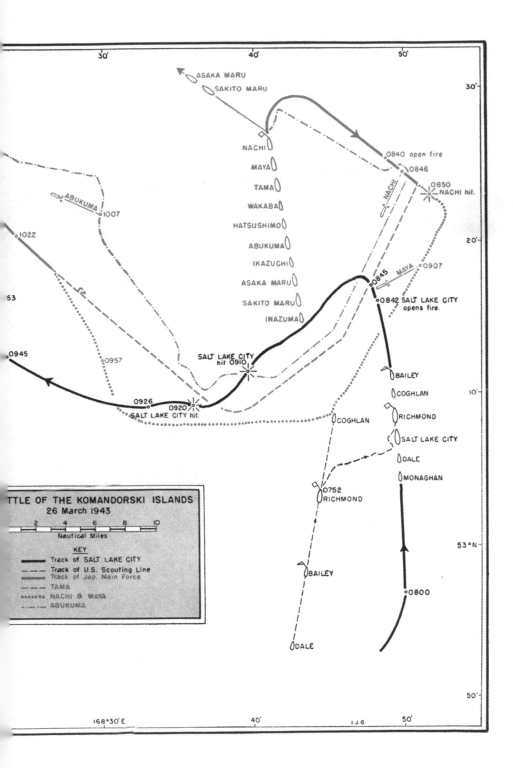

ASAKA MARU
SAKITO MARU

NACHI
MAYA
TAMA
WAKABA
HATSUSHIMO
ABUKUMA
IKAZUCHI
ASAKA MARU
SAKITO MARU
INAZUMA

ABUKUMA 1007

1022

53

0945

0957

0926

0920
SALT LAKE CITY hit.

SALT LAKE CITY
hit 0910

0840 open fire
0846
0850
NACHI hit.

NACHI

MAYA 0907
0845
0842 SALT LAKE CITY
opens fire.

BAILEY

COGHLAN

RICHMOND

COGHLAN

SALT LAKE CITY

DALE

MONAGHAN

0752
RICHMOND

53°N

BAILEY

0800

DALE

TTLE OF THE KOMANDORSKI ISLANDS
26 March 1943

2   4   6   8   10
Nautical Miles

KEY

Track of SALT LAKE CITY
Track of U.S. Scouting Line
Track of Jap. Main Force
TAMA
NACHI & MAYA
ABUKUMA

168°30'E.   40'   I.J.G.   50'

30'

20'

10'

50'

hit each other at a range of about 24,500 yards; the Japanese cruiser slowed down and was seen to be smoking heavily.[10] Apparently the shell that stopped her was a destroyer's 5-inch which passed through a gun port of No. 1 turret, exploded inside and killed the entire gun crew; other 5-inch shells burst above the main deck and killed men topside.

All enemy ships now checked fire. McMorris, hoping that he had knocked out the smoking cruiser, and bent on getting a crack at the transports, made a wide right turn, bringing his column around to due north, between 0926 and 0953. At 0930, when *Nachi's* main battery resumed working, she, *Maya* and the four destroyers straightened out in pursuit, crossing the American wakes at 0952 about five miles to the rear. All this time both sides were slugging their best. Although *Maya* and *Nachi* were faster than *Richmond* and *Salt Lake*, they took it out in zigzagging; for a pursuing ship in a stern chase can come bows-on only at the expense of masking her stern guns, and must reckon with running into torpedo water if she closes. Hosogaya's tactics were to concentrate on *Salt Lake* with a minimum of risk to his ships.

Captain Rodgers, observing that light cruiser *Tama* had worked up to about 18,000 yards on his starboard quarter, an excellent position to spot for *Nachi* and *Maya*, obtained permission from the Admiral to sheer out and take her under fire at 0945. *Salt Lake* fired 8 salvos at the light cruiser and forced her to make a 360-degree turn to evade. *Richmond's* officers on the bridge had time for a good laugh over a dispatch from Admiral Kinkaid at Adak, sent to McMorris half an hour earlier, "suggesting that a retiring action be considered." He added cheerfully that Army bombers would be due to arrive in about five hours' time!

Salt Lake's steering gear, which had given trouble before, came near letting her down badly at 1002, just as *Maya* and *Nachi* began to straddle her. The hydraulic unit on the steering engine was

---

[10] About this time the float plane from *Nachi* was spotted and fired on by both cruisers and destroyers; it disappeared into a cloud, smoking, at 0931 and did not again tangle with them; but Cdr. Hashimoto says that it spotted for the Japanese forces throughout the action.

carried away by the shock of her own gunfire. This limited rudder changes to 10 degrees for the rest of the action; even that
was possible only by use of a diesel boat engine that the ship's
crew had rigged in preparation for just such an accident. Her
movements became erratic but she kept up a high rate of fire from
her after turrets. *Maya* and *Nachi,* both apparently in the best of
health, closed range under 20,000 yards, steering so as to throw
full salvos. The enemy cruiser which fired blue-dyed projectiles
was particularly obnoxious; some 200 of her shells fell within
50 yards of *Salt Lake City,* which again and again was concealed
from view of her consorts by the splashes; many times they
thought she was lost, but she emerged intact from this shower
of 8-inch armor-piercing projectiles, except for one high-trajectory
hit at 1010 which penetrated her main deck and passed out through
her hull below the waterline.

The last hope of working around the enemy's van toward his
transports had now vanished; McMorris's one object was to save
his ships. Captain Rodgers, now that *Salt Lake* was taking water
and steering with difficulty, expected the enemy to close and requested a smoke screen, which the Admiral promptly ordered.
Conditions were ideal for laying smoke: a retiring action on a
windless day, with high humidity and the temperature just above
freezing. *Bailey, Coghlan* and *Salt Lake* used both chemical and
funnel smoke very effectively from 1018 until the end of the
fight. At 1028 the Admiral changed course to 240° in order to take
advantage of this cover. The enemy fired whenever he caught
sight of his quarry through holes in the smoke, or on information relayed by his light forces, which now and again closed
range although promptly slapped down by *Richmond* and Riggs's
destroyers whenever they did. *Maya* fired four torpedoes at so
great a range that no American ship even sighted their wakes.

As eleven o'clock approached, McMorris was pushing westward at 30 knots in the direction of Kamchatka. *Richmond* was in
the van with *Salt Lake* 3000 yards astern; and the four destroyers on *Salt Lake's* port beam and quarter were diligently

making smoke. They had now arrived at a point about 550 miles from Adak but only 420 miles from the Japanese base at Paramushiro. The Army bombers were not due for another four hours; Mitsubishis from the Kuriles might well get there much earlier. The enemy was making about two knots' more speed than the Americans. "The chance of breaking away to the south with a view to later turning east seemed fair," observed Admiral McMorris. "Determined to act accordingly," at 1100 he ordered a turn southward inside of the Japanese track, to course 210°. *Maya* and *Nachi*, presumably baffled by the smoke screen, continued for several minutes westward before turning south, and when they did so the flagship fired eight torpedoes; the light cruisers cut the corner, taking the inside track, and at 1115 *Abukuma* fired four torpedoes. None of these caught up with the Americans.

Salt Lake received her fourth and last hit at 1103,[11] as a result of which the after gyro room and engine room flooded, the latter to a depth of four feet.[12] Valiant work was done by damage control, men calking leaks in the outer skin with their own shirts while standing chest-deep in oil sludge and icy water. The flooding was serious enough to give her a five-degree list to port, yet she never ceased firing, and was still able to keep up full speed. But when the after fireroom went out of commission at 1125, as a result of damage to the after oil manifold, speed fell to 20 knots. McMorris ordered a torpedo attack by three destroyers, then canceled the order at 1138 because *Salt Lake's* speed had picked up as the fuel oil system was unsplit and suction was taken on the forward fuel line. The enemy managed to close only about 3000 yards during this slowdown, as he did a "ships right" to avoid the torpedo attack that he expected from the destroyers' movements, but which never was launched.

[11] Capt. Rodgers's Action Report states that she was hit also at 1059 on the starboard plane, which was jettisoned; but the "exec.," navigator and gunnery officers with whom the writer conversed on 6 Nov. 1943 were positive that the plane was hit and jettisoned at 0910 and that there was no hit at 1059.

[12] To control this flooding, the main circulator pump of No. 3 main engine was periodically used to take suction on the after engine room bilge. When the main circulator was so used, the engine was stopped.

From a painting by Albert K. Murray USNR

Rear Admiral McMorris on Bridge of U.S.S. *Richmond*

U.S.S. *Salt Lake City* at the Battle of the Komandorskis

U.S.S. *Pennsylvania* bombarding Attu

In the Aleutians

At 1150, *Salt Lake's* situation became very unhappy. Arctic sea water in the fuel oil snuffed out all the burners,[13] steam pressure dropped, power was lost, main engines stopped and she drifted to a halt. At 1155, the signal "Speed Zero" was hoisted, and also sent out over voice radio after an 8-inch projectile passed through the "Zero" flag. The ship was then 105 miles south of the Komandorski Islands and 190 miles west of Attu. Few impartial observers would have bet five dollars on her chance of survival. *Maya* and *Nachi* were at 19,000 yards' range on her port quarter, firing steadily and closing rapidly. The light cruisers were at about the same range on her starboard quarter. Japanese destroyers would soon be at effective torpedo range; *Hatsushimo* in fact sent a spread of six torpedoes her way at 1154, but they failed to score. "Swayback Maru" was still firing with her after turrets, but her ammunition was 85 per cent expended, and as a "sitting duck" she had little chance against two healthy hunters of her own class.

Yet within five minutes the picture completely changed.

At 1154, when his ship went dead in the water, Captain Rodgers asked the Admiral to order a torpedo attack and McMorris promptly complied. He also closed the stricken cruiser in *Richmond* with the object of taking off her crew, and Captain Riggs sent *Dale* on the same rescue mission. *Salt Lake* still lay behind the destroyers' smoke screen, her plight concealed from the enemy, when at a minute or two before noon [14] *Bailey, Coghlan* and *Monaghan* reversed course to deliver a torpedo attack on *Maya* and *Nachi,* distant 17,000 yards. It was a "magnificent and inspiring spectacle." The destroyers had some distance to go under fire before releasing torpedoes, but before they had been gone five minutes there occurred what seemed almost a miracle: the enemy column turned from a southerly to a westerly course.[15]

[13] This happened because the engineers, attempting to correct the list by pumping salt water ballast from port tanks, inadvertently connected the ballast-transfer line to the one fuel line in use.

[14] The time given by Capt. Riggs is 1154 but his clock must have been a bit slow or else *Salt Lake's* were fast. Admiral Pye thought the time was 1159.

[15] The time, as far as we can make out, was 1203.

Could Hosogaya be breaking off the action? That is exactly what he was doing.

There were several reasons for this decision by the Japanese commander. His fuel supply was low and he wished to be certain of enough to get home. His ammunition was "below the minimum prescribed by doctrine." [16] He was disgusted with the performance of his destroyers. Nobody told him that *Salt Lake* lay dead in the water because the only Japanese who could see her through the smoke was the pilot of *Nachi's* spotter plane, who either could not get through to the Admiral with this vital piece of news, or did not try. Hosogaya figured that American bomber-plane support, already overdue, might arrive at any moment. Indeed, he thought it was already there. *Salt Lake*, which had been firing blue-dyed armor-piercing shells, ran out of them at this point, and the white plumes raised by near-misses of her undyed HC shells looked to Captain Rodgers like splashes from aërial bombs dropped from above the overcast. Obviously the Japanese thought so too, as they were observed to be firing their anti-aircraft guns at high elevation. Finally (in the words of a participant),[17] "Our flagship, the *Nachi*, was hit by effective shots from an outstandingly valiant United States destroyer, which appeared on the scene toward the end of the engagement."

Bailey, the "outstandingly valiant destroyer," with *Coghlan* and *Monaghan*, tried her best to overtake *Nachi* and *Maya*. The Japanese returned the destroyers' gunfire briskly, apparently smothering them with splashes; it seemed impossible that they could survive, but still they bore in. Lieutenant Commander Atkeson, *Bailey's* skipper, chased the salvos expertly. Presently an 8-inch shell exploded at the galley door on *Bailey's* starboard side.[18] Cap-

---

[16] Cdr. Hashimoto in *Inter. Jap. Off.* p. 112. If figures in "Northern Area Operations" p. 32 are correct, *Nachi* had expended only 59 per cent and *Maya* 75 per cent of her 8-inch ammunition, but *Salt Lake* had expended 85 per cent of hers.

[17] Name unknown; the account is the one Mr. Salomon obtained through SCAP.

[18] The torpedo attack developed so quickly that only a part of *Bailey's* crew were warned, and when this shell exploded the damage control party was in the galley gangway getting lunch to serve to the gun crews. The key damage control men were killed or wounded.

tain Riggs decided to launch torpedoes immediately at a range of some 10,000 yards, rather than risk destruction of the ship before he could get them away. At 1203, just as her five torpedoes hit the water, *Bailey* received a second hit which cut all electric power; she turned away and her sister destroyers followed, without launching. Captain Riggs wished to send them back in, but Mc-Morris, knowing how difficult it is to score with torpedoes in a stern chase, ordered them to retire with him.

Salt Lake City remained dead in the water only four minutes. In complete darkness and during the heat of battle, damage control purged the salted fuel lines, cut in other oil tanks and relighted fires in the forward fireroom. At 1158 the forward engines began to show life. When eight bells struck, she was making 15 knots, which gradually built up to 23 as power was restored to the after engines. Captain Rodgers resumed gunfire with his after turrets at 1202, but the enemy was now opening range so rapidly that he ceased firing at 1204; *Richmond* and some of the destroyers continued until 1212, when the action broke off.

By 1215 the Japanese ships were hull-down. *Salt Lake*, with five feet of water in the after engine room bilges, was capable of making 30 knots and fighting until her ammunition was exhausted — as it almost was. Admiral McMorris gave his group the course for Dutch Harbor.

Thus *Salt Lake* was extricated from her predicament, and with her sister ships lived to fight another day. They had conducted a brilliant retiring action against heavy odds, and were able to get home under their own power. Their casualties were incredibly low: 7 killed (2 in *Salt Lake*, 5 in *Bailey*); 7 hospital cases and 13 minor injuries.[19] All sailors topside were soaked through their winter "zoot suits" by the shell splashes, and thoroughly chilled, for the water temperature was 28° and that of the air 30° to 40°. All hands in *Salt Lake* were served a shot of "medicinal alcohol"

[19] Japanese casualties were 14 killed, 26 or 27 wounded, all but one in *Nachi* (WDC No. 160623 NA No. 11,784 "Tabular Records of Japanese Heavy Cruisers"). Cdr. Miura in *Inter. Jap. Off.* p. 99 says 40 men were killed topside; he must have meant total casualties.

and worked cheerfully at damage control for hours before securing; but there was none of that for the destroyer sailors. *Bailey's* men, with a demolished galley, had cold comfort from a diet of ham, crackers and apple juice until they reached port. She and *Salt Lake* went on to Mare Island for repairs; and when *Bailey* was dry-docked a good third of her underwater plates were found to be wrinkled and dented from near-misses.

Air participation in this action was limited to one or two float planes from *Nachi*. Why no Japanese bombers came out from Paramushiro has never been explained, but there were plenty of "alibis" for the American air forces. Two PBYs on routine patrol were ordered by Admiral Kinkaid at 0844 to make and keep contact with *Asaka Maru* and *Sakito Maru*, but did not find these ships until 1410; they carried no bombs and their contact reports were poor and belated. A minor strike of B-25s from Amchitka, the new emergency airstrip 450 miles from the scene of action, was delayed owing to the necessity of installing auxiliary gas tanks. Three B-25s and eight P-38s took off at 1330 and received a report from Admiral McMorris telling where to find the two *Marus*, but turned back for lack of fuel; a second strike also failed. The Adak-based bombers, 150 miles farther eastward, were even more tardy. McMorris's first contact report found them armed with general-purpose bombs, readied for a strike on Kiska. An attack on ships required the substitution of armor-piercing bombs. These had to be gathered from various storage places where they were frozen in, and auxiliary tanks had to be installed in the B-25s. Four hours were spent in making the change, and then a snowstorm socked Adak in for two hours. The bombers finally took off in time to view McMorris's force on its homeward passage, when they had insufficient fuel to pursue the enemy.[20] But the two Japanese transports and the freighter returned to Paramushiro without touching Attu; their mission was thwarted. So, by any standards, Admiral McMorris had won.

[20] Cominch "Battle Experience Solomons and Alaska" pp. 43–2; Craven and Cate *Army Air Forces in World War II*, IV 377.

Radio Tokyo claimed the usual annihilating victory, and took great umbrage at the American radio release claiming that the Japanese had fled,[21] but Admiral Hosogaya's conduct was not pleasing to his superior officers. They saw no reason why he should not have disposed of *Salt Lake City*, relieved him within a month, and sent him into the reserve. Flagship *Nachi* retired to Sasebo for repairs.

Although retiring actions never seem as glorious as advancing ones, the odds against which McMorris fought, his bold handling of the task force, and the magnificent manner in which all ships responded to his leadership should make Komandorski a proud

AMMUNITION EXPENDITURE, BATTLE OF THE KOMANDORSKIS

By United States Ships [22]

	8" AP	8" HC	6" Common	5" & 3"	40-mm	21" Torpedoes
SALT LAKE CITY	806	26	—	95	—	—
RICHMOND	—	—	271	24	—	—
BAILEY	—	—	—	482	—	5
COGHLAN	—	—	—	750	—	—
MONAGHAN	—	—	—	235	48	—
DALE	—	—	—	728	—	—
Total	806	26	271	2314	48	5

By Japanese Ships [23]

	8"	5.5"	5.1"	24" Torpedoes
NACHI	707	—	276	16
MAYA	904	—	9	8
ABUKUMA	—	95	—	4
TAMA	—	?	—	4
WAKABA	—	—	?	6
HATSUSHIMO	—	—	6	5
Total	1611	95 +	291 +	43

[21] "We had purpose in that our fleet went in westerly direction in order to pursue American fleet. There is only shock at such base means of propaganda taken by America." (Tokyo broadcast 30 March 1943.)

[22] O.N.I. Combat Narrative *The Aleutians Campaign* p. 64.

[23] *Inter. Jap. Off.* pp. 401–2 and "Northern Area Operations" pp. 26–32, which seem to be the most reliable, except for *Nachi* whose tabular records are in WDC. We have no figures for main batteries of *Tama* or the 4 destroyers. Those for main battery *Abukuma* are small because she fired for 10 minutes only.

name in American naval history. That moment in the gray sub-arctic noon just as the enemy turned away, when *Salt Lake City* lay dead on a glassy sea but still firing, with *Richmond* firing as she closed, and three destroyers going in for a torpedo attack, deserves to be depicted by a great marine painter.

As one bluejacket remarked, "The way Captain Rodgers handled the ship had a good deal to do with it, but there was more to it than that." Ensign F. R. Lloyd usnr of *Salt Lake* thus concluded her log for 26 March: "This day the hand of Divine Providence lay over the ship. Never before in her colorful history has death been so close for so long a time. The entire crew offered its thanks to Almighty God for His mercy and protection."

CHAPTER III

Attu Regained[1]

April–May 1943

1. Preparations and Approach

IN THE SPRING of 1943 the Americans were still beginners in the science of amphibious warfare. They had been fortunate in the only two invasions that they had yet undertaken, Guadalcanal and North Africa. An assault on Attu offered plenty of opportunity for a shift of fortune. The Battle of the Komandorskis had demonstrated that tactical air support in the Aleutians was as uncertain as the weather. A whole gale with blinding snow during the passage to Attu, or a sudden williwaw whistling out of a mountain gorge as the boats advanced to the landing, might break up an invasion before it fairly started.

The North Pacific Force had plenty of time to plan this offensive. Under Admirals Nimitz and Kinkaid in the chain of command, Rear Admiral Francis W. Rockwell[2] was appointed Com-

[1] In addition to sources cited in chap. i footnote 1, see Com Amphibious Force North Pacific "Operations against Attu May 1943"; Action Reports of participating ships, especially *Pennsylvania;* Cominch Secret Info. Bulletin No. 9 "Battle Experience, Assault and Occupation of Attu" (1943); Lt. Col. L. D. Smith USA "Preliminary Report on Attu Landing," Western Def. Command and Fourth Army, 30 May 1943; Jicpoa Item No. 4986 "Professional Notebook of Ensign Toshio Nakamura."

[2] Francis W. Rockwell, born S. Woodstock, Conn., 1886; Naval Academy '08, and after various duties afloat helped fit out *Jarvis* and served in her 1912–14. Instructor in elect. engineering and physics Naval Academy 1914–17 and again in 1920–23 and 1926–29. During World War I, in *New Jersey* and with DDs based at Queenstown, rising to be C.O. *Winslow*, and in 1919, of *Thatcher*. Gunnery officer *Tennessee* 1923–26; C.O. *Robert Smith, Dorsey* and *Medina*, "exec" of *Mississippi* and duty in Navy Dept., 1929–39. C.O. *Nevada* 1939; Rear Adm. and Com. 16th Naval Dist. 5 Nov. 1941 (see Vol. III of this History). After evacua-

mander Amphibious Force North Pacific to conduct the landing. At San Diego in January 1943 he organized a joint staff to which Admiral Kinkaid and the Army contributed. The 7th Infantry Division United States Army, which had been training in the Nevada desert, now began amphibious practice at Ford Ord near Monterey under conditions as unlike those of Attu as could well be. To strengthen gunfire support, Admiral Nimitz assigned three of the older battleships, *Pennsylvania, Idaho* and *Nevada*. Their crews, nicknamed the "Market Street Commandos" during the months of frustration when based on San Francisco, were delighted with the prospect of action. "Pennsy" had had her face lifted since Pearl Harbor; she now sported a single tripod foremast, eight 5-inch dual-purpose guns and ten 40-mm quads besides her 14-inch main battery. Also, for the first time in the Pacific, an escort carrier, *Nassau,* was assigned to provide close air support.

In late April the 7th Division embarked in transports at San Francisco while the bulk of the naval force got under way from San Pedro Roads to make rendezvous at sea. Sundry "cloak and dagger" measures were taken to keep the destination secret. A false training order was given wide circulation; medical officers lectured on tropical diseases; stacks of winter clothing were hidden; commanding officers allowed themselves to be seen studying sailing directions for the North Atlantic and charts of the Argentine Republic.

Cold Bay at the end of the Alaskan Peninsula, the chosen rallying point for the expeditionary force, proved to be well named. On 1 May the mountains that surrounded the harbor were covered with snow down to about 200 feet above water level. No signs of civilization except a huddle of wooden houses and Quonset huts; airfield out of sight from the anchorage. "The ships look out of place in a world that belongs so little to man," wrote a

---

tion from the Philippines, appointed Com 'Phib Forces Pacific Fleet, where he supervised planning for the Aleutians. Duty in Navy Dept. at end of 1943; Com 'Phib Training Command Atlantic Fleet 1944; retired as Vice Admiral 1948.

young officer of the Marine guard in *Pennsylvania*.[3] Upon arrival
of the West Coast contingent, Admiral Kinkaid commanded a
force of three battleships, three heavy and three light cruisers, one
escort carrier, 19 destroyers, four attack transports, chartered S.S.
Perida, and a variety of tenders, oilers, minesweepers and smaller
craft.[4] Conferences among top-flight officers went on day and
night, as last-minute intelligence and hydrographic information
required many changes in the operation plan.

During the first week of April, 100-knot winds and stinging
snow buffeted the Aleutians. Then the XI Army Air Force renewed its efforts, and by the 21st had rocked Kiska with 83 raids;
distant Attu received only minor attention. Submarines, Catalinas and Venturas assured that no Japanese would approach undetected, and McMorris's cruisers and destroyers patrolled the
western Aleutians, ready to intercept.

This striking group had undergone several changes since the
Komandorski fight. The new light cruiser *Santa Fe* had relieved
damaged *Salt Lake City*, old light cruiser *Detroit* had joined; of
the four destroyer veterans of Komandorski, only *Coghlan* stayed,
but five new ones were added. "Soc" McMorris was the harbinger
of woe for the Japanese Attu garrison. His victory off the Komandorskis had lost them their last hope for reinforcement. Two
destroyers on 10 April attempted an Arctic Express run, but a
PBY spotted them, dropped bombs and sent them scampering back
to Paramushiro, although the bombs failed to go off. On 25/26
April a Japanese lookout on Shimushu in the Kuriles, less than
two miles from the Kamchatka Peninsula, excitedly reported "a
large vessel of unknown nationality firing and is proceeding to
the northeast." So, instead of sending torpedo-toting "Bettys" to
Attu, where they would have caught McMorris's force delivering
a 25-minute bombardment, Admiral Kawase dispatched ships and

[3] Capt. John Elliott USMCR War Diary. "On one watch," he wrote, "I wore an
ordinary suit of underwear, two woollen suits (long handles), khaki trousers,
flannel shirt, windbreaker (lined), muffler, massive sheepskin coat with waterproof
outside, two pairs of woolen socks, field boots, galoshes and woolen cap."
[4] See Appendix I for Task Organization.

planes to Shimushu, only to find that the mysterious vessel was a Russian ship laying mines in Soviet waters.

Word now came through from Tokyo that Attu, not Kiska, was to be the focal point of Aleutians defense — evidently there had been a leak of the American plan. Kawase decided to defer reinforcement until late May, when a daily fog could be expected and the Japanese transports would have obtained radar equipment.[5] The Attu garrison in the meantime would have to fend for itself.

Weather, as usual, upset the American timetable. At daybreak 4 May, already 24 hours late, Admiral Rockwell's assault force of 29 ships weighed anchor in Cold Bay. In a sea so rough that the battleships had to elevate their forward guns so the breaking waves would not rip off their muzzle bags and bloomers, the ships steamed along the south side of the Aleutian chain, entered the Bering Sea by Amukta Pass, and to avoid detection steered well north of Kiska to the run-in point 115 miles NE by N of Attu. Planes scouting Attu predicted a hazardous high surf on 7 May; so Rockwell postponed landing to the 9th. Expecting that an alerted enemy would have deployed surface forces, he sent his battleships westward to see what they could pick up. They departed in high feather, hoping for a second Battle of the Komandorskis; but the only force that Kawase then had at sea was *Kimikawa Maru* under light escort bringing a few scout planes to Attu, and the American battlewagons missed her.

Weather was so foul on 8 May and the sea so high that waves swept right over the forward 40-mm mounts on the battleships. D-day was postponed again to the 11th and the task force fueled again at sea about 150 miles north of Attu. Dense fog concealed the ships from enemy air and submarine snooping; radar was supposed to prevent collisions while the shift from cruising to approach disposition was made. This complicated procedure required an interchange of ships between transport and battleship groups as well as changes within each formation. At twilight 10 May the battle-

---

[5] "Northern Area Operations" p. 17. Vice Admiral Shiro Kawase had relieved Hosogaya.

ships returned from their fruitless search westward, in order to make rendezvous with the transports. In a pea-soup fog they joined the disposition, a hazardous maneuver even with radar navigation. For hours the ships groped carefully and fearfully. Destroyer-minelayer *Sicard*, distrusting her SC radar, followed the wake of the ship ahead as long as she could, and when fog blanked out this nebulous watermark, resorted to stopwatch and maneuvering board to hold station. Destroyer *MacDonough*, when changing course to conform to the movements of the transports, got between *Sicard* and the ship ahead and was rammed by the minelayer. Nobody in either ship was hurt and both made port safely, but their absence was keenly felt, since *Sicard* was to have been control vessel for the landing and *MacDonough* had a special fire control mission.

After a delay of three hours, the task force turned south and headed for Attu, planning to land troops at 1040 May 11.

2. *The Landings, 11 May*

Attu Island, 35 miles long and 15 miles wide, presents a forbidding aspect. Mountain ranges slope down to treeless muskeg-grass valleys which debouch into the sea on rough, surf-rimmed bays. On the eastern end of the island before the war had been the American weather station and an occasional hut of Aleut trappers. Here also, at the head of Holtz Bay, the Japanese had established their base and built their airstrip. For the invader, treacherous currents, uncharted rocks and almost continuous fog promised trouble. The old Arctic navigator's rule was never to approach nearer the land after you began to hear the bark of sea lions, but these ships had to close to perform their missions. Yet there was one advantage in Attu which many operations in southern waters did not have: a choice of several neat little sand beaches.

Two major landings were contemplated, one west of Holtz Bay

on the northern side of the island, the other in Massacre Bay on the southern side. Preliminary landings on the northern side, where the selection of beaches had yet to be made, came first. Submarines *Narwhal* and *Nautilus*, which had been reconnoitering these beaches for five days, each sent about 100 scouts ashore in rubber boats at Beach Scarlet, northwest of Holtz Bay, between 0309 and 0510 May 11. Destroyer transport *Kane*, coached in by *Pennsylvania's* radar, put a reconnaissance troop of 400 soldiers ashore several hours later. These men joined the scouts and moved up a mountain valley, searching for the pass to Holtz Bay, which they reached in midafternoon but found impassable for the time being. Exhausted from scrambling over rocks, they dug in for the night.

On board transport *J. Franklin Bell*, which carried the main body of troops for the northern landing, no word came from Beach Scarlet, and by 0900 visibility narrowed to a ship's length. Colonel Frank L. Culin USA, commanding the 32nd Infantry, did not relish the idea of rolling about in the fog all day, so he took off with two landing craft, each towing plastic dories. Under his personal command was the Alaska Scout Detachment which included Aleut Indians. Destroyer *Phelps* shepherded them through the fog. Half a mile from the shore the Aleuts transferred to the dories and landed on Beach Red, just outside Holtz Bay. With no enemy in sight, six more boats which had followed *Phelps* in landed troops promptly, and Beach Red became the site of the major northern landing. By nightfall about 1500 troops were ashore here.

The southern group of the expeditionary force, with three transports, nine destroyers and battleship *Nevada*, took position off Massacre Bay in early morning, lowered landing craft and embarked the troops. Fog closed in and the Admiral ordered the landing delayed until visibility improved. Fortunately the temperature was high (48°F.) and the sea calm, so the troops did not suffer much from spending a foggy day in landing craft. After noon came word that, clear or thick, the landing would take place at 1530. The first wave started for the shore, following destroyer *Pruitt's* tooting whistle. Two more waves followed shortly; the fog partially lifted, and the rest was easy. By 2000 May 11, some 2000 troops were ashore at Massacre Bay, with command posts and communications established on beachheads extending a mile inland, and contact made with the enemy in Massacre Valley.

Where were the Japanese? *Nassau's* planes, striking Attu before the fog closed in, had seen none. A radar-controlled bombardment of Chichagof Harbor by *Pennsylvania*[6] and *Idaho* for an hour that morning had flushed none. But they were not surprised. Admiral Koga had given them two days' warning. A local radio monitor had picked up American ship transmissions on invasion morning, and *Nassau's* planes dropped what the Japanese called "absurd leaflets urging surrender." Landing craft from *J. Franklin Bell* were sighted at 1500, and the Massacre Bay landing took place two hours later. Colonel Yamazaki had only 2630 men to defend Attu, and his defense installations — 12 anti-aircraft and a few coast defense guns — were inadequate. There was no sense in dividing this small force to defend all possible landing beaches. His best chance for a delaying action, the only one possible, lay in blockading the valley connecting Massacre and Holtz Bays. With no illusions as to his ability to hold out, Yamazaki had all secret documents burned and prepared to sell Attu dear.

Admiral Kawase at Paramushiro was in a similar fix, amply warned but wanting means to act. After diverting three transport submarines to Kiska and ordering land-based bombers and the planes in *Kimikawa Maru* to attack the American transports, he departed in heavy cruiser *Maya* with destroyer *Usugumo* to join the *Kimikawa* convoy, leaving word that one heavy and two light cruisers and two destroyers shortly due at Paramushiro were to join him as soon as possible.[7] The new Commander in Chief Combined Fleet, Admiral Koga, assigned heavy cruisers *Myoko* and

[6] "Pennsy's" first offensive salvo of her main battery, when approaching her 27th birthday!

[7] Details on Japanese dispositions and decisions from Jicpoa Item No. 4986, Ensign Nakamura's notebook, and "Northern Area Operations" p. 11.

Haguro to Kawase's command, augmented air and submarine strength in Arctic waters and on 16/17 May in flagship *Musashi*, accompanied by *Kongo, Haruna,* carrier *Hiyo,* cruisers *Tone, Chikuma* and five destroyers, sailed from Truk to Tokyo Bay, arriving the 21/22nd. Carriers *Zuikaku, Shokaku* and *Zuiho,* heavy cruisers *Suzuya, Kumano* and *Mogami,* light cruisers *Agano* and *Oyodo,* 11 destroyers and a suitable train were already at Tokyo. This move came too late to help Yamazaki, but, indirectly, it afforded Admiral Turner an unopposed landing at Rendova in the Solomons in late June.[8]

3. *One Week's Struggle*

The soldiers who landed in the north crushed enemy outposts and advanced toward Holtz Bay until fog closed in and darkness fell. When the fog lifted next morning they found themselves half a mile short of their first objective, a snow-splotched hill, and waited for artillery support. At 1600 it arrived in the shape of 105-mm and 75-mm howitzers, augmented by gunfire from *Phelps.* Planes from *Nassau* crisscrossed the hill with bullets and bombs; *Pennsylvania* and *Idaho* bombarded targets on Holtz Bay at 14,000 yards' range. The troops came to their feet, engaged in close fighting, and by midnight held all but a single knob of the hill.

Throughout this second day *J. Franklin Bell* discharged cargo at Beach Red. Planes from *Nassau* and Army bombers from Adak and Amchitka worked over both arms of Holtz Bay in the face of lively flak. *Pennsylvania, Idaho* and *Phelps* plugged away at enemy positions, particularly anti-aircraft emplacements. At 1825, off Holtz Bay, a PBY warned *Pennsylvania* that a torpedo wake was headed her way. The old battlewagon dodged the "fish" and a PBY teamed up with *Edwards* and *Farragut* to hunt down the submarine. Around midnight depth charges brought *I-31* to the surface; she submerged under gunfire, and the destroyers thought they had sunk her but they were mistaken; she survived until 13 June,

[8] See Volume VI of this History pp. 146–53.

to be sunk by *Frazier*. The same thing happened at 1140 on 15 May; torpedo wakes passed astern of *Pennsylvania*, and destroyers peeled off in a fruitless hunt for the culprit.

On the Massacre Bay front the 12th opened with a bombardment by *Nevada*. While the sweepers swept and survey ship *Hydrographer* sounded the channel, the transports resumed unloading

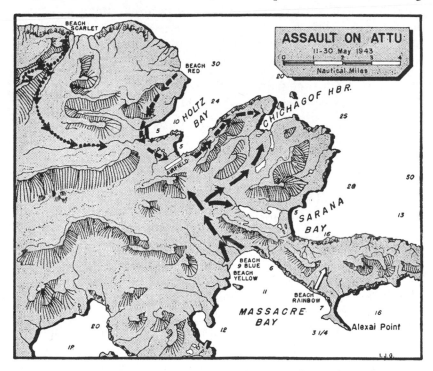

and continued all day, enlivened by the growling of naval guns as call fire was delivered. The troops of the southern force were in a bad tactical position under enemy observation and gunfire from three sides. Only 44 Americans were killed on Attu in the first two days, but among the number was Colonel Edward P. Earle, commanding the 17th Infantry of the southern force. The worst natural obstacle was muskeg and the underlying mud which resisted the movement of trucks and tractors.[9]

[9] *The Capture of Attu*, in the *Infantry Journal* Fighting Forces Series (1944), is the best account of the ground fighting that has yet appeared.

On the third day, 13 May, the Army planned an attack in force but again thick fog blanketed the terrain. Japanese anti-aircraft guns continued to lay down annoyingly accurate fire on Beach Red. The troops west of Holtz Bay knocked the enemy off the knob of the hill taken the day before, and then settled down to wait out the fog. This northern contingent, under the direct command of Major General A. E. Brown, was not doing too well; the men were glad to see the first reinforcement echelon arrive — transports *Grant* and *Chirikof* escorted by gunboat *Charleston*. *Chirikof* was dispatched to Beach Red where she began unloading her combat team that night. In the southern area, *Grant* quickly disembarked her troops but the attack transports and *Perida* still had bulging holds. *Nevada* got off four bombardments, of doubtful value since the planned infantry attack had been canceled.

Expenditure of naval ammunition so far had been generous, but the results were disappointing. Japanese defense positions were well dug in on steep ridges and the sides of deep ravines, very difficult to reach; and, since the troops had advanced but slightly since D-day, naval gunfire had merely been neutralizing positions which the enemy would bring "back to battery" as soon as the shooting stopped. General Brown felt that he could do little without more reinforcement, and on the evening of the 13th requested Admiral Kinkaid to provide it.

On 14 May Colonel Culin attempted a breakthrough to the west shore at the head of Holtz Bay. Weather prevented air support, but *Pennsylvania* hammered the shores of Holtz and Chichagof with 14-inch and 5-inch fire, from a range of 13,300 to 15,000 yards. After two and a half hours' steady bombardment, all 14-inch high-capacity ammunition was spent. The shore fire control party, which had directed her shooting, thanked *Pennsylvania* for her efforts but begged her to resume fire with the armor-piercing projectiles that she was carrying for possible encounter with enemy ships. This request made her sailors indignant: "What! wear out our big guns, waste our AP, when the soldiers are supposed to be doing the fighting ashore!" Nevertheless, she closed again to 14,000 yards and delivered 600 rounds of rapid fire from her 5-inch secondary battery on wanted targets before securing for the day, and for the campaign.

Not only "Pennsy" but all fire support ships in the Attu operation exhausted their bombardment ammunition, and they could get no more short of Adak, where *Shasta* was waiting to replenish.[10] *Phelps* also closed in at 2043 and fired in support of the troops' advance, which amounted to only 500 yards before dark.

On the southern front, advance was again postponed by fog. At the General's urgent request, *Nassau* catapulted one strike against southern targets, but williwaws seized these planes as they flew up valleys beneath overcast and three were lost.

By this time Admiral Kinkaid in Adak was becoming restive. The troops had advanced only 4000 yards in 48 hours. If the Japanese intended to counterattack, they would have had time to assemble a large naval force which might arrive unannounced through the fog. General Brown blamed the terrain and enemy strength, greater than he had anticipated. He wanted still more troops and road-building equipment. An officer of *Pennsylvania*, who visited shore headquarters, heard him predict that it would take six months to capture Attu. The Admiral decided to relieve him.

On 15 May several things brightened, but not the sky. Colonel Culin's soldiers came down out of the fog toward Holtz Bay so rapidly that the enemy left stores and weapons which were put to good use. Through a mountain pass from the west came the troops who had landed at Beach Scarlet; they had been lost for five days and were suffering from frozen feet. And four Japanese submarine torpedoes intended for *J. Franklin Bell* passed clear. In the southern sector the front line remained static.

[10] The fuel oil supply also was cause for anxiety, as available storage tanks were small, 173,000 bbl. at Dutch Harbor, 10,000 at Kodiak. The task force had oilers *Guadalupe* and *Neosho* for fueling at sea, and *Neches* at Cold Bay. *Neosho* and *Pecos* had to make 3 round voyages of 6000 miles to San Pedro between May and September to feed storage tanks and tankers in the Aleutians each time with 95,000 bbl. fuel oil, 300,000 gals. avgas, and 95 tons provisions. W. R. Carter "Beans, Bullets and Bulkheads" ch. vii.

Next day started badly for the 32nd Infantry. Carrier *Nassau's* planes, unaware of American advances made the previous night, bombed and strafed these troops, who had no ground panels to indicate front lines. There was a long delay before Culin's men started again, but once under way they moved fast to the shores of Holtz Bay. When night fell they kept on, having learned that fog and darkness afforded opportunities to surprise a dug-in foe.

While this attack went forward and the troops in the south were still held to slight gains, Admiral Rockwell withdrew three unloaded transports and stationed his fighting ships north of Attu. That evening, 16 May, Major General Eugene Landrum USA steamed up to Attu in destroyer *Dewey*, went on board *Pennsylvania* in a breeches buoy and reported that, according to orders from Admiral Kinkaid, he was relieving General Brown as ground force commander.

On the afternoon of 17 May, Colonel Culin's men made contact with a battalion of the southern force. By that time Holtz Bay was cleansed of the enemy, who had retired to Chichagof Harbor for a final stand. Now that the defenders were concentrated, they made easier targets for bombs, shells and bullets.

Admiral Kinkaid now felt it was time to remove Rockwell's ships from the dangerous waters around Attu. General Landrum took command of such naval forces as remained — destroyer *Phelps* and gunboat *Charleston* for call fire, seaplane tender *Casco* to service the Catalinas, the unloaded transports and their escorts.

Admiral Rockwell's force had been maneuvering within sight or hearing of Attu surf for a week, a dangerous business; but the only enemy counterattacks, by submarines, had failed. Where was Kawase's try for an Arctic Battle of Savo Island? The fog, so heartily damned by the invaders, had really been shielding them. Twenty torpedo bombers sent out from Paramushiro 13 May had been driven back by weather, and each day thereafter had waited in vain for a break. Nor could *Kimikawa Maru* fly her planes. Since Attu radio reported battleships and carriers operating so close to the island, Admiral Kawase, who did not wish to pit his heavy cruisers against them, never ventured closer than 400 miles.

4. *The Final Assault, 19–29 May*

Imperial Headquarters vacillated. It first ordered Admiral Koga to send his carriers and heavy cruisers to seek battle with Rockwell. But on 21/22 May, just as Koga arrived at Tokyo Bay with reinforcements from Truk, it postponed this move "to await developments." Reports of the mighty American force off Attu were obviously a deterrent.

Something did happen, however, on 22 May. Nineteen torpedo-carrying "Bettys" from Paramushiro finally found a clear spot off Holtz Bay, and at 1548 surprised *Phelps* (Lieutenant Commander John E. Edwards) and *Charleston* (Commander Gordon B. Sherwood) who, because of mountain interference, had missed a radio warning. The two intended victims built up speed, maneuvered violently and sent up a terrific clatter of anti-aircraft fire which exploded one torpedo in midair, shot down one plane and fatally crippled another. All torpedoes dropped were evaded. Seventeen Japanese pilots returned to report sinking a cruiser and a destroyer and setting fire to a third ship that was not there. Next day the Japanese tried again. Just as they made landfall on western Attu, five Army Lightnings vectored to the scene with the aid of radar, jumped the formation and shot down five "Bettys" at a cost of two of their own. The Japanese jettisoned bombs and fled.

On shore, between 19 and 25 May, the developments awaited by Imperial Headquarters were not long coming. Colonel Yamazaki's troops retreated, fighting stubbornly all the way, into the fishhook-shaped ridge between Chichagof Harbor (which it commanded) and Sarana Bay. Colonel Wayne C. Zimmermann USA, who had succeeded Colonel Earle, directed the attack. On the 27th his men captured the barb of the hook. Next day a PBY circled low over the ridge and dropped an invitation to surrender, which

Yamazaki scorned. Under cover of night he led his men from the heights to the plateau where the main American force was concentrated; and at first light, about 0330 May 29, directed one of the biggest banzai charges of the war. Into a temporary gap in the American lines poured a howling mob a thousand strong, armed with everything from automatic weapons to bayonets lashed to sticks, and screaming slogans such as "Japanese drink blood like wine!" They overran two command posts, killed Lieutenant Colonel James Fish, charged into the medical station to stab wounded soldiers and the chaplain, and were finally brought to bay by a detachment of Army engineers. Frustrated at last, 500 of them committed suicide with hand grenades. The battle continued with decreasing violence all day. Next morning remnants of the force delivered a weak final attack in which all who were not killed, killed themselves.[11]

That ended organized resistance. Ground fighting at Attu cost the Japanese 2351 killed and 28 prisoners. In return they killed about 600 and wounded some 1200 Americans[12] out of a landing force of 11,000.

Attu was American again, this time for keeps. The operation succeeded, although clumsily executed. The loading and unloading of transports was badly done, naval bombardments were delivered from unnecessarily long ranges, and the 7th Division, owing to initial training for desert warfare and poor top leadership, showed little dash or initiative. After all, Attu was only the third American amphibious operation of the war, and the reports of it, studied and pondered by amphibious force commanders such as Turner and Wilkinson, prevented similar mistakes in the future. In the course of this volume a vast improvement will be noted. Off

[11] Notes by Mr. Robert Sherrod, who viewed the scene the day after; his articles in *Time* magazine 5 July 1943 pp. 28–29, and *History in the Writing* (1945) pp. 194–97.

[12] The official figures at the time were 552 killed, 1140 wounded; but these are certainly too low. Mr. Sherrod, who remained on Attu for some time, counted 565 buried there, and in addition some men drowned at the landings and some of the wounded died in hospitals later or en route thither. The Army Historical Division has not arrived at a final count.

Kwajalein, only nine months later, old "Pennsy" closed to within a mile of the shore for her shoot, and the 7th Division, under a resolute commanding officer, proved itself second to none as an amphibious assault force.

Imperial Headquarters, unaware of the progress of events since Radio Attu had gone silent, on 28/29 May ordered an evacuation of the Attu garrison similar to that of Guadalcanal. Kawase's Fifth Fleet was to draw off Rockwell while destroyers entered Chichagof Harbor to rescue the Sons of Heaven. Shortly thereafter, they heard from American broadcasts what had happened, belayed the plan and turned their attention to Kiska.

By way of compensation, the Japanese government squeezed propaganda value out of Attu. A campaign of attrition was presented to the world as one great "suicidal charge" of 2300 heroes, "a tremendous stimulant to the fighting spirit of our nation." Congratulations poured in from Axis military attachés and ambassadors of puppet governments. The Japanese ambassador to Russia wrote that Stalin, deeply impressed, had ordered the story of the Attu "suicidal charge" to be inserted in primary school textbooks, "in order to promote the spiritual education of the people and to help them understand the Japanese people." [13]

---

[13] "Aleutian Islands Campaign" (No. 851–51) pp. 178–79.

CHAPTER IV

The Aleutians Secured[1]

May–October 1943

1. Airfields and S-boats

GUNS were still barking on Attu when Army engineers surveyed that island for airfield sites. Disdaining the uncompleted strip of Holtz Bay which had cost the Japanese so dear, they selected a spot on the east side of Massacre Bay, started work at once, and on 8 June opened for business. Another engineer outfit landed on uninhabited Shemya, the only flat island in the Aleutians, 25 miles east of Attu, to construct a field for B–29s; and by 21 June that too was ready for medium bombers.

These new fields served a triple purpose: to protect the Aleutians, to base bombers for hitting the Kuriles, and to put the squeeze on Kiska. For the time being, the last purpose was paramount. A new plan to take Kiska was ready before Attu fell, but the veterans of the recent assault needed reorganizing, and fresh troops wanted training before storming an island known to contain at least twice as many defenders as Attu. This time the North Pacific Amphibious Force would conduct realistic rehearsals north of the 50th parallel.

The old S-boats of the North Pacific Force were very active in May 1943. Each patrol was a test of human ingenuity and endurance, and the 10- to 12-knot speed, poor maneuverability, great

[1] In addition to sources for chaps. i and iii: Admiral Kinkaid's Report, "Evacuation of Kiska by Japanese"; Maj. R. I. Delacroix USA "Report on the Occupation of Kiska"; "Report of Withdrawal from Kiska," furnished Mr. Salomon through SCAP, 1946; diary of Capt. John Elliott USMCR, and notebook of Mr. Robert Sherrod.

age [2] and general crankiness gave S-boat skippers little chance to score. "Unsuccessful for the purpose of combat insignia award," read the majority of the endorsements on their patrol reports. Most of the few contacts made could not be exploited, and such modern wrinkles as evasive tactics and effective silent running were beyond their power.

The sixth patrol of *S–41* (Lieutenant Commander Irvin S. Hartman) was one of the few to score. On the morning of 27 May off Paramushiro an auxiliary seaplane tender ran away from her, but later a large schooner under sail hove in sight. At last *S–41* had a target that was slower than she, if only by a few knots. Two torpedoes were fired and one hit amidships; all four masts came down and the schooner sank. Proving that submariners were still sailors, Commander Hartman commented, "The sails on the main and mizzen masts did not appear to be well tended." On 31 May *S–41* wound up this patrol by torpedoing a small freighter. It blew up with a tremendous explosion, sending flames a thousand feet into the air and spattering the scene with debris.

Throughout the summer the patrols continued. *S–30* got a 5000-ton freighter on 11 June off Paramushiro; *S–35* sank a large crab-cannery ship on 2 July off the coast of Kamchatka, and *S–28* sank the auxiliary gunboat *Katsura Maru No. 2* on 19 September in the Sea of Okhotsk. But the final submarine event in these waters was the loss of *S–44* (Lieutenant Commander F. E. Brown). This boat already had three sinkings to her credit in Solomons waters,[3] but her luck ran out in the Arctic. On the night of 7/8 October, shortly after entering the Sea of Okhotsk, she made a radar contact evaluated as a small merchant vessel. Opening fire with her deck gun, she was presently overwhelmed with gunfire from her assailant, a destroyer. The skipper took her down, but she was too badly holed and only two men survived.[4] After this loss, Vice

[2] The Washington Treaty of 1936 declared the life expectancy of a submarine to be 13 years, but these boats were 20 years old in 1943.

[3] See Volume V of this History p. 61 for sinking of CA *Kako*. The other two were auxiliary gunboat *Keijo Maru* on 21 June 1942, and salvage vessel *Shoei Maru* 12 May 1942.

[4] *U. S. Submarine Losses World War II* p. 63.

Admiral Charles A. Lockwood pulled all "Sail"-boats out of Aleutians waters. Turned over to training commands, they served to very good purpose through the rest of the war.

2. *Concentrating on Kiska*

Admiral Kinkaid established a destroyer blockade of Kiska shortly after the fall of Attu and announced that the island would be bombed several times every day, weather permitting. Cruiser-destroyer task forces stood by to repel any forward move by Kawase's Fifth Fleet. There was no longer any danger of this, however, because on 28/29 May Imperial Headquarters definitely rescinded its order to Admiral Kawase to engage the North Pacific Force, and sent attached units of the Combined Fleet to the Inland Sea for training and upkeep. Submarine *Trigger*, patrolling off Tokyo Bay, got a torpedo into carrier *Hiyo* as she sortied on 10/11 June, but light cruiser *Isuzu* towed her into Yokosuka.[5]

Admiral Kinkaid's injunction to the XI Air Force to hit Kiska daily was faithfully followed. The Army pilots, discarding the old Alaskan weather rule, "Never take a chance," adopted a new slogan, "Never miss a break." They solved the fog problem by letting Navy Venturas equipped with special radar guide them to the target. From 1 June until 15 August these fliers made 1454 sorties and delivered 1255 tons of bombs on Kiska. The Japanese anti-aircraft gunners occasionally scored, but most American plane losses were operational. Motor torpedo boats from Lieutenant Commander James B. Denny's Squadron 13 (which had relieved McKellar's division) took station as lifeguards west of Amchitka, saved at least one crew of a plane that splashed, and gave the rest confidence.

The Navy also helped the air campaign by carrying out night bombing raids with Catalinas, but its biggest contribution to the harassment of Kiska came from the muzzles of ships' guns. The first bombardment of that island in 11 months took place on

---

[5] Salomon documents obtained through SCAP, 1946.

Vice Admiral Hosogaya, Vice Admiral Kawase, Rear Admiral Kimura

After the suicide charge, Attu

Japanese Planning

Staff planning for Kiska

Seated, left to right: Rear Admiral Rockwell, Vice Admiral Kinkaid, Major General Corlett, Lieutenant General Buckner, Major General Butler, Major General Pearkes RCA

Chichagof Harbor, Attu, 31 May 1943

Aleutians Campaign

6 July 1943 when Rear Admiral Robert C. ("Ike") Giffen in *Wichita* herded in from a prowl off Attu the task group that he fondly called his Alley Cats: three heavy cruisers, one light cruiser and four destroyers. He waited 40 miles southwest of Kiska until destroyer *Aylwin* radioed that the morning fog had burned off, then headed north. When within gun range of Kiska, "Ike" turned his ships east in column to parallel the southern shore. Neither in technique nor in results was this 22-minute bombardment any improvement over "Poco" Smith's of the previous August; all firing was indirect, spotted by the cruiser planes, and no shore battery replied.[6] After firing 312 rounds of 8-inch, 256 rounds of 6-inch and 1250 rounds of 5-inch projectiles, Giffen retired south and the fog shut down. Probably more effective were five "nuisance" night bombardments by destroyers *Aylwin* and *Monaghan* between 8 and 20 July.

The Navy scheduled a grand slam on Kiska for 22 July. Battleships *Mississippi* and *New Mexico*, neither of which had ever seen action, had been gathering barnacles for two months. Now they were to fight in company with five cruisers and nine destroyers, a powerful bombardment force for that era of the war. Vice Admiral Kinkaid[7] placed the battleships and cruiser *Portland* in one group under Rear Admiral Robert M. Griffin, and three heavy cruisers and a light cruiser in a second group under Rear Admiral Robert C. Giffen.

The morning of 22 July dawned clear as a bell; not in two months had the sailors seen such a sparkling day. At noon both groups shaped a course for Kiska Volcano, which stood out diamond-sharp 35 miles to the south. Few battleship sailors took time to admire the view. Gunner's mates sorted ammunition and tested machinery, surface lookouts kept eyes lowered lest they miss the frothy wake of an oncoming torpedo. On ships' forecastles boatswain's mates bellowed and cursed as they rigged the fussy,

[6] This bombardment brought the total casualty figures on Kiska, from the beginning of the campaign, up to 107 killed, and the number of buildings destroyed to 70. "The Aleutian Islands Campaign" p. 178.

[7] Promoted 7 June 1943.

complicated paravanes, those bird-shaped mine-cutters so designed that they streamed from the bows like escorting dolphins. Below decks the damage control parties checked doors, ventilators and valves.

While Griffin's battleships jarred the Japanese around Kiska Harbor, Giffen's cruisers churned up the muskeg and chipped the rocks on Little Kiska, South Head and Gertrude Cove. No interference was offered; the only enemy fire observed was directed at Army planes. Kiska received 212 tons of high explosive from the firm of Griffin & Giffen. Half an hour after they retired, 20 Lightnings swooped in low to strafe troops and 10 Mitchells to bomb, with more American and Canadian fighter planes following; only one was lost. On the ground a Japanese soldier who had earlier noted American marksmanship as "a sad case," recorded in his diary, "Today's battle was the most furious since landing on Kiska." [8] The troops were so well holed in, however, that none were killed, and the net result of all this shooting and bombing was the destruction of one barracks and damage to two others.

The Japanese on Kiska rightly regarded the 22 July bombardment as a prelude to invasion. Under normal circumstances they would have been resigned to die fighting. But, having been promised by Imperial Headquarters a transfer to the Kuriles, they counted on a new lease on life and the prospect of dying for the Emperor on Kiska failed to arouse the proper emotion.

3. *A Slick Evacuation, 28 July*

Thirteen big I-boats, transport submarines which had run the Kiska blockade once every three days on the average, reported to Admiral Kawase for evacuation duty. *I–7*, initiating the operation, exchanged a cargo of weapons, ammunition and food at Kiska for 60 evacuees on 26/27 May. She made another successful round

---

[8] "Diary of Takahashi" Enc. A with Comnorpac 11 Oct. 1943 "Evacuation of Kiska by Japanese, Supplementary."

trip with 101 passengers; but on her third she had a fight with
Monaghan (Lieutenant Commander Peter H. Horn) and was
driven ashore, damaged, on 22 June. Refloated, she was trying to
escape when three United States patrol craft attacked and forced
her ashore again, where she was lost with most of her crew. *I–9*,
after one successful round trip, encountered *PC–487* (Lieutenant
Wallace G. Cornell USNR) near Shemya Island on the foggy morning of 10 June. A classic anti-submarine battle followed; the PC
first picked up propeller noises by sonar, then came a radar contact 750 yards distant in the fog and in a few minutes the twin peri-
scopes loomed up. Cornell closed in as the enemy submerged, and
dropped five depth charges. Up came the submarine as though
lifted by a giant hand. The patrol craft, one eighth the tonnage of
I–9, rammed at 19 knots. Her bow rode right over the boat's hull,
her bottom bumping across its deck. She came clear, circled, delivered 3-inch and 20-mm fire, and rammed again. Cornell expected his vessel to break in two, but it was the sub that rolled
over on its side and sank. *PC–487* slowed down to repair damage
to several flooded compartments, then proudly sailed into Attu.
I–31 was sunk by destroyer *Frazier* (Lieutenant Commander Frank
Virden) by gunfire off Kiska on 13 June. *I–24* went missing, an
operational victim apparently; *I–155* suffered hull damage in a
storm and turned back; *I–2* and *I–157* scraped the rocky bottom
off Kiska and returned without accomplishing their missions. Thus,
7 of the 13 submarines allotted were lost or crippled in evacuating
820 men.[9] On 21 June Admiral Kawase canceled further underwater evacuations.

Japan could now abandon Kiska or inaugurate a "Tokyo Express," Guadalcanal style. Kawase took the bold course, planning
to dash into Kiska under cover of summer fog, in the face of obstacles such as searching Catalinas, surface patrol forces, Army
planes bombing the Kuriles, destroyer blockade and naval bombardment. Operation KE, as the Japanese called it, was admirably
conducted. The old light cruiser *Tama* was chosen as flagship.

[9] "Northern Area Operations," pp. 40–42; "Report of Withdrawal from Kiska."

Rear Admiral Shofuku Kimura commanded the transportation group comprising light cruisers *Abukuma* and *Kiso* and six destroyers. Captain Shigetaka Amano commanded a screen of five or more destroyers. Oiler *Nippon Maru,* with escort vessel *Kunashiri* as screen, tagged along.

For a week or more Kawase waited assurance that he could count on thick weather. Having obtained it, on 21/22 July his force departed Paramushiro and steered SE to avoid air detection. Four days later it arrived at a point 500 miles SSW of Kiska, where the destroyers were fueled and preparations made for the final dash. American search planes could not find them in the dense fog, but that same fog was not entirely friendly. On the 25/26th there were two collisions, as a result of which destroyer *Wakaba* had to return to Paramushiro, and *Hatsushimo,* "incapable of combat," joined the oiler's screen.

At noon on the 28/29th Kawase ordered Kimura's transportation group to start the final 50-mile run to Kiska while he remained behind in *Tama,* as distant cover. Kimura now headed north through the fog.

At Kiska the days subsequent to the 22 July bombardment had been hell for the Japanese. Every time they sighted bombers, the troops imagined that Americans were about to land. A false report of American transports in the offing threw the garrison into despair. Adjutant Terai collected flowers as a diversion, but his spirits drooped like the short-lived blossoms. Others went fishing to eke out the meager rations. On the morning of 28 July a brisk northwest wind carried fog over the harbor and word came that the evacuation ships would make port that afternoon. Soldiers prepared demolition charges, set booby traps and scrawled insults to Americans on barracks walls. At 1840 Kimura's ships anchored in the fog-smothered harbor. The evacuees quickly touched off the demolition charges, set fire to stores, buildings and shops and assembled on the shore, taking with them only a few personal belongings. Boats hustled from shore to ship and, in the incredibly short time of 55 minutes, Rear Admiral Shozo Akiyama, officers, enlisted men and civilians to the number of 5183 were jammed on board two cruisers carrying 1200 apiece, and six destroyers averaging 470 passengers each. "The fog miraculously lifted" as Kimura's Express filed out of the harbor and steamed southward to rejoin Kawase. Following the same roundabout track as on the outbound trip, the force reached Paramushiro on 31 July/1 August without firing a shot, except at Little Kiska which the Japanese mistook for an enemy submarine. This daring and brilliant achievement remained a complete secret to the Americans for three weeks. It was the second time in 1943 that they had been completely fooled by a Japanese evacuation.[10]

How did the Japanese get away? Why could not scouting planes, prowling task forces or destroyer blockade have intercepted this 16-ship task force? Japanese savvy, American bungling, Aleutian weather and good fortune are the answers. If Kawase had not bided his time in leaving Paramushiro, he would certainly have been discovered. If the whimsical fog had lifted, he would have been pounced upon. If blockading destroyers had been on station on the 28th, they would have sighted Kimura's transport group, called for reinforcements, and fought a battle. None of these "ifs" materialized.

The most serious bit of American bungling led to a famous phantom battle and at the same time cleared the course for Kimura. It started 23 July with a Catalina's radar contact on seven vessels 200 miles southwest of Attu. Just what really was behind this contact, nobody knows. It may have been enemy picket boats, it may have been nothing; but Norpac headquarters believed it to be a reinforcement convoy bound for Kiska. Admiral Kinkaid alerted the Giffen-Griffin team covering the approaches; and the two destroyers blockading Kiska, *Aylwin* and *Monaghan*, were pulled off station to join up.

On the evening of 25 July, Rear Admiral Giffen was forming the same force that had bombarded Kiska into an approach disposition at a point 80 miles SW by S of that island. His plan was

[10] See Vol. V 364–71.

to steam westward at full speed to intercept the seven ships reported by the PBY. His men were spoiling for a fight and received word of impending action with enthusiasm. Overhead an unfamiliar sliver of moon shone out of a surprisingly cloudless sky and gave promise that if the Japanese came north that night the fight would be in the clear. At 0007 July 26, while on course 95°, *Mississippi* reported radar contacts 15 miles on the port bow. *Idaho, Wichita* and *Portland* chimed in that they "had 'em too." In every ship the General Alarm tolled excited sailors to battle stations as "Ike" Giffen jockeyed his disposition into battle formation and set course due north. When the strange contacts registered eight miles from the cruisers and twelve from the battleships, the Admiral altered course to 340° to clear enemy torpedo water. Battleships and cruisers opened fire at 0013, throwing shells at the places where radar indicated that the enemy lay, while destroyers were detached to deliver torpedo attacks. Radar spotters gave salvo corrections; lookouts reported torpedo wakes, flares and lights; men below decks felt concussions similar to those that they had experienced of near-misses; gunners noted star shell apparently thrown up by the foe; there was even a mental breakdown by a neurotic sailor! It seemed odd, though, that no return fire came from the enemy, and that neither *San Francisco* nor a single destroyer had any radar contact whatsoever.

When the Admiral ordered Cease Firing at 0044, because the radar screens were clear of targets, the battleships had expended 518 rounds of 14-inch shell and the three cruisers 487 rounds of 8-inch. When dawn broke Giffen circled back to the vicinity of the "battle" and launched a plane which found nothing — no ship, no debris, no wreckage, not even a dead whale; nothing but the cold, gray surges of the North Pacific. Suspicion had already dawned that the "targets" had been mere radar phantoms, and suspicion now became certainty. What had shown up on the radar were return echoes from the mountains of Amchitka and other islands 100 to 150 miles distant.

"The Battle of the Pips," as this episode came to be called, provoked much humorous and sarcastic comment. Admiral Giffen put a good face on it as the most realistic battle exercise he had ever experienced, but the waste of ammunition and the wear and tear on big guns were not appreciated by the ordnance and supply branches of the Navy.

While the Giffen-Griffin team slugged it out with spooks, Kimura's evacuation group was loitering 500 miles below Kiska, planning to ride in on a weather front that their aërologists had predicted. Next day, 27 July, Kinkaid ordered the victors of the phantom battle to fuel from *Pecos* at a point 105 miles SSE of Kiska. They made the rendezvous at 0900 on the 28th, leaving a wide-open ocean for Kimura's approach.[11]

4. *Bootless Bombardment and Bloodless Occupation*

American action against Kiska after 28 July, when the last Japanese soldier left its spongy soil, was also mildly ridiculous. On the 30th *Farragut* and *Hull* slapped 200 rounds into vacant enemy positions. Three days later, two battleships, two heavy cruisers, three light cruisers and nine destroyers hurled upon the abandoned island 2312 shots of all calibers from 14-inch down to 5-inch. During the following fortnight, destroyers enlivened the weary hours of blockade with individual bombardments and on 12 August two heavy cruisers, three light cruisers and five destroyers returned to shoot 60 tons of shells at Kiska. Every day the XI Army Air Force was over the island early and late, bombing and strafing.

Whenever the fog permitted, photo missions were flown, but the fog prevented between 26 July and 2 August. On the latter date, cameras had a good look at the enemy's main camp and submarine base. Two days later Kinkaid's intelligence officer handed the Admiral a memorandum noting that the photographs showed "remarkable changes" and that "never before since the initial occu-

[11] *Farragut*, detailed to reëstablish the Kiska blockade, had to fuel too, and so missed the enemy. *Hull* was patrolling independently in an area north of Kiska and Segula Is. on 28-29 July.

pation of Kiska has so much destruction been created in an equivalent period of time." [12] Twenty-six buildings had been destroyed including radio stations, garages and barracks. Of a score of barges in the harbor the week before, only one remained. Wonderful shooting, if bombardment had done all that! But how could one explain why motor trucks, which the Japanese customarily dispersed, were now clustered near the harbor shore? Or why Radio Kiska had gone off the air 28 July and never come back? Or why coast defense guns failed to fire on destroyers closing the island's coast? Or why pilots flying the daily bombing and strafing runs received no anti-aircraft fire, or why the gun positions appeared to be completely abandoned? All this added up to something, but nobody knew what. For there were several "facts" that appeared to contradict the theory of evacuation: air spotters of the 2 August bombardment reported "light flak," certain Army fliers saw "tracers," one pilot even told a story of strafing a Japanese soldier and seeing him fall flat! Major General Holland M. Smith USMC, observing that the green aviators alone saw things, wanted Admiral Kinkaid to send scouts ashore at night from rubber boats to solve the question, but it was not done.

If the Americans had been dealing with a conventional enemy, they might have hit upon the truth, but trickery was always expected of the Japanese. Weren't they hiding to make us think the landing would be easy, or saving ammunition against the invasion? Admiral Kinkaid demanded and obtained more and better photographic coverage, but still the evidence was inconclusive. So he decided that the operation must proceed.

Proceed it did, and on a colossal scale. Major General Charles H. Corlett USA commanded 34,426 troops, 5300 of them Canadian.[13] Lieutenant General John L. DeWitt of the Fourth Army, the Honorable John J. McCloy, Assistant Secretary of War, and General H. M. Smith came along as passengers. Admiral Rockwell

---

[12] Lt. Cdr. Blake L. Lawrence "Preliminary Photo Interpretation Memo No. 30" Advanced Intelligence Ctr. Norpac 4 Aug. 1943.

[13] Including the 1st Special Service Division, Col. Robert Frederick USA, part Canadian and part American, which later helped save the day at Anzio.

had nearly a hundred ships in his amphibious force. It assembled in the big harbor at Adak, where the soldiers spent several days on landing rehearsals and practice-marching on soggy muskeg.

The expeditionary force departed Adak on Friday the 13th and began arriving off Kiska during the midwatch of the 15th. Minesweepers turned-to, clearing transport areas; battleships, cruisers and destroyers hammered at enemy gun positions and transports maneuvered into station southwest of Gertrude Cove. Five strange-looking craft darted shoreward, loaded to the gunwales with troops; they did not land, for the troops were wooden dummies and the craft were PT boats disguised as landing boats. This was a demonstration to fool the foe into thinking the Americans were attacking Gertrude Cove, while the real landing from the new-fangled LSTs, LCIs and LCTs took place at a beach midway on the western side of the island. By 0840 3000 troops and tons of equipment cluttered a beach which the flowing tide would soon claim. By the end of the second dogwatch 7300 soldiers were ashore and spreading out inland looking for the enemy. Next morning troops were landed on another beach four miles south of Kiska Volcano. Patrols advanced rapidly across the throat of the island and occupied Gertrude Cove.

On 17 August the troops, groping through a clammy fog, reached the enemy's main camp. Everywhere were signs of evacuation, so hasty that food, stores and weapons had been only partially destroyed. Poking through a deserted camp under swirling mists turned out to be a dangerous business. Patrols on occasion pulled triggers by mistake against friends; 25 men died and 31 suffered wounds from such errors on Kiska. And there were more casualties at sea. A Japanese mine broke loose from its mooring and drifted into the path of *Abner Read* at 0134 August 18, when she was making a routine night patrol off the northwestern beach. A violent explosion crumpled the ship's stern. Smoke from a ruptured smoke tank seeped below and paralyzed the respiratory muscles of trapped men so that they could breathe neither in nor out. It was a relief when the stern broke off near the after gun mount and carried them down into cold water. Some were saved by the ship's motor whaleboat; many were drowned. Destroyer *Bancroft* passed a line to her, and *Abner Read* minus her stern was towed to Adak. She lost 70 men dead or missing, 47 wounded.

From 18 through 22 August the Americans continued their search for the enemy in vain. A message came through from Washington that a doctor who had been on the island in 1902 remembered there were two big caves each capable of holding a thousand men, and suggesting that they be searched! But alas, the only living things the Japanese had left behind were three or four mongrel dogs.[14] "We dropped 100,000 propaganda leaflets on Kiska," said an aviator, "but those dogs couldn't read."

Safe in Paramushiro, the rescued Japanese heard with glee of the elaborate bombardment and the landing on empty Kiska. It seemed to them "truly the height of the ridiculous." [15] They were certainly entitled to their fun. Admiral Halsey could have used some of those ships and men to speed up the capture of New Georgia; General MacArthur, at the end of the line, might have employed a few of them to help drive the Japanese from Huon Gulf and the Bismarcks Barrier. Less than 10,000 Japanese troops, a skeletonized fleet and a few squadrons of seaplanes had tied up a much greater body of United States troops — rising over 100,000 in August — a formida-

---

[14] The dogs gave rise to a sarcastic ballad, "Tales of Kiska," part of which goes as follows: —

You've heard the bloody tales of old
Of fearless knights and warriors bold,
But now the muse pens Tales of Kiska,
Or, how we missed them by a whisker.

One hundred thousand men at muster,
Admirals, generals adding luster;
Two hundred planes, as many ships —
All were bound for Kiska's Nips.

And now we come to how and when
"Dog-day" got its cognomen —
"Dog-day's" evening found our log
Quoting capture of one dog.

"Dog-day" plus 1 and 2 and 3
Found three more in captivity;
But as for Japs we couldn't say
We'd seen one either night or day.

We searched volcanic craters vast
To catch a glimpse of one at last;
It took three days before we learnt
That more than dogs there simply weren't.

Refrain

O here's to mighty ComNorPac
Whose kingdom lay at cold Adak,
Whose reign was known in fame for fog
And capture of two couple dog!

[15] Notebook of Ens. T. Nakamura (Jicpoa Item No. 4986).

ble naval task force, and the XI Army Air Force, with its Canadian allies, for over a year. But the evacuation of Kiska did not aid the Emperor. He had lost his last foothold in the Aleutians. His troops had abandoned valuable weapons, supplies and equipment; his navy had lost three destroyers, six submarines and nine *Marus* in re-inforcing Kiska and Attu.[16] If a moral victory were claimed, the Americans had it, for now the "sacred soil" of Alaska was cleansed; while thinking Japanese wondered whether a series of "brilliant evacuations" were the pattern for victory.

5. *Aleutians Secured*

Now that the Allies had recovered the western Aleutians, what would they do with them? Use them as a short invasion corridor to Japan? That idea, often discussed and even promoted by air power fanatics, had been ruled out since the airmen had discovered for themselves what flying along the Aleutians was like. Or, should Adak, Kiska and Attu be used to mount an invasion of Paramu-shiro? That project was discussed by the J.C.S. on 7 September 1943 and submitted to their joint planning committee which, after discussing the matter with representatives of the area command, made a negative recommendation on 18 September. The capture of Paramushiro would require more forces than could be spared, with the Gilberts and Bougainville invasions timed for November. And possession of the Kuriles base would confer no benefit on the Allies unless it were exploited for a further advance into Hokkaido, a project which the C.C.S. had rejected. Paramushiro in enemy hands was only a minor threat to the Aleutians.[17] The joint planners recommended that an Army base be developed at Adak, and air

[16] "Northern Area Operations" p. 51, and JANAC.

[17] On 4/5 August Imperial Headquarters abolished the Northern Area Force and combined the Fifth Fleet and the Twelfth Air Fleet, based at Ominato and Paramushiro, as the Northeast Area Fleet under Vice Adm. M. Tozuka, for the defense of the Kuriles. The surface components of this Fleet comprised but one heavy and two light cruisers, two desdivs, 7 transports and a number of small craft, and remained under the command of Vice Adm. Kawase.

bases established there and on Attu. They pointed out that recent reductions of air strength in the Aleutians would rule out a continuous bombing offensive against Paramushiro.

On 5 October 1943 the J.C.S. approved a gradual strengthening of the western Aleutians, with a view to reviving the Paramushiro project in the event that Russia entered the war against Japan. But they ordered that forces should not be built up to invasion size until and unless that contingency occurred.[18]

After 11 September 1943, when Major General Davenport Johnson usa took command of the XI Army Air Force, a series of harassing raids were delivered against Paramushiro. On 11 October Vice Admiral Kinkaid, relieved by Vice Admiral Frank Jack Fletcher, left to command the Seventh Fleet in the Southwest Pacific. The North Pacific Force was reduced on the eve of Operation "Galvanic," but on 2 February 1944 a striking force under Rear Admiral Wilder D. Baker (*Richmond, Raleigh* and seven destroyers) pulled off a very creditable bombardment of the Kuriles base.

During the rest of the war the Aleutians sector offers little of interest to the military or the naval historian. Harassing air raids on Paramushiro were varied by occasional shore bombardments and feeble Japanese retaliatory raids on Attu, Kiska and Adak. But there was a constant improvement both of bases and of flying efficiency in these difficult northern areas; and that was all to the good. For it may well be that, in the future, the Bering Sea, and not the Caribbean or the South Pacific, will be America's "Sea of Destiny."

[18] Craven and Cate *The Army Air Forces in World War II*, IV 392–97.

PART II

The Gilbert Islands Recovered

(Operation "Galvanic")

West Longitude dates, Zone plus 12 time, in the Gilberts.[1]

Disembarkation was a matter of extreme difficulty for these reasons: the boats drew too much water to be run ashore except where the coast was steep-to; the troops, besides being ignorant of the terrain, were loaded down by the great and oppressive weight of their equipment, and with their hands full had at the same time to leap overboard from the boats, stand firm in the water, and fight the enemy.

— CAESAR: *De Bello Gallico* iv. 24

---

[1] Although the Gilberts are in East Longitude, so much of the operation was mounted in Hawaii that West Longitude dates were used throughout the operation, and so here. The dates of the Southern Attack Force when still in South Pacific waters are, however, East Longitude. The Japanese used East Longitude dates and Tokyo time.

CHAPTER V

Plans and Preparations

1. *The Spider's Web*

DURING the last months of 1943, when Allied forces of the South and Southwest Pacific were hammering at islands and airfields in the Bismarcks and Bougainville, Admiral Nimitz organized two massive amphibious operations. The first planted American power in the Gilbert Islands, the second in the Marshalls.

These two groups of coral atolls are included with the volcanic Carolines and the lush Marianas under the name Micronesia, the "tiny islands," as distinct from Polynesia, the "many islands," and Melanesia, the "black men's islands." Micronesia, insignificant in world economy, was vital in the strategy of World War II. The Gilberts, Marshalls, Carolines and Marianas sprawled across the main sea lanes between the United States and the Philippines, China and Japan like webs of a giant tropical spider. Kwajalein in the Marshalls, Truk in the Carolines and Saipan in the Marianas were each the center of a defensive system easily supported and supplied from Japan, within which air and naval forces could be assembled and deployed, planes and ships serviced, air and surface raids organized. No search planes could reach them from existing Allied bases; the nearest Marshall Island lay 1100 miles from Guadalcanal, 1130 from Canton and 1230 from Johnston.

If these islands were "made to order for Japan," as Admiral Nobumasa Suetsugu once said, they might equally well serve the enemies of Japan. Certain Allied strategists proposed simply to ignore them, arguing that Micronesia might be by-passed with impunity. Why not creep up on Japan via New Guinea and the Philippines, or by the Aleutians route? But the farther west that America projected her sea power, the more dangerous it became to leave in enemy possession such ample means for flank attacks on Allied lines of communication, and the more urgent it became to capture his airfields and fleet anchorages. Eniwetok, lying a little more than a thousand miles from Saipan, would be worth a dozen Wakes. The Carolines not only included the naval bases of Truk and Palau; they threatened General MacArthur's advance after the Bismarcks Barrier was broken. Saipan and Guam in enemy control screened the Philippines; in Allied possession they might bring B–29s within range of Japan. The Marshalls' spider web could entangle any westward advance from Pearl Harbor; that of the Gilberts enabled man-made insects to pounce on the America-Australia lifeline.

The Gilberts and the Marshalls, with which we are immediately concerned, are uniform in physical character. Each unit is a coral atoll consisting of a string of twenty to fifty islands, islets and reefs. If you took twenty necklaces of different lengths composed of beads of different shapes and sizes, threw them into the bottom of a tank and let in just enough water to cover the smaller beads, you would have a fair chart of the Marshalls. Kwajalein, the largest atoll in the world, encloses a lagoon over 60 miles long by 30 miles wide, but some of the smaller atolls are only a few hundred yards in diameter. A ten-foot rise in the Marshalls is accounted a hill, and the highest point in the archipelago is only 21 feet above sea level; sailors sight the tops of palms before they can see the land. The soil is too poor to be valuable for coconut plantations, rainfall seeps through rapidly and vegetation is sparse.

Yet the same physical features that make these atolls uninviting to seamen and travelers render them highly interesting to military men. Each of the larger atolls includes at least one island capable of development as an airfield. On their level surfaces, composed of coral rock and sand, bomber and fighter strips can readily be constructed and easily maintained.

The Marshalls Archipelago, named after the master of an East

Indiaman which sailed among them in 1788, comprises 30 to 35 coral atolls [1] between lattitudes 5° and 12° N, and longitudes 160° and 172° E. Claimed though never occupied by Spain, the Marshalls were annexed by Germany in 1884. In World War I both this group and the Carolines were captured by Japan and awarded to her in 1920 under a mandate from the League of Nations. Article 22 of the League of Nations Covenant and the terms of the mandate forbade Japan to establish military or naval bases, erect fortifications, give the natives military training, or make any military use of the islands. Although Japan seceded from the League on 27 March 1935, she retained the mandate to the South Sea Islands, as she called them, together with the same responsibilities and obligations.[2]

Shortly after, Japan dropped a thick curtain of secrecy around the Marianas, Carolines and Marshalls. No foreign ship was allowed to enter their harbors or lagoons, no foreign national to take passage thither on a Japanese ship, no foreign warship to make a courtesy visit. Everyone suspected that this secrecy covered a progressive militarization of the islands, and the suspicion was correct. At the war crimes trials at Tokyo in 1946–47, the defense pretended that all buildings constructed on the islands prior to the outbreak of war were for "cultural purposes," and that the airfields were intended only to facilitate "rescue work in case of shipwreck," or "to assist fishermen in locating schools of fish." The tribunal was not convinced that military barracks enhanced Micronesian culture, or that the chain of airfields and seaplane bases extending from Saipan to Palau and from Truk to Wotje, constructed between 1934 and 1941, were benevolent devices for air-sea rescue and the spotting

[1] Depending on whether one counts some of the hourglass-shaped atolls as one or two.

[2] Quincy Wright in *Am. Journ. International Law* XXIII (1939) 347. This was explicitly recognized by the Japanese government, which continued to make its annual reports on the islands to the League until 1938. See Marquis Ito's speech in *League of Nations Permanent Mandates Commission, Minutes of 28th Session* (Oct. 1935) p. 184. In this connection, a recent advisory opinion of the International Court of Justice declared, 11 July 1950, that the Union of South Africa was still under the same obligations as mandatory power over Southwest Africa, even though the League of Nations had expired.

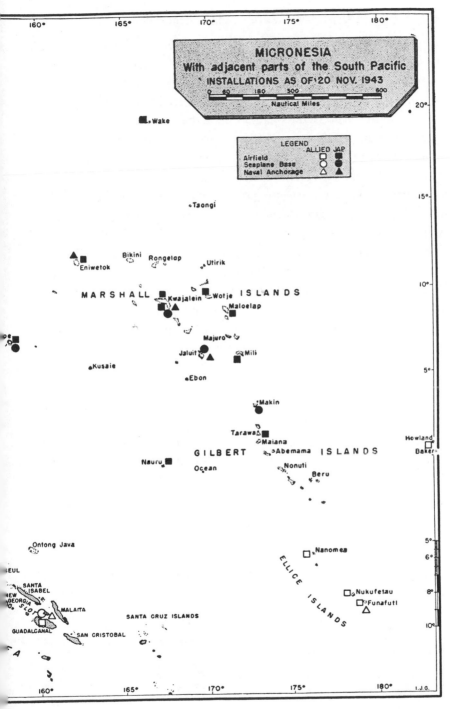

of fish. The natives, previously well treated by the Japanese, were the first victims. Forced to labor on "cultural" runways for a very low wage, and kept at work under pain of severe beatings, they welcomed the American invasion as a release from servitude.

Early in 1937 the islands came under the administrative control of Japanese naval officers; next year Japan ceased to make reports to the League of Nations, and the systematic militarization of Truk and the Marshalls began in November 1940. At least 40 vessels were constantly employed in carrying out men and materials from Japan, and Admiral Shigeyoshi's Fourth Fleet as well as part of the Sixth (submarine) Fleet was based at Truk and Kwajalein.

Saipan in the Marianas, Truk, Ponape and the Palaus in the Carolines, Kwajalein, Wotje, Jaluit and Maloelap in the Marshalls, were well enough developed to be designated as supply bases in Admiral Yamamoto's Combined Fleet Secret Operation Order No. 1 of 5 November 1941, the blueprint for the first, the offensive, phase of the Pacific war.[3] Some of them were put to use immediately. The submarines that attacked Pearl Harbor started from Kwajalein, as did the expeditionary force against Wake. The assault troops that wrested Wake from the Marines belonged to the Marshalls garrison; the big bombers that attacked Major Devereux's Marines flew from Roi and Wotje. The amphibious force that took Guam started from Truk, and Jaluit was already an important base for scouting seaplanes.[4]

Development speeded up after the war began, and by the time the Central Pacific advance opened the islands were indeed formidable. Kwajalein had become the most important base in the Marshalls. Roi and Namur islets on the northern end of the lagoon had been turned into an airdrome; Roi had one 1330-meter and two 1100-meter runways, and "every facility" for basing 72 torpedo

---

[3] See Vol. III of this History p. 84; but the date given in the first printing (1 Nov.) is incorrect.

[4] These paragraphs on military developments 1935–43 are based on the USSBS Naval Analysis Div. publication *The American Campaign Against Wotje, Maloelap, Mille and Jaluit* (1947); on relevant documents, affidavits and testimony before the International Military Tribunal for the Far East (IMTFE) 1946–48, still in typescript; and on data obtained by Mr. Pineau and myself in Japan.

bombers and 100 fighter planes including barracks for an ample garrison on adjoining Namur. The naval base was located at the southern end of the lagoon off Kwajalein Island, and on that island there were a supply depot, torpedo station, advanced naval base headquarters, and a 1200-meter runway, whose discovery by air reconnaissance, as we shall see, materially altered American plans. On the nearby Ebeye islet two squadrons of scout seaplanes were based.

At Jaluit in the southern Marshalls, a seaplane base able to take care of two squadrons of 4-engine flying boats and one of fighter seaplanes had been completed by April 1941; but not much was done to develop Jaluit during the war. Mili, the atoll nearest the Gilberts, had two 1200-meter runways, barracks, and bomb and torpedo storage buildings completed by September 1943. Taroa Island of Maloelap Atoll had two airstrips, 1500 and 1300 meters long, completed before the war began, with so many buildings that pilots from *Enterprise* who took part in Halsey's strike on Taroa, 1 February 1942, reported that base to have been "better equipped than Ford Island," Pearl Harbor. At Wotje an extensive plan for installations, dated August 1940, had been largely completed by the time war broke out. There were two runways, 1500 and 1050 meters long, and a seaplane base; more than fifty buildings, plenty of dual-purpose and coast defense guns installed, and a connecting system of roads and trenches.

All these fortified islands in the Marshalls had ample radio facilities and some of them had search radar. The airfields and installations were protected by well-designed machine gun, antiaircraft and coast defense emplacements, and by garrisons of sufficient strength to make any amphibious invader pay a very high price for them. Only Eniwetok, westernmost of the Marshalls, was ill protected, because the Japanese never expected they would have to fight for it. The two runways on Engebi Island at the northern end were intended for staging only; the barracks and other installations were few and inferior.

*   *   *

In the early months of the Pacific war the Japanese seized a southeastern annex to the Marshalls — or, one might say, spun a fifth spider's web — in the Gilbert Islands.

That archipelago of 13 to 16 atolls lies SSE of the Marshalls' axis, straddling the Equator between longitudes 173° and 175° East. Discovered by the Portuguese navigator Quiros on his return from Espiritu Santo in 1606, it was named after Thomas Gilbert, master of an East Indiaman, in 1788. Lieutenant Charles Wilkes USN visited the Gilberts in the course of his famous exploring expedition in 1841. He reported the women to be the prettiest in the South Seas, and the men, armed with ten-foot spears barbed with sharks' teeth, to be formidable warriors. His chart of Tarawa was not the worst of those furnished to the Fifth Fleet in 1943. After 1856 the Reverend Hiram Bingham and Protestant missionaries from Boston were active in the Gilberts, weaning the natives from their favorite sports of internecine warfare and the murder of trading schooners' crews. Robert Louis Stevenson spent several months in the Gilberts in 1889 and called attention to them by writing *In the South Seas;* the British government took them under its protection in 1892. Not long after, they were included with the Ellice, Phoenix and Union groups, and Ocean Island, as "the Gilbert and Ellice Islands Crown Colony." Under a British régime which respected their tribal customs, the Gilbertese prospered and multiplied while retaining their upstanding physique and frank, friendly bearing. The last pre-war Gilbert Islands census, counting over 26,000 natives and only 109 whites and Chinese, proved these islands to be the most densely populated in the Pacific.

Their nearness to the Marshalls and distance from Allied bases made the Gilberts easy meat for the Japanese at the outset of the war. On 10 December 1941 the Japanese Navy occupied Makin and set up a seaplane base, left a token force on Tarawa, and placed coastwatchers on some of the other atolls.

This threat to the America-Australia lifeline could not be ignored, but it was dealt with prematurely. In August 1942, Lieutenant Colonel Carlson's Marine Raiders, carried by submarines *Nautilus* and *Argonaut,* pulled off a spectacular hit-and-run raid on Butaritari Island, Makin. As General Holland M. Smith wrote, this "piece of folly" merely stimulated Japan to fortify the Gilberts and make the ultimate American task far more costly.[5]

Imperial Headquarters dispatched from Yokosuka a fresh garrison and construction battalion which, dividing at Jaluit, arrived Makin 12 September 1942 and Tarawa 15 September. A detachment of the Tarawa force occupied Abemama a few days later, and mopping-up parties were sent in a destroyer and two gunboats to Kuria, Maiana, Tabiteuea, Abaiang, Nonuti and Beru Atolls. These rounded up all the New Zealand coastwatchers, who, together with a trader, a dispenser and a Protestant missionary from Beru, were tortured and murdered.[6] Thus, the effect of Carlson's raid was to increase Japanese garrisons in the Gilberts from fewer than 100 to 1500 men, and to destroy Allied means of intelligence.

Already, in the last week of August, the Japanese had seized the two phosphate islands, Ocean and Nauru. On the latter they constructed an airfield of three runways (800, 1200 and 1300 meters long) from which, by the end of January 1943, planes were searching 600 miles out. By the middle of 1943 the Japanese garrison at Nauru numbered about 1400 men and defense facilities were ample. The menace of bombers based there confined Allied shipping to the south of the line Funafuti–Santa Cruz–Solomons. This threat to the sea routes between the United States and Australia was augmented by the new airfield on Betio Island, Tarawa, which the Japanese began to use 28 January 1943, and the seaplane base at Makin which was ready six months earlier. Planes based there raided as far as Canton Island, 960 miles to the SSE, so that for a time American transport aircraft bound from Pearl

[5] *Coral and Brass* p. 132; see Vol. IV of this History pp. 235–41 for the raid. Previously, in the spring of 1942, Capt. Emil M. Krieger USMC had made a reconnaissance of the Gilberts in a New Zealand sailing vessel with a native crew.

[6] The Catholic clergy, mostly French, were unmolested, since, as the Japanese commander leeringly informed them, that "made good propaganda." (Record of interview with Msgr. Octave Terraine, Bishop of the Gilbert Is., and four French priests, 2 Dec. 1943.)

Harbor to Nouméa had to take the Palmyra–Wallis route. By July 1943 the formidable defenses of Tarawa that the Marines were to encounter in November had been almost completed.

Tarawa received significant reinforcements in March 1943, but not all the troops destined for it got there, thanks to the enterprise of United States submarine *Pollack* (Commander B. E. Lewellen). Patrolling close aboard Jaluit on 20 May 1943, she was alerted by the presence of two Japanese patrol craft. Lewellen, husbanding his torpedoes for bigger game, found it that afternoon in the shape of 5400-ton auxiliary cruiser *Bangkok Maru* carrying 1200 troops to Tarawa. *Pollack* planted four torpedoes which blew the *Maru's* stern to bits. One third of her passengers went down with her; the rest, without their equipment, got ashore at Jaluit, where they spent the rest of the war. Other units intended for Tarawa were diverted to Bougainville and the Shortlands to meet the impact of Halsey's advance in the South Pacific. The ground forces which the Americans encountered at Tarawa in November were little stronger than they had been in March; but they were much more deeply dug in.[7]

The next Allied countermove after the Makin raid was the occupation of Funafuti Atoll in the Ellice group, a good 700 miles SE of Tarawa, on 2 October 1942.[8] Elements of the 5th Marine Defense Battalion, commanded by Lieutenant Colonel George F. Good USMC, were brought up from Samoa in four transports escorted by cruiser *Chester* and a number of destroyers.

The Marines were given a warm welcome by the natives and by the garrison — one lieutenant and one corporal of the New Zealand Army. Naval units in the occupying forces at once began dredging Te Buabua Pass and marking shoal spots, so that eventually the lagoon was able to accommodate over a hundred ships;

[7] Thomas Wilds "Japanese Forces in the Gilbert Is., 10 Dec. 1942–Nov. 1943"; ms. prepared in 1950–51 for Office of Military History, Special Staff, Dept. of the Army.

[8] Log of the Naval Local Defense Force, examined by the writer in July 1944, and other information obtained on the spot. This occupation was not publicly announced or even generally known in the Navy until April 1943. The name of this atoll is pronounced "Funnafutti," all vowels short and no accent.

Seabees immediately started work on an airfield, and made it operational within a month. A bomber and a PT boat based there picked up Captain Eddie Rickenbacker and his companions on 12 November 1942 after their 21-day voyage in a rubber boat.

Secrecy was so well maintained in the occupation of Funafuti that the Japanese apparently did not discover it until April 1943. On the 22nd of that month their bombers came over in two waves. At the first alert, 680 Ellice Islanders took refuge in the concrete-walled, pandanus-thatched church. Corporal F. B. Ladd of the 5th Marine Defense Battalion undertook, on his own responsibility, to get them out of there and into dugouts; and within ten minutes after the church was cleared, a large bomb came through its roof, exploded, and completely blasted the interior. That was the last important bombing attack on Funafuti. The new airfield was ready for launching photographic missions against Tarawa, Mili and Jaluit by mid-June.

2. *Micronesia in Pacific Strategy* [9]

In Allied circles, very little was known of enemy activities in the Gilberts and Marshalls. Photographic reconnaissance could not stretch up to the Marshalls, even from Funafuti. Submarines *Pompano, Stingray* and *Plunger* reconnoitered Rongerik, Bikini, Eniwetok and several minor atolls between 21 February and 15 March; but a fish-eye view does not reveal what is going on ashore, and in those particular Marshalls the Japanese were then doing nothing important.[10] The Imperial Combined Fleet might have rendezvoused in Kwajalein Lagoon and half a dozen new airfields might have been constructed without the news reaching Pearl Harbor.

Admiral King, always alert to seize opportunities, on 9 February 1943 invited Admiral Nimitz's comment on an operation to secure

[9] See Vol. VI chap. i for earlier strategic planning in the Pacific, and planning procedures at Pearl Harbor.
[10] Theodore Roscoe *U.S. Submarine Operations in World War II* (1949) p. 508.

the Ellice and Gilbert Islands. Cincpac thought the suggestion premature. The Central Pacific Force of the Pacific Fleet, created in mid-March 1943 and consisting of old battleships, a couple of carriers and a few cruisers and destroyers, was far too weak to support an amphibious operation. No ground troops were yet available. Three divisions, all that the Joint Chiefs felt they could then spare for the Central Pacific, were wanted by the Army for the defense of the Hawaiian Islands. None had been amphibiously trained. The enemy still held the western Aleutians, and no forces could be spared from the Central Solomons operation, which began in June.

Modern warfare has to be planned far ahead; improvisation may lead to disaster. It will be interesting to find out why the Marshalls became a priority target in the Joint Chiefs' Strategic Plan for the Defeat of Japan which was accepted by the Combined Chiefs of Staff on 20 May 1943.[11] The object of this plan was to attain positions in the Western Pacific from which Japan's unconditional surrender could be forced, possibly by air action alone, probably by invasion after repeated air strikes on her industrial cities. In the choice of such positions, the Kuriles were dismissed on account of persistent foul weather, and because Siberia could be used only if Russia entered the Pacific war. The planners did not believe that the Bonins, Okinawa or Formosa would be big enough or near enough to Japan. A major base on the coast of China would be necessary, and Hong Kong appeared to be the most suitable beachhead.

The problem then resolved itself into ways and means of reaching Hong Kong. Even if the Burma Road could be recaptured, most of the necessary men and supplies would have to come by sea, and the transpacific route could be opened only by seizing intermediate objectives, and maintained by destroying the Japanese Fleet. The Royal Navy might crash through the Malacca

[11] C.C.S. 220. To be exact, the Marshalls were in C.C.S. 239/1 "Operations in the Pacific and Far East in 1943–44," a J.C.S. paper approved by the C.C.S. 21 May. The person largely responsible for bringing up the Marshalls was Capt. Carl J. Moore, who subsequently became chief of staff to Admiral Spruance.

Straits and recover Singapore, but the most feasible approach for the United States Navy would be through the Celebes and Sulu Seas between North Borneo and Mindanao. General MacArthur at that time was in favor of concentrating everything on this New Guinea-Mindanao axis. But, said the Joint Staff planners, an advance along only the South Pacific route would leave the Japanese in possession of their freedom of maneuver on the Allied flank, abundant opportunity to strike at the long Allied lines of communication, and would certainly not precipitate a decisive naval action.

Moreover, if the Allies adopted a single line of advance, the enemy would naturally concentrate against it. *If, on the contrary, an offensive through the Marshalls and Carolines were pushed at the same time as in the Bismarcks,* it would at once protect Southwest Pacific operations from flank attack and deceive the enemy as to our ultimate route to his home waters. And these war planners ventured the prophecy that the offensive possibilities of the aircraft carrier, permitting a large concentration of aircraft at any desired point and time, would first be realized in the Marshalls and Carolines. The positive measures in this master plan for the Pacific may be summarized as follows: —

1. Simultaneous carrier and amphibious operations to open lines of communication to the Celebes Sea through (*a*) Micronesia, (*b*) the Bismarcks; (*c*) a British operation to recapture Burma, to be correlated with them.
2. Royal Navy to open Malacca Straits while United States forces commence liberation of the Philippines.
3. American amphibious operation coördinated with Chinese forces, to capture Hong Kong and control of the South China Sea.
4. Development of air bases in China.
5. Bombing offensive by B–29s, to be followed if necessary by the invasion of Japan.

One may speculate whether this plan was better or worse than the one subsequently followed, but the hard fact is that it could not be followed, even through Phase 1. The British were unable to play their assigned part in Burma; Churchill's estimate of Chiang Kai-shek proved to be better than Roosevelt's, and China had to be by-passed on the road to Tokyo. But the strategy of Phase 1 was sound, and two thirds of it was realized. By moving forward in two powerful columns by air, sea and land, through the Bismarcks and Micronesia, the Allies applied pressure to the enemy at a variety of points, dispersed his forces and chose where and when to strike next. It was assumed, though not explicitly stated, that by the time the Nimitz column had absorbed Truk it would combine with the MacArthur-Halsey column to invade Mindanao. But, as we shall see, Truk was by-passed; the Fifth Fleet sailed straight from the Marshalls into the Marianas and joined the MacArthur column in Leyte Gulf.

In mid-June 1943, the Joint Chiefs of Staff directed Admiral Nimitz to submit a plan for occupying the Marshalls about 15 November. Without waiting for his reply, the Joint War Plans Committee on 17 June reported an outline plan providing for the initial seizure of Kwajalein, Wotje and Maloelap by 1 December, with an alternate plan for the Gilberts. Cincpac staff felt certain that in any case the Gilberts must be secured before the Marshalls were attacked. Earlier amphibious operations such as Guadalcanal and North Africa had proved the need of intensive and long-continued photographic reconnaissance to provide information of approaches, beaches and enemy defenses. Air mastery up the Slot, made possible by Henderson Field, would have been worth the cost if the runways had been paved with gold. Adequate photographic coverage of the Marshalls could not be obtained until and unless the Gilberts were secured, and it was only in the Gilberts that a new air attack springboard for the Marshalls could be built.

Admiral Nimitz had long been trying to obtain intelligence of enemy activities in the Gilberts. Until the fall of 1943 he was dependent on carrier raids and submarine reconnaissance, and on the VII Army Air Force (Major General Willis H. Hale usa) based at Pearl Harbor. A number of Hale's Liberators equipped for photography were moved up to Canton Island and staged to Funafuti. On 26 January 1943, three of them made a combined bombing attack and photographic reconnaissance of Tarawa, 704 miles away, discovering the airstrip on Betio Island. Butaritari Island (Makin), photographed on 17 February, was found to be a strong seaplane base. All this was very disquieting. If progress continued at the same rate, the Gilberts might be rendered impregnable.

Nauru was another cause of anxiety. On 20 April General Hale in person led a raid of 22 Liberators from Funafuti, dropped numerous bombs and took 240 photographs. Japanese planes followed the Liberators home, and in the small hours of 21 April delivered an attack on Funafuti which destroyed two planes on the ground and killed six men. Two days later, Liberators visited Tarawa again.

The intelligence obtained on these raids helped Admiral Nimitz to convince the J.C.S. that the Gilbert Islands and Nauru, or some of them, must be taken before the Marshalls. Additional pressure in the same direction was applied by the British. Admiral Mountbatten was planning an amphibious operation against Akyab and the Ramree Islands in the Bay of Bengal, with a parallel land drive from Imphal into Burma, for the fall of 1943. Since the Marshalls operation could not start before the New Year, he hoped that the United States Navy would do something in the fall of 1943 that would keep the Japanese Navy off his neck. The J.C.S. pointed out that it would be mutually helpful if Nimitz hit the Gilberts at the same time that Lord Louis struck at Burma. On 20 July they issued the necessary directive to Cincpac to organize and train amphibious forces for the capture of the Gilbert Islands and Nauru around 15 November, and, by 1 September, to submit preliminary plans for taking the Marshalls early in 1944.

The Burma operation never came off; Mountbatten's forces were pulled out of Ceylon to take part in the invasion of Italy. In order to forestall a wrong conclusion that Americans reconquered the Gilberts at British request, one must reiterate that both the spark and the current in Operation "Galvanic," as the Gilberts campaign was called, were American.

Thus, on 20 July 1943, the J.C.S. decided to take two Gilbert

Islands plus Nauru first, and the Marshalls next. The objectives of both operations, as defined in this directive, were (1) to capture, occupy and control the Marshalls; (2) to improve Allied lines of communication across the Pacific; (3) to support other operations in the Pacific, partly to take the heat off other Allied operations but primarily to open through Micronesia a second "road to Tokyo" which in time would unite with the one that Admiral Halsey and General MacArthur were about to break through the Bismarcks Barrier.

On 20 August, Admiral Nimitz presented the J.C.S. with a tentative plan for simultaneous occupation of Kwajalein, Wotje and Maloelap in the Marshalls. The J.C.S. observed that the area which Nimitz proposed to seize was too narrow. At the Quadrant Conference at Quebec on 24 August, the Combined Chiefs of Staff, in their final report to the President and Prime Minister, proposed that the forthcoming advance in the Central Pacific should be divided into six phases: (1) Gilbert Islands and Nauru; (2) Marshall Islands, Wake and Kusaie; (3) Ponape; (4) Central Carolines including Truk; (5) Palaus and Yap; (6) Marianas. The J.C.S. passed on the first two in a directive to Cincpac dated 1 September.

The immediate practical questions were, Which Gilberts? And why Nauru? There was no doubt that Tarawa, with the only finished airfield in the Gilberts, should be the main objective. A second airfield could easily be constructed at Abemama. Nauru was included in order to "broaden the base," as one of the generals said; it seemed unwise to leave an island with an airfield only 380 miles from Tarawa in enemy hands. But, the more Nauru was studied, the less anyone liked the idea of assaulting it. For Nauru is a solid island with no harbor or lagoon, shaped like a hat with a narrow brim of coastal plain where the enemy had built his airfield, and a crown where he had mounted coast defense artillery. The hilly interior was full of holes and caves where phosphate rock had been excavated — just the sort of terrain that the Japanese liked for defensive operations. General Holland M. Smith pointed out that a whole division would be little enough to take Nauru, and the

Fleet had not enough transports to take it there at a time when Tarawa was being assaulted. But one regiment should suffice to take Makin. Admiral King, after contemplating a scale model of Nauru, agreed that it would not be worth the cost of capture. So, on 27 September, Admiral Nimitz obtained permission from the J.C.S. to substitute Makin for Nauru — a very wise change.

3. *Organization and Training*

The wisdom of this westward advance through Micronesia seems obvious now, but in the summer of 1943 many strategists regarded it as very risky because it would take ships beyond the range of Allied land-based air power. Air power advocates had been preaching the danger of sending even carriers into an area buzzing with enemy shore-based planes; had not the Japanese carriers got sunk at Midway by doing that? [12] In the Solomons the Navy had never ventured more than 300 miles from a friendly airfield; when escorting troops, it operated within 150 miles of one. But Tarawa lay 704 miles from the nearest Allied field, at Funafuti. There might be some justice in calling the Navy's earlier Pacific strategy "island hopping," although the Navy always resented the term; but now it was to be island leapfrogging with a new brand of seven-league boots — the *Essex*-class carriers.

Essex herself joined the Pacific Fleet in June 1943. Next month new *Yorktown*, new *Lexington* and light carriers *Independence*, *Belleau Wood* and *Princeton*, with 20 new 2100-ton destroyers and a couple of cruisers, came out. The new fast battleship *Alabama*, and *South Dakota* with her Guadalcanal scars healed, arrived in August. And the J.C.S. informed Admiral Nimitz that by October he might expect to have five new battleships, seven old ones, ten fast carriers, seven escort carriers, eight heavy and four light cruisers, 66 destroyers, 27 attack transports and cargo carriers, and

---

[12] They had not, as readers of Vol. IV know; but the myth of the Japanese carriers' being sunk by land-based planes died hard.

nine merchant ships suitable for transports. For air forces he could have all Pacific Fleet aircraft not assigned to Admiral Halsey in the South Pacific and the VII Army Air Force then based in Hawaii. In addition, the new Kaiser-built escort carriers began to join the Fleet in August, and Admiral Nimitz planned to use these to provide close support for the amphibious operations and for the ground troops ashore, as had been done by *Nassau* at Attu. The prewar battleships which had already proved their value as bombardment ships in the Aleutians were to be used in "Galvanic" to pound down the islands before the landings, while the new fast-stepping battleships would operate with the fast carrier forces.

At last the Central Pacific Force — Fifth Fleet after 15 March 1943 — was really formidable. It included practically the entire Pacific Fleet except Admiral Halsey's South Pacific Force and Admiral Fletcher's North Pacific Force. Vice Admiral Raymond A. Spruance, victor of Midway [13] and subsequently Admiral Nimitz's chief of staff, became Commander Fifth Fleet on 5 August 1943 and so also of the Gilbert Islands expeditionary force. When engaged in amphibious operations, ships of the Fifth Fleet were under the tactical command of the amphibious force group commander (Turner, Hill and, in the Marshalls, Conolly) to whom they were assigned. But there was always a plan for a major fleet action in case the Japanese Fleet challenged; in that event, the fleet commander would pull out all combatant ships that could be spared from protecting the landing force, in order to join the fast carrier forces and engage the enemy.

Within the Fifth Fleet the V Amphibious Force was set up on 24 August 1943 to plan, train and conduct the landings in Micronesia. The "V 'Phib," as it came to be called, organized a continuous training program for troops and ships and established close liaison with the aircraft belonging to assigned escort carriers. All attack transports (APA) and attack cargo vessels (AKA) in the Central

---

[13] Admiral Spruance, in commenting on the first draft of this volume, requested that I delete "victor of" and substitute "who commanded a carrier task force at"; but, for reasons which readers of Vol. IV will appreciate, I have let it stand.

Landing officer signaling to a Hellcat

Lieutenant Commander Edward H. O'Hare in his Hellcat

Action, Gilberts

U.S.S. Essex *during Operation "Galvanic"*

Pacific, all beaching craft (LST, LCT, LCI), all landing craft not yet attached to ships, and the new LSDs (landing ships, dock) were assigned to V 'Phib.

Rear Admiral Richmond K. Turner assumed command of the V Amphibious Force on the day it was created, relinquishing to Rear Admiral Wilkinson that of the Central Solomons operation which he had planned and inaugurated. Captain Paul S. Theiss, who had commanded the transports at Rendova, became his chief of staff. Pending conversion of command ship *Rocky Mount,* battleship *Pennsylvania* was assigned to Turner as his flagship. Proud old "Pennsy," sometime flagship of the United States Fleet, had been claimed sunk by Radio Tokyo no fewer than six times. The sailors at the submarine base, Pearl Harbor, jibed at her crew — "Ten to one you'll never get back this time!"

Turner divided the V 'Phib into two amphibious groups corresponding to the twin objectives of the Gilberts operation; he personally took charge of one and gave the other to his second in command, Rear Admiral Harry W. Hill. All ground troops under the force constituted the V Amphibious Corps, commanded by one of the fathers of modern amphibious warfare, Major General Holland M. Smith USMC.

"To assemble forces from such widely separated areas, adequately train them for the specific operation, deliver detailed plans, conduct a final rehearsal, and make a coördinated attack against separated objectives, . . . required the greatest of coördination and coöperation." [14] This was one of the rare understatements of Major General Holland M. Smith. Training for a big amphibious operation is probably the most difficult branch of military preparation. It never even approaches perfection because the units employed cannot be trained as a team. Circumstances are such that they can never be brought together before the actual operation. No base is big enough to hold them all; and even if one were the conditions of the operation could not be reproduced. A division, corps or even an army can be trained together for a land objective and the com-

[14] Commander V 'Phib Corps Report on Gilbert Islands Operation Jan. 1944.

manding general can inspect every regiment and know every colonel. A naval task force can be trained together for almost any sort of battle that is likely to occur, and the flag officer in command may know every ship and its captain. An air group can be trained to fight, bomb or scout, and the group commander can acquaint himself with the capabilities of every type of plane and almost every pilot under him. Contrast the situation of Admiral Turner. In an operation requiring the most detailed planning and the nicest timing, he commanded men of the Army, Navy and Marine Corps attached to ships, planes and ground forces in points as far apart as New Zealand, Hawaii, San Diego and Alaska, organized in units very few of which he could even see before D-day. It was as if a football coach were required to form a team from different parts of the country, brief them with a manual of plays, and, without even lining them up, send them against a champion opponent. To make the parallel complete, this All-American team would not even know on what field it would play. Security was so essential that the great majority of officers engaged in training did not even know, until after the troops were embarked, what islands they were to attack.

In addition to these organic and inescapable difficulties, Admiral Turner was allowed too little time. When he took command on 24 August, V 'Phib existed largely in blueprint. Most of its ships were not yet available; some were in the South Pacific, others in the Atlantic or the Aleutians, a few were not even in commission. The ground forces were in Hawaii, New Zealand, California and Samoa. Many commanders in his position would have demanded postponement of D-day at least a month. But "Kelly" Turner is a man of steel. Tireless himself, he expects unceasing work from his subordinates. A firm believer in the Navy way of doing the best you can with what you have, rather than waiting for better equipment and more training, he refused to contemplate any delay in starting the drive into Micronesia. D-day as finally set, 20 November 1943, was only five days later than the tentative date named in the J.C.S. directive of 20 July.

Before taking command of the V 'Phib Corps, General Holland M. Smith USMC had trained the troops that occupied Attu and Kiska. The General reported at Pearl Harbor 4 September, but neither he nor Turner learned until the 15th the composition of the Corps or its assignment: one regimental combat team of the 27th Division, then in Hawaii, to take Makin; the 2nd Marine Division, then in New Zealand, to take Tarawa; three defense battalions (two Marine, one Army), then at Samoa, Wallis and Pearl, for garrisons.

Admiral Spruance flew down to Wellington, New Zealand, about 3 August to confer with Major General Julian C. Smith USMC. The problem of getting troops ashore over a fringing coral reef was uppermost in Spruance's mind. Accordingly, he called at Canton, Upolu and Funafuti to study reef conditions, and communicated his findings to the Marines.[15] They started intensive amphibious training immediately.

The famous amphtracs or LVTs with which the Marines practised landings were track-driven amphibious vehicles propelled by gasoline engines. A development from the "alligators" manufactured by the American Food Machinery Corporation for rescue work in the Florida Everglades, their possibilities for landing operations were appreciated before the war by the Marine Corps, which had an improved model (LVT–1) built. The few employed at Guadalcanal and the Morocco landings in 1942 were not successful because they threw their tracks, wore them down quickly on shore, and stalled easily in the water. The Marines, however, had faith in the amphtrac as the only practicable method of getting assault troops over a fringing coral reef, and went on experimenting and making improvements. These hippo-like objects were 25 feet long by 10 feet 8 inches wide, weighed 23,000 pounds, carried 20 men or 6500 pounds of cargo and a crew of three to six, mounted one or two

---

[15] At Funafuti the manufacturers of the dukw or amphibious truck conducted a demonstration for the Admiral but not enough dukws could then be obtained for use in the Gilberts. Later, with minor improvements, they became very valuable in the landing of matériel for amphibious operations. But the dukw was never an assault craft and never played the decisive rôle in amphibious warfare that Vannevar Bush assigns to it in *Modern Arms and Free Men* (1949).

machine guns and cost about $35,000. The advantage of amphtracs over landing craft was that they could do everything but fly. They could make 4 knots in the water, ride over shoals and reefs, crash through wire entanglements and do 15 miles per hour on land, loaded. The 2nd Division had about a hundred of them at New Zealand, and selected the best 75 to take along; 25 of these were loaded deep in the AKAs and so were unavailable for the assault, but 50 more were combat-loaded. In addition, the initial landing waves had 50 of the latest 1943 model (LVT–2) which were sent directly from the West Coast via Samoa as there was not time for them to join the division at Wellington.

The Marines in 16 transports, escorted by a destroyer division, sailed 1 November from Wellington for Efate where they were joined by Rear Admiral Hill's battleships, cruisers and destroyers that had left Pearl Harbor 21 October. All except the air elements of the Tarawa attack force now being assembled,[16] rehearsals were held off Fila Harbor and a landing practised at Mele Bay, Efate. Fueling completed on 13 November, the Southern Attack Force sailed from Efate for Tarawa. This 2nd Marine Division was in fine shape physically, hardened by Guadalcanal experience, the best unit that the United States had ever sent into an amphibious operation.

At Oahu the Northern Attack Force for Makin was mounted. The 27th Infantry Division, a New York National Guard outfit commanded by Major General Ralph C. Smith USA, had been there for a year and a half. One of its regiments, the 165th Infantry (the old 69th or "Fighting Irish" of World War I), was reinforced by additional artillery, engineers and other specialists to become the 165th Regimental Combat Team. This RCT, commanded by Colonel Gardiner Conroy USA, was selected by the Commanding General U.S. Army Forces Pacific [17] to capture Makin. Unfortunately the 27th Division had lost its fighting edge. First mobilized in 1940, it had been pulled out of maneuvers to "defend the West

---

[16] With the exception of a few naval units that accompanied the Northern Attack Force from Pearl and LSD *Ashland* which loaded the 2nd Division's tanks at Nouméa and joined at Fila.

[17] Lieutenant General Robert C. Richardson USA.

Coast" after Pearl Harbor, and in April 1942 was sent to augment the Hawaii garrison. Its company officers were too old, the morale of the men had declined from too long a stretch of garrison duty, and their amphibious training on Oahu was inadequate for want of tanks, air support and other essential elements.

Upon completion of a rehearsal at Maui and Kahoolawe 3 November, troops of the Northern Attack Force returned to their base camp on Oahu for six days while the transports were reprovisioned and refueled, and the V 'Phib staff planners held conferences with troop and ship commanders to discuss difficulties and make minor changes in plans.

Throughout the summer of 1943, there were fleet maneuvers, target practice and shore bombardment, and anti-aircraft fire at towed sleeves and "drone" planes. Over half the ships of the Fifth Fleet were new, and very few of its sailors knew battle. So vast had been the expansion of the Navy since Pearl Harbor that even veteran ships were now officered over 75 per cent by reservists, and manned almost 50 per cent by men who had never even been to sea. They had to be prepared not only for scheduled operations but for a fleet action in case the Japanese chose to challenge. Vice Admiral Raymond A. Spruance, energetic without waste motion, thoughtful and economical of speech, spared neither himself nor his small staff nor his men; but battle practice is one thing that the American bluejacket never grumbles about, at least when he expects a real fight.

The new carriers with partly trained air squadrons offered a particular problem. Escort carriers had not proved very useful in the Pacific, and the recent history of fast carriers was such that problems of protection, tactics and employment gave Vice Admiral John H. Towers, Commander Air Force Pacific, plenty to worry about. Fast carriers had saved the day at Coral Sea and Midway, and in two of the Solomons battles; but all except *Enterprise* and *Saratoga*, which were damaged, had ended on the bottom. The flattops with their attendant battleships, cruisers and destroyers wanted training in teamwork, and their aviators needed combat practise.

Consequently they were tried out on a series of raids conducted more for training and tune-up than from any expectation of positive military benefit.

4. *Preliminary Operations*

a. Fast Carrier Strikes, 1 September–6 October

Marcus Island, 1568 miles from Midway and less than 1000 miles from Tokyo, was worked over on 1 September by a task group built around carriers *Yorktown*, *Essex* and *Independence*, commanded by Rear Admiral Pownall. Hellcat fighters, Dauntless dive-bombers and Avenger torpedo-bombers made six strikes totaling 275 combat sorties. Several Japanese "Bettys" were destroyed on the ground; three Hellcats and one Avenger were lost.

Admiral Pownall now led another carrier task force built around *Lexington*, *Princeton* and *Belleau Wood* in a raid on the Gilberts. On 18–19 September seven strikes were made by the carrier planes on Tarawa and Makin. Again, four were expended, but this attack did plenty of damage. Half of the 18 planes present on Tarawa were destroyed, and "a great number" of soldiers killed and wounded; "The island is a sea of flames," recorded a Japanese diarist; the "Water Defense Section" (three picket boats and minecraft) was wiped out and a *Maru* in the lagoon was sunk. Makin "shivered in the shower of bombs all day." [18] But the really important booty from this raid was the set of low oblique photos of the lagoon side of Betio, taken by *Lexington's* planes, which were most useful in the detailed planning for the assault on Tarawa.

Wake Island's turn came 5 and 6 October when the largest fast carrier force yet organized, *Essex*, *Yorktown*, *Lexington*, *Cowpens*, *Independence* and *Belleau Wood* under Rear Admiral Alfred E. Montgomery, made six strikes totaling 738 combat sorties, but at heavy cost — 12 planes lost in combat and 14 operationally. About

[18] Lt. Roland Boyden's "Notes on Carrier Raids" prepared for Operational Information Section Comairpac; Jicpoa Items Nos. 3872 and 4991, captured diaries.

three times the weight of bombs was dropped on Wake as on Marcus, and the target was also shelled by battleships and cruisers. As to Japanese planes, 22 (out of 65 claimed) were destroyed, and only 12 were left, so air reinforcements were sent up from the Marshalls.[19]

After these preliminary workouts the fast carrier forces received a brief rest before firing the opening guns of Operation "Galvanic."

The value of these raids on Marcus and Wake, as well as of a bombing strike on Nauru in early November by the VII Army Air Force, was questioned. Why expend valuable pilots and aircraft on targets that one has no intention of capturing? Planes splash or get shot down and trained aviators are lost; the enemy promptly repairs damage and flies in reinforcements. But, in naval warfare, battle is the best battle practice. If a fleet proposes to win, it must seek out tough assignments and accept casualties, for military power too long saved and husbanded has a way of turning sour.

Vice Admiral Charles A. Lockwood, Commander Submarines Pacific Fleet, at the request of Rear Admiral Pownall, stationed submarines off Marcus and Wake Islands at the time of the strikes with a primary mission to rescue fallen aviators. *Skate* (Commander E. B. McKinney), assigned to Wake, was strafed at dawn 6 October by a Japanese plane which seriously wounded one of her officers. Next morning she sighted American planes, apparently looking for the target, and gave them the correct course. McKinney then moved his boat up to a patrol line about six miles off the reefs, but a Japanese coast defense gun got *Skate's* range and forced her to submerge. When she surfaced at 1130,

[19] *Inter. Jap. Off.* p. 133. The gunfire ships took so long to silence coastal batteries that Capt. R. W. Bates, commanding cruiser *Minneapolis*, felt compelled to write a letter to Admiral Nimitz, urging that "both air power and ship-based gun power in *great quantity*" be furnished at Tarawa "to insure that the enemy batteries have been silenced," and predicting "that *even then* it may be expected that the landing will be opposed in strength and that considerable losses will fall to the attackers." There is a vivid account of this raid by Robert Sherrod in Gordon Carroll (ed.) *History in the Writing* (1945) pp. 283–88.

McKinney received word that three American aviators had splashed. He conned her shoreward through shellfire from the beach and picked up one aviator from the water and another from a rubber boat but, when searching for the third, was attacked and forced under by a Japanese dive-bomber. *Skate's* wounded officer, Lieutenant (jg) W. E. Maxon, was in so critical a condition that, on Admiral Lockwood's orders, McKinney headed for Midway at top surface speed. But she had not gone far when a message came through from Rear Admiral Montgomery, commanding the carrier strike, stating that nine more aviators were adrift on rafts near Wake. Back went *Skate* and succeeded in rescuing four of them. Lieutenant Maxon died of his wounds, but this boat had proved the value of submarine "lifeguarding," which became doctrine for carrier strikes beyond the range of Dumbo rescue planes. And the morale of carrier aviators was enhanced by the knowledge that submarines were standing by.

After the conclusion of *Skate's* mission, Commander McKinney received this message from Captain Stump of *Lexington:* "Anything in *Lexington* is yours for the asking. If it is too big to carry away, we will cut it up in small parts!" [20]

b. Baker Island Reoccupied [21]

While battle practice and carrier raids were going on, Americans were moving into the friendly Ellices north of Funafuti, and into Baker Island. Between 18 and 28 August, elements of the VII Army Air Force and a battalion of Seabees, conveyed by carriers *Independence* and *Princeton*, occupied Nukufetau and Nanomea. Work on airfields there started immediately with equipment begged, borrowed and stolen from Espiritu Santo, Wallis, Tutuila and Hawaii. Nanomea, the more advanced of the two, had a bomber field with a mile-long runway ready on 27 October,

---

[20] Theodore Roscoe *Submarine Operations World War II* pp. 281–82.
[21] Report by Capt. W. J. Jennings of Admiral Lee's staff, later island commander.

and was already supporting an occupation and service force of 2300 men.

Baker offered a new and profitable staging point for air search and photo reconnaissance. This tiny elliptical island, an American possession for almost a century, rises from great depths to mark the Equator at long. 176°28′ W. It is about a hundred miles nearer than Funafuti to the northern Gilberts, and almost on the direct line from Canton to Maloelap.

Rear Admiral Willis Augustus Lee, in what must have seemed to him a strange sort of flagship, naval freighter *Hercules*, commanded a small task group which landed on Baker, 1 September 1943, an engineer battalion of the VII Army Air Force and other base troops. *Ashland*, first of the new LSDs, brought up 23 LCMs preloaded with bulldozers in her womb-like dock, supposedly a snug harbor for them to operate from. But the ground swell caused her to roll so heavily that the gear carried away and her offspring, half full of water after sloshing around inside, had to be hoisted out by cranes — an LSD Caesarian, as it were. Nor was that the end of their troubles. There is no bottom off Baker that ground tackle can reach, and the current runs parallel to the lee shore; so the transports could unload only by heaving-to broadside to the swell and lowering both men and cargo over the lee bulwarks, while ship and landing craft rolled and drifted down-wind together. LCM crews had not acquired sufficient seamanship to enable them to cope with such conditions, and 11 out of 23 of these craft were sunk or damaged beyond repair.

Air cover for the Baker occupation was furnished at night by Navy Venturas from Canton Island, in daytime by Hellcats from light carriers *Princeton* and *Belleau Wood* under the command of Rear Admiral Radford [22] with a fighter-director team in de-

[22] Arthur W. Radford of Iowa, born Chicago 1896, Naval Academy '16, battleship duty in World War I, and after winning his wings in 1920 closely associated with naval aviation. Commander Fighter One in *Saratoga* 1930; two tours of duty in Buaer and two on staff of Commander Aircraft, Battle Force; Commander N.A.S. Seattle 1937; "exec." of *Yorktown* 1940. As director of aviation training Buaer from outbreak of war to April 1943, he organized the vastly expanded program of training naval aviators, and deserves great credit for keeping up high

stroyer *Trathen*. On three different occasions the Hellcats were vectored north on radar contact, and each time they shot down an "Emily" 4-engine flying boat from Makin, so quickly and neatly that the Japanese pilots were unable even to report what hit them. Their squadron commander, fearing that some operational defect had caused their disappearance, stopped sending them out after losing these three, as was subsequently learned from his diary captured at Makin.

On 11 September the new airstrip on Baker was ready and an Army fighter squadron flew in to base there. Two days later a reconnaissance party landed on nearby Howland Island to inspect the 2400-foot airstrip which had been prepared for Amelia Earhart in 1937. Early in the war it had been bombed by American planes so that the Japanese could not use it, and by the Japanese so that the Americans could not use it; but both sides were poor marksmen and the strip was soon put into condition for use for emergency landings.

c. Photographic Reconnaissance

Before December 1943, land-based air operations in the Central Pacific were few in number and of slight importance, owing to the vast distances involved. Between 1 January and 1 September, only 102 combat sorties had been flown; in October, only 71. Admiral Fitch's planes made 3187 combat sorties in the South Pacific that month. Even in November, while Operation "Galvanic" was on, land-based Navy and Army Liberators made only 259 sorties against the Gilberts and Marshalls, as compared with 2284 sorties on the same targets by carrier aircraft, and dropped only 275 tons of bombs, as compared with 917 from carrier-based planes. "These attacks," concluded the analyst for Commander

---

standards under pressure. Comcardiv 11 from July 1943, chief of staff to Comairpac from Dec. 1943, asst. deputy C.N.O. for Air from May 1944, Comcardiv 6 in the Iwo Jima and Okinawa campaigns, deputy C.N.O. for Air Dec. 1945, Com 2nd Task Fleet Feb. 1947, Vice C.N.O. 1948, Cincpac April 1949.

Air Force Pacific Fleet, "did little damage of any military importance, and there is no indication that any fields were closed for more than the duration of the attack." [23]

So far, Army Air Force bombers had carried the camera from land bases; the Navy now began to help. Fleet Air Photographic Squadron VD–3 (Commander Robert J. Stroh), eight Liberators with an operational radius of 1100 miles, moved in to Canton Island in early October; the new Baker and Nanomea fields were useful for staging their missions, and Marine Corps Fighter Squadron 111 moved up from Samoa into Nukufetau for intercepting enemy counterattacks. Squadron VD–3 first photographed Makin on 13 October and Tarawa on the 20th, besides covering the other Gilbert Islands thoroughly and ascertaining that no enemy forces of any consequence were in them. Early in November, reinforced by more Liberators, this squadron extended its operations to the Marshalls, photographing Mili on the 5th, Wotje and Maloelap on the 13th, Tarawa again and Jaluit on the 16th (in company with some VII Army Air Force Liberators from Nanomea) and Wotje on the 17th. The photographs of Mili showed a large airfield; it received much attention from carrier planes during the Gilberts operation.[24]

Fortunately the planners at Pearl Harbor did not have to wait for photos by land-based planes. Those of Tarawa taken by *Lexington's* planes on 18 September [25] gave sufficient information about the beaches and tides to determine D-day. Admiral Nimitz on 5 October recommended that it be 19 November, and Cominch approved. But the most useful intelligence of Tarawa was obtained by submarine *Nautilus*. Her periscope was fitted with a camera bracket and she was supplied with three cameras which proved unsatisfactory; but fortunately her "exec," Lieu-

[23] Comairpac "Analysis of Pacific Air Operations" for Sept.–Nov. 1943.
[24] *Review of Gilberts and Marshalls Campaign* (VII A.A.F. Gen. Intel. Bulletin No. 21); data from "Prisic" (Photo Reconnaissance and Interpreter Section Intelligence Center), Cincpac; Squadron VD–3 War Diary.
[25] The VII A.A.F. participated in this attack, dropped bombs, claimed shooting down 7 enemy fighters (Japanese sources say none got off the ground) and took photographs; but *Lexington's* low obliques were the more valuable.

tenant Commander R. B. Lynch, an ardent "shutter-bug," saved the day with his own German-made camera. *Nautilus* arrived off Tarawa 25 September and spent 18 days making a thorough reconnaissance of it, as well as of Abemama and Makin. The periscope was rotated at each exposure and a long roll of film taken, so that a continuous panorama of the coastline was obtained.[26] Owing to these efforts, added to those of the planes, intelligence of the defenses of Tarawa and of the approaches through the lagoon to Betio Island was virtually complete. *Nautilus* did not return to Pearl until 7 October, and Admiral Hill's staff had to work day and night to incorporate her information in a revised operation plan, dated 4 November, in time for distribution to every ship of the Southern Attack Force.

As naval vessels, great and small, from newest battleship down to beaching craft, with troop-laden transports, supply ships and fleet oilers, began to converge from sixteen points of the compass toward their Gilbertese objectives, the land-based planes of Army, Navy and Marine Corps were marshaled at Canton Island, Funafuti, Nukufetau and Nanomea. Rear Admiral John H. Hoover, his flag in tender *Curtiss*, commanded all land-based air forces for this operation, no matter what service they belonged to.

Preliminary air bombing began 13 November when 17 Army Liberators hit Betio. Every day for the next week, Tarawa or Makin or both had a similar visitation. In the Marshalls at the same time, Mili was bombed four times, Jaluit twice and Maloelap twice, and a number of planes that might have interfered with Operation "Galvanic" were eliminated. The enemy twice struck back, at Nanomea and Funafuti, destroying one B–24 and damaging two. Intensive air searches by the VII Army Air Force began from Baker and Nanomea on 16 November over segments of a circle with an 800-mile radius that reached a point east of Maloelap in the Marshalls and, in conjunction with the searches from

---

[26] Roscoe *U.S. Submarine Operations World War II* pp. 282–84. *Permit* and *Porpoise* had taken photos of Kwajalein, not good enough for Intelligence, in early September.

Espiritu Santo and other South Pacific bases, effectively covered the waters from Midway down through the southern Marshalls and up to the southern fringe of the Carolines.[27]

The initial sortie of surface forces from Pearl Harbor took place on 21 October: three carriers, four battleships, four cruisers, two oilers and 14 destroyers departed to join the Marines off Efate. Even after these had left, 196 combatant ships were counted in Pearl Harbor. Never before had there been such intensive activity there, and in the Fijis and New Hebrides, as during the last days of October and the first of November 1943. Then, suddenly, each harbor and roadstead was deserted. Over two hundred sail, the Fifth Fleet carrying 108,000 American soldiers, sailors, Marines and aviators under the command of taut Spruance, gallant Hill, and bristling Turner, were on the high seas. By various and devious routes they were converging on two coral atolls whose names will be remembered as long as men prize valor: Makin and Tarawa.

[27] Data on searches from overlays in Operations section Cincpac staff.

CHAPTER VI

Logistics Afloat in the Pacific[1]

NAVAL LOGISTICS is commonly supposed to be a very dull subject; few naval historians tell one anything about how a fleet manages to get supplied with food, fuel, ammunition and countless other items which fighting men afloat must have in order to wage war. But in the Pacific war logistics problems were so vast and so novel that the story of how they were solved is of surpassing interest.

As a result of the United States Fleet's cruise around the world in 1907–09, the Navy built a small number of destroyer and submarine tenders, fleet repair ships, supply ships and colliers (later replaced by oilers). It also adopted the policy of effecting a ship's repairs by her own crew as far as possible despite opposition by unions and politicians interested in "making work" at navy yards. The striking success of the tenders based at Queenstown and Brest in servicing destroyers in World War I confirmed this trend toward self-sufficiency and lessened dependence on navy yards. Shortly after that war, the Navy established the Base Force, which later became the Service Force, to give mobile logistic support to the fleet. Ammunition ships and other special types were

---

[1] This chapter attempts to deal only with the special problems created by the Central Pacific advance. Initially compiled from oral information obtained during the war from Vice Adm. W. L. Calhoun and several members of his staff, from Capt. W. M. Callaghan, Capt. C. R. Eagle and Lt. Cdr. T. A. Brown of the Logistics Section of Cincpac-Cincpoa staff, it has been revised after discussions with Commo. Worral R. Carter, wartime commander of Servron 10, who lent me his ms. study of Pacific logistics called "Beans, Bullets and Bulkheads," and Capt. H. E. Eccles, head of the Dept. of Logistics at the Naval War College, who has issued a number of mimeographed books and pamphlets, especially *Pacific Logistics* (1946), *Establishment of Advance Bases* (1946) and *Operational Naval Logistics* (revised ed. 1950).

developed. Even so, the vast problems involved in extending a naval war across the Pacific were only in part anticipated.

On 12 March 1942, the same day on which the President appointed Admiral Ernest J. King Chief of Naval Operations, he designated, at King's suggestion, Vice Admiral Frederick J. Horne Vice Chief of Naval Operations; and to him King virtually delegated the responsibility for logistics planning, procurement and distribution. Horne worked in close coöperation with Lieutenant General Brehon B. Somervell, head of the United States Army Service of Supply, and with the Assistant Secretary of the Navy for Air, who looked out for naval plane procurement; with Mr. James Forrestal, Under Secretary of the Navy, and with Rear Admiral Ben Moreell, Chief of the Bureau of Yards and Docks and father of the famous Seabees. But Admiral Horne [2] was the key figure. "Placed at the crossroads of civilian-military pressure," he was able to see the problem as a whole, to reconcile incongruities in the system as he found it, and to persuade discordant elements to work together harmoniously.[3]

As far back as 1904, Civil Engineer A. C. Cunningham USN had proposed that the Navy establish a mobile service force made up of floating dry docks, colliers, repair, supply and hospital ships that would move with the Fleet and provide the services of a naval base.[4] This farseeing suggestion could not be acted upon until the necessity arose. Congress never liked appropriating money for bases outside the continental United States, but it was even

[2] Frederick J. Horne, b. New York 1880, Naval Academy '99, served in *Texas* at Battle of Santiago. Various sea assignments as engineer or navigating officer or "exec." 1899–1915, when he began a 4-year term as naval attaché at the American Embassy, Tokyo. C.O. successively of *Von Steuben, Buffalo* and *Birmingham,* 1919–21. At Naval and Army War Colleges, 1922–23; C.O. *Omaha,* 1924–26; qualified as naval aviation observer, 1926; C.O. aircraft tender *Wright.* War Plans Division under C.N.O., 1927–29; C.O. *Saratoga* to 1930; aircraft squadrons commander Scouting Fleet, chief of staff 14th Naval Dist. and Com. Training Squadron 1 to 1933, when promoted Rear Admiral. Comcrudiv 6 in 1935, Comaircraft Battle Force, 1936; General Board 1938 to 27 Dec. 1941, when appointed Vice Chief of Naval Operations, a post which he held until Jan. 1946.

[3] Duncan S. Ballantine *U. S. Naval Logistics in the Second World War* (1947) p. 149.

[4] "The Movable Base," U.S. Naval Inst. *Proceedings* III No. 1 (March 1904) p. 181.

less willing to provide a large and expensive fleet train in time of peace. And the logistics problems of World War I were relatively simple, with but one ocean to cross and friendly bases overseas.

During the first year and a half of the Pacific war, logistics requirements for ships operating thousands of miles from United States territory were partly met by building advanced bases [5] where supplies of various sorts could be stockpiled, and where combatant ships and auxiliaries could get what they needed. The United States lost Cavite and Guam to Japan, leaving only Pearl Harbor, Dutch Harbor and Pago Pago as extra-continental Pacific bases. Base facilities were now built or leased at Bora Bora in the Society Islands, Nandi and Suva in the Fijis, Nouméa in New Caledonia, Havannah and Fila in Efate, Segond Channel in Espiritu Santo, Tulagi in the Solomons, Wellington in New Zealand, Brisbane and Sydney in Australia. Some of these could be used as springboards for portions of American forces assaulting the Gilberts and Marshalls; but Espiritu Santo lies over a thousand miles from Tarawa; and Nandi, a little farther, is almost 3000 miles from Pearl Harbor over the route that the Japanese then compelled Allied ships to use. In any case, now that a massive and swift transpacific advance was planned, fleet maintenance could no longer be carried on merely by building new advanced bases. It would take too long, and if the advance was successful, each base would have to be "rolled up" almost as soon as it was ready for use. Some new advanced bases were indispensable, if only to operate and defend new airfields; but the Pacific war could never have been won without mobile logistic bases.

Pearl Harbor, 2100 miles distant from Tarawa, was the great store center and naval base for the Central Pacific. Its facilities, fortunately built up by the President's decision in 1940 to base the Pacific Fleet there,[6] and as fortunately spared by the Japanese

[5] See Volume IV of this History pp. 242–53, 263 for a brief account of bases in the South Pacific in 1942; the full story is told in the official publication *Building the Navy's Bases in World War II*, Vol. II (1947).
[6] See Volume III of this History p. 47.

Taken by Lexington planes. Note the wide apron of reef, with native fish traps and wire obstacles

Air Photos of Betio 18 September 1943

Vice Admiral William L. Calhoun

on 7 December 1941, had been constantly expanded and developed ever since. But Pearl Harbor could not take care of all the Fleet's requirements in Operation "Galvanic." Service Force Pacific Fleet must now supply and service an amphibious force approximately twice as great as the one which had taken French Morocco, and in an area where there were no large land masses, no labor, no supplies or facilities of any kind. Admiral Spruance could not afford the time and fuel to send his ships on a 4000-mile round trip to Pearl every few weeks. How could this logistics problem be solved?

At Pearl Harbor the two principal organizations concerned with the logistic support of the Pacific war were Service Force Pacific Fleet, commanded by Vice Admiral William L. Calhoun, and the Logistics Section of Cincpac-Cincpoa staff. "Uncle Bill" Calhoun [7] had already initiated and established the supply system for the South Pacific. A man who inspired deep affection from those who came into contact with him, he allowed no difficulties to daunt him. As Admiral Spruance said, "There was nothing the Fleet wanted that Uncle Bill wouldn't get." Loyalty was perhaps his outstanding quality: loyalty to the Fleet and to Admiral Nimitz, loyalty to his subordinates and his staff, which comprised a number of very able officers. There were Commodore Allen G. Quynn, his chief of staff; [8] Rear Admiral Charles A. Dunn, his Fleet Maintenance Officer; [9] Captain Henry E. Eccles of his Ad-

[7] William L. Calhoun, b. Florida 1884, Naval Academy '06; served as junior officer in various ships until 1915, when he qualified as a submariner and also as inspector of ordnance and machinery. Commanded Subdiv 1 and sub base at Coco Solo, 1917–19; gunnery officer *Mississippi;* helped fit out *California;* C.O. *Young* 1921–23; navigator of *Maryland* until 1925; inspector of ordnance at Mare I., Comdesdiv 31 1927–29; Naval War College course; C.O. *Rochester* 1932–33; duty in N.O.B. San Diego, 1934–37; C.O. *California;* Com Base Force Pacific Fleet (which became Service Force Pacific Fleet in 1942) from Dec. 1939 to Mar. 1945; Comsopac to Oct. 1945; retired 1 Dec. 1946. Away back in his gunnery officer days, after his ship had won the fleet gunnery trophy, a bluejacket was overheard saying, "Uncle Bill is a talkative old so-and-so, but he delivers the goods."

[8] Except Feb.–Oct. 1943 when Capt. H. M. Scull was chief of staff.

[9] Relieved May 1944 by Rear Adm. Harold T. Smith. Cdr. L. B. Stuart, who ran surface operations of the Service Force under this office, was so able that it was said of him that he could arrange to have the same tug towing at two different places at the same time!

vanced Base Section; Captain Carleton R. Eagle, his Supply Officer, who was responsible for provisioning the Fleet; Captain Augustine H. Gray, the "oil king of the Pacific"; Captains Herbert M. Scull, Worrall R. Carter and Jasper T. Acuff, who commanded the mobile service squadrons. Although he loved detail himself, Admiral Calhoun gave his subordinates complete authority and never interfered with their conduct of their several and complicated tasks. "Most coöperative man I ever worked under," said one of them.

Service Force Pacific Fleet implemented all strictly naval logistic plans of Admiral Nimitz's staff, except those relating to the naval air arm which were the province of Vice Admiral John H. Towers, Commander Air Force Pacific Fleet. Army plans were implemented by the Army Service of Supply; Marine Corps plans by the Marines' own logistics organization. The important thing is that these Army, Navy, Marine and Air plans in the Pacific all emanated from the same source. Admiral Nimitz's joint staff was "joint all the way through";[10] its logistics Section (J–4) eminently so. Under an Army officer, Major General Edmond H. Leavey USA, it was organized as follows: —

J–41 Transportation and Priorities, Captain William M. Callaghan
J–42 Fuel and Lubricants, Captain Russell M. Ihrig
J–43 Supply, Captain Carleton R. Eagle, Supply Corps[11]
J–44 Planning, Captain William G. Greenman[12]
J–45 Medical, Captain Thomas C. Anderson, Medical Corps
J–46 Construction, Colonel Ralph G. Barrows USA, Engineer Corps
J–47 Administration and Statistics, Lieutenant Commander Thomas A. Brown, Supply Corps

[10] Letter of Capt. Eccles to writer, 3 Oct. 1950. See Vol. VI 11 for complete list of sections of Cincpac-Cincpoa staff. An earlier Joint Army and Navy Logistical Board set up at Pearl Harbor in March 1943 had proved ineffective because its powers were advisory only. The Joint Logistics Section was an integral part of Cincpac-Cincpoa staff, and its directives had the force of command.

[11] This division determined who was to supply what materials when, where and in what quantities. The execution then became a responsibility of one of three agencies: Service Force Pacific Fleet, Air Force Pacific Fleet, or Commanding General Hawaiian Dept. Capt. Eagle "wore two hats" — he was also Supply Officer of Serforpac, as we have seen.

[12] This was the old Advanced Bases Planning Unit of Serforpac. Col. B. F. Hayford USA relieved Capt. Greenman about 1 Jan. 1944.

In addition, two divisions of the Operations Section of the Joint Staff, Combat Readiness (J–31), headed by Captain Thomas B. Hill, and Communications (J–35), headed by Captain John R. Redman, were made responsible to the head of the Logistics Section for planning the supply of ammunition and communications matériel, both of which the Pacific war consumed in enormous quantities and infinite variety, as new weapons and radar were developed. And, just before the Marshalls operation, a new section was added to Cincpac-Cincpoa staff, the Central Shipping Control Agency under Captain John F. Rees, aided by Colonel Frederic H. Nichols USA. With this addition, the shore-based logistics machinery that lasted through the Pacific war was complete. (The naval bases in the Pacific never were placed under Service Force; they were a direct responsibility of Cincpac working through area and island commands.)

Despite defects, the new setup worked very well. General Leavey, one of the most intelligent and hard-working officers at Pearl Harbor, soon grasped the essential needs and principles of fleet supply. His division heads were zealous and industrious. Admiral Calhoun's Service Force became far more effective when told well in advance by the planners what was required, and when and where. Logistics Section and Service Force, housed in Cincpac-Cincpoa headquarters at Makalapa,[13] together worked out revolutionary innovations in logistics to meet the special needs of the Pacific war.

The first great problem to be faced in the Central Pacific advance was that of resupplying the Gilbert Islands after their capture, simultaneously with the rapid approach of D-day for the Marshalls. Building up bases in the Gilberts would require more matériel from Pearl Harbor than had ever before been sent to the Fleet at sea, and the Marshalls would need still more and at a greater distance; Kwajalein lies 2137 miles from Pearl Harbor. What could be done to take care of both simultaneously?

[13] Early in 1944 Service Force moved into the adjoining building especially erected for it (see illustration in Vol. VI 19); but Logistics Section remained in the Cincpac Building.

A mobile supply base, Cunningham's suggestion of 1904, was the answer. This innovation in the art of naval warfare was worked out by Service Force Pacific Fleet, just before Operation "Galvanic." On 1 November 1943 Service Squadron 4, the first floating base in any navy, was commissioned, with Captain Herbert M. Scull, Admiral Calhoun's chief of staff, as commander. The initial composition of this squadron on 20 November 1943 will be found in the organization table in Appendix II. It consisted of tenders, repair ships, tugs, minesweepers and a collection of three 366-foot concrete fuel barges, six 2000-ton-capacity steel barges for general stores, two 500-ton lighters for receiving and sorting, and two for ammunition.[14]

This mobile base carried a thirty-day supply of food and medicine for 20,000 men, three units of anti-aircraft fire for guns, one unit of fire for ground weapons, ten of aviation bombs, 15 days' fuel for vehicles, distillers, ranges and various machines carried by the landing force, and ample spare parts and repair facilities. Servron 4 began assembling in Funafuti lagoon well before D-day. Its barges, accompanied by destroyer escorts, floated supplies up to the Fleet and to the amphibious forces in the Gilberts almost daily, and provided repair and salvage facilities. The scheme worked very well and Servron 4 was absorbed into a new and larger mobile service base, Service Squadron 10, Captain W. R. Carter's, which moored in Majuro Lagoon after the capture of Kwajalein in January 1944.[15]

---

[14] The barge business is a story in itself. The first acquired by Servron 4 were big steel Mississippi River sugar barges which had been towed from New Orleans to Nouméa early in 1943 to relieve the unloading bottleneck there. The reinforced concrete oil barges were built in Miami for carrying fuel along the inland waterways in 1942 when the U-boats were sinking tankers off the East Coast. Each carried 66,000 bbl. of oil and had living quarters; they were invaluable for fuel storage in advance bases. In addition, before the end of 1944, thirteen large 366-foot concrete barges, each with a crew of 58, were used for the storage and issue of fresh and dry provisions, clothing, small stores and many other items. Some had bakeries and butcher shops on board to permit crews of patrol and other small craft to have as varied a diet as those of larger ships.

[15] Servron 10 comprised provision ships, barracks ships, tankers, hospital ships, DD tenders, a survey ship, net tenders, repair ships, a pontoon assembly ship, SCs, PTs, YPs, buoy boats, harbor and salvage tugs, a floating dry dock, a degaussing

A mobile supply base was the logistic counterpart to the airplane carrier. While flattops projected naval air power within striking distance of the enemy, Servrons 4 and 10 acted as a logistic annex to Pearl Harbor for servicing the Fleet at sea. Advanced naval bases were still needed; but it was the mobile base, in conjunction with the fast carriers, that permitted leapfrogging with seven-hundred-league boots.

Fuel supply, the persistent logistics problem ever since navies abandoned the use of sail, became one of increasing urgency as ever greater numbers of ships, landing craft, planes, vehicles and shore installations consumed astronomical amounts of petroleum derivatives.[16] The technique of oiling at sea had been solved by the United States Navy in World War I, but never before had the problem arisen of how to fuel some 200 combatant ships at sea for 30 days without sending them into port. The situation was met by Service Squadron 8, commanded at Pearl by Captain Augustine H. Gray. All ships' fuel tanks were topped off before they left port, and each attack force was accompanied by two fleet oilers; but this was far from enough to maintain a fleet that was expected to do a lot of high-speed steaming. Accordingly, a task group drawn from Servron 8 was set up as a roving fueling group. Fleet oilers in "deuces" and "treys," escorted by destroyers, were dispatched to designated ocean positions near the Gilberts in order to fuel relays of combatant ships, according to a prearranged schedule; other oilers shuttled between these rendezvous and Pearl. Every fighting ship knew where she could oil up if caught short. And, in addition, commercial tankers were sent to Nandi and Funafuti to provide refills for the fleet oilers.

As so organized, fueling the Fifth Fleet in the Gilberts operation was easily effected by 13 fleet oilers, mostly of the *Cimarron* class, each of which carried 80,000 barrels of fuel oil, 18,000 bar-

---

vessel, a floating crane, and various craft down to and including the humble but indispensable "honey barge."

[16] Information on fueling from Commo. A. H. Gray, Lt. E. R. Smith, and documents in Service Force files. The oilers also carried limited amounts of provisions and other stores for transfer at sea during oiling.

rels of aviation gasoline and 6782 barrels of diesel oil, while nine commercial tankers brought in fuel at the rate of 600,000 barrels a month to the nearest bases; and another fleet of commercial tankers kept the great underground "surge tank" at Oahu filled. In an operation like this, a nice balance had to be effected between tanker time and fleet time. Fewer tankers might have been used, but more fueling time would have been required; and ships oiling up would have been held down longer to the standard fueling speed of 8 to 12 knots. More tankers might have been found, but only by robbing Admiral Halsey. As it turned out, no ship wanting fuel was delayed longer than an hour, and more than enough oil was provided.[17] In the Marshalls operation no fewer than 28 oilers were employed.

During the Gilberts operation, it was possible to operate the fueling groups in stretches of ocean beyond the range of enemy land-based air; but when the Fifth Fleet penetrated the Marshalls that was no longer feasible. A division of escort carriers to provide air support for the oilers and their customers, and also to deliver replacement planes at sea, was added to the task group and the whole placed under the command of Captain Edward E. Paré of Servron 8.

The plan for Operation "Galvanic" called for over 35,000 soldiers, sailors and Marines to be landed on Makin, Tarawa and Abemama within five days. Admiral Nimitz's staff planners were greatly concerned with "troop lift" — the means of getting them there — and with the even greater problem of transporting 85,000 troops to the Marshalls ten weeks later. Distances were too great to send in assault troops in slow LSTs, LCIs and other beaching craft, although these could be used for the garrisons that relieved them. At that time, 12 attack transports (APA), 3 attack cargo ships (AKA) and 1 landing ship dock (LSD) were required to move a reinforced division of 20,000 to 21,000 men consisting of

---

[17] An average daily consumption of 80,000 bbls. was provided from 10 Nov. to 10 Dec., but, owing to the wind's being just right, the carriers, our greatest fuel consumers (*Essex* used 74,000 bbls. in this operation) did not have to use full speed to launch and recover planes, and so saved a great deal of oil.

three regimental combat teams with their ammunition, about 1500 vehicles and initial supplies. Four regimental combat teams had to be lifted to the Gilberts and at least twice as many to the Marshalls; but in July 1943 only 19 APAs and AKAs were even in sight. Several of the largest transports had been sunk in the Solomons, and many that the Pacific Fleet counted on were tied up in the Sicilian operation or were still on the ways. Admiral Halsey, it is said, had to "talk tough" at Pearl Harbor to get six transports for the landings at Empress Augusta Bay.

This troop-lift bottleneck illustrates the essential difference between short and long amphibious operations. For the assault on Hitler's *Festung Europa*, American troops could be shifted to North Africa, Italy and Great Britain by what amounted to colossal ferryboat operations. The troops could be trained at forward bases and, when wanted, conveyed to the points of enemy contact by beaching craft, APAs being used only for assault waves. In the Pacific, however, the only places where you could give a body of 50,000 troops "room and board" while they were waiting to fight were the Hawaiian Islands, Fiji, New Caledonia, Australia and New Zealand; and only the last two could help feed them from local resources; merely maintaining men in these places required a great volume of merchant shipping. Then, in order to carry them to the point of attack in combat-loaded transports, with the vast quantities of armor, artillery, vehicles and supplies that modern warfare demands, the armed forces required about one large ship to every 1100 men. And, what with training troops on board, combat-loading, rehearsing, getting there, unloading and standing by, these specially equipped transports could do nothing else for at least two months. Merchant ships and LSTs had to be ready to carry up reinforcements promptly in case the going was tough, or the assault force might be annihilated; for there was no hinterland on these coral atolls, no jungle or mountains where they could dig in, no chance for a perimeter defense as on Guadalcanal and Bougainville; either they must exterminate the enemy within a few days or be thrown out. Every blow struck in the Central Pacific had to be swift, sure and powerful; and that meant loading overwhelming forces for the initial attack.

On 6 August 1943 came the welcome word that the Chief of Naval Operations was shifting from the Mediterranean to Admiral Nimitz's command six APAs and two AKAs, which brought up the total to 20 (not counting Halsey's APAs); but that was still not enough. In the Gilberts operation, 15 chartered merchant ships and ordinary APs had to be used to help out. On 21 September seven more APAs were allotted to Cincpac, but they arrived only in time to carry troops to the Marshalls.

Food was another urgent problem. The service squadron in Admiral Halsey's command saw to stocking up the Marines before they left Wellington. Captain Eagle, who had personally set up "reverse lend-lease" from Australia and New Zealand on a business-like basis, had to find the rest. His feeding plan called for Navy rations to 87,854 men in 38 battleships, cruisers and carriers and in 122 destroyers and smaller vessels; and Army B rations for the 20,491 garrison forces to be left in the Gilberts. After 30 days the Army provided the food ashore, but the Navy had to get it there. Considering that it takes one ton (70 cubic feet) of shipping space to keep one soldier supplied with food, fuel, clothing, ammunition and small stores for one month,[18] and that the Navy was very short of "reefers" (refrigerator ships), this problem taxed Navy resources. As a starter, storeship *Boreas* (Commander E. E. Burgess) arrived at Efate on 27 October to provision all ships there to capacity; *Aldebaran* (Captain James L. Wyatt) went to Espiritu Santo, and *Bridge* arrived at Funafuti 24 November from Pearl Harbor to provision ships proceeding thither after the landings. The rest of the provisioning was effected by fleet freighters going direct from Hawaii to the scene of operations, while merchant vessels kept the vast warehouses at Pearl Harbor filled.[19]

[18] In a temperate or warm climate; 90 cu. ft. in the Arctic.

[19] There were good reasons for not bringing food direct from the West Coast: (1) it was more economical to use large ships on the route West Coast–Pearl and small ones from Pearl on, especially since we were not certain that even a Liberty ship could enter the Gilberts' lagoons; (2) it was desirable to keep the merchant marine out of the combat zone.

Naval provision storeships (AFs) by this time had worked out a system known as unit or vertical loading, which assured that the last warship supplied would receive the same assortment as the first. *Aldebaran*,[20] on her maiden voyage from San Francisco to Espiritu Santo 6 October to 24 November, discharged to shore activities and to 61 different naval vessels at Havannah, Segond Channel and Pallikulo Bay 1438 tons of fresh food, 2153 tons dry stores, and 1273 tons chilled and frozen provisions.[21] To Admiral Lee's battleships 1833 tons were delivered, in 44 hours, faster than their crews could strike the stuff below decks. In the Marshalls operation, ancient *Bridge*, whose tall stack had been familiar to the Fleet since 1917, made an even more remarkable record under Lieutenant Commander Robert R. Stevens USNR. In 40 hours she delivered 2080 tons of provisions to 80 different ships, receiving the high compliment of Admiral Turner's "appreciation of the efficiency, dispatch and patience" with which her mission was performed.[22]

In addition to feeding American sailors, troops and aviators, Service Force Pacific Fleet had to take care of the Gilbertese natives. With the help of some British evacuees from Makin, Captain Eagle worked out requirements for 30,000 natives for one month in terms of beef and flour, fishhooks and knives, calico and blackstrap tobacco.

Ammunition of all kinds for the Micronesian campaigns was planned for and procured by the combat readiness section of Cincpac staff. Captain Tom Hill, Commanders Ernest M. ("Judge") Eller and Mell A. ("Pete") Peterson, the bright lights of this section, despite their long hours and appalling responsibilities, kept such a blithe spirit that they were locally known as the "Pearl Harbor Gun and Fun Club." One of their many problems was to

[20] "Since taking command of the *Aldebaran* about one year ago, it is my pleasure to report that she has never failed to meet her schedule, and has delivered 22,918 tons of cargo without loss, and has traveled 61,115 miles." Capt Wyatt's report.

[21] Including enough for all hands' Thanksgiving dinners at sea; *Bridge* dispensed 60,000 lbs. of turkey on her provisioning voyage at this time.

[22] *Bridge* Ship's Memorandum No. 19, Feb. 18, 1944.

provide enough HC 14-inch ammunition for the battleships scheduled to do most of the shore bombardment, and yet have enough
AP shells on board in case Koga's Combined Fleet came roaring over from Truk. The Marines carried five units of fire ashore
at Tarawa and the soldiers wanted four times that amount at
Makin. Combat Readiness beat them down to 15 units, of which
the 27th Division actually used one unit to destroy enemy resistance; the other 14 went to the garrison.[23] All combatant ships
were given their total supply for the Gilberts operation before
leaving port, either from the magazines at Pearl Harbor or from
AEs (ammunition ships) *Lassen*, *Rainier* and *Shasta* at the New
Hebrides and Fiji. As these facilities were insufficient for the
Marshalls, and as only one more AE was in sight, ammunition
barges were added to the mobile service base in order to supply
the Fleet in forward areas.

Every island recovered from the enemy had to be put into a
defense perimeter and several were to be improved as bases. Consequently, Service Force Pacific Fleet had to provide for a continuous supply of rations, fuel, medicaments, construction materials, clothing, ammunition and small stores, and the Navy had
to find the shipping to carry it there. By 20 September, pools of
supplies were already being accumulated in Oahu to service our
expected acquisitions during the next eight months.

Behind Pearl Harbor lay a logistic network which extended
through Western Sea Frontier at San Francisco, with its warehouses at Alameda and Oakland, to the great collecting depot at
Clearfield, Utah, which had been set up on the eastern slope of
the Continental Divide in order to relieve railway congestion in
the Rocky Mountain passes; to Admiral Horne and General
Somervell at Washington; and thence into every city and town
and almost every farm in the United States. Planning, procurement, processing and transportation over this vast network were as
important for winning the war as the efforts and procedures we

---

[23] A unit of fire is a theoretical day's battle expenditure for each kind of
weapon. A unit of fire of aviation bombs is called a "mission."

have just described. But all these matters lie outside the scope of this History; we shall have to be content, here, with describing the end product at the battle theaters of the Pacific Ocean. The logistics aspects of Operation "Galvanic" may stand as an example of what took place with ever increasing variety, quantity and mobility through the rest of the Pacific war.

CHAPTER VII

Organization and Approach

November 1943

TO appreciate the size and complexity of Operation "Galvanic," the reader must consult the task organization in Appendix II and glance at the track chart here reproduced, which shows the ingenious method of bringing approximately 200 sail of ships carrying or escorting 27,600 assault and 7600 garrison troops, 6000 vehicles and 117,000 tons of cargo[1] to their destination.

The principal divisions of the task organization to keep in mind are: —

1. NORTHERN ATTACK FORCE (TF 52), commanded by Rear Admiral Richmond K. Turner in *Pennsylvania*, mounted at Pearl Harbor and destined for Makin. Six transports carrying one RCT of the 27th Division; four battleships and four cruisers for fire support, and three escort carriers for air support; an LSD full of tanks; three LSTs steaming ahead to get the amphtracs there on time. These and other slow ships departed first and followed a direct course. The main force started off as though destined for somewhere in the South Pacific, steaming well below the Line (which greatly pleased the crews, since it permitted their initiation as "Shellbacks"), fueled 15 November at a point about half-way between Baker and Canton Islands, steered due west to the international date line and then headed straight for Makin.

2. SOUTHERN ATTACK FORCE (TF 53), commanded by Rear Admiral Harry W. Hill, mounted in New Zealand and Efate and

[1] Figures from Turner Report on Gilberts, Enc. 1.

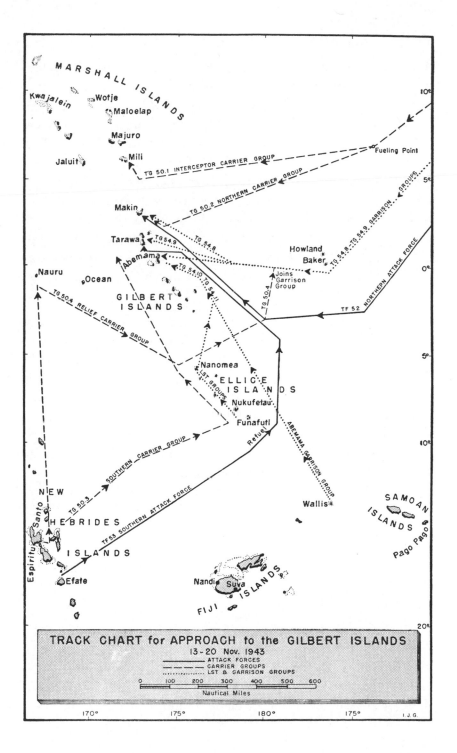

TRACK CHART for APPROACH to the GILBERT ISLANDS
13-20 Nov. 1943

ATTACK FORCES
CARRIER GROUPS
LST & GARRISON GROUPS

0   100   200   300   400   500   600
Nautical Miles

MARSHALL ISLANDS

Kwajalein   Wotje
Maloelap
Majuro
Mili
Jaluit

TG 50.1 INTERCEPTOR CARRIER GROUP

TG 50.2 NORTHERN CARRIER GROUP

Makin

Tarawa   TG 54.9   TG 54.8   TG 54.8-TG 54.9 GARRISON GROUPS

Abemama

TG 54.10 TG 54.11

Nauru   Ocean

GILBERT ISLANDS

Howland
Baker

Joins
Garrison
Group

TG 50.4

TF 52 NORTHERN ATTACK FORCE

TG 50.4 RELIEF CARRIER GROUP

Nanomea

ELLICE ISLANDS

LST GROUPS

Nukufetau

Funafuti

Refuel

NEW

ESPIRITU SANTO

HEBRIDES

ISLANDS

Efate

TG 50.3 SOUTHERN CARRIER GROUP

TF 53 SOUTHERN ATTACK FORCE

ABEMAMA GARRISON GROUP

Wallis

Nandi   Suva

FIJI ISLANDS

SAMOAN ISLANDS

Pago Pago

10°

5°

0°

5°

10°

20°

170°   175°   180°   175°

I.J.G.

destined for Tarawa. Sixteen transports, three battleships and five cruisers for fire support, five escort carriers for air support, 21 destroyers and one LSD with tanks. Admiral Hill went on board flagship *Maryland* at Efate on 5 November, together with General Julian C. Smith of the 2nd Marine Division. Most of Task Force 53 sortied from Havannah Harbor 12 November. It was joined next day by the escort carriers from Espiritu Santo, and on the 16th by three light cruisers under Rear Admiral DuBose, which had been covering troop movements to Bougainville. TF 53 fueled about 75 miles east of Funafuti, steered north and made a "dog leg" to Tarawa, paralleling TF 52 the last two days. The LSTs carrying amphtracs started from Samoa and came up through the Ellice Islands.

3. Fast Carrier Forces Pacific Fleet (TF 50), commanded by Rear Admiral Charles A. Pownall. This was the greatest carrier force hitherto assembled anywhere, yet only a nucleus of the famous TF 38. Four new *Essex*-class carriers, five light carriers, veteran *Enterprise* and venerable *Saratoga* who, with her old-fashioned superstructure, suggested a nineteenth-century ship of the line among the first ironclads. For escorts, TF 50 had six new battleships, three heavy cruisers, three anti-aircraft cruisers and 21 destroyers — which were not enough.

It was divided into four groups, each of which had a special mission. Two of them had been lent to the South Pacific to pound Rabaul, and Spruance did not know until the day he sailed whether Halsey would be through with them in time for him to use them; the other two groups as well were very busy during the ten days before the Gilberts were invaded. Here is a summary of the actions of all four: —

(*a*) *Carrier Interceptor Group* (TG 50.1), commanded by Rear Admiral Pownall in the new *Yorktown*, included the new *Lexington* and light carrier *Cowpens*. Starting from Pearl, it fueled and met supporting battleships at lat. 7° N, long. 174° W, on 19 November struck Jaluit once and Mili thrice, and kept that nearest Marshalls field to the Gilberts well pounded down by repeated strikes on four succeeding days. All this "contributed greatly to the success of the landings at Makin and Tarawa." [2] TG 50.1 also helped the escort carriers of the Amphibious Force to maintain local air supremacy over the Gilberts. On 23 November it intercepted 20 enemy planes coming down from the Marshalls, shot down all but three, and repeated the performance next day.

(*b*) *Northern Carrier Group* (TG 50.2), commanded by Rear Admiral Arthur W. Radford in *Enterprise*, who, with light carriers *Belleau Wood* and *Monterey*, sortied from Pearl Harbor 10 November in company with group (*a*) above, met supporting battleships and fueled at the same position. They then parted; TG 50.2 worked Makin over on 19 November, again next morning (D-day), after which it stood by TF 52 as a striking group and took the rap of several air attacks.

(*c*) *Southern Carrier Group* (TG 50.3), commanded by Rear Admiral Alfred E. Montgomery in *Essex*, including *Bunker Hill* and *Independence*, had struck Rabaul on 11 November.[3] It fueled at Espiritu Santo and, at a point close to Funafuti, was joined by four cruisers and three more destroyers from Pearl. After fueling again from fleet oilers, TG 50.3 then supported the Southern Attack Force, bombing Tarawa on 18, 19 and 20 November. The three heavy cruisers of this group, and two destroyers, bombarded Betio briefly on the 19th.

(*d*) *Relief Carrier Group* (TG 50.4), *Saratoga* and *Princeton* commanded by Rear Admiral Frederick C. Sherman, struck Rabaul thrice between 1 and 11 November. It fueled at Espiritu Santo on the 14th and departed next day to neutralize Nauru. That it did on 19 November, following a strike by Admiral Hoover the previous day, and to such good purpose that Nauru was unable to support the Japanese in the Gilberts. TG 50.4 then

[2] Admiral Spruance's Endorsement on Report of CTG 50.1.
[3] See Vol. VI of this History ch. xviii.

fueled at a point near Nanomea and provided the Makin and Tarawa garrison groups with air coverage until they reached their destinations.

4. LAND-BASED AIRCRAFT (TF 57), commanded by Rear Admiral John H. Hoover. *Curtiss,* the frequently bombed tender in which he flew his flag, anchored in Funafuti Lagoon well in advance of D-day; headquarters VII Army Air Force, Major General Willis H. Hale USA, moved up too. Over 100 Liberators, 24 Catalinas and 24 Venturas based at Funafuti and Canton searched the Gilberts every day from 16 November, bombing incidentally, and also assisting the Interceptor Carrier Force in pounding Mili and Maloelap. Some Liberators flew 1100 miles from Nukufetau to Mili, staging through Nanomea; others, based at Canton, flew over 1500 miles, staging at Baker, to drop bombs on Maloelap. These, it is claimed, were the longest continuous combat missions yet recorded in any theater of the war. The Liberators also dropped 75 tons of bombs on Tarawa and Makin.

The damage done by these air strikes was not great, and much of the intelligence that they brought in was inaccurate. "CTF 57 reported that our bombers over Tarawa observed no enemy planes, vessels or signs of life from 2500 feet, with weak anti-aircraft fire from end of Betio Island." [4] This message, received by Admiral Turner 17 November, would have raised false hopes that the defenders of Tarawa were either dazed or dead, if his staff had not learned to discount observations from such an altitude.

The first ships, other than submarines, to see action in Micronesian waters were the LSTs bringing up amphtracs. Because of their 8-knot speed, they had to be sent ahead of the attack forces in order to arrive in time for assault troops to use the LVTs. Thus they ran a grave risk of being jumped by enemy aircraft; but the Navy had learned through South Pacific experience how to protect LSTs.[5] The Makin group, discovered 18 November when at

[4] Turner Report on Gilberts Enc. A, p. 2.
[5] See Vol. VI 338–40.

no great distance from the islands, was attacked by enemy planes that evening and again on the 19th; but Commander Hurst handled his box-like ships well; the anti-aircraft gunners beat off every attack, and all escaped damage.

Nautilus, the big submarine which had already spent late September and early October photographing the Gilberts, departed Pearl 8 November under Commander William D. Irvin, carrying a scouting party of 78 troops, mostly Marines. Off Tarawa on 18–19 November she observed weather, surf, landing hazards and the results of recent bombardments, and radioed this last-minute information to Admiral Hill. Japanese coastal batteries opened up at extreme range but apparently did not see her when she closed to within half a mile. Anyway, they failed to hit her; unfortunately her friends were better shots.

Admiral Spruance, flying his flag in cruiser *Indianapolis,* sortied from Pearl 10 November with the main body of the Northern Attack Force, of which Admiral Turner in *Pennsylvania* had tactical command. There was little rest for anyone on the nine-day passage to Makin. Turner knew from abundant experience the value of constant training, and some of the ships under him were fresh from shakedown. A prearranged zigzag plan was imposed on the basic course, but the task force seldom followed it an hour without Turner's ordering some sort of workout. Radio silence was maintained, but signal flags snapped and blinkers flashed his orders; groups of cruisers or battleships deployed to repel imaginary air or submarine attacks or steamed over the horizon to practise division tactics; transports, looking like indignant old ladies being pushed around, made emergency turns and steamed in line of bearing; carriers swung into the wind to launch or recover planes as their pilots played at submarine hunting, searching 175 miles northward of the formation; destroyers continually dashed about, screening other vessels or shooting at towed sleeves. Not one submarine or air contact was made en route, but this training was all to the good. Each ship was a floating college of naval warfare; officers studied intelligence material, digested the thick operation plan and held classes on damage control, anti-aircraft gunnery and all manner of subjects. A succession of perfect winter tradewind days slipped by with everyone busy and in high spirits, eager for a fight and confident of victory.

Shortly after break of day 19 November, the Northern and Southern Attack Forces sighted each other's superstructures over the horizon. Frequent reports of hostile planes approaching sent everyone to general quarters as the two forces assumed anti-aircraft dispositions; but the Japanese planes confined their attacks to the LSTs. As night fell, Admiral Turner sent to all hands this calm, cheering message: —

Units attached to this force are honored in having been selected to strike another hard blow against the enemy by capturing the Gilbert Islands. The close coöperation between all arms and services, the spirit of loyalty to each other and the determination to succeed displayed by veteran and untried personnel alike, gives me complete confidence that we will never stop until we have achieved success. I lift my spirit with this unified team of Army, Navy and Marines whether attached to ships, aircraft or ground units, and I say to you that I know God will bless you and give you the strength to win a glorious victory.

Eight bells announce D-day, 20 November. Admiral Pownall's carriers register on radar screens and are assumed to be enemy; line of battle is being formed when they are identified and the ships return to approach disposition. Breakfast is over by 0330; General Quarters at 0350. A gibbous moon about 40 degrees above the horizon affords enough light for the lookouts to pick up the objective, toward which the pointers of the Bear and that favorite navigators' sequence, Sirius, Betelgeuse, Nath and Capella, seem to converge. A greenish glow of pre-dawn is in the sky at 0525 as signal is made — Take Stations for Attack! Battleships and cruisers launch spotting and anti-submarine patrol planes. Butaritari is now dimly visible, six miles distant. The transports are moving into their assigned area; assault-wave boats are swung out, ready to lower. H-hour is at hand.

CHAPTER VIII

Makin [1]

19–29 November 1943

1. *Plan and Initial Landings*

MAKIN was a pushover for the ground troops, but cost the Navy heavily.

Butaritari Island of Makin Atoll (which we may as well pronounce "Muckin" or "Muggin" as the British and Gilbertese do) [2] is shaped like a long, crooked-handled hammer. Flink Point, the head with a spike in it like a fireman's ax, is 3½ miles long; and the handle is about 11 miles long. For the invaders the most important part was a section of the handle about 3000 yards long and 400 wide, contained between two deep tank traps which ran across the island from shore to shore. From a ship one could look right through a tank trap and see the lagoon, which elsewhere was concealed by tall coconut palms. The principal Japanese defenses were between traps and on the beach where Carlson's Raiders had landed in August 1942. Apparently the Americans were expected to call there again; but this time they preferred two beaches on the hammer-head, facing west and so offering a partial lee from the tradewinds.

[1] Rear Adm. Turner's Report on Gilberts Operation 4 Dec. 1943. Historical Branch G–2 War Dept. Report "Makin Operation" compiled by Capt. J. M. Baker USA; information obtained at 27th Div. Hqrs. shortly after the action; information from observers, Cdr. E. M. Eller and Lt. Col. S. L. A. Marshall USA; Hist. Div'n War Dept. *The Capture of Makin* (1946) and ms. "Japanese Forces in the Gilberts" by Mr. Thomas Wilds.

[2] The name is properly applied only to Makin Meang or Little Makin, north of the main atoll which, down to World War II, was called Butaritari after the name of its largest islet. But the American operation plan, following an inaccurate chart, consistently referred to the whole atoll as Makin, so we follow suit.

Butaritari was defended by very few guns[3] and less than 800 men. A junior grade lieutenant, Seizo Ishikawa, commanded 284 troops of the Special Naval Landing Force. In addition there were 100 aviation personnel, 138 of the 111th Pioneers and a detachment of the 4th Construction Unit comprising 76 Japanese and 200 Koreans, few if any of whom had been trained to fight.[4] Lieutenant Kurokawa, commanding the Pioneers, appears to have been the senior officer on the island. These men had not even a picket boat to help them defend the island. Their float planes escaped in time, except one disabled "Emily" whose crew of nine neatly draped themselves on the wings and fuselage and committed suicide before the Americans landed.

To conquer this small garrison with its few defenses, Admiral Turner's Northern Attack Force brought up 6472 assault troops — the 165th Regimental Combat Team and a battalion landing team of the 105th Infantry ("Apple-knockers"),[5] both of the 27th Division, Major General Ralph C. Smith USA. They were supported by eight battleships and cruisers, thirteen destroyers, and planes from one large, one medium and three escort carriers. Such excess of force might seem faintly ridiculous but for the air menace of the Marshalls, and the desire to take Makin promptly and construct an airfield. The Japanese had air bases at Jaluit about 250 miles and at Mili less than 200 miles away, and one had to assume that they would reinforce them. Fortunately they had no planes to spare after concentrating their air strength at Rabaul. Unfortunately the ground forces that we landed on Butaritari were "infuriatingly slow."[6]

The operation plan worked out by the staffs of Admiral Turner and the two Smiths called for two landings in the morning —

[3] Wilds ms. p. 60 states that all there were on D-day, above 7.7 mm light machine guns, were six 8-cm, three 70-mm, howitzers, six 37-mm field guns, two 13-mm double-mounted machine guns.

[4] Jicpoa Bulletin 8–44 "Japanese Forces in the Gilbert Islands," based on captured documents; Mr. Wilds, however, estimates total as 741, including only 300 "combat effectives."

[5] So called because the 105th, when a National Guard Regiment, had been recruited in the orchard region of central New York.

[6] Holland M. Smith *Coral and Brass* p. 125.

assault troops on the Red beaches in the middle of the hammer-head, divisional artillery on Ukiangong Point — and a third landing, in the afternoon, on the Yellow beaches on the lagoon side. The Japanese were expected to deploy their main force against the Red beaches and be caught as in a nutcracker after the lagoon landing took place. But they did not coöperate. Their commander may have been only a lieutenant, but he had the sense to stay in his prepared positions between the two tank traps, as the best way to sell his island dear. Even the few men he could spare for defending the ax-head were very effective in holding up the American advance.

Rear Admiral Richmond Kelly Turner directed the capture of Makin from the bridge of *Pennsylvania*. Troops as well as ships were under his command until General Ralph Smith signaled him, on the fourth day, "Makin taken." The Admiral had characteristically chosen to direct the Northern Force because that would bring him nearer the Japanese Fleet if it sortied from Truk. With "Kelly" Turner as the central figure, there was something Ossianic about the scene. The spectacular tradewind clouds scurrying to leeward, the flash and rumble of great ordnance seemed more appropriate to the harsh crags of Morven than to this soft Micronesian dream world, now about to become a tough new field of battle for the "Fighting Irish." Turner's long upper lip, bushy black eyebrows and gray hair, steel-gray eyes shooting furious glances when anything went wrong, might have been those of a Celtic chieftain. "Fingal comes, the first of men, the breaker of the shields. The waves foam before his black prows. His masts with sails are like groves in clouds. Blow, ye winds that rush along my isle of mist. Come to the death of thousands, O king of resounding Selma!" [7]

Before 0500 the low-lying island was visible, dimly lighted by a quarter moon and rising Venus. At 0540 the fire support ships, already within three miles of the island, commenced launching spotting planes. There was as yet no sign of life from the enemy.

The six transports reached their designated area 5000 to 7000

[7] MacPherson's Ossian, *Fingal* Book ii.

yards off Beach Red at 0601, only one minute late. *Leonard Wood*, manned by coastguardsmen, commenced lowering her LCVPs at 0603, with soldiers already in them. As the sun rose over dark clouds at 0631, carrier planes were finishing a twenty-minute air bombardment. Nine minutes later, naval bombardment opened with the sullen *woof . . . woof* of 14-inch salvos from *Pennsylvania, New Mexico* and *Mississippi*. Light and heavy cruisers joined in; the sharp bark of the destroyers' 5-inch .38 was heard; and the whole fire support group roared and flashed away until 0824. By that time the island was hidden by a dark haze of smoke and dust, with one large fire blazing in the center. There was no reply; the enemy had nothing to reply with. During the shoot a turret explosion occurred in unlucky *Mississippi*, killing 43 men and wounding 19 more.

In the meantime boat waves were assembling in the transport area to the west of Flink Point. The classical ship-to-shore technique was employed, with amphtracs the one innovation. Sixteen LVTs carrying the first wave of assault troops were discharged from each of two LSTs, a process that looked like small fish swimming out of a whale's mouth.

Perfect weather for an orderly landing; a long tradewind swell and light chop with occasional whitecaps. The assault, as seen from the bridge of a cruiser, looked like a race. Destroyers *Phelps* and *Macdonough* defined the starting post, the line of departure; the amphtracs jockeyed about while ordinary landing craft kept out of the way; *Phelps* hoisted the Blue Peter as a sign to the amphtracs to form up; and, as her chief signalman snapped it down at 0813 like the starter of a horse race, all 32 LVTs went roaring full speed across the line. Cruisers and fire support destroyers, with big battle ensigns displayed, threw a last shower of steel at the largely nonexistent enemy behind Beach Red; a few flashes from dark trees on the beach marked a couple of Japanese machine guns. As the bombardment of the interior continued, mangled coconut trees arose in the air, and their tops came down slowly like shuttlecocks. Fighter planes from the carriers swooped low, strafing the beach as the line of amphtracs galloped forward in a flat arc, each trailing a long white wake like the tail of a charger, their machine guns and rockets spitting fire, plumes of white water arising from numerous misses on both sides. There is nothing more beautiful in war than an amphibious operation when it clicks; and this one did.

The first amphtracs touched shore at 0832. One could see them crawling up on the beach like prehistoric monsters foraging for game, while the second and third waves of landing craft pressed in, throwing spray. Carrier planes, having completed their beach strafing, were now dropping bombs behind the beachhead; clouds of yellow-brown smoke billowed up and a thick, black column burst out of a fuel tank near the center of enemy power. There was no opposition on the beach. By 0845 two tanks and several machine-gun and rifle companies were ashore.

At 0855 an American carrier plane, after flying the length of Butaritari, reported "only desolation." There were mingled shouts and groans on the flag bridge to the effect that the Japanese had "escaped us again." Opinions were voiced that the remaining bombardment schedule should be called off as useless. Admiral Turner snorted at this, saying he had not come all that distance to abandon his plan on the say-so of one aviator, and that one could not go wrong to continue naval gunfire. Events proved him to be right, as usual.

After the assault waves landed, the beaches began to get congested. It was nobody's fault; owing to irregular tides there was less water in the approaches than had been anticipated. The amphtracs, after landing about 400 men, were pressed into service by the Navy beachmaster to take men and equipment from regular landing craft outside the reef and ferry them in. At 0904 all transports closed to one mile from shore for quick unloading. But the landings were so slowed down that on D-day only 31 of a possible 250 LCVP loads, and 18 of 28 possible LCM loads, actually got ashore on the Red beaches — an average of only five landing craft an hour. Here was a first lesson in getting ashore on a coral atoll; others were learning it at Tarawa in the most costly manner.

Fortunately, only a few score natives were on the western end of the island; the Catholic Fathers had taken the hint and removed the rest in time. Those left were embarrassingly friendly. They swarmed all over the LVTs and gave valuable information about the Japanese. Lieutenant Clarence B. Selden, the Navy Beachmaster, encountered a native chief who said, all in one breath: "I-am-so-glad-you-have-come-we-have-waited-many-months-we-are happy-you-have-come-may-I-get-your-men-coconuts?" Lieutenant Colonel James Roosevelt, who had been with Carlson's Marine Raiders in 1942 and now accompanied the 165th RCT as observer, was greeted with, "Welcome back, Mr. Roosevelt!" By noon, when the natives were beginning to get under foot, they were given Spam and K rations and led by an MP lieutenant to a safe area around Flink Point.

At 1000 Lieutenant Colonel Joseph Hart of the 3rd Battalion 165th RCT reported that the western beachhead was secured. LCMs began unloading 105-mm guns with D–4 tractors at 1100. Within two hours they had taken up prepared positions on Ukiangong Point, from which they could support troops advancing down the handle.

The 1st Battalion 165th followed a plantation road eastward through coconut palms, halting frequently to shoot at real or imaginary snipers. Progress was held up by a huge shell crater in the road at a point where marsh and jungle made by-passing impossible. About 150 yards short of the western tank trap, where the road passes between the lagoon and a swamp, several hundred troops of this battalion were stopped by about fifteen Japanese riflemen and one machine gun. A few tanks were present, but their drivers would take orders only from their own commander back on the beach, with whom the infantry had no means of communication. Colonel Gardiner Conroy of the 165th was walking ahead of his troops to make a personal appeal to the tank drivers, when a rifle bullet hit him between the eyes.[8]

[8] Capt. Baker's "Makin Operation" and conversations with him. A different account of the Colonel's death is given in *The Capture of Makin* (1946),

2. *Lagoon Landings*

While troops who had come in over the outer beaches were securing the hammer-head, the late morning landing was taking place
on beaches inside the lagoon. Minesweeper *Revenge*, which entered
the lagoon first, was followed by a motley procession: control destroyers *Phelps* and *Macdonough*, *LST–179* carrying the rest of
the amphtracs in her belly and an LCT on her back, and LSD *Belle
Grove* teeming with tanks preloaded on LCMs. The LSD took
station just inside the entrance and started flooding her dock.

"The lagoon is shoal. The tide being out, we waded for some
quarter of a mile in tepid shallows, and stepped ashore at last into
a flagrant stagnancy of sun and heat." So wrote Robert Louis
Stevenson of his landing at Butaritari in the reign of King Teburei-
moa; [9] so it was 54 years later in the reign of King George VI.
R. L. S. and his party waded ashore on beach Yellow 2 between
On Chong's and King's Wharves. Here and at Tarawa American
landing forces encountered the same physical conditions. So we
may pause a moment to make clear what manner of reefs Stevenson called "tepid shallows."

Reefs they were, not in the ordinary sense of rocky shoals, but in
that of an irregularly surfaced, hard coral rock sloping gently from
the beach to deep water, corresponding to the mud flats that are
commonly found at low water on many shorelines in the United
States and Europe. As the word "reef" is used in describing lagoon
shallows in the Gilberts and Marshalls, it is simply a continuation
of the beach under water. In air photographs it looks like a sort
of apron around the island. At high water the reef at Butaritari
would be covered with three to four feet of water, and landing
craft could easily float over it. But on 20 November there was an
irregular tide so that only the outer fringe of the reef could be
negotiated by boats; only amphtracs could push in over the "tepid
shallows" until they reached dry land.

[9] *In the South Seas* Part III chap. i.

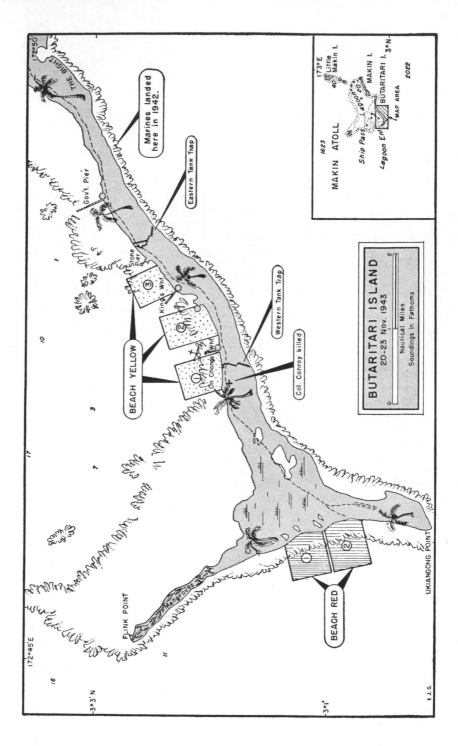

BUTARITARI ISLAND
20-23 Nov. 1943

Nautical Miles
Soundings in Fathoms

MAKIN ATOLL

BEACH YELLOW

BEACH RED

Marines landed here in 1942.

Eastern Tank Trap

Western Tank Trap

Col. Conroy killed

Gov't. Pier

Stone Pier

King's Whf.

On Chong's Whf.

FLINK POINT

Mangroves

UKIANGONG POINT

THE BIGHT

173° E
Little Makin I.
MAKIN I.
BUTARITARI I., 3° N-

Ship Pass

Lagoon Ent.

MAP AREA

Lagoon

1623
2022

172°50'

172°45'E

-3°3'N

-3°1'

10

17

3

7

16

11

I.J.G.

The 2nd Battalion Landing Team of the 165th Infantry, commanded by Lieutenant Colonel John F. McDonough, was brought to a point outside the lagoon in transport *Neville* and there transferred to amphtracs and LCVPs. At 1015, when the landing craft were well started, *Phelps* and *Macdonough* moved over to the edge of the lagoon for their direct-lay bombardment.

Captain Baker gives a vivid account of the scene as the landing craft neared shore at Beach Yellow: —

At 1020 the alligators (LVTs) were about halfway across the lagoon with between three and four thousand yards more to go. The light wind had veered almost to the east, and the smoke from exploding fuel dumps a mile or so apart was rolling over the tree tops thousands of feet west of each fire. The low swells that backed up into the lagoon from the ocean to the west were spilled into choppy little waves by the breeze that knocked the top off a few of them. About nine hundred yards behind the alligators the tank lighters forming the second wave bunted their way through the lagoon. They formed the semblance of a line, traveling along a couple of hundred yards apart and piling several feet of spray against their blunt, sloping bows. Nine hundred yards behind the tank lighters and a couple of thousand yards north-west of Flink Point were the smaller landing craft of the third wave. . . .[10]

The first wave headed for Yellow Beach. The boats moved calmly in. Some of the men read magazines. Although there was singing all along the line of landing craft, a few men fell asleep. Others . . . were eating cold lunches and horsing around, all the way in. . . .

Lieutenant Colonel McDonough now takes up the story as he saw it:

The alligators moved slowly towards shore and this caused them to reach the shoreline at 1040 instead of 1030. As they neared the edge of the reef they received heavy small-arms fire. The bullets were dropping all around them and the boats of succeeding waves. With naval gunfire exploding ammunition and fuel dumps on the shore, planes strafing and bombing the beach, the alligators firing their rockets and machine guns and the "M" boats[11] conveying the medium tanks

[10] His account of the wave formations is incorrect; see diagram in *Neville* Action Report.
[11] The LCMs floated out of *Belle Grove*.

(right on the tail of the alligators) firing their machine guns, it was almost impossible for anyone to certify just where the enemy fire was coming from. . . .

The alligators on landing carried out their prearranged plan of overrunning the beach and then splitting their force in order to secure the flanking wharves. The west group engaged and silenced a machine gun at the foot of On Chong's Wharf. The east group encountered and engaged machine guns at the seaplane basin. In accordance with the prearranged plan the left flank alligators moved to the seaplane ramp at the end of King's Wharf. . . . This group encountered and engaged a couple of light machine guns. . . .

Like the tanks, the assault waves, landing in good order and in accordance with schedule, were forced to debark on the edge of the reef and wade through waist-high water for a distance of approximately 300 yards to the beach. At this time they presented a perfect target for enemy fire from the flanks but suffered only a few casualties.

Finally, we have a yeoman's shorthand record of the radio telephone conversation between the pilot (whom we will call "Clare") of a liaison observer plane from carrier *Enterprise* and the air coördinator (whom we will call "Victor"), in another plane from the same carrier — with occasional remarks to pilot "Bill" of a third plane.[12]

(0958) CLARE TO VICTOR: Salvos falling near tank trap. Heavy fires have started at middle of island and natives assembled on Red beaches under guard.
(1001) VICTOR TO CLARE: If you see any nice females down there, save me one.
(1006) C. TO V.: DDs in lagoon have opened up.
(1008) C. TO V.: Looks like all the girls have skivvy shirts on.
(1009) V. TO C.: Aw, that's too bad!
(1009) V. TO BILL: Fighters in position to strafe upon firing rockets.[13]
(1010) V.: Let's put on a big show for the big shots. They are all out there with their glasses and sunbonnets.
        (*Bill moves in, apparently bent on strafing.*)

[12] *Enterprise* Air Combat Action Reports Gilbert Islands Operations, Enclosure in Report No. 8.
[13] Firing of rockets from landing craft was the signal for the close strafing of beaches to commence.

(1010) V. TO BILL: Ha, ha, ha! Give 'em hell, keed!

(1010) (*Somebody cuts in*): Let's have a little less bull from the bull.

(1011) V. TO ANYONE: Somebody has lost their sense of humor.

(*At 1013, 66 boats are counted in the lagoon.*)

(1019) V. TO C.: Will you call me when the rockets are discharged?

(1025) C. TO V.: Boats are about 2000 yards from the beach.

(1029) C. TO V.: I took a good look at the beach but can see no activity.

(1029) V. TO C.: You're breaking my heart.

(1036) C. TO V.: No rockets fired yet, though boats are about 500 yards from the beach at King's Wharf. Fighters are going in now. (1037) Rockets firing. (1041) No boats are being fired upon. (1042) Boats reached King's Wharf. (1044) Boats beaching all along now.

(1045) V. TO C.: Well done, report to base.

(1046) C. TO V.: Amphtracs almost across island now. One gun firing at troops in landing boats. (1047) All TBFs gone down and all bombs clear. Boats with tanks have disembarked 300 yards from beach. They are cutting through the water. (1055) An enormous blast went off in square 849, but not from bomb.[14] (1104) Troops from H landing[15] have reached Western Tank Trap. (1105) A small green sedan is parked in the road down there. Maybe it has four good tires on it.

(1115) V. TO C.: Request reconnaissance of square 978 through 910 all the way out to . . . island,

(1123) C. TO V.: No Nip activities in area requested investigated.

(1126) Have had bad gas leak — request permission to return to base.

(1126) V. TO C.: Roger. You have done good job, Clare.

On landing at 1135 "Clare" found that shrapnel had cut his gasoline and that about three inches of gasoline were sloshing around near the bomb bay.

The banter and wisecracks with which the pilots interlarded their information was sternly discouraged by air group and other commanders because it kept important data off the circuit. And ground-air communications at Makin, though better than those between different ground units, were weak. In this respect, as in many others, the Gilberts were a laboratory of amphibious warfare, and ground-air communication later improved until, at Okinawa, it was nearly perfect.

[14] A fuel dump going up.
[15] On Beach Red 2.

3. *Makin Taken*

After these successful landings on the Red and the Yellow beaches, the troops should have overrun this weakly defended island and secured it by nightfall. Apologists for the 27th Division have always maintained that they did as well as could be expected. This writer, after a careful examination of facts and arguments, regretfully agrees with General Holland M. Smith USMC that they put up a miserable, dilatory performance, giving the enemy ample time to reorganize and dispute every step.

Although outnumbering the enemy at that point about ten to one, the troops who landed on Beach Yellow took until noon to secure a continuous line across the island from On Chong's Wharf, with their right flank on the western tank trap. On the other side of the trap were the men who had landed on the western beaches. These troops, who had lost their commanding officer, allowed themselves to be pinned down interminably by small knots of enemy snipers, and did not cross the western tank trap until 1030 next day, 21 November.

In the direction of the eastern tank trap, the enemy had a few machine-gun nests and pillboxes similar to those that the Marines encountered at Tarawa. These held up the infantry until they could be dealt with by tanks. In the meantime there was confusion, almost chaos, in the American ranks. Trigger-happy soldiers fired on imaginary snipers in coconut trees while overlooking concealed nests in the ground or among mangrove roots lining the lagoon. After one squad of riflemen had passed through an area and cleared it, the next would shoot into the same coconut trees, with the result that those ahead thought they were under fire from the rear. General Ralph Smith in the regimental command post had such poor communications that he knew little of what was going on.

Operations on the east flank of Beach Yellow were similar to those on the west flank. The 105th BLT became widely scattered and suffered a few casualties from heavily protected dugouts in and around the sandspit west of King's Wharf. Artillery at Ukiangong Point first opened fire on one of these installations at about 1310 November 20, but so inaccurately that it had to be wiped out by a light tank.

In the late afternoon all naval combatant ships except one cruiser and three destroyers retired to operate off shore with the Northern Carrier Group. Just before sunset the entire task force half-masted colors while battleship *Mississippi* buried her dead. The sun set over Makin at 1810 in an angry red sky whose reflections turned the gun-metal sea to the color of imperial purple. And a hideous night followed for the soldiers on Makin, with Japanese infiltrating and green troops firing at anything and everything.

On the second day, 21 November, the Americans were so closely tangled with the Japanese that little could be provided in the way of call gunfire to help the situation ashore. An unfortunate accident occurred when a plane from *Enterprise*, mistaking the western tank trap for the eastern one, which was still in enemy hands, dropped a 2000-pound "daisy-cutter" bomb which killed three and wounded several Americans. Army units were making such miserably slow progress that General "Howling Mad" Smith stormed ashore to see what was the matter. He passed one of his worst nights in the Pacific at General Ralph Smith's command post; the danger came not from the enemy but from Army sentries, who put bullets through the command post tent and clipped coconuts off the palms.[16]

Early 22 November the 3rd Battalion 165th Infantry, which had been held in reserve, crossed the eastern tank trap without opposition, and by 1100 was almost halfway to the bight on the south shore, near which Carlson's 1942 landing had taken place. A company of the 1st Battalion landed on the lagoon side of the bight to support them. At the same time, a detachment of the 105th was boated by LVTs to Kuma, island next to Butaritari, in order to cut off the enemy's retreat. Friendly natives greeted the troops with such gusto that the amphtracs gave them a joy ride; a fleet of LVTs

[16] *Coral and Brass* pp. 127–28.

filled with laughing Gilbertese afforded comic relief to a tedious operation.

At nightfall the 3rd Battalion established a skirmish line across Butaritari within 50 yards of prepared enemy positions. Under cover of darkness the few Japanese defenders of this line tried every trick in their bag. Firecrackers were thrown to draw rifle fire; Gilbertese natives were driven toward the American lines with Japanese snipers intermingled; soldiers followed, imitating babies' cries so that the Yanks would take them for native women and children; taunts and threats were shouted and individual soldiers were called by name; Japs jumped into foxholes to shoot and stab. In 27th Division folklore this is known as "the Massacre" or "Sake Night," as the Japanese had been working up enthusiasm with that pleasant liquor. The Americans lost only 3 killed and 25 wounded, but 51 enemy dead were found next morning.[17]

That was the last organized resistance. By 1030 November 23, the 3rd Battalion reached the eastern end of Butaritari and at 1300 General Ralph Smith signaled to Admiral Turner, "Makin taken."

An important island base had been secured, at a loss to the 27th Division of only 64 killed and 150 wounded;[18] but it cost the Navy heavily — as we shall see presently. Counting the naval casualties, the enemy exacted at least one American life for each of his. The United States paid relatively dearer for Makin than for Tarawa.

Unloading supplies from the transports commenced at 1400 on D-day and continued until dark. It was interrupted then only because underwater obstructions made the western beaches unusable at night,[19] and those in the lagoon were supposed to be under sniper fire. After 21 November the large transports discharged continuously from outside the lagoon to landing craft and LCTs, while

[17] *The Capture of Makin* p. 120.
[18] *The Capture of Makin* p. 132.
[19] Some efforts were made both here and at Abemama to dynamite the coral heads and blast out a channel, but the explosions resulted only in killing fish. Lt. Cdr. Draper L. Kauffman USNR was working on this problem, and the Underwater Demolition Teams solved it in the Marianas.

the LSTs found spots inside where they could lay their ramps ashore. Some unloaded in pairs on King's Wharf, a flimsy construction that almost collapsed under the weight of Army equipment.

Across the golden sunrise of 21 November appeared a column of strange aspect to sailors' eyes — six LSTs as evenly spaced as if they were camels crossing a desert. These were Makin LST Group No. 2. *Revenge* herded them into the lagoon, where they commenced unloading promptly. Dawn also revealed a cheery group of strayed LCMs, well off shore. They had missed *Belle Grove* when trying to return to her bosom after dark, and so had secured to snatch a little sleep. Fortunately, they were not picked up by any friendly radar screen until there was light enough to permit identification.

By the close of 22 November the five attack transports were almost discharged. The lagoon afforded good anti-submarine protection for LSTs and smaller craft, but was not yet charted with sufficient accuracy to be used by transports or ships larger than a destroyer. These had to cruise off shore every night, awaiting such time as the Army would be ready to reload the assault troops with their equipment and turn the island over to the garrison force. This force arrived as scheduled, at noon 24 November, in four chartered transports screened by two destroyer escorts. By that time, suitable berths had been charted, and the transports went inside the lagoon.

CHAPTER IX

Japanese Reaction and Counterattack

October–November 1943

JAPAN reacted weakly and uncertainly to the Gilberts and Marshalls operations.[1] Imperial Headquarters had a simple plan for the defense of Micronesia: the Combined Fleet would sortie from Truk and, with the support of land-based air forces and local garrisons, "annihilate" the invaders. According to the "New Operational Policy" of September 1943, the Gilberts and Marshalls must be defended *à l'outrance* in order to delay and wear out Allied offensives against the inner Japanese perimeter.

The secret of the impending American attack on the Gilberts was well kept. Not until 19/20 November, when Admiral Sherman's carriers struck Nauru, and a scout plane sighted Admiral Turner's force, did Tokyo guess what was up. The news caught the Japanese off balance, powerless to support their garrisons in the Gilberts. During the previous month, Admiral Koga had been shifting the Combined Fleet about to no good purpose. Eager like his predecessor Yamamoto for a big fleet action, he interpreted the American carrier strike of 5–8 October 1943 on Wake, and the few ships seen at Pearl Harbor by a Japanese scout plane on 17 October, to mean that the Pacific Fleet was all out to assault Wake. So Koga sailed

---

[1] Movements of Japanese ships and air forces from a variety of Japanese sources obtained by us in Tokyo, from Wilds Ms. (see chap. v footnote 8); WDC 161,407 Tabular Records of Japanese CL Movements; WDC 160,623, same for CAs. For events here mentioned in connection with Rabaul see Vol. VI of this History pp. 26, 286, 323–26. The details in *Inter. Jap. Off.* p. 411 and *Campaigns of the Pacific War* pp. 191, 200–03 are undependable.

his fleet up to Eniwetok in order to be in a position to join battle, tarried there a week while scout planes searched fruitlessly for Nimitz's fleet, decided that Wake was a false alarm, and on 24 October sailed back to Truk. He then stripped all his carriers of their air groups in order to reinforce Rabaul.

One week later the news of Admiral Wilkinson's landing at Empress Augusta Bay, Bougainville, caused Koga to shift his naval strength southward. On 5 November Admiral Kurita's heavy cruiser force, assembled at Rabaul in preparation for a destructive sortie against Wilkinson, got so badly battered by planes from *Saratoga* and *Princeton* that it retired to Truk. All but one of the stripped Japanese carriers were now in home waters.[2] Thus, when D-day dawned for the Gilberts, the only undamaged warships at Truk were the two immense battlewagons *Yamato* and *Musashi*; smaller battleships *Nagato*, *Fuso*, *Kongo* and *Haruna*; heavy cruisers *Kumano*, *Chokai*, *Suzuya* and *Chikuma*; five light cruisers, less than three destroyer squadrons, and 18 submarines.

Defending coral atolls posed new problems to the Japanese, as taking them did to the Americans. Admiral Koga, remembering the tough defense the Sons of Heaven had put up at Munda and elsewhere, expected his men in the Gilberts to hold out for a long time. So he endeavored to reinforce Tarawa and other atolls that he expected would be attacked shortly.

On 21 November light cruisers *Isuzu* and *Naka* with two destroyers departed Truk for Ponape, loaded troops there and went on to Kwajalein, whither headquarters Fourth Fleet (Vice Admiral Masashi Kobayashi) had already been transferred by air. It was Admiral Koga's intention to reinforce Tarawa with these troops. But by the time they reached Kwajalein, Tarawa had fallen, and the men debarked at Mili instead. Cruiser *Nagara* arrived there with more troops about 1 December, depth-charging United States submarine *Plunger* en route, but without result. She then transferred

---

[2] *Zuikaku*, with empty decks, was at Truk 26 Oct.–7 Dec. when she went to Kure to train new air groups. *Zuiho* and two escort carriers ferrying planes arrived Truk 21 Nov. and departed for Kure 30 Nov.

some aviation ground crews to Wotje and returned to Kwajalein, arriving in time to provide a target for Rear Admiral Pownall's raid of 4 December. Heavy cruisers *Kumano, Chokai* and *Chikuma,* light cruiser *Noshiro* and a number of destroyers dashed up to Kwajalein 26 November, made a round trip to Eniwetok, and departed Kwajalein 3 December in time to escape Pownall's visit. There were other inter-island surface movements, too, all useless and wasteful of fuel.

So much for the innocuous surface movements of the enemy. His air counterattacks were somewhat more serious, although only 46 planes were left in the entire Gilberts-Marshalls area after 27 long-range bombers had been dispatched to Rabaul on 12 November.[3] The first air counterattack, and the only one of any consequence during the first six days, was delivered by 16 torpedo-bombers (half from Roi, half from Maloelap) on the evening of 20 November. Admiral Montgomery's carrier group lay about 30 miles west of Tarawa, recovering planes, when these planes were sighted coming in low over the water. All ships opened fire, and fighter planes in the air attacked the bold bombers, nine of which broke through the anti-aircraft fire and split into three equal groups. Three attacked *Essex* and *Bunker Hill,* inflicted no damage, and were shot down. The other six concentrated on *Independence,* dropped at least five torpedoes and made one hit. Eight of the planes were shot down. *Independence* lost 17 killed and 43 wounded and retired to Funafuti for repairs. It was no minor job for Commander W. T. Singer and his crew of repair ship *Vestal,* for the carrier's after engine room, fireroom and magazine were flooded, many bottom plates were damaged, and she had a wobbly shaft and a ruptured fire main. Yet they got her in shape to depart for Pearl Harbor under her own power on 7 December.

The Japanese submarines sustained heavy losses but they did accomplish something. A force of eight I-boats and one RO-boat, commanded by Captain H. Iwagami in *I–19,* were sent out from Truk and Kwajalein, or diverted from other patrols, to scout pos-

[3] Wilds Ms. p. 53.

sible American movements in the Gilberts and do what damage they could.

The first to reach the islands, *I–35*, did so on 22 November. She approached the Tarawa transport area, attracted by the large number of fat targets, but had the misfortune to be picked up on a sound contact by destroyer *Meade* (Lieutenant Commander John Munholland) at about 1519. After a depth-charge attack had failed, and the contact had been lost, *Frazier* (Lieutenant Commander Elliott M. Brown) joined the chase, regained contact and depth-charged twice between 1715 and 1727. *Meade's* second load of "ashcans," delivered shortly after, blew *I–35* to the surface broadside to *Frazier* and a mile astern of herself. Both destroyers opened gunfire, then checked as *Frazier* rammed the boat just abaft the conning tower. *Frazier's* crew with pistol fire prevented the Japanese from manning their deck guns. As the destroyer backed off the submarine settled, then plunged stern-first, followed by depth charges from planes of the American anti-submarine patrol. Both destroyers launched boats to recover four swimming survivors, one of whom fired on his would-be rescuers and was killed; the other three were picked up. *Meade's* whaleboat, while returning with the Japanese prisoners, was mistaken by a plane from *Suwannee* for a submarine's conning tower and so favored with a 500-pound bomb. It exploded under water only a yard away and lifted the boat into the air. "Occupants were somewhat shaken," according to *Meade's* action report. The destroyer, unable to see the plane's markings, fired back, scoring two hits; but the plane managed to make its carrier and nobody was badly hurt on either side of this "friendly" brawl.[4]

The scene now shifts to waters off Makin where *I–175*, Lieutenant Commander Tadashi Tabata, arrived on the 23rd.

Before dawn 24 November a temporary task group built around the three escort carriers under Rear Admiral Mullinnix, commanded by Rear Admiral Robert M. Griffin in *New Mexico*, was steaming

---

[4] *Meade* Action Report. Enc. in Comdesdiv 14 to Cincpac 16 Dec. 1943. C.O. *Frazier* to Cincpac 30. Nov. U.S. Fleet *A/S Bulletin* Jan. 1944 p. 26.

at 15 knots about 20 miles southwest of Butaritari. There was a gentle swell and a light SE breeze; clouds obscured the moon, the carrier crews were about to go to flight quarters and to fuel planes for dawn launchings. One destroyer was detached for special duty at Makin, leaving only four in the screen. "Bogeys" — unidentified planes — were about. At 0435 destroyer *Franks* reported a dim, flashing light. Admiral Griffin ordered her to investigate, and her departure made a hole in the already thin screen. Shortly after, *New Mexico's* SG radar screen showed a surface contact a little E of N. After four minutes it faded; *I-175* had submerged. False contacts, however, were frequent on radar screens at that period, and as no sound contact had been obtained by the destroyers the formation carried out prearranged simultaneous turns in a northerly direction. Carrier *Liscome Bay* went to general quarters at 0505. *Franks* reported at 0508 that the light "appeared to be" a flashlight from a raft. Actually it was a float light dropped by a Japanese plane as a signal to other planes in the vicinity that targets were near.[5] Two minutes later, the formation turned right to 55° — NE by E — presenting a perfect target for the submarine, which happened to bear almost due north.

The first light of day was in the sky at 0513 when a torpedo hit *Liscome Bay* amidships. There was a terrible explosion. A column of bright orange flame rose a thousand feet in the air. Within a few seconds the aircraft bombs stowed in the hold detonated, and with a mighty roar the carrier burst apart as though she were one great bomb, tossing men, planes, deck frames and molten fragments so high that the deck of *New Mexico* 1500 yards to leeward was showered with fragments of steel, clothing and human flesh. The entire after third of the escort carrier was demolished. Flames raced through her interior and arose from her flight deck as from a giant torch. Ammunition exploded, sending huge bouquets of fire upward, the flight deck caved in, and only 23 minutes after being hit,

---

[5] After the event, it was thought that a plane had dropped this float light as a signal to the submarine; but the Japanese Navy had no air-underwater coördination, and it was pure chance that a submarine happened to be in the vicinity.

the doomed ship flared up for the last time and sank hissing into a 2000-fathom deep.

Pitifully few survived to fight for their lives in a spreading pool of burning oil. Admiral Mullinnix, Captain Wiltsie, 51 other officers and 591 enlisted men were lost; 55 officers and 217 men were rescued,[6] mostly by destroyers *Morris* and *Hughes*. Many were in a frightful condition, with shattered limbs, internal hemorrhages, head concussions and horribly disfiguring burns; all were thickly covered and many blinded by viscous, stinging fuel oil. Yet many a man in the water when approached by a destroyer's whaleboat said, "Never mind me; others need the boat more," and, if taken on board, turned to and helped the boat's crew rescue others. The energy and courage of the rescuers also was beyond praise. Electrician's Mate T. R. Furnas repeatedly dove into the oily sludge to get wounded men on board.[7]

The destroyers were too busy recovering survivors to go submarine hunting, and *I-175*, which had destroyed an escort carrier and 644 men, returned safely to Truk after firing a torpedo, which missed, at another escort carrier.[8]

We now return to air counterattacks. There would have been more of these but for the concentration of carrier air power that Admiral Spruance brought up to the Gilberts. Planes from *Lexington* and *Cowpens* intercepted and thwarted every daytime attack. During the three days' fighting on Makin, not a single enemy plane appeared over the island.

[6] Bupers figures, 1950.

[7] Rear Adm. Griffin to Cominch 11 Dec. 1943, enclosing reports of the other shops; Comcardiv 24 (Capt. J. G. Crommelin) Action Report 8 Dec. 1943; conversations shortly after with Cdr. Lidstone, C. O. *Franks*, and with Capt. Crommelin; Buships War Damage Report No. 45, Mar. 10, 1944. The Buships damage report ascribes primary responsibility for the sinking to the massive explosion in bomb stowage, which was at or very near the spot where the torpedo hit. In these Kaiser-built carriers, bomb stowage was provided with no protection against fragments from torpedo or shell hits. *Sangamon*-class CVEs, converted from oilers, were afforded such protection in the form of a bulkhead around bomb stowage after the loss of H.M.S. *Avenger* 15 Nov. 1942. Following the *Liscome Bay* explosion, steps were taken to provide liquid protection for all bomb magazines in vessels of the "Kaiser" class.

[8] Japanese records report her as missing after 10 Feb. 1944, in waters around Kwajalein.

One "Betty" flew over the lagoon on 27 November and was driven off by anti-aircraft fire but claimed to have sunk a cruiser that was not there.[9] Against Tarawa only two minor strikes got through and no damage was done. Unloading was not once interrupted by enemy air attack; a new record for Pacific amphibious operations. In the Gilberts the one torpedo hit on *Independence*, 20 November, represents the total damage done by enemy aircraft. And eight of the 46 Japanese planes in the entire area were lost in that attack. Three days later, 21 more were flown up to Roi from Truk, and in the next two days 32 carrier planes and 15 others arrived at Roi. Owing to the rapid plane attrition at Rabaul no more could be spared. But, by 25 November, the Japanese were ready to go after the tempting targets off the Gilberts.

That evening 13 "Bettys" attacked Admiral Turner's group of three battleships, two cruisers, two escort carriers and seven destroyers, operating about 60 miles east of Butaritari. At sunset several Japanese snooper planes skirted this formation. "The night is gathering around," one could imagine them saying, like Ossian's Cuthullin; "Where are now the ships of Fingal? Here let us pass the hours of darkness, here wish for the moon of Heaven." Wishing brought no moon that night, but the snoopers carried something almost as good. On each side of Turner's formation, three to five miles away and parallel to his course, they dropped a string of blinking float lights. These were followed by parachute flares, and then two groups of attack planes bore in. There followed a contest of wits between the Japanese and Admiral Turner in which the Admiral won every trick. Enemy pilots would catch sight of his task force in the light of the flares and attempt to deliver a torpedo attack from both flanks. The Admiral waited until the flares were halfway down, at their best illuminating position; and then, calculating correctly that the enemy planes were about to deliver, presented the sterns of his ships to them by simultaneous turns. So numerous, radical and well executed were these turns,[10] that the

---

[9] Fourth Fleet War diary (WDC 160,336; Nat. Arch. No. 11,398).

[10] Twenty emergency turns, averaging 64° each, were made in 76 minutes. (Turner Report on Gilberts, "Air Attack on TF 52, Nov. 25, 1943.")

Mississippi bombarding Makin

Landing craft approaching lagoon beaches

Butaritari, Makin, 20 November 1943

Rear Admiral Henry M. Mullinnix

enemy in spite of his superior speed never could get in position to score with bombs or torpedoes. Thus Turner's constant drill in simultaneous ships' turns on the voyage from Pearl to Makin, paid handsome dividends.

Another group of enemy planes was driven off that night by Admiral Radford's Northern Carrier Group. And on the evening of the 26th they tried again. The enemy was ill-advised to pick on this 47-year-old carrier commander, since "Raddy" was the first to organize a radar-equipped night combat air patrol.

This air battle, said to be the first of its kind over the Pacific or any other ocean, began at 1735 when the first shadower was shot down. Combat air patrol was promptly recalled and the night fighter group, consisting of one radar-equipped Avenger and two Hellcats, was launched; but, owing to excessive zeal of the fighter director in *Enterprise*, they were sent off before joining each other. Brilliant flares, blinking float lights — red, white and green — lit up the night as enemy torpedo-bombers began to close in. Lieutenant Commander John L. Phillips, piloting the Avenger, shot down the "tail-end Charlie" on radar contact and gave the rest of the Japanese such a surprise that they broke formation and started shooting at one another; in the mêlée the Hellcat piloted by Lieutenant Commander E. H. ("Butch") O'Hare, which had not yet joined Phillips, was shot down; by whom nobody knows. So died that gallant and resourceful pilot, one of the best in the Navy.[11]

But not a single ship was hit. "Believe this is the first time a night interception was made from a carrier," concluded Admiral Radford, "and judging from the events of the last two evenings, we had better hurry with proper equipment." For the Japanese were getting better and better in night torpedo-bombing, which they had invented. "Thirty to forty planes put on a beautiful show — don't believe we have an outfit who could touch them at this sort of thing." [12]

Radio Tokyo's report of this air attack created great amusement

[11] See Vol. III p. 267 and Vol. IV p. 14.
[12] CTG 50.2 to Cincpac, 28 Nov.; *Enterprise* and TG 50.1 Action Reports on Gilberts Operation; conversations with Admiral Radford, 1950.

in the Fleet. Imperial Headquarters claimed one big carrier "instantly sunk," another not quite so instantly, two cruisers sunk, one battleship or cruiser heavily damaged and "set ablaze." And in accordance with Bougainville precedent this fruitless attack was named "the Air Battle of the Gilberts."

Following the air attack of 25 November one of the destroyers in the Northern Carrier screen, appropriately named *Radford*, added fresh luster to her name by sinking Japanese submarine *I–19*. Shortly after 2000, several ships of the screen made radar contact bearing due north, eight miles away, and about 60 miles west of Makin. *Radford* (Commander Gale E. Griggs), sent to investigate, got a sound contact and depth-charged. After contact had been regained and lost several times, sonarmen F. R. Buckley and W. C. Wells picked up the "mush" from the submarine's screws and the destroyer made three more depth-charge attacks. At 2344 a loud and violent underwater explosion was heard. Commander Griggs swept the area for eight hours, and after daylight, with the help of two Avengers, located a mass of debris. *Radford* was awarded a "probable" kill only, but *I–19* never surfaced again.

RO–38, the one boat of that type deployed in this operation, never returned; and *I–40*, which departed Truk 22 November, was never heard from. United States Navy records throw no light on what happened to them.

On the evening of 28 November a group of "Bettys" made a feeble and fruitless attack on Admiral Sherman's carrier group, first ganging up on destroyers *Bradford* and *Brown* which had escorted *Monterey* from Admiral Radford's command to this new hot spot. By skillful maneuvering and accurate anti-aircraft fire, the two destroyers shot down a couple of planes and escaped being hit themselves; the Japanese claimed to have sunk two carriers, one cruiser and one other ship in this attack.

By the end of November most of the American carriers had retired from Gilbertese waters. Their operations that month, seen in retrospect the next year, appeared little better than warming-up exercises. But carrier inexperience was so great in the Gilberts that maintaining combat air patrol steadily for almost ten days seemed to exhaust their deck, engineering and flight crews. Either because their tires were of poor quality or because their pilots landed too violently, many Hellcats became inoperative from blowouts and consequent crashing on landing.

Including the carrier raids on the Solomons and New Britain that preceded D-day, as well as strikes on Micronesia and Wake, American plane losses for November were 47 in combat and 73 operational out of a total of 831 planes carried — an attrition of almost 14 per cent. The American estimate of 101 enemy planes destroyed during Operation "Galvanic"[13] was probably not far wrong; for Japanese records show a loss of at least 122 planes based on Marshall Island fields between 14 November and 13 December 1943.[14]

On the last day of November the transports that had brought up the Makin garrison, together with all ships of the Northern Attack Force not required to screen the fast carriers, departed for Pearl Harbor. Admiral Turner, still in tactical command, sent a well-deserved "Well Done!" to his forces; but no small part of the success was due to the "Old Man" himself. He had held every line of that northern team in his hands; leading, encouraging and cracking the whip at the right spot, keeping an off eye on Admiral Hill's team at the same time. His sleepless, steel-like strength and capacity for accurate thought and instant decision impressed all who were with him on the bridge of *Pennsylvania*. This was the third amphibious operation that he had conducted and the second that he had planned. And it was far from being his last.

[13] Comairpac Analysis of Air Operations Pacific Nov. 1943 pp. 10, 36.
[14] Figures obtained by Mr. Salomon, 1946. This breaks down into 26 interceptors that didn't return, 31 plus shot down in aërial combat over bases, 29 in attacks on Pownall's carriers 4–5 Dec., 65 destroyed on ground. Capt. Ohmae in 1950 said 152 planes were destroyed from 19 Nov. to end of year, viz. 61 fighter planes, 58 land bombers, 21 bombers from carriers, 1 flying boat and 20 scout seaplanes.

CHAPTER X

Tarawa[1]

19–23 November 1943

1. The Japanese Defensive System on Betio

TARAWA lies about 100 miles south of Makin and only 80 miles north of the Equator. A triangular coral atoll, its eastern and southern legs, respectively 18 and 12 miles long, are composed of a string of long, narrow, coconut-planted islands; the third or western leg is all barrier reef except for two deep-water passes into the lagoon.

Betio,[2] the fortified island with the Japanese airfield which was the American objective, occupies a position at the southwest corner of the atoll, corresponding to that of Butaritari in Makin. It is even smaller than Butaritari — about 291 acres by rough measurement. Every square foot of it could be defended, and almost every foot was defended.

[1] Pronounced "Ta-ra-wa," slight accent on the "ta" and all a's short. The basic sources are CTF 53 (Rear Adm. Hill) War Diary for Nov. 1943, Op. Order No. A101–43 revised and Action Report Tarawa 13 Dec. 1943; the Turner Report; Maj. Gen. Julian C. Smith Report to Com Gen V 'Phib Corps 23 Dec. 1943; V 'Phib Corps G–2 Report on Gilbert Is. Operation. I discussed the operation not long after with Gen. Julian Smith and other participants and read many reports by company and boat-wave officers which have not been preserved. There is a long and careful analysis by Capt. Ralph C. Parker in the Cincpac Monthly Analysis for Nov. 1943. Since then have appeared Robert Sherrod *Tarawa, the Story of a Battle* (1944), a vivid and accurate account by a participant; Capt J. R. Stockman USMC *The Battle for Tarawa* (1947), a detailed and carefully documented Marine Corps monograph, and Jeter A. Isley and P. A. Crowl *The U. S. Marines and Amphibious War* (1951) which I read in proof; Richard W. Johnston *Follow Me! The Story of the 2nd Marine Division* (1948). Japanese material on Tarawa is both scarce and untrustworthy; the official report published 3 May 1944 by Imperial Headquarters is translated by Hist. Div. Army Pacific Section as "Captured Japanese Doc. No. MR–50 (D–65): Military Action in the Gilbert Islands."

[2] Pronounced "Bay-shio"; the spelling "Bititu" on old charts is incorrect.

In shape Betio resembles an old-fashioned muzzle-loading musket, complete with stock, lock and barrel, pointing a little south of east. The total length, 3800 yards, is short of two miles; the width, 500 yards at the stock (Beaches Green 1, Red 1) 600 at the lock (Beaches Red 2 and 3), tapering off to a point on the barrel. The airfield, with a strip over 4000 feet long and triangular taxiways, was in the wide center part. Part of the stock had been cleared of trees in order to lengthen the runway. The rest of the island was covered with a stand of coconut palms under which was installed the most complete defensive system that oriental or any other ingenuity could have devised. Here is a summary of the defenses of Betio: —

1. Outside the beaches, mined concrete tetrahedron boat obstacles; coral cairns; barbed-wire and log barricades designed to divert landing boats into lanes covered by artillery.

2. Along the edge of the island, a few feet behind the beach, a barricade 3 to 5 feet high, mostly of coconut logs wired and stapled together.

3. Behind this barricade, sited to fire over it or through ports, a system of 13-mm and 7.7-mm machine-gun emplacements, some dual-purpose, others covered by coconut logs, coral sand and, occasionally, concrete or armor plate, connected by revetted trenches with rifle ports, command posts and ammunition dumps.

4. At the corners of the island and at various other points along shore, 14 coast defense guns ranging from 5.5-inch to 8-inch. The latter were British Vickers naval guns, said to have been captured at Singapore. All had bombproof shelters for crews, underground storage vaults for ammunition, and fire control systems.

5. Along and inside the beach, (a) 25 field guns (37-mm and 75-mm) in covered emplacements, mostly in pillboxes well protected from shrapnel blast by thick coverings of logs and sand, sometimes reinforced by armor plate or concrete caps, and immune to direct hits from all but the largest guns; (b) a number of 13-mm to 5.1-inch anti-aircraft guns; (c) immobile tanks containing fourteen 37-mm guns.

6. A system of bombproof shelters, some in barracks and headquarters areas, others behind the beach. Built of coconut logs strengthened by angle irons, their roofs, six feet and more thick, were so constructed of sand, logs and corrugated iron that only heavy-caliber AP or other delayed-action shells could penetrate. Many were compartmented in-

side by partitions like baffle plates so that the inmates were protected from explosives hurled through the ports. The Japanese when cornered used these bombproofs for defense and their impressive size attracted the attention of photographers; but they were not nearly so lethal to the Marines as the other defenses.[3]

Since no part of Betio Island is as much as 300 yards from the beach, almost all these defenses could be brought to bear on a landing force. Fortunately for the Americans, the Japanese had not yet got around to mining the lagoonside beaches or to constructing formidable obstacles to a landing at that point. No military historian who viewed these defenses could recall an instance of a small island's having been so well prepared for an attack. Corregidor was an open town by comparison. Parts of Iwo Jima, Peleliu and Okinawa were as well fortified, but these islands were high enough for subterranean defenses to be constructed.

The Japanese installations were not only skillfully planned but amply manned and bravely defended. The best enemy troops were those of the Sasebo 7th Special Naval Landing Force, 1497 officers and men under Commander Takeo Sugai, stout fellows who could take a lot of punishment. The 3rd Special Base Force, a naval landing force of 1122 men who had been there since March 1943, were almost as formidable. The defenses had been constructed by the 111th Pioneers (a unit corresponding to our Seabees), 1247 strong, and by the Fourth Fleet's construction unit of 970 men, of whom over half were Koreans. Subtracting these, and men killed or wounded in previous bombardments, there were over 4500 troops on the island 20 November, all well fed and hard as nails. The atoll commander, Rear Admiral Keiji Shibasaki, killed 21 November in his concrete command post, was reported by a prisoner to have declared that the Americans could not take Tarawa with a million men in a hundred years. He gave orders "to defend

[3] "Study of Japanese Defenses of Betio Island (Tarawa Atoll) Part I — Fortification and Weapons." Prepared by Intelligence Section 2nd Marine Div. and Jicpoa, 20 Dec. 1943; Thomas Wilds Ms. "Japanese Forces." The Japanese at Tarawa had no naval defense; all their small craft had been sunk in earlier air raids.

to the last man all vital areas and destroy the enemy at the water's edge. In a battle where the enemy is superior, it is necessary to lure him within range of our fixed defense installations, and then, using all our strength, destroy him." [4] Such were the standard Japanese defensive tactics, which never succeeded. But the Japanese on Tarawa did fight almost "to the last man." Only one officer, 16 enlisted men, and 129 Koreans were taken prisoner.

Admiral Montgomery's carrier group had done appreciable damage to Betio in its plane strikes of 18–19 November. Two of the four 8-inch coast defense guns, and three of the seven tanks, had been destroyed or damaged. But the chief advantage of these raids (and earlier land-based air raids) lay in the large amount of ammunition they had caused the defenders to shoot off. On 20 November the Japanese had left only 4800 rounds of 75-mm and 127-mm anti-aircraft ammunition and only 15,000 rounds of 13-mm machine-gun bullets.

2. *Plan, Leaders, Approach*

Betio had been so thoroughly reconnoitered by aircraft and submarine that the Japanese defenses were well known in advance to the officers entrusted with its capture. Even the number of defenders had been estimated correctly, to within a hundred men.[5] The large-scale chart (250 yards to the inch) prepared by Jicpoa

[4] Jicpoa Bulletin No. 8–44 "Japanese Forces in the Gilbert Islands"; Wilds Ms. estimates total as 4715, of which 35 had been killed and 169 wounded in the air attacks of 13–19 Nov.; he doubts whether there were more than 3000 combat effectives on 20 Nov.

[5] An ingenious method was used for the estimate of personnel. A vertical air photograph taken by an Army plane 20 October revealed a number of multi-holed wooden privies sticking out into the lagoon. Their dimensions, checked by those of a Japanese plane of known size shown in the same photo, indicated the number of holes; and Jicpoa, by one of those uncanny procedures which Intelligence officers prefer to keep secret, knew Japanese military doctrine with respect to the ratio of men to hole. The resulting calculation worked out at exactly 64 men more than the number of troops actually on Betio. The story of this Intelligence effort has been told with characteristic humor by Capt. John L. Zimmerman USMCR in a privately printed pamphlet appropriately entitled *Ars Longa, Vita Brevis, or, Some Secrets of Japan's Inner Circles Revealed by Captain Z.*

from photographs taken up to one month before the attack, left nothing out but a few bombproof shelters which were invisible from the air.

The invaders had a choice of three places to land: (1) on the southern beaches; (2) on the western beach at the butt end of the stock, and (3) on the lagoon side where a pier stuck out 750 yards over the coral reef to deep water. The first two were where the Japanese hoped we would land,[6] because the shores at both places made reëntrant angles which exposed an invader to enfilading fire. Along the south shore a series of log barriers and mined wire and concrete obstacles were so placed as to divert landing craft into approaches over which large and small guns were sighted. Certain armchair strategists and after-the-battle sightseers pointed out the western beach as the place where the Marines should have landed, because it was on the lee side with a shorter approach and few natural obstacles and because the enemy had no rifle pits there behind the log barricade. But that place, Beach Green, was prepared to give invaders the hottest kind of reception. Two lines of concrete blocks on the reef, and mines between, would have canalized approaching landing craft into the field of fire of three pedestal-mounted 3-inch guns.

There remained, then, as the least of three evils, the beaches designated Red 1, 2 and 3 on the lagoon side, where troops could land on a broad front. There was one bad reëntrant angle on Beach Red 1, but, from the Japanese point of view "the beaches where the enemy landed were the points where both our fortified positions lacked equipment and our troop disposition was weak, and . . . where there were no anti-tank obstacles." [7]

The Marines hoped, by landing on a three-battalion front on these lagoon beaches, to sweep across the island, capture the airfield and pin the enemy down on the barrel of the Betio gun, where he could be finished off next day.

Although a lagoon landing was the least of three evils, it re-

---

[6] Interrogation of a Japanese ensign taken prisoner.
[7] Official Report (see footnote 1 to this chapter).

quired a complicated plan and a very long run for the landing craft. The nearest corner of the transport area lay 10 miles northwest of the butt end of Betio. The boats, after forming up in an area between the transports and the pass, would have to run three and one half miles to the line of departure within the lagoon, make a 75-degree turn and run another three miles to the beach. And unless the tide gave them a break, the Marines would have to wade or crawl over the reef for the last 300 to 500 yards.

But it was the Japanese who got the break in the tide. No accurate tide tables for the Gilberts existed. They were unpredictable. No one could foretell whether there would occur on 20 November a so-called "dodging" tide.[8] That is an irregular neap tide which ebbs and flows several times a day, at unpredictable intervals, and maintains a constant level for hours on end. For instance, the dodging tide that occurred in the following lunar month rose to a level 4 feet above the outer edge of the reef and stood still for 3 hours, fell 1 foot in the next 3 hours, stood still 2½ hours more, fell 2 feet more by 1815 and gradually rose to a 3.4-foot level at 2000, stood still 2 hours, and so on. That was a "high dodging" tide which would have helped the Marines by keeping a sufficient depth of water over the reef to float landing craft. But on 20 November they had the bad luck to draw a "low dodging" tide that would admit no boats over the reef. It was impossible to predict whether there would be a low or a high one or an ordinary neap tide, which would have been all right for at least six hours on the 20th. It was fairly certain that the "dodgers" would be over by the 22nd, but Admiral Turner decided not to postpone D-day for three reasons: (1) high water would come an hour later every day, and so delay the landing of artillery and heavy equipment; (2) for every day postponed, the greater became the danger of the wind's setting in from the west; and a west wind on Tarawa kicks up such a short steep sea as to make landing impossible; (3) spring tides, due 22

---

[8] Tide information from Lt. Cdr. Heyen RANR, a former resident of the Gilberts who was on Admiral Turner's staff. Cdr. N. P. Badger who commanded "Prisic," Cincpac-Cincpoa staff, warned Fifth Fleet against taking a chance on those tides.

November, would cover the entire beach up to the enemy barricades. So, because there was a two-to-one chance that the tide on the 20th would be favorable, Turner took the long chance, and lost.[9]

Rear Admiral Hill[10] in battleship *Maryland* commanded the Southern Attack Force that took Tarawa. In contrast to the dour and saturnine Turner, Harry Hill was a sanguine, genial officer who still thought and talked like a young man and preferred to lead rather than drive. Lean in body and quick in his movements, he had a full head of hair just beginning to turn gray, a square chin, blue eyes and a pleasant expression that was constantly breaking into a merry smile. One could still see him as bow oar of the Academy crew or the springy champion of the high hurdles. He had plenty of the latter in the Pacific.

Major General Julian C. Smith,[11] commanding the 2nd Marine Division after a service of thirty-four years in the Corps, also sailed in *Maryland*. A student of the art of war and of human nature, he had the complete confidence of his officers and men. He well knew that Tarawa could not be taken without heavy casualties.

[9] The spring tides 27 November would have been high about 0500 and 1700, too early for a daylight landing and too late to permit securing a beachhead before dark.

[10] Harry W. Hill, b. Oakland Calif. 1890, Naval Academy '11; served in armored cruiser *Maryland*, whose fine silver plate inspired his book *Maryland's Colonial Charm Portrayed in Silver*. Engineer officer *Perry* and *Albany*, and assistant gunnery officer *Texas* to 1917–18. Flag lieut. to Rear Adm. R. E. Coontz, gunnery officer *Concord* and *Memphis* 1923–26 and of *Maryland* 1928–31; staff gunnery officer to Admiral Reeves. C.O. *Dewey* 1934–35; Naval War College course; war plans officer on staff of Admiral Bloch and in office of C.N.O.; C.O. *Wichita* 1942 in Murmansk convoys. Commanded amphibious groups Sept. 1943 to April 1945 when he relieved Admiral Turner as Com V 'Phib at Okinawa. Comdt. National War College 1945–49, chairman General Board of Navy to March 1950, when he became Supt. U.S. Naval Academy. Admiral Hill was accused by Gen. H. M. Smith in *Sat. Eve. Post*, 6 Nov. 1948, of having issued a silly message about "obliterating" Tarawa before the operation started. But it was not Admiral Hill who made this foolish boast.

[11] Julian C. Smith, b. Elkton Md. 1885; U. of Del. '07; 2nd Lt. MC 1909. Served in Cuba, Canal Zone, Vera Cruz and in Hispaniola 1912–16; instructor in various MC schools; service in Nicaragua 1930–33 and in operations and training divisions of MC; colonel of 5th Marines 1938–40, chief of staff at Quantico 1940–41, naval observer in England 1941, C.O. Camp Lejeune 1942. Deputy Com. Fleet Marine Force 1944; Com. expeditionary troops Third Fleet at Palau 1944; Com. Gen. Dept. of Pacific 1945–46, when he retired with rank of Lieutenant General.

Maryland, one of the rehabilitated victims of Pearl Harbor, was unsuitable as a command ship. Her quarters were inadequate for the staffs and her communications, primitive at best, had an annoying habit of conking out on every main-battery salvo.

The Southern Attack Force was larger than the Northern, but weaker in ratio of attack to defense. As against 6472 troops in the northern assault, about 18,600 Marines were to be landed on Betio,[12] but the Makin force outnumbered the Japanese 13 to 1, while the Tarawa force was less than four times as numerous as the defenders. Makin, moreover, was comparatively unfortified. So the two tasks, though similar, cannot be equated on the scale of toughness. Fortunately the 2nd Marine Division was very, very tough. All its components had fought on Guadalcanal.

At daybreak 19 November, the Southern Attack Force, covering an eight-mile square of ocean, was steering northwesterly for a designated point, lat. 1°6′ N, long. 174°50′ E. One of *Suwannee's* planes shot down a Japanese search plane 45 miles away. Destroyers *Ringgold* and *Dashiell*, scheduled for an early entrance into the lagoon, transferred their secret codes to the flagship. A possible shoal entered on the chart as "discolored water reported 1914" was investigated by two other destroyers and found to be nonexistent. At 1451 the designated point was reached and the formation swung to a due west course; at 1700 it took approach disposition.

Just before sundown, the LSTs bringing amphtracs up from Samoa were reported, welcome news for Admiral Hill. They crossed his bow and took station to starboard. Speed dropped to 10 knots as wind and current were pushing the ships along too quickly, and *Ringgold* thrust ahead to locate the next turning point, north of Maiana, by radar bearings.

Admiral Hill's approach narrowly avoided being spoiled by poor charts. Commodore Wilkes's hundred-year-old chart of Tarawa was not too bad, but on the latest Admiralty productions

[12] Not counting the 1211 men in LST Group 2, or the 1927 garrison troops to follow. (Turner Report, Enclosure I.) See table at end of next chapter for breakdown of the force actually engaged, numbering 18,593 officers and men.

Betio was oriented wrong, the gun-barrel axis pointing 139° instead of the correct 128°. Fortunately submarine *Nautilus* had reported the error and a new approach chart of the atoll had been improvised on board *Maryland,* with the compass rose rotated 11 degrees clockwise. Thus, accurate radar fixes were obtained on the land and the approach was made properly. (Dead reckoning could not be relied on because of a strong westerly set between Tarawa and Maiana, the small atoll 17½ miles to the southward.)

Nautilus was ill rewarded for her excellent reconnaissance. About 2200, as *Ringgold* and *Santa Fe* were pushing ahead of the Southern Attack Force, they picked up a pip on the radar screen moving south at 20 knots. Everyone had been warned to look out for *Nautilus*, but word came that afternoon that she had gone westward to pick up an aviator, and it was assumed that she would submerge if she encountered friendly forces. Being near a dangerous reef, she did not submerge. Hill felt he could not run the risk of this contact's being an enemy patrol vessel and gave the order to fire. *Ringgold's* first salvo hit *Nautilus;* a 5-inch shell passed through the base of the conning tower, rupturing her main induction valve but, fortunately, not exploding. Commander Irvin took her down quickly and she was in "dire circumstances" for two hours; but her damage control people worked so well and so fast that she was able to carry on to Abemama and complete her mission.[13]

When eight bells struck for D-day, 20 November, the force guide had reached a point a few miles northwest of Maiana. Admiral Hill signaled a 45-degree right turn and the fire support ships began to haul out toward their stations. At 0045 the Marine buglers commenced sounding reveille and, to their amusement, the moon promptly rose. Scrambled eggs, beefsteak and coffee were served to the troops around 0100. At 0205 the last 45-degree wheel was made to a course due east in order to close the land while it was

[13] *Nautilus* War Patrol Report, in Ms. "Submarine Operational History World War II"; Rear Adm. A. D. Bernhard's Report on Shelling of *Nautilus* 24 Dec. 1943; conversation with Admiral Hill, who said, "The responsibility is entirely mine."

silhouetted by the moon. Forty-five minutes later, Betio was sighted from the flagship's bridge. The transport commander, Captain H. B. Knowles in *Monrovia*, reported at 0355 that all 16 transports were in position. Before eight bells struck again, the buglers were sounding "Boats away!" and rail-loaded landing craft were being lowered.

On board the transports there was intense activity, but in the battleships and cruisers all was calm and silent. A peaceful picture of moonlight in the South Seas lay before them; low-lying Betio was merely a shadow in the moon's path, a threat or a promise as you chose to look upon it. Not a light could be seen ashore. Hypocritical regrets that the Japanese had "done a Kiska on us" were voiced. Stale gags about native girls in grass skirts and Lamours in sarongs passed between Marines and the sailors on watch. Ships moved purposefully to their fire support stations but the enemy showed no sign of awareness. There is nothing like a night amphibious operation to stress that poignant contrast between the beauty, sweetness and serenity of nature and man-made noise, horror and destruction.

The Marines were wearing mottled green cloth-covered steel helmets and green dungarees, except for those who were sporting an experimental uniform. This was a reversible, snap-fastened coat and trousers, the outside camouflaged in shades and blocks of green and the inside in brown, with the idea that it could be reversed if one moved from coconut grove or jungle to bare earth or dead grass. It proved to be much too hot, made the men sweat to the point of exhaustion, and was never used again. Each Marine carried, besides his weapons and one unit of fire, three units of K rations, two canteens of water, shaving kit, toothbrush and spoon. Chaplains passed the word: "In a few minutes you will be over there. . . . This will be a great page in the history of the Marine Corps. . . . Wherever you men are, stop and give a prayer. . . . God bless you all."

3. *Betio Assaulted, 20 November*

By 0430 most of the six transports carrying the initial assault had completed lowering boats, which were circling nearby or hustling over to one of three LSTs in order to transfer Marines to amphtracs. At 0441 a gun on the south shore of Betio fired a red star cluster, first sign that the ships' presence was detected. Nothing else happened for almost half an hour. At 0505 destroyer *Meade* laid a smoke screen on the shore side of *Maryland* to conceal the flash of the battleship's catapult as she launched her spotting plane. Apparently the enemy saw the flash, however, for just two minutes later shore batteries opened up and shots began falling around the flagship. She silenced the two 8-inch guns on the southwestern point of Betio with ten 16-inch salvos. "The whole island of Betio seemed to erupt with bright fires that were burning everywhere." [14] Counter-battery fire continued until 0542, which was the moment for the bomber planes to take over. The sky was just beginning to lighten in the east.

At this juncture there occurred the first delay in a very tight schedule. The planes of Rear Admiral Montgomery's Southern Carrier Group, scheduled for a dawn air strike at 0545, did not appear until 0610. There had been a misunderstanding: the aviators supposed that they were not wanted until 0615, the hour of sunrise.[15] And there was no way to hurry them up, because *Maryland's* radio circuit that communicated with the carriers had conked out on her first 16-inch salvo and required some time to repair. Counter-battery fire, accordingly, was resumed at 0605. But the Japanese shore batteries had been afforded 20 minutes for shooting at the transports without opposition. *Zeilin* and *Heywood*, still in the delicate situation of loading troops into landing craft along-

---

[14] Sherrod *Tarawa* pp. 61–62.

[15] Explanation given by Capts. Tate and Whitehead to Gen. Julian Smith. Admiral Montgomery, who had been pounding Rabaul only 9 days earlier, was unable to be present at the conference at Efate, where the misunderstanding could have been cleared up.

side, were straddled by shells from shore batteries at a range of 11,000 yards. Admiral Hill, accordingly, ordered all transports to move out of range at 0619, and they did not return to the unloading area until 0707. This did not delay the initial waves, because all attack transports had already boated their troops.

Counter-battery fire from the warships ceased as bombers from carriers *Essex, Bunker Hill* and *Independence* appeared over Betio. The air bombardment was over in seven minutes; at 0622 commenced the scheduled naval bombardment — not counter-battery fire, but a systematic going-over of the whole island.

Naval practice and tradition had long opposed risking capital ships within close range of shore batteries; but after the successful performance of fire support cruisers in closing the range at Fedhala, in November 1942, bolder gunfire plans were in order. Admiral Hill opened fire on the strong points of Betio's stock and barrel from a range of 10,000 to 15,000 yards and closed to 2000 yards. The cruisers followed the battleships at 20- to 30-minute intervals, closing the range as firing progressed, and were followed by the destroyers. During this phase, which lasted 80 minutes, shore batteries continued to reply and the ships frequently shifted to counter-battery. At 0735 the fire support ships moved up north of the "gunstock" and lay-to, and at 0745 began to deliver enfilading fire along the Red beaches where the troops were about to land. With some interruptions, to avoid hitting friendly planes, this phase lasted 70 minutes. H-hour for the first wave to hit the beach was announced to all hands as 0830.

Two and a half hours of gunfire from three battleships, four cruisers and a number of destroyers, throwing about 3000 tons of naval projectiles[16] was expected to knock out Betio shore defenses and leave the defenders dazed and groggy. This was a gross miscalculation. Nobody realized how much punishment Japanese could take when protected by several thicknesses of coconut logs and coral sand. There should have been at least three times as

[16] Isley p. 230. Even lightly defended Butaritari had been given 1700 tons before the landing.

much gunfire, supplemented by 2000-pound bombs dropped by Liberators,[17] and by vertical fire from rockets or mortars. Close-range naval gunfire has too flat a trajectory to wreck a low, flat island. Much good, however, was accomplished: many of the enemy's above-ground installations were destroyed; his communications were knocked out, which prevented him from organizing a counterattack on the American beachhead; his control instruments were hit, which made his shooting at the ships inaccurate; many of the coast defense guns and some of the larger anti-aircraft guns were silenced; and many Japanese were killed before the landing.[18]

Minesweepers *Pursuit* and *Requisite*, screened by smoke, swept a channel from the transport area into the lagoon while the bombardment was going on, and answered enemy shore fire with their 3-inch guns. Lieutenant Commander R. A. MacPherson, flying one of *Maryland's* planes, then guided *Pursuit* on a buoying mission, dropping smoke-pots to indicate shoal spots, while *Requisite* returned to lead in *Ringgold* and *Dashiell*. They were a gallant sight as they tore through the pass into the lagoon, enemy shells falling all around them. Only *Ringgold* was hit, and she by duds, one of which knocked out the port engine. Since larger vessels could not as yet venture into the lagoon, these two destroyers and the two minesweepers dished out all the frontal fire that the

---

[17] H. M. Smith *Coral and Brass* p. 131 and J. R. Stockman *Tarawa* p. 5 state that the VII Army A.F. had been requested by the Marines before the operation to provide such a bombing mission, but that the request was not honored. Dr. A. F. Simpson, the Air Force historian, tells me that there is no record of its having been received. There is a rumor that the mission took off but bombed the wrong atoll.

[18] "This writer believes that approximately 40 per cent of the Japanese casualties were due to this bombardment." (Gen. Holland Smith's Report, section on naval gunfire, p. 2.) In his *Sat. Eve. Post* articles in 1948 the General bitterly complained of the inadequacy of naval gunfire support, but after being reminded by Admiral Hill that his staff had participated in the gunfire plan and shared responsibility for it, he wrote a less devastating account in *Coral and Brass* p. 132. Most of the CD guns were silenced, but very few were disabled. One 8-inch gun on the SE part of Betio resumed fire about 1430 but was then knocked out by a battleship. Col. Carlson, a trained observer, said that not more than 5 guns bigger than an automatic rifle were firing at the LVTs when he came ashore around 0945, and there had been at least 45 guns on that side of the island alone.

beach defenses received; and that they did so lustily that more ammunition had to be lightered out to them before the day's end.

Following this bold quartet, the next ship to enter Tarawa Lagoon was high-bosomed *Ashland*, "pregnant with tanks impatient to be freed," to paraphrase a line of Dean Swift on the Trojan horse.

The hundred amphtracs (LVT–2s) that made up the first three assault waves had been disgorged by their LSTs or lowered from transports at first light, those from the LSTs picking up Marines from LCVPs. All were buzzing about the boat rendezvous area by 0620. Colonel David M. Shoup USMC commanded the assault.

The first wave consisted of 48 amphtracs, timed to land at H-hour; the second, of 24, to land at H plus 3 minutes; the third, of 21, to land at H plus 6 minutes; the following waves were composed of landing craft, some bringing troops, others vehicles and supplies. Each wave carried elements of all three landing teams, which were composed as follows: —

LANDING TEAM ONE, to land on Beach Red 1. 3rd Battalion 2nd Regiment 2nd Marine Division, Major John F. Schoettel. From *Heywood*.

LANDING TEAM TWO, to land on Beach Red 2. 2nd Battalion 2nd Regiment, Lieutenant Colonel Herbert R. Amey. From *Zeilin*.

LANDING TEAM THREE, to land on Beach Red 3, 2nd Battalion 8th Regiment, Major H. P. Crowe. From *Arthur Middleton*.

According to plan, the distance from the boat rendezvous area to the line of departure was over three and a half miles, and thence to the beaches another three miles. All three waves left the boat rendezvous at 0645. The amphtracs were expected to reach the line of departure by 0745, but they could not do it. The distance was greater than had been expected, because *Pursuit* was somewhat out of place in marking the line of departure, and because a strong westerly set outside, and a heavy chop running with it, reduced the amphtracs' speed. At 0748 Admiral Hill's spotter plane reported that they were still half a mile from the line of departure. At 0803 he postponed H-hour to 0845, but as the first wave did

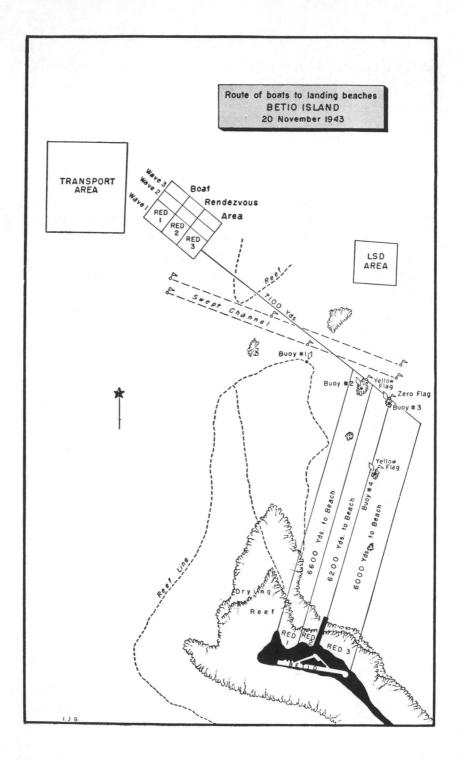

not cross the line of departure until 0825, he had to change it again to 0900. Gunfire support ships were ordered to resume fire at 0840 and to continue for 15 minutes, when the escort carriers' Hellcats would take over and strafe beaches until the Marines landed. Even these postponements were not enough; the first LVTs hit the beach at 0913.[19]

Admiral Hill did not order naval bombardment to continue after 0855, because the island and parts of the lagoon were now under a heavy smoke pall and he feared lest shells fall among the landing craft; only the two control destroyers and *Pursuit* continued to fire on Beach Red 1. Thus the enemy, already alerted by the amphtracs' movements, had 20 to 30 minutes' additional grace to transfer troops from the southern shore to man the rifle pits and machine-gun nests on the lagoon side. (The plane strafing did not bother him much, since the Hellcats' .50-caliber bullet could not penetrate his emplacements.) This last-minute transfer of Japanese fighting men to the point of impact was one principal reason for the high initial casualties at Betio. The other was the dodging tide.

As the amphtracs approached the three beaches, their passengers could dimly see through the smoke a narrow sand beach fringed by shattered coconut palms, a few wooden buildings and a long, narrow pier poking out to the edge of the reef. The Marines, 20 to 25 in each LVT, had already been boated for four hours and were eager to get ashore and "push the Japanese into the sea." The amphtracs, still undamaged, hit the coral-reef apron to the beach and crawled along it, just as they were designed to do.

Landing Team Three found two thirds of Beach Red 3, the

[19] Timetable of boat waves from *Heywood* and *Monrovia* Action Reports, corrected from other sources: —

	Wave 1	*Wave 2*	*Wave 3*	*Wave 5*	*Wave 6*
Left Transport Area	0540	0540	0540	0705	0730
Left Boat Rendezvous	0645	0645	0645	—	—
Left Line of Departure	0825	0828	0831	0853	0902
Arrived Beach Red 1	0913	0915	0917	0920	0925
Arrived Beaches Red 2 and 3	0922	0922	0922	0933	—

one east of the pier, so cluttered with coral blocks that the 17 amphtracs destined for that beach all landed on the western half of it, opposite the apex of the airstrip triangle. The enemy opened with machine-gun and small-arms fire, but not severely; he had not yet completely manned his beach defenses at this point and only a few Marines were wounded before the first LVT hit Beach Red 3. Two or three amphtracs, finding no beach barrier here, continued about a hundred yards inland and there discharged their complement of Marines intact; but these men soon found themselves outflanked and had to retire.

The first wave of Landing Team Two reached Beach Red 2 at 0922 without much opposition, but Colonel Amey was shot dead while wading ashore. When these Marines hit the beach, they were literally up against it. From undamaged coconut-log gun revetments the enemy dealt out such terrible punishment that most of the troops crouched on the narrow beach under the barrier.

Landing Team One suffered heavy casualties in steering for the strongly defended Beach Red 1. The reef apron there is wide, and the beach line forms a sharp reëntrant angle between stock and lock of the Betio musket. Japanese troops stationed here waited until the amphtracs were within a hundred yards of the beach, then opened up with coast defense guns, rifles, light and heavy machine guns, mortars and anti-boat guns. Amphtrac drivers were killed, their engines disabled, their fuel ignited, and several of the craft were completely knocked out before they reached the beach.

Here is how it looked to one Marine who landed in the first wave on Beach Red 1: —

Bullets pinged off that tractor like hailstones off a tin roof. Two shells hit the water twenty yards off the port side and sent up regular geysers. I swept the beach, just to keep the bastards down as much as possible. Can't figure how I didn't get it in the head or something.

We were 100 yards in now and the enemy fire was awful damn intense and gettin' worse. They were knockin' boats out left and right. A tractor'd get hit, stop, and burst into flames, with men jumping out like torches.

The water here was only about three feet deep, just covering the coral reefs, which the tractor'd bounce onto and over. Bullets ricocheted off the coral and up under the tractor. It must've been one of these bullets that got the driver. The boat lurched, and I looked in the cab and saw him slumped over, dead. The lieutenant jumped in and pulled the driver out, and drove, himself, till he got hit.

That happened about thirty yards off shore. A shell struck the boat. The concussion felt like a big fist — Joe Louis maybe — had smacked me right in the face. Seemed to make my face swell up. Knocked me down and sort of stunned me for a moment. I shook my head. Shrapnel was pinging all around. Nicked hell out of my face and hands. One piece, about an inch long, tore into my back. A fella later pulled it out on shore.

I looked around. My assistant, a private with a Mexican name, who was feeding my gun, had his pack and helmet blown right off. He was crumpled up beside me, with his head forward, and in the back of it was a hole I could put my fist in. I started to shake him and he fell right on over.

Guys were sprawled all over the place. I looked across at my buddy, who was only five feet from me. He was on his back and his face was all bloody and he was holding his hand over his face and mumbling something.

Our boat was stopped, and they were laying lead to us from a pill box like holy hell. Everybody seemed stunned, so I yelled, "Let's get the hell outa here!" I grabbed my carbine and an ammunition box and stepped over a couple of fellas laying there and put my hand on the side so's to roll over into the water. I didn't want to put my head up. The bullets were pouring at us like a sheet of rain. . . . Only about a dozen out of the twenty-five went over the side with me, and only about four of us ever got evacuated.[20]

4. *"Issue in Doubt"*

The fourth wave, consisting largely of 37-mm guns and their crews boated in LCVPs, could not pass the edge of the reef owing to the low tide; these boats retracted and waited until nightfall to land. The fifth wave, LCMs from *Ashland*, had to dis-

[20] Pvt. N. M. Baird usmc, an Oneida Indian, as told in *Sea Power* April 1944 by J. Campbell Bruce as "One Square Mile of Hell." These extracts are from the original script, furnished by the editor, Mr. Roger Kafka.

charge its Sherman tanks in three or four feet of water. Eleven of them crawled over the reef and reached Red beaches 2 and 3 by 0933; the rest, disabled by enemy fire, stopped dead.[21] The tank battalion commander, Lieutenant Colonel Alexander B. Swenceski, had as tough an experience as did any officer who survived. Badly wounded in shallow water, he dragged himself on top of a heap of dead bodies to avoid drowning in the flood tide, and lay there for dead until well on into the next day.

Along the Red beaches and for a few yards inland there was close, bloody and bitter fighting. The Marines soon discovered that rifle fire and hand grenades were of little use against their holed-up enemy, and began attacking the machine-gun nests and pillboxes with flame throwers, of which they had too few, and blocks of TNT used as hand grenades, which they had learned to use at Guadalcanal. In addition to meeting fierce opposition in front, they were subjected to severe artillery fire from enemy emplacements in the eastern or barrel end of Betio.

Colonel David M. Shoup reached the pier before 1100 with Lieutenant Colonel P. M. Rixey of the 75-mm pack howitzer battalion. Colonel Shoup, Major Tom Culhane, and a sergeant with a radio on his back, all three waist-deep in water, directed the desperate battle as best they could from a position alongside the pier.

By 1000 the reef opposite Beaches 2 and 3 was being swept by cross fire from behind the beaches, from the barrel, and from a grounded hulk northwest of the pier. At least 20 amphtracs and two LCMs, full of dead and wounded, were stuck on the reef. One large gun on the barrel was horribly accurate; several times it dropped a shell right on a landing craft just as the ramp came down, spreading a pool of blood around the boat. Colonel Shoup radioed General Julian Smith in *Maryland* for all possible fire sup-

---

[21] These tanks followed the then tank doctrine, based on experience in Africa, of advancing alone to overwhelm enemy machine guns and anti-tank weapons. Rolling up from the beach through a gap in the wall, they charged blindly about the interior of the island, doing themselves no good and the enemy little harm. Only two survived until the third day. Then, with the light tanks which had landed at Beach Green, guided by foot soldiers to point out targets and pick off magnetic mines, they helped to break up the remaining enemy defenses.

port on the barrel; and at 1034 *Tennessee, Anderson* and *Russell* began dishing it out as requested. Carrier aircraft bombed and strafed the lock, where the line between Marines and Japanese was too close and fluctuating for naval gunfire.

Colonel Shoup had already ordered into Beach Red 2 his regimental reserve, the 1st Battalion 2nd Regiment commanded by Major Wood R. Kyle. General Smith now decided to commit the 3rd Battalion 8th Regiment (Major Robert H. Ruud), half of his divisional reserve. This landing team was ordered into Beach 3 to reinforce the badly shot-up eastern flank of the 2nd Battalion. It was the calculated hour of high water, but the tide still dodged and the sea level was so low that Ruud's men were forced to disembark opposite the end of the pier and wade in for nearly 700 yards, suffering heavy casualties in spite of the cover provided by the pier. Thus, the reinforcements for Beach 3, instead of arriving with élan and fresh enthusiasm, reached the beach wet, exhausted and decimated.

It was now noon. For another two hours the situation remained very critical. Most of the amphtracs had been knocked out; and owing to the tide's refusal to rise, no landing craft could float over the reef. Everything was stalled; reinforcements could not land and some 1500 Marines were pinned down on the narrow beach under the coconut-log and coral-block wall, unable to advance or retreat. A few hundred bold spirits had crossed this barrier and were engaged in killing and being killed, but the beachhead was almost nonexistent.

Only two companies of Major Schoettel's Landing Team One under Major Michael P. Ryan had succeeded in reaching the butt end of Beach Red 1, where they were holding their own; the cove on their east flank was swept by so murderous an enfilading fire that Major Schoettel hesitated to land the rest of his team. The middle of Beach Red 2 was covered by heavy machine-gun fire, fatal to approaching men and boats.

On the eastern end of that beach, Landing Team Two held a 200-yard front. Their commanding officer, Colonel Amey, had been killed; and in the absence of his executive officer, who had been taken into the wrong beach, Colonel Walter I. Jordan, an observer from another Marine division, was trying without much success to organize the battalion. Jordan led one company about 100 yards inland, but at 1154 he radioed to Colonel Shoup, "We need help. Situation bad."

Around noon Colonel Shoup set up a command post on the seaward side of a Japanese coconut-log bombproof shelter. Japanese were inside the shelter but the Marines could not get them out without blowing up their own colonel, so sentries were posted at the entrance to contain them. Communications between the commanding officer and his landing teams were still very tenuous.

On Beach 3, east of the pier, the 2nd Battalion 8th Regiment, led by two courageous and resourceful officers — Major Henry P. Crowe, a prodigious redhead who had risen from the ranks, and Major William C. Chamberlin, short, blond and wearing glasses, who had been a professor of economics when the war began — held a front of about 250 yards and a beachhead of about 100 yards' depth. But the premier killers ashore were the 34 members of Lieutenant William Deane Hawkins's Scout-Sniper Platoon. These picked troops, trained to conceal themselves, to fire quick and sure, and to strike home with the knife, killed at least ten times their number of Japanese, shooting them out of trees and blowing them out of holes. Hawkins was seen riding in an amphtrac, bullets zinging about his head, to clean up machine-gun nests. He continued fighting with two bullets in his shoulders and died on the second day from loss of blood.

In the early afternoon Colonel Shoup sent Colonel Carlson out, in an amphtrac that was evacuating wounded, to request of General Julian Smith that reserves, water, ammunition and the division artillery (none of which had yet been landed) be sent in to the pier, where a narrow corridor was relatively safe from enemy fire. Colonel Carlson did not reach *Maryland* until well into the evening. General Smith had received very few messages from the beach, as most of the Marines' radios had been knocked out

Battle

Destruction on Beach Red 2, Betio

Marines

Battle conference: Lieutenant Colonel Shoup in center, holding map; Captain Ware talking to him; Colonel Carlson seated; Major Culhane at left; Colonels Holmes, Edson and Rixey in center

Brigadier General T. E. Bourke, Colonel M. A. Edson and
Major General Julian C. Smith

Marine Officers at Tarawa

and their communications crews killed, but the pilots of *Maryland's* Kingfisher planes, after repeatedly flying low over Betio, told him the essence of the critical situation. He feared lest too many reinforcements make a "Spotsylvania bloody angle" out of the beachhead; but if he sent too few the Marines might be smothered by enemy counterattack. At 1330 he radioed General Holland M. Smith, who was with Admiral Turner in *Pennsylvania* off Makin, requesting release of the corps reserve. This message concluded with the ominous words, "Issue in doubt." [22]

A ship-to-shore movement with a long distance to cover and a tight schedule is very difficult to stop when once started. If Colonel Shoup could have called a halt on transport unloadings at noon and obtained only needed reinforcements, water and ammunition, his situation would have been much better. But all the troops supposed to land on D-day, as well as supplies not needed for several days, were already boated by the time the first attack waves reached shore. Boats kept pouring into the lagoon all that afternoon. LVTs which had retracted, and a few LCVPs still trying to land elements of the regimental reserve, hovered off the edge of the reef and jammed approaches to the pier, providing fine targets for the enemy. The amphtrac battalion's commanding officer, Major Henry C. Drewes USMC, had been killed and the LVTs were leaderless. Some drifted in the lagoon, their reduced and exhausted crews awaiting oral orders since most of their portable radios had been drowned or shot out; others valiantly took men off stranded landing craft and brought them in over the reef. The transport commanders, eager to discharge and retire, continued to unload their ships according to plan. [23] So by midafternoon over 100 landing craft, mostly loaded with unwanted supplies,

[22] Gen. Julian C. Smith's D–3 Journal. He received a favorable answer at about 1500, and decided to land the Corps reserve next day. Col. Carlson was here as an observer from the 4th Marine Division, then in training.

[23] For instance, 2 LCMs loaded each with a bulldozer and metal beach mat early on D-day to go ashore in the 4th wave could not discharge for 48 hours (*Harry Lee* Report). Some landing craft had cargo on board for 3 days before being able to get rid of it.

were milling around in the lagoon. That part of the divisional reserve not yet committed, the 1st Battalion 8th Regiment, lay in its boats all night awaiting orders to land that had been sent but not received.

By the end of D-day about 5000 men were ashore and about 1500 of them had been killed or wounded.[24] Several hundred of the wounded were evacuated from the beach. Navy medical corpsmen [25] showed great ingenuity and fortitude, working all day under fire and all night without rest, ferrying the wounded out over the reef in large rubber rafts for transfer to landing craft which took them to the transports.

Throughout D-day destroyers *Ringgold* and *Dashiell,* relieved by *Frazier* and *Anderson,* continued close gunfire support on call from Navy fire control parties ashore, and this was what most helped the Marines. Bombing and strafing by carrier planes went on almost continuously until sunset, against targets recommended by ships, shore parties and *Maryland's* planes; 32 strikes in all, one of them by 80 planes. Rear Admiral Ragsdale's five escort carriers maintained combat air and anti-submarine patrol over the area and supplied planes for strikes, as did the big carriers of Admiral Montgomery's Southern Group. But the air support provided at Tarawa was slight in strength and elementary in technique compared with what was done 18 months later at Okinawa.

As daylight faded, all combatant ships except three destroyers, together with the transports, withdrew to designated offshore areas for protection against submarine and air attack. The transports returned at 2140. *Ringgold* anchored inside the lagoon, *Anderson* cruised off the south shore, and *Frazier* off the butt end, to supply the Marines with call fire throughout the night.

The divisional artillery, commanded by Lieutenant Colonel Presley M. Rixey USMC, landed on Beach Red 2 after nightfall. Their 75-mm pack howitzers could not be rolled down the pier

---

[24] See casualty statistics at end of chapter xi, but all figures for D-day alone are a guess; this is General Julian Smith's.

[25] U.S. Marines do not have their own medical service but use that of the Navy; more than 20 pharmacist's mates were killed at Tarawa.

under fire, so the cannoneers carried the pieces ashore on their backs. Water, blood plasma and ammunition also were landed on the pier, and reinforcements straggled in that way all night. That pier was a great asset to the Marines. Constructed of coconut logs in cribwork, it offered good protection from enemy gunfire to men wading ashore on the western side.

By 1800 the Marines controlled the beach from a point 300 yards west of the long pier to the short Burns Philp wharf 400 yards east of the pier, with an average depth of 300 yards, halfway across the island. At the very butt end of Beach Red 1 was a second beachhead which Major Ryan had been stoutly defending all day; this he expanded after dark to an area 150 yards wide and about 500 deep, extending along Beach Green, by using units from different battalions which happened to land there.

The Marines secured for the night, half of them standing guard while the other half slept in improvised foxholes. Their situation seemed more precarious than it actually was. A vigorous counterattack, at any time that night or next morning, might have swept them into the lagoon; but Rear Admiral Shibasaki could not counterattack. Half his men had already been killed, naval gunfire had broken his communications, he had no control over units outside his command post, and the only part of the island where he could have found troops for counterattack was the musket barrel, which was under almost continual bombardment by the destroyers. Individual Japanese infiltrated that night, but almost all were disposed of by the Marines, who kept excellent fire discipline, as veterans of Guadalcanal had learned to do.

D plus 1 day, 21 November, opened with the second half of the divisional reserve fighting its way ashore. During the night several enterprising Japanese had swum out to reoccupy a freighter hulk grounded northwest of the pier; others had crawled into disabled tanks and amphtracs stranded on the reef, or set up machine guns in wooden latrines that projected over the lagoon. So, when Major Hays's reserves started to land, after spending almost 20 hours in their boats, they suffered heavy casualties on the reef. The first of three waves hit the center of the reef opposite the eastern end of Beach Red 1 at 0615. As soon as the ramps were down, murderous fire poured into these boats from machine guns on the beach, from the nearby hulk, and even, as it seemed, from the pier.[26] The boats were too far in for naval gunfire support to function, so the troops had to jump overboard into waist-deep water and wade ashore. "We suggested to the men in the water," reported the Navy "jg" in charge of this wave, "that they had better keep near the boats to protect themselves; but they told us to follow plan and retire so other waves could get in to help them take the beach." [27] Carrier planes promptly bombed and strafed the infested hulk, and a Marine mortar ashore demolished a privy that harbored a machine gun, but the enemy continued to rake the reef from other positions. In order to avoid one field of fire, some Marines waded into the cove of Beach Red 1 between stock and lock, where they were shot down almost to a man. During the five hours or more that Major Hays's men required to complete landing, their losses were greater than those of any battalion that landed on D-day.[28]

On 21 November there was a normal neap tide which threatened to drown wounded men who had fallen on the reef. Two salvage crews from transport *Sheridan*, which had been in the lagoon all night, collected landing boats for rescue work. While some pulled wounded Marines out of the water, one LCVP silenced an enemy machine gun with its .30-caliber, worked over a wrecked landing craft to kill a Japanese sniper there, and then joined the rescue party. The cool, impeccable seamanship of this boat's unidentified coxswain was admirable. He "kept perfect control of his boat

---

[26] Many believed that the Japanese had established a machine-gun nest under the pier along which men and supplies had been coming all night, but the fire from that direction came from two guns on the lagoon shore east of Beach Red 3, shooting over the pier.

[27] Boat Wave officer, Lt. (jg) H. N. Stephens USNR, in *Sheridan* Action Report.

[28] The losses of this 1st Battalion 8th Marines — 4 officers and 106 men killed, 9 officers and 225 men wounded — are almost identical with those of the 2nd and 3rd Battalions which had landed on Beach 2 the previous day; but the reserves incurred almost all their losses on the reef.

against a strong current, holding her off the wounded men and yet close enough to lift them from the water, and not ground the boat. . . . Finally the last of the wounded men, 13 in all, were lifted into the boat, leaving about 35 men in the water, unharmed as yet but without rifles. They refused to come into the boat, and asked this officer to bring them back something to fight with." The coxswain backed out while bullets were zinging around his head and the men on board were stamping out incendiary bullets which threatened to ignite his cargo of drummed gasoline.[29]

Landing craft were now brought under control by Captain John B. McGovern, designated boat-control officer by Admiral Hill. He set up his command post on board *Pursuit*, rounded up about 18 amphtracs, bellowed orders to landing craft through a bull horn, and straightened out the unloading schedule. Hitherto, if a unit ashore wanted ammunition, water or food, four or five transports had attempted to fill the same order, wasting boat time. But Captain McGovern "with meager and often conflicting information, did the things that needed to be done, and did them in the order of their importance to the accomplishment of the mission."[30]

Things could not straighten out fast enough for Colonel Shoup, still in his sand-hole command post alongside an enemy-held bombproof shelter. "Imperative you land ammunition, water, rations and medical supplies in amphtrac on Beach Red 2 and evacuate casualties," he radioed to *Maryland* at 0852; and to the assistant division commander: "Imperative you get all types ammunition to all landing parties immediately." At 1100 he remarked to Mr. Sherrod, "We are in a mighty tight spot," and half an hour later he radioed to General Julian Smith, "Situation doesn't look good ashore." Major Schoettel, the Landing Team One commander who was still afloat in an LCVP, sent Shoup a message at 1133 that troops who had just attempted to land on Beach Red 1 had been driven back to their boats by heavy machine-gun fire. "We were

[29] Lt. (jg) E. A. Heimberger USNR in *Sheridan* Action Report.
[30] Col. Carlson's Report.

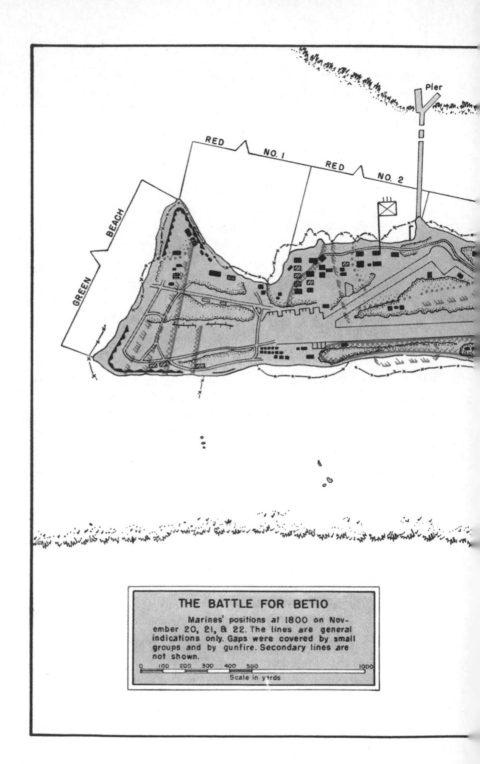

THE BATTLE FOR BETIO

Marines' positions at 1800 on November 20, 21, & 22. The lines are general indications only. Gaps were covered by small groups and by gunfire. Secondary lines are not shown.

0 100 200 300 400 500   1000

Scale in yards

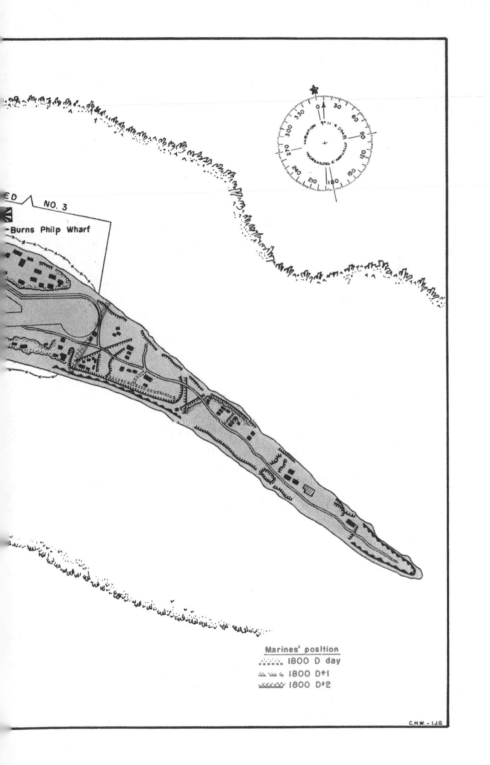

ED NO. 3

Burns Philp Wharf

Marines' position
1800 D day
1800 D+1
1800 D+2

C.H.W. - I.J.G.

not all heroes," said one officer to the writer. "I started inland with about 100 Marines to take out a machine gun that was giving us trouble, but by the time we got there only two or three were with me."

5. Betio Secured

Around noon, when the laggard tide finally did its duty, the tide of battle turned. In preparation for others to land on Beach Green, Major Ryan's men broke out of their narrow beachhead on Red 1, and with the help of call fire from destroyers, overran three 80-mm coast defense guns that commanded the beach approaches. At 1225 they announced that they had reached the southwest corner of the island. General Julian Smith immediately ordered the 6th Marines, the corps reserve, to land on the southern half of Beach Green and advance to the western end of the airstrip. Amphtracs went in first to clear the way for landing craft and pull two broken-down tanks off the beach. While Major Ryan's men held the beachhead, the 1st Battalion 6th Regiment (Major William K. Jones) landed in rubber boats late in the afternoon, dug themselves in and called for bombing of positions along the south shore.

By 1700 November 21 several Marine units formerly pinned down in the beachhead on each side of the long pier had fought their way across the airfield, under Lieutenant Colonel Jordan, and established a small perimeter on the south shore of Betio. For the time being they were isolated; the enemy still held the lock area that commanded the reëntrant angle of Beach Red 1, and laid down such heavy fire on the Marines' eastern flank, resting on the Burns Philp wharf, that they could make no advance in that direction. Light tanks which had landed at high water rumbled about firing high explosives through the slits of pillboxes and bombproofs. As a precaution against the enemy's escaping, a landing team of the 6th Regiment took possession of Bairiki, the island next east of Betio; they were followed thither by a part of the divisional artillery which did some useful shelling of Japanese positions in the gun-barrel end of Betio, on which the 75-mm pack howitzers in the beachhead were already sighted.

Colonel Shoup, reporting on the situation at 1600, felt justified in concluding, "We are winning." And he was justified, for both beachheads had been expanded, the Japanese defenders had been split into two groups which could be dealt with separately, and the movement of reinforcements had been properly organized. Urgently wanted supplies were brought in and casualties evacuated by a shuttle service of LVTs; one of them traveled right across the island to bring food and water to Colonel Jordan's men. At 1803, the first two jeeps came rolling along the pier, towing 37-mm guns. "Sign of certain victory," noted correspondent Sherrod. "Who will carve a monument to the embattled jeep as the Wheeled Victory of Tarawa?"

Another good portent that evening was the arrival of Colonel Merritt A. Edson, General Julian Smith's chief of staff, at Colonel Shoup's command post, to take command of all troops on Betio. Colonel Shoup could now concentrate on his own combat team. Both colonels were up all night making plans for next day and arranging for naval gunfire support.

No Marine slept easy that night for fear of counterattack; but none developed. Early next morning, 22 November, the Japanese radio on Tarawa sent out its last message: "Our weapons have been destroyed and from now on everyone is attempting a final charge. . . . May Japan exist for ten thousand years!" [31] Throughout the day the enemy-held part of the island diminished fast. Major Bill Jones's reserve battalion, which had landed on Beach Green, marched along the south shore. Light tanks rolled ahead, pouring shellfire into the embrasures of pillboxes and bomb shelters; Marine riflemen followed with grenades and TNT blocks; flame throwers scorched what life was left. This went on all day. The heat was terrific, the resistance desperate, water and food ran out; but the

[31] Official Report p. 10.

6th Marines pressed resolutely on, and by nightfall had established themselves between the south shore and the east end of the
airfield. The big bombproof in the hammer position, on the
boundary between Beaches Red 1 and 2, was the only strong point
at the western end still in enemy hands.

At the close of this third day, 22 November, General Julian
Smith felt far from hopeful of a rapid cleanup. Heavy casualties
among his officers weakened leadership in command. Naval gunfire and bombing by planes had failed to smash the strong points
behind Beach Red 1 and at the east end of the airfield. But events
that night, the third ashore, cast a different light on the situation.
Thrice the Japanese on the eastern end staged heavy counterattacks on the positions which had been taken up by Major Jones's
battalion at nightfall. All were repulsed with artillery, machine-
gun and rifle fire, hand grenades and the bayonet, while destroyers
Schroeder and *Sigsbee* pounded areas still under enemy control.
Some 325 Japanese dead were counted next morning, but about
500 were still alive on the barrel end of Betio.

On the fourth day, 23 November, two things remained for the
Marines to accomplish. The 3rd Battalion 6th Marine Regiment
(Lieutenant Colonel Kenneth F. McLeod), relieving Major Jones's
tired troops, swept down the barrel of Betio, liquidating Japanese
who seemed to have lost all will to fight after the failure of their
night counterattacks. McLeod reached the eastern end of the
island at 1300. Another team ganged up on the enemy pocket back
of Red 1 — including the big bombproof that no naval shell had
been able to penetrate. The final storming of this shelter was
attended by correspondents, photographers and other sightseers.

All that morning, Marine engineers and Seabees had been repairing the main airstrip, and at noon a carrier-based plane landed
there. General Julian Smith then reported to Admiral Hill, inviting
him to come ashore and study "the type of hostile resistance which
will be encountered in future operations," predicting "complete
annihilation of enemy on Betio this date." By the early afternoon
of November 23, it had been accomplished.

On the beach, end of D-day

Official U.S. Marine Corps photos

Marines advancing inland

Marines on Betio

Japanese command post

Official U.S. Marine Corps photos

First United States plane lands at Abemama

CHAPTER XI

Tarawa and Abemama Secured

24–27 November 1943

1. Bairiki to Buariki[1]

ALTHOUGH Betio Island was the one needed for an air base, the rest of Tarawa Atoll could not be neglected. A string of islands and islets connected by reefs fordable at low tide stretched for about 12 miles eastward from Betio, turned a corner, and extended another 18 miles northwestward. These two sides of the triangle (the third being nothing but reef) had to be secured in order to make Betio safe, and also to obtain a site for a second airfield. This task was assigned to the 2nd Battalion 6th Marine Regiment, commanded by Lieutenant Colonel Raymond L. Murray, and to an artillery detachment of the 3rd Battalion 10th Marine Regiment.

The first landing outside Betio was made by Colonel Murray's battalion on Bairiki, the next island to the east, on 21 November. No live Japanese were there, only a machine-gun unit of about 15 men who had been killed by the explosion of a gasoline drum on which one of the cruisers' Kingfisher planes had obtained a lucky hit. So next morning Murray was ordered back to Betio to help out at Beach Green. Not being needed there, his men were reëmbarked in landing craft with orders to proceed to Eita, the next large island eastward, and thence sweep up the atoll.

Landing there at 0900 November 24 they found it to be cluttered with abandoned gasoline drums and bombs. A narrow road,

<hr>

[1] The following account was obtained orally from Col. Murray.

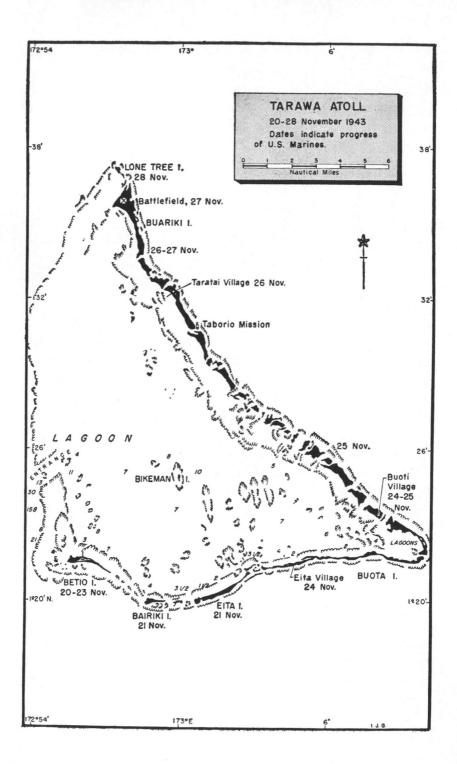

TARAWA ATOLL
20-28 November 1943
Dates indicate progress
of U.S. Marines.

0 1 2 3 4 5 6
Nautical Miles

LONE TREE I.
28 Nov.

Battlefield, 27 Nov.

BUARIKI I.

26-27 Nov.

Taratai Village 26 Nov.

Taborio Mission

25 Nov.

L A G O O N

Buoti
Village
24-25
Nov.

BIKEMAN I.

LAGOONS

BETIO I.
20-23 Nov.

Eita Village
24 Nov.

BUOTA I.

BAIRIKI I.
21 Nov.

EITA I.
21 Nov.

I. J. G.

interrupted only by the fordable reefs, ran along the lagoon side of the atoll right up to the northern end; and along it the 2nd Battalion marched. But they had plenty of company for, beginning at Eita, they were joined by natives who increased in number to over 200 as the column advanced. These Gilbertese wanted nothing from the Marines, not even food; they looked on the expedition as a huge lark and were eager to get in on the inevitable fight when the Japanese were cornered. The boys — well built, ruddy brown in color and wearing only lava-lavas — flashed smiles with their white teeth; the girls, natural, unaffected (and by no means unattractive), in grass skirts, were eager to help and so were allowed to carry some of the troops' equipment on their bushy heads.

It was a pretty picture: the lean, unshaven Marines in their steel helmets and green coveralls trudging under coconut palms and pandanus trees with laughing, half-naked boys and girls springily keeping pace. A Tarawan named Tutu, who had studied at the medical college of Fiji and spoke excellent English, interpreted for Colonel Murray and kept good order among his compatriots. Every night, Marines and natives bivouacked at discreet distances apart and amused each other with song; the Gilbertese singing hymns in their own language, and the Marines "From the Halls of Montezuma" and other well-known Leatherneck songs. Even with this encouragement, the march was a tough one for the Marines, for they had to take turn as scouts and flankers in the heavy underwood and wade with their packs through the tide-swept channels between islands.

On 25 November the Marines got into trouble fording a channel between two islands where the tide rose very quickly. Mr. Tutu swam across with a few natives and brought back three canoes that served as ferries. By the following night the column was half-way up the northeast leg of the Tarawa triangle. A couple of amphtracs carrying supplies stayed with the Marines and were replenished by boats from Betio.

On the afternoon of 26 November the column reached the

Catholic mission station of Taborio on Taritai Island where three Sacred Heart Fathers and several nuns resided. A few had been there through the Japanese occupation; others had recently been paddled over from Abaiang after the natives had informed them that the Japanese were planning to kill them off. The clergy appreciated the Marines' K rations and, in return, broke out some excellent French wine that they had managed to hide away.

At nightfall on the 26th, the Marines bivouacked on Buariki, the island at the north end of Tarawa Atoll. They were fagged out. A company sent ahead by Colonel Murray to reconnoiter discovered about 160 stout fellows of the Japanese Special Naval Landing Force, armed with rifles, hand grenades, two knee mortars and at least ten machine guns. They had taken up positions in a line of taro pits that ran about halfway across the northern end of this island, and were protected by a wild coconut grove full of dense undergrowth. Two Marine companies attacked simultaneously at 0700 next morning while a third was held in reserve. Colonel Murray tried to induce the natives to stay in the rear. The boys insisted on coming up to see the fight, but the girls obeyed orders and helped care for Marine casualties in a deserted native village where a first-aid station was set up. They made palm-frond pillows for the wounded, fanned away flies, brought fresh water and made themselves generally useful, while Mr. Tutu proved that he knew how to handle surgical instruments.

The Battle of Buariki was soon over. The Japanese simply fought from the taro pits until they were exterminated. The killed, who were cheerfully buried by the natives, numbered 156; and eight more were later caught on tiny Lone Tree Islet to the north. No prisoners were taken.[2] The Marines lost 34 killed and had 56 wounded. Next day the 2nd Battalion was evacuated by landing craft to Betio.

About 25 November the Tarawa Garrison Group, four char-

[2] Two Korean prisoners were taken in the march up the island. One of them made himself so useful that the Colonel wished to keep him as an orderly; but that was against regulations, and this P.O.W. wept bitterly when parted from his new friends.

tered merchantmen commanded by Captain Herbert O. Roesch and escorted by two destroyer escorts, had arrived off Betio and entered the lagoon. They carried 1900 men, including an Acorn detachment with the necessary equipment to build an airfield, and a carrier aircraft service unit to take care of it. This garrison group had been inefficiently loaded and arrived much earlier than it was wanted. Nothing was accomplished during the first three days because the pier and beaches were being used to reëmbark Marines, and some of the matériel discharged into landing craft could not be put ashore for several days more. Unloading was still "the world-wide difficulty of amphibious operations," as Admiral Wilkinson remarked; for it was almost impossible to anticipate what facilities there would be at an objective, or what could be accomplished promptly. Shipping control, especially of supply echelons, was still being inefficiently handled; when the transports of the Tarawa Garrison Group withdrew on 7 December, one of them still had 1250 tons of cargo on board that nobody ashore would accept.[3] Not until the Marianas operation was shipping so effectively controlled from Pearl Harbor as to obtain quick turnaround.

2. *Abemama* [4]

An almost bloodless side show was the occupation of Abemama. This "Land of Moonshine," as the name signifies, lying about 75 miles southwest of Tarawa, is the most salubrious and beautiful of the Gilberts. Robert Louis Stevenson resided there a few months

[3] Capt. Roesch's Report; "A Service Force Officer's Observations on Tarawa," enclosed in Cincpac to Comcenpac 4 Dec. 1943.

[4] Capt. J. L. Jones Action Report. Cdr. C. E. Anderson's Report of Unloading at Abemama and Report of Comtransdiv 6 (Capt. T. B. Brittain) enclosed in Admiral Hill's Report on Abemama Operation; Sgt. Frank X. Tolbert "Apamama, a Model Operation in Miniature" *Leatherneck* Feb. 1945 p. 26; the writer's observations in 1944 and conversations with Capt. Jones, Cdr. Anderson and Lt. George Hard of the Australian Army. The atoll is usually spelled Apamama in U.S. naval documents, but the Gilbertese consonant equivalent to both *b* and *p* was officially made *b* in 1934, and Abemama is the official spelling of the Gilbert and Ellice Islands Colony.

in 1889 as the guest of Tem Binoka, the philosopher-king who held absolute sway over Abemama, Aranuka, and Kuria. Later Abemama became the center of missionary effort. In 1943 the natives were friendly, healthy and numerous, for the soil is richer and the vegetation more abundant than at Tarawa and Makin. Uncultivated coconut groves are mingled with pandanus, the fleshy-leaved uri tree with fragrant white flowers, the mao or salt bush, and trees and shrubs of many other varieties. The Japanese, after occupying the atoll in some force, had withdrawn most of their men to Tarawa but they had plans to return and build an airfield.

Abemama was invaded by the 5th Amphibious Reconnaissance Company, 68 Marines and 10 bomb-disposal engineers, commanded by Captain James L. Jones USMCR, and brought to their destination by submarine *Nautilus*. Although she was fired on by "friendly" forces on the night of 19 November, expert damage control allowed her to proceed to Abemama. At midnight between the 20th and 21st, she lay-to 3000 yards off Kenna, the southern islet of the atoll.

The troops, embarked in six large rubber landing boats with outboard motors, had a very unhappy trip to shore. A nasty cross-sea and frequent rain squalls spun the doughnut-shaped boats around like chips in a whirlpool; the outboard motors frequently stalled; the current swept them to leeward of their intended beach, and only by the most strenuous efforts, after four hours at sea, did they succeed in touching the very last point where they could land before being involved in the barrier reef.

When day broke, these weary raiders who had striven with the elements all night carried their weapons and fifteen days' supplies along the water's edge to the planned beachhead. There they found a windfall in the shape of a Japanese whaleboat. A native who recognized Lieutenant George Hard, the Australian scout officer who accompanied the detachment, indicated the enemy position on an island two miles northward and correctly described their armament and strength — 25 men. Between the raiders and the enemy was a Catholic mission station, staffed by four French or Belgian priests and a few Sisters of Charity who had stood by throughout the Japanese occupation. They knew nothing of what had gone on in the world since the middle of 1942. They supposed Marshal Pétain to be still ruling North Africa, and that the Japanese had invaded Australia. "We don't want to be involved in the war," said they; but — as in the case of many million other people who felt just the same — the war had caught up to them, in this far-off Land of Moonshine.

Captain Jones and his Marines were supposed only to scout for an assault force due 26 November, but as one of them said, "We had to stay there five days, and there wasn't room for the Japs and us too." So, with native guides, they advanced to the enemy position. It was a strong one, separated from the mission island by a fordable channel, and with all possible approaches well covered by machine-gun fire. *Nautilus* was still standing by, and Captain Jones had arranged with her commander a signal code of naval mattress covers hung in palm trees. By this means he indicated his own position and called for gunfire, which the submarine delivered. The Japanese appeared to be unimpressed, as they fired vigorously on the raiders' approach, killing one Marine. Captain Jones saw no reason to lose lives rushing the enemy position, and waited. Shortly after noon 25 November, a native came in and reported that the Japanese were all dead. Fourteen had been killed or wounded by naval gunfire and the rest had committed suicide.

Transport *Harris* brought over from Tarawa the 3rd Battalion 6th Marines on the 26th. They landed before noon on the principal island of the atoll, which forms its northern curve, and set up defensive installations to protect the projected airfield. Next morning appeared the Abemama Garrison Group, consisting of transport *President Monroe* and three chartered steamers, escorted by two destroyer escorts. The commodore of this task group, Commander Carl E. Anderson USNR, promptly constituted himself beachmaster and took charge of the unloading.

The beaches here were about the worst for unloading purposes ever encountered in the Pacific, but "Squeaky" Anderson was the best man in the Navy to cope with them. An Alaskan sourdough nearing sixty, he had operated steamers and managed canning factories between wars, and had been recalled to active duty in 1940 in order to organize an Aleutian patrol. After he had helped to clean up that part of the world, Admiral Hill gave him something new to tackle. Coral reefs ran out a thousand yards into the lagoon, and there was no pier. Undaunted, Anderson used bulldozers to dig two channels wide enough to admit LSTs; the dirt they threw up in the center became a dry causeway to deep water. "When I came aboard LSTs and requested coöperation," reported Commander Anderson, "an amphibious regulation was shoved in my face indicating that they could not be ordered by the beachmaster to participate in an unloading operation." These delusions of grandeur on the part of the "jg's" who commanded the LSTs were promptly dissipated by the verbal lash of authority picturesquely laid on by the Commander. He was also troubled by beach and shore parties' scattering through the coconut groves sightseeing, instead of helping his crew to unload. For, as he observed to this writer, "De girls vos very pretty, und dey vear no vests around der chests!"

Everything was put ashore in nine and a half days — about the time it had taken these ships to load at docks in Pearl — and Commander Anderson was commended for "his tireless energy and skill in this work." The Abemama airfield, as we shall see, was highly useful as a base for pounding down enemy airfields in the Marshalls.

3. *Conclusions and Casualties*

Tarawa was the first place in the Pacific where an American amphibious landing had been vigorously opposed on the beach. Ignorance of how to tackle a strongly defended coral atoll surrounded by a fringing reef was responsible for most of the errors in this attack. The principal mistakes were a naval bombardment that was not long, heavy or accurate enough; a badly timed air bombardment before the landing, and badly executed air support of troops; too few amphtracs and they not good enough.[5] Hindsight reveals no errors in appraising the situation, or in the plan of attack, other than the unavoidable bad guess about the tide. Errors in timing and communications failures, incident to most amphibious operations, were largely due to the imperfection of matériel,[6] and to deficiencies inevitable in the training of so big an amphibious team. Of preventable blunders, there were none of any consequence.

Indignation swept over the participants when they read the accounts of this operation in home newspapers. A flock of war correspondents had been taken to Tarawa, the Navy hoping thereby to give fresh and accurate news to the public. Some of these correspondents, especially Robert Sherrod, wrote accurate and informing reports; but others, supported by those who stayed at Pearl Harbor, stressed sensationally the "horrors of Tarawa" and created the impression that the attack had been a sort of Charge of the Light Brigade, gallant but futile; "someone had blundered." Editorial writers and armchair strategists elaborated on the theme of "tragic Tarawa." Some, ignoring the strategic value of the Gilberts, even insisted that the entire plan was wrong; we had shed good American blood for a few acres of worthless coral.[7] On the contrary — the Battle for Tarawa was a

[5] Gen. Holland M. Smith, before the end of the month, requested that highest priority be given to providing each operating amphibious division, whether Marine or Army, with 312 LVT A-2s, 75 LVT A-1s and 100 dukws. These recommendations for the most part were carried out, but another thing that he urged, a Marine Corps air wing on escort carriers, was not honored until the end of the war, when fortunately it was carried out in time to be used effectively in Korea in 1950.

[6] Especially of communications matériel taken ashore in landing craft. Ever since Operation "Torch" a year earlier, the Navy had been complaining about the radios furnished, as being inadequate; but the Bureau of Ships had not yet managed to provide better equipment. (Report of V 'Phib Corps observers.)

[7] This, to the writer's astonishment, is the conclusion of Gen. Holland Smith in *Sat. Eve. Post* 6 Nov. 1948 p. 15, and in *Coral and Brass* chap. vi. He declares that we could well have leapfrogged the Gilberts and gone right into Kwajalein, the center of enemy power in the Marshalls. To this theory the story of the 4 Dec. carrier strike on Kwajalein, told in chap. xiv, is sufficient answer. If we had invaded Kwajalein in November without taking the Gilberts, we would have made

magnificent victory, well planned and bravely executed, illustrating the finest qualities of American manhood, training the armed forces for still greater and more profitable captures along the road to Tokyo.

Lieutenant General Robert C. Richardson usa at Pearl Harbor, in congratulating General Julian Smith and the 2nd Marine Division on the very afternoon that Betio was secured, declared, "The lessons learned from our battle on Betio Island will be of greatest value to our future operations." That was the exact truth and an excellent prophecy. The battle for Tarawa was probably the toughest single fight that the Marine Corps had as yet sustained; but there were plenty more, and even worse. The lessons there learned were of inestimable value in the planning and executing of later operations. Even before the end of November, detailed reports — by admirals, generals, observers, transport commanders and officers, right down to ensigns commanding boat waves, all pointing out flaws in their performance and suggesting remedies — came pouring into amphibious force headquarters at Pearl Harbor, where plans were being perfected for the next big push into Micronesia.[8]

Tarawa cost us, as the following tabulation shows, the lives of 980 Marines and 29 sailors. Not one died in vain, nor did the 2101 men wounded in action and who recovered, suffer in vain. Every man there, lost or maimed, saved at least ten of his countrymen

---

exactly the same mistakes as at Tarawa and encountered infinitely greater opposition; probably the assault force would have been annihilated. The relatively easy conquest of Kwajalein in January was due (1) to lessons learned at Tarawa; (2) to a perfect take-off position, the triangle Tarawa–Makin–Abemama, in November; (3) to using this position and the fast carriers for photographic reconaissance and for neutralizing enemy air power in the Marshalls before D-day. Admirals Spruance, Turner and Hill disagreed with General Smith completely.

[8] Admiral Turner sent a dispatch on 30 Nov. to amphibious force headquarters that radically changed the plan for taking the Marshalls. Admiral Hill issued a document the same day called "Lessons Learned at Tarawa." On 23 Dec. Admiral Turner issued a mimeographed document called "Extracts from Observers' Comments" on Operation "Galvanic"; and Capt. James Steele, Admiral Nimitz's planning officer, compiled a report entitled "A Hundred Mistakes Made at Tarawa." The most detailed critical discussion of the mistakes is in Isley's work pp. 230–35, 251–52.

NUMBERS AND CASUALTIES

OF

GROUND UNITS PARTICIPATING IN ASSAULT ON TARAWA

Total Strength in Action Casualties corrected to 8 April 1944.

From the official compilation in the hands of Major General Julian C. Smith USMC

K & D = Killed in Action and Died of Wounds.   W = Wounded in Action

The Navy elements with the Marines were mostly Medical Corps officers and men.

	MARINE CORPS						NAVY						
	Officers			Enlisted			Officers			Enlisted		
	Total	K&D	W	Total	K&D	W	Total	K&D	W	Total	K&D	W
2nd Regiment Marines	143	22	33	3366	354	763	16	2	1	109	10	24
6th Regiment Marines	143	7	10	3127	91	237	18	0	0	111	5	9
8th Regiment Marines	138	12	35	3049	297	686	13	0	0	109	9	12
10th Marines (Artillery)	178	1	4	2695	9	23	11	0	0	53*	0	0
18th Marines (Engineers)	66	6	0	1280	53	83	18*	0	0	574*	1	1
Special Troops:												
Headquarters Battalion	58	3	1	544	27	36	7	0	0	16	0	0
Tank Battalion	22	2	1	463	24	27	2	0	0	12	0	0
Special Weapons Battalion	9	0	0	300	0	0	0	0	0	2	0	0
Service Troops:												
LVT Battalion	26	4	5	623	59	98	1	0	0	11	1	1
Medical Battalion	0	0	0	93	1	3	29	0	0	277	1	2
Other	5	0	0	87	0	0	0	0	0	0	0	0
Temporarily Attached:												
2nd Defense Bn. (Spec. Weapons)	10	1	0	278	3	0	0	0	0	0	0	0
Air Liaison Group & Fire Control Party, V Amphibious Corps	13	0	0	82	4	5	10	0	1	0	0	0
Argus, Radar, Casu Units	0	0	0	0	0	0	12	0	0	100	0	0
Total Engaged and Total Casualties	811	58**	89	15,987	922	1961	137	2	2	1374	27	49

Total engaged all ranks and both services: 18,313

Total casualties all ranks, both services: 3,110 = 17%

* Seabees.

** Also 1 officer observer from 4th Division Medical Corps killed.

as the Navy plunged deep into enemy waters and sailed irresistibly on through Micronesia. All honor, then, to the fighting heart of the United States Marine. Let that small stretch of coral sand called Betio be remembered as terrible indeed, but glorious, and the seedbed for victory in 1945.

Amphtrac Losses, Tarawa *

125 LVTs were brought to Tarawa, 50 of them in LSTs, 75 in APAs and AKAs. They were operated by 500 men, 323 of whom were killed, wounded or missing from the organization at the end of the operation. Here is what happened to the amphtracs: —

Sunk in deep water by gunfire	35
Sunk on reef from gunfire	26
Burned up by gas tanks igniting from gunfire	9
Wrecked by underwater mines	2
Wrecked on the beaches	10
Wrecked by mechanical failures	8
Total losses	90

* Data supplied by Maj. Gen. Julian C. Smith.

CHAPTER XII

Scouting Submarines and Carrier Strikes

13 November–8 December 1943

1. Loss of CORVINA and SCULPIN

DURING Operation "Galvanic," United States submarines in the Pacific Ocean continued to diminish the Japanese merchant marine; in November they hung up a new record of 45 *Marus* sunk, amounting to 232,119 gross tons. The story of their far-ranging patrols must be postponed until our next volume. Here we shall confine ourselves to the fine work done by the ten submarines [1] directed by Admiral Nimitz to scout for his surface forces in the Gilbert Islands and to act as a harassing defense force in case the Japanese Fleet came out.

Thresher, *Apogon* and *Corvina* covered quadrants on three sides of Truk, to report movements of the Combined Fleet. *Sculpin* and *Searaven* took stations near Oroluk between Truk and Ponape. *Seal* watched Kwajalein and *Spearfish* Jaluit. *Plunger* lifeguarded the carrier plane strikes on Mili on 20–21 November, picked up an aviator, and while so doing was attacked by a Japanese plane which wounded six men by strafing. She then took station off Wotje. *Paddle*, with an aërologist and his instruments embarked, acted as "rainmaker" off Nauru, transmitting weather reports every sunset from 15 to 24 November inclusive. *Nautilus*, as we have already seen, had a very special rôle in taking Tarawa and Abemama.

---

[1] For names of boats and C.O.s see Appendix II.

Pickings were rather slender, and losses were serious. *Thresher* sank a 4600-ton transport off Truk on the 13th, but an engine breakdown forced her to return prematurely to Pearl Harbor. *Apogon* sank a 3000-ton auxiliary gunboat; *Searaven* sent down a 10,000-ton naval oiler north of Ponape on 25 November. *Seal*, on station off Kwajalein, sent in a steady stream of valuable reports on ships and shipping within the lagoon, but was unable to close either of the two cruiser formations that she sighted. *Corvina* (Commander Roderick S. Rooney), cruising on the surface 85 miles SW of Truk, was sighted on 16 November by *I-176*. The Japanese fired three torpedoes and made two hits. *Corvina* exploded and her entire crew of 82 was lost.[2]

She was not the only victim. *Sculpin* (Commander Fred Connaway) of the Oroluk patrol had on board Captain John P. Cromwell, who was to have taken command of a wolf-pack including *Searaven* and a third boat. On the night of 18–19 November *Sculpin* sighted a fast enemy convoy and at dawn attempted to attack it, submerged, but was detected and forced deep. When she surfaced about an hour later, she was immediately forced down and depth-charged by destroyer *Yamagumo*. When the diving officer tried to bring her to periscope depth the depth gauge stuck at 125 feet and *Sculpin* broached. As *Yamagumo* roared in to attack, the submarine dove deep but a close string of 18 depth charges followed her down. The explosions threw the boat out of control, distorted her pressure hull, started leaks, jammed her rudders and diving planes. As a desperate expedient Commander Connaway ordered "Blow all ballast!" and then, as *Sculpin* rose from the depths, gave the signal for gunfire action, "Battle surface!"

Sculpin's one 4-inch and two 20-mm guns had no chance to fight off a Japanese destroyer with six 5.1-inch guns, torpedo tubes and numerous automatic weapons. She took one lethal hit in the

[2] Naval Technical Mission to Japan *Japanese Submarine Operations* (S-17) pp. 148, 160, item 257. She was the only U.S. submarine sunk by a Japanese submarine as against 23 of the latter sunk by U.S. submarines and 2 more by R.N. submarines.

main induction valves. A second, penetrating the conning tower, killed Commander Connaway, his "exec" and the gunnery officer. Lieutenant G. E. Brown, senior surviving officer, ordered "Abandon Ship." All vents were opened and at flank speed *Sculpin* dove for the last time. The "wolf-pack commander" and a dozen others rode her down, Captain Cromwell deliberately sacrificing his life because, familiar as he was with American plans for the Gilberts and Marshalls, he feared lest information be extorted from him by torture.

Forty-two of *Sculpin's* crew were picked up by *Yamagumo*. One, severely wounded, was thrown overboard and another escaped the same fate only by wrenching free of his captors and mixing with the other prisoners. The destroyer took the remaining 41 submariners to Truk, where they were transferred to escort carriers *Chuyo* and *Unyo*. En route to Japan on 4 December *Chuyo* fell victim to a torpedo attack by United States submarine *Sailfish*, and only one of the prisoners on board her survived.[3] He and the 20 prisoners in *Unyo* were forced to work in the copper mines at Ashio until released at the end of the war.

2. *Strikes on Kwajalein and Nauru, 4–8 December* [4]

The Gilberts operation was quickly followed by a fast carrier strike on Kwajalein, center of Japanese air power in the Marshalls, with an incidental pass at Wotje. As the execution of this raid was contingent on an early decision in the Gilberts, the operation order was hurriedly drafted at an Admirals' conference on board ship and was not delivered to the vessels concerned until the first day of December. Enemy merchant shipping and four cruisers were

[3] When *Sailfish* (ex-*Squalus*) sank off Portsmouth, N.H., in June 1939, it was *Sculpin* who came to her rescue. The story of her last fight and Cromwell's heroic death is told in the Comsubpac publication *U.S. Submarine Losses World War II* p. 73.

[4] Narrative in Cincpac Monthly Analysis Dec. 1943; the Comairpac Monthly Summary is less detailed. Action Reports of Rear Adm. Pownall and of ships concerned; comments of Com Air Group 9 and Cdr. A. D. Chandler "Memorandum on Recent Operations," 8 Dec. Japanese data obtained by Mr. Salomon in Tokyo, 1946.

reported to be in the lagoon, and photographs of Kwajalein were urgently wanted to help the next operation.

The carriers that had had the Rabaul and Buka assignments in early November were excused, and the task force was made up as follows: —

TF 50, Rear Admiral Charles A. Pownall [5]

	TG 50.1, Rear Admiral Pownall	TG 50.3, Rear Admiral Montgomery
Carriers	YORKTOWN, LEXINGTON	ESSEX, ENTERPRISE
Light Carriers	COWPENS	BELLEAU WOOD
Heavy Cruisers	BALTIMORE, SAN FRANCISCO, NEW ORLEANS, MINNEAPOLIS	PORTLAND
Light Cruisers	OAKLAND	MOBILE, SANTA FE, SAN JUAN, SAN DIEGO
Destroyers	NICHOLAS, TAYLOR, LAVALLETTE, BULLARD, KIDD, CHAUNCEY	FLETCHER, RADFORD, JENKINS, ERBEN, HALE

Plane Availability 1 December 1943

	Fighters (F6F)	Dive-Bombers (SBD–5)	Torpedo-Bombers (TBF)	Total
YORKTOWN	38	28	18	84
LEXINGTON	38	28	18	84
COWPENS	21	0	9	30
ESSEX	38	28	18	84
ENTERPRISE	34	20	17	71
BELLEAU WOOD	24	0	9	33
	193	104	89	386

Subtracting combat air patrol and reserve left 249 planes for striking, of which 158 were bombers and the rest fighter and photo reconnaissance planes.

This powerful task force headed east and then swung north in order to make a wide sweep around the Marshalls before striking quick and hard at the center of that spider's web. An ocean rendezvous was made between the two task groups, and with fleet oilers from Pearl Harbor, at lat. 13° N, 179° E on 1 December. From that point the force steered almost due west. At 0800 on the

---

[5] For commanding officers of ships and air groups, see list Appendix II.

3rd, Admiral Pownall made signal, "Be ready for anything after 1700 today. Be accurate, keep cool, and hit 'em hard."

The two groups were then parallel about 12 miles apart, just within sight of each other and northeast of their objective. At lat. 15°27′ N, long. 172° E, they changed course to the rhumb line for Kwajalein, heading right into the spider's nest at 20 knots. Bikar, northeasternmost of the Marshalls, was left about 40 miles on the port hand, and the Rongerik–Rongelap group to starboard. This line of approach was unexpected. The Japanese picket boats and air searches were covering sectors south and east of Kwajalein, expecting any attack to come straight up from the Gilberts.

Promptly at 0600 December 4, after reaching a position about 36 miles ESE of Rongerik Atoll and 25 miles to leeward of the striking position, the big flattops swung ENE into the tradewind, facing a rosy dawn. *Cowpens* showed her red preparatory signal, flashed her green launching light and presently threw into the air the combat air patrol for her group. Over the horizon, *Belleau Wood* was doing the same for Admiral Montgomery. In the morning twilight each carrier seemed to be merged in the purple sea. From the cruisers one could not even see the planes launching, but presently one was aware of dark wings crossing the rose-pink clouds of dawn as combat air patrol formed a flying vault over the operation. At 0630 *Lexington* and *Yorktown*, a thousand yards apart, commenced launching their contributions to this first strike, about 60 to 65 planes each, at rapid intervals. A pale, lemon-yellow sun rose at 0653. Twelve minutes later the two commanders signaled "Launching complete." A roar of engines filled the air and planes in lines, planes in columns and planes in wild-goose Vees were crossing the bright clouds of a perfect tradewind day. By 0715 they were all away and silence fell as the ships, now 116 miles NNE of Roi Island, turned easterly toward the agreed rendezvous.

A strategic but not a tactical surprise was achieved. The Japanese had concentrated the bulk of their fighter and search strength at Maloelap, thinking Pownall would attack there or at Mili. The task force, no inconspicuous flotilla, had approached within 120 miles of the center of their web without detection. But the Roi radar, or perhaps a search plane, saw the wings coming in time for the Japanese to get about 50 fighters into the air and to throw up a heavy anti-aircraft barrage, so "solid" at 8500 feet that the American planes dove under it to 5000 feet. By 0750 they were over the target.

The American pilots were hampered by want of accurate information on Kwajalein topography, and the headwork of the acting air group commander was none too good.[6] Owing to a failure in communications, only twelve Hellcats dropped down to strafe the bomber-packed Roi airfield, and they, with no photographs to guide them, were deceived by the Japanese camouflage. Consequently only three bombers and 16 fighter planes were destroyed on the ground, leaving 30 to 40 undamaged in their revetments. In addition, 18 fighters and 10 long-range bombers were destroyed aloft.

At the same time, 41 SBDs and 36 Avenger torpedo planes from *Essex* and *Lexington* went after light cruiser *Isuzu,* a large freighter and several small craft in the lagoon. This attack, too, was only moderately successful. The bombers, who had had no recent practice on moving targets, were easily evaded by the Japanese ships and only 4 or 5 out of 36 torpedoes launched by the Avengers made hits. *Asakaze Maru* (6500 tons), the largest transport present, blew up with a gusto that suggested she was carrying ammunition. *Isuzu* was hit by two bombs, one of which knocked out her rudder, but she too escaped sinking. United States submarine *Seal* was waiting outside the lagoon, but she found no victims.

While *Essex* and *Lexington* aviators were fumbling matters over Roi, those from *Enterprise* and *Yorktown* were looking for targets off Kwajalein Island at the southern end of the lagoon. This was the principal naval and submarine base in the Marshalls, with an airfield under construction. Out of the thirty vessels lying in the lagoon, the Avengers, armed with bombs, disposed of three *Marus*

[6] Cdr. C. L. Crommelin in *Yorktown* should have been in command, but he had lost the use of an eye in one of the interceptor affairs of November and had to stay on board. He is a brother to Comdesdiv 50 in *Ringgold* who played so important a rôle in the taking of Tarawa, and to the chief of staff of Admiral Mullinnix.

for a total of 10,375 tons, and hit light cruiser *Nagara*. Another group of planes attacked the seaplane base at Ebeye Island and destroyed 18 float planes there.

In about 45 minutes the American planes had destroyed four ships and 55 Japanese planes, losing only five of their own. From a military point of view this was small pickings. Most of the enemy merchant shipping, all his men-of-war, 30 to 40 bombers and many fighter planes escaped. The "Big E" had done relatively better when Admiral Halsey directed the first strike on Kwajalein, 1 February 1942.[7]

Although the operation plan called for a second strike at noon, Admiral Pownall decided to call everything off except a scheduled strike on Wotje, and retire. He believed that the pilots had not yet recovered from their long grind at the Gilberts and he wished to put a long distance between his force and Japanese air bases since, unlike Admiral Radford, he had no adequate defense against night attack. But there are two opinions as to whether these reasons justified a retirement when the task was not half accomplished. The pilots had had a week to recover from the wear and tear of combat air patrol; every squadron leader on board *Yorktown* begged to be allowed to make another strike; nobody realized how few planes were then available to the enemy in the Marshalls. There were enough, however, to give trouble.

Although Admiral Pownall's decision pleased neither his own aviators nor the higher command, that does not prove his judgment to have been unsound. In carrier strikes the equation of risk against probable result, when the birds are once flushed, is strongly in favor of the enemy. The loss even of a destroyer would have been too heavy a price to pay for the planes left at Kwajalein. Unlike the hit-and-run raids on peripheral islands like Wake and Marcus, this one was delivered in the center of a defensive system, and the longer the flattops stayed around the more enemy planes could presumably be staged through Kwajalein, Wotje and Maloelap to hit them on their way home.

[7] See Vol. V xii and III 262.

From 1000 to 1100 the carriers were busy recovering, and at noon *Yorktown* commenced launching 29 planes for the Wotje strike.[8] Four minutes later, the enemy delivered his first counter-attack, directed at *Lexington*. It was a gorgeous day — sapphire sea and purple cloud shadows, the ships heading into a brisk NE trade-wind that had risen to force 7, the destroyers throwing spray mast-head high. Three "Kate" torpedo-bombers from Roi or Maloelap[9] skimmed in low over the water and were first sighted by *Lexington's* lookouts. All three, hit by anti-aircraft fire from the carrier, burst into orange flame and splashed close aboard. One launched a torpedo which passed only a hundred yards astern of *Lexington* after she had completed 30 degrees of a full right rudder turn.

During this attack *Yorktown* was launching her Wotje strike. At 1248, when combat air patrol was playing around like swallows chasing gnats in June, four "Kates" sneaked in low to get her. They too eluded radar and were first seen by human eyes. Cruiser *San Francisco* and destroyers *Taylor* and *LaVallette* shot down two. They splashed between cruiser and carrier,[10] one so close to the stern of *Yorktown* that her humorous flight surgeon reported the Japanese pilot's teeth to be defective! A third torpedo-bomber, discouraged by anti-aircraft fire, sheered off without closing; a fourth passed down the center of the formation between five or six ships spitting fire, turned right and splashed. This action took place about 20 to 25 miles north of Utirik.

At 1500, having recovered the planes of the Wotje strike, Admiral Pownall signaled, "Mission completed, retire northeastward course 35°, speed 25 knots." This proved to be more than the destroyers could make against a brisk gale and high-crested sea. Speed of advance had to be lowered to 18 knots, and at that rate the force would not be out of enemy bombing range until the following evening, if then. Everyone expected a rough night, and nobody was disappointed.

[8] This accomplished little except photographic reconnaissance.
[9] Eight bombers were launched from Maloelap and seven from Roi.
[10] *Nicholas* Action Report 7 Dec. 1943.

None of the carriers in this force had trained a night combat air patrol. Fortunately, however, there had been enough enemy night air attacks during the previous month to teach their sailors what to expect. These attacks followed a definite pattern.[11] A little before sunset, one or more snoopers trailed the formation, waiting for darkness when they dropped a string of float lights marking the direction from which the striking planes would approach. These lights also served to mark the point of rendezvous. When the striking planes arrived, the snooper flew ahead of them high over the ships and dropped bright parachute flares. As the target became illuminated, groups of three or four "Kates" or "Bettys" armed with 'torpedoes launched attacks from favorable positions, one after the other, over a period of 30 to 45 minutes. Japanese night tactics were economical, as they required no fighter escort, and they were far more effective than the German Luftwaffe's night attacks on Mediterranean convoys in the spring of 1944. This technique, first practised in Solomons waters, reached a new pitch of perfection on the night of 4–5 December 1943.

Snoopers began circling above Pownall's carriers at 1945, and from then until after moonset at 0124 December 5 there was an almost continuous performance. When "Bettys" were not attacking, they were circling or ganging up for a fresh strike, so that bogeys were constantly on the radar screens. Thirty to 50 planes were involved; 14 distinct raids were made by single planes and groups of 4 to 12, concentrated into two half-hour periods. During this time each task group maneuvered independently and radically. Heavy flak was thrown up, with *Oakland* leading off from her position six miles nearer the enemy than the carriers were.

No damage was done during the first half-hour. But at 2255 planes began to come in again from port and starboard, and at 2300 Admiral Pownall signaled his support ships, "Anyone with

---

[11] Lt. Roland Boyden "Analysis of Enemy Night Torpedo Attacks in the Central Pacific, 18 Nov.–5 Dec. 1943," an illuminating paper by the operations information officer, Comairpac staff. A more detailed account from a captured document is given as an addendum to Cincpac-Cincpoa *Weekly Intelligence* I No. 15 (20 Oct. 1944).

a good setup, let 'em have it!" Under a clear sky the moon, on the
port quarter of the base course, was so bright that every ship in
each group could see every other one. At 2323, just as gunfire
was being opened on radar contact, the enemy dropped three very
brilliant parachute flares from 5000-foot altitude, two miles away
and broad on the formation's port bow. A plane approached down-
moon, headed for *Yorktown*. Her gunfire and that of destroyer
LaVallette chased it away; but at 2333 a plane approaching from
the starboard hand scored a torpedo hit on *Lexington's* stern.

The detonation destroyed *Lexington's* steering engine, jamming
the rudder hard left, killed nine men and wounded 35. Admiral
Pownall ordered Admiral Montgomery's group to stand by. The
calm voice of Captain Stump was heard over radio telephone, informing other ships of his situation. "She can make speed but cannot steer . . . We are putting five submersible pumps in to clean
out ship. . . . *We are going to find a way out of this thing.*"
His men had installed an emergency hydraulic unit in the steering-
engine compartment before leaving port, but the petty officer there,
who alone knew how to operate it, was knocked out by the torpedo and his mates had to be instructed by telephone what to do,
since the access trunk was flooded and the emergency pumps kept
clogging with the rags and culch that bluejackets are apt to leave
around. After 20 minutes' work Chief Electrician's Mate L. R.
Baker and Quartermaster D. E. Woods brought the rudder amidships. *Lexington* could now steer with her engines, although one
shaft had been ruptured by the torpedo. By midnight she could
make 21 knots. While all this was going on, and until 0041, several
more attacks were made on the carrier and were beaten off by her
anti-aircraft fire.

At 0124 December 5 the moon set and all enemy planes retired
to base. They had shot their bolt. At 0205 Admiral Pownall signaled, "Consider present emergency over. All hands relax and be
ready to go first thing in the morning." Then the sweet word was
passed "Secure from General Quarters, set Condition Yoke."

A peaceful sabbath was made the more enjoyable by listening

to Radio Tokyo's version of the battle. A hundred American planes had attacked the Marshalls but caused "absolutely no damage," and 20 of them had been shot down. Japanese "eagles" had counterattacked with the following results: "One large carrier and one large cruiser sunk instantly; one carrier and one cruiser severely damaged and probably sunk." [12]

Actually they attempted another attack on Sunday while the task force was within bombing range of Wotje. Large groups of aircraft appeared on the radar screens at 1400. But they never succeeded in locating the carriers.

On Monday 6 December faithful oilers met the task force at an appointed rendezvous and on the 9th all entered Pearl Harbor, where *Lexington* was expeditiously repaired.

Admiral Pownall and his chief of staff, Captain Truman J. Hedding, had handled the task force during this series of counterattacks in a masterly fashion, and maneuvered it smartly. With an unusually small screen and no night fighters, they thwarted the enemy's attack at a cost to him of 29 planes, 18 of them long-range bombers.

As Admiral Halsey objected to being deprived of the battleships formerly included in his South Pacific Force, Admiral Nimitz returned them to him as soon as the Gilberts were secured; but they were required to work their passage. As Admiral Spruance suspected that the "Bettys" which had attacked his forces had landed at Nauru, he decided to give them a pounding before they could go elsewhere.

The force assigned to this operation, commanded by Rear Admiral Willis A. Lee, consisted of carriers *Bunker Hill* and *Monterey*, five fast battleships and twelve destroyers. At about 0500 December 8 they arrived at a position 50 miles northeast of Nauru and divided into bombardment and carrier groups, each taking half

---

[12] Japanese claims, however, were no more fantastic than those of the American aviators, as reported by the U.P. and International News correspondents in Honolulu *Advertiser* 10 Dec. 1943. The same paper, 11 and 13 Dec., has some good stories of the raid.

the destroyers. The former group threw 810 sixteen-inch and 3400 five-inch projectiles into the island from a distance of only 1500 yards; the carrier planes dropped 51 tons of bombs and strafed enemy positions. But the birds had flown. Barely a dozen planes were observed on Nauru, and eight or ten of these were destroyed at a cost of four to us, and damage to destroyer *Boyd*. She, when investigating a life raft about two miles off shore several hours after the bombardment had ceased, was fired on by a shore battery. A shell exploded in one engine room, killing ten men, and another went off inside the forward stack. *Boyd* retired, zigzagging violently at 27 knots, straddles and near misses following her out more than seven miles from the shore. She managed to make base under her own steam.

Captain John P. Cromwell

Carrier sailors in *Lexington's* ready room

Seated: Commander E. M. Snowden, Lieutenant Commander R. H. Isely, Captain Felix B. Stump, and (at the mike) Lieutenant (jg) E. F. Ternasky

Carrier Strike on Kwajalein, 4 December 1943

Light cruiser *Isuzu* in the lagoon

Torpedo plane attack on *Lexington*

"Kate" shot down

Carrier Strike

PART III

The Conquest of the Marshalls[1]

All dates are West Longitude, except in chapter xx.
Zone plus 12 time, unless otherwise noted.

In the Marshalls and at Truk the Navy has done more than to win a good victory over the enemy. It has won a resounding victory in the hearts and minds of our people over the anxiety and the doubt which have, since the close of the other war, divided and confused us.

— WALTER LIPPMANN in *New York Herald Tribune*, 21 Feb. 1944

[1] The basic reports for the Marshalls campaign are those of Admirals Spruance, Turner, Conolly and Hill and Generals Holland M. Smith, Corlett and Harry Schmidt. Before the end of the war Maj. William G. Wendell USMCR prepared for the Historical Division of the Corps an excellent preliminary study "The Marshall Islands Operation." Lt. Col. S. L. A. Marshall's *Island Victory* (1944) in the *Infantry Journal* "Penguin" series covers the Kwajalein Island conquest in great detail, and Lt. Gen. Robert C. Richardson's *Participation in the Marshall Islands Operation by the U.S. Army Forces Central Pacific Area*, in the form of a Report to General Marshall, 30 Nov. 1944, includes the Operation Reports of the 7th and 27th Infantry Divisions, the VII A.A.F. and the 7th Division Engineers as annexes, in a second volume. Since the end of the war have appeared J. A. Isley & P. A. Crowl *The U.S. Marines and Amphibious War* (1951) containing a thorough and well-balanced study of this campaign; and W. F. Craven & J. L. Cate *The Army Air Forces in World War II* Vol. IV (1950), covering the land-based air aspect.

CHAPTER XIII

Getting Set for the Marshalls

June–December 1943

1. Which Marshalls? [1]

SINCE the Marshall Islands were the original — and always the principal — objective in Micronesia, planning for them began early. On 20 July the Joint Chiefs of Staff, as we have seen, ordered Cincpac to prepare to take the Marshalls in January next. Admiral Nimitz's planners were then exceedingly busy with "Galvanic," but they managed to grind out a tentative plan by 20 August, which proposed to take Kwajalein, Wotje and Maloelap Atolls simultaneously. This plan was taken up by the Quadrant Conference of the Combined Chiefs of Staff at Quebec. The Combined Chiefs, in their report of 24 August to President Roosevelt and Prime Minister Churchill, described the Marshalls as too narrow a base for the great Central Pacific advance.[2] The J.C.S. accordingly, in a directive to Admiral Nimitz of 2 September, ordered him, after the Gilberts, to take the Marshalls in two bites, with Wake and Kusaie, Ponape, Truk and other eastern Carolines added as seasoning; Palau and Yap to follow as the next course.[3]

This plan was not acceptable to Cincpac staff; it called for too much. The only point in recovering Wake was for photo reconnaissance, and for that the Gilberts would be sufficient. Wake was

---

[1] Records of V 'Phib Planning Section; conversations with Capt. J. M. Steele, Col. Ralph R. Robinson usmc and many others.

[2] See chap. v sec. 2.

[3] J.C.S. 461, adopted 31 Aug. but sent to Nimitz 2 Sept.

a drain upon the enemy's transportation and supply, and could be of but slight use to us; yet a division of infantry or a brigade of Marines would be required to capture and hold it. Kusaie, easternmost of the Carolines, would not be too difficult to take, but its climate was too wet to permit the building of a major air base. Eniwetok, farthest west of the Marshalls but one, provided everything needed for a temporary naval and air base en route to the Carolines, Marianas and Tokyo.

So too thought the planning section of the V Amphibious Force, created in early October out of Turner's old III 'Phib staff, augmented by recent graduates of the new Joint Staff College.[4] And, after sundry communications between Cincpac and the J.C.S., Wake and Kusaie were eliminated. Two main questions remained, Which Marshalls should be attacked? And how?

Before the first could be decided, experience at Tarawa gave most of the answers to the second question. A paper by Admiral Turner on "Lessons Learned at Tarawa," dated 30 November on board *Pennsylvania* and flown to Pearl Harbor, blew previous tactical planning masthead-high. A remarkable document, it proved this master of amphibious warfare to be as quick to learn as he was brisk in execution. Turner pointed out that the defenses of Betio had been greatly strengthened during the three months previous to the assault and that Kwajalein should be at least as strongly protected; that the Japanese would have had time to mine channels and beaches, build more pillboxes, emplace more guns and provide more troops. He concluded that United States forces would need more and better air reconnaissance; more submarine scouting like the performance of *Nautilus* at Betio; more ships and landing craft, especially destroyers, destroyer escorts, LVTs and converted LCI gunboats which had proved useful in the South Pacific; and the expenditure of at least three times as much bombardment ammunition as at Tarawa "in order to ensure the troops' getting

---

[4] Detailed planning from a log kept by Lt. Col. D. Z. Zimmerman USA, assistant planning officer V 'Phib Force, unfortunately destroyed when the staff was merged with Cincpac-Cincpoa.

ashore with losses that we can sustain." He wanted continuous heavy attacks by shore-based aircraft on stores, troops and installations; several days' bombardment by carrier planes; several days' naval bombardment by battleships, cruisers and destroyers, with their ammunition supply replenished if necessary from Makin. All fire support vessels must train intensively, since "observation of the firing at Makin shows that with more care and training the effectiveness of the bombardment ought to be increased 50 per cent."

Admiral Spruance approved these recommendations on 2 December and Admiral Nimitz directed that the planners act accordingly. But the want of enough attack transports to float two divisions made it impossible to prepare for a Marshalls landing in thirty days. Accordingly, with J.C.S. permission (4 November), the target date was postponed from 1 to 17 January, and later to the 31st. The operation, originally called "Bankrate," was redesignated "Flintlock."

During the first two weeks of December, with the aid of photographs brought in almost daily by reconnaissance planes flying from Tarawa, the question *"which?"* was threshed out by the Cincpac and V 'Phib staffs. Hitherto the proponents of leapfrogging the eastern Marshalls and going directly into Kwajalein had been overruled by the argument that military principles required the taking of an atoll with a completed bomber strip, which meant Wotje or Maloelap. Everyone assumed that there was no airfield big enough for bombers on Kwajalein Atoll, and no opportunity to activate one promptly.[5] But one of the carrier planes in Admiral Pownall's 4 December strike took a photograph of Kwajalein Island, at the southern end of the atoll, that showed a bomber strip about 70 per cent completed. Rear Admiral Forrest Sherman, chief of staff for operations, brought this photo in and showed it to Colonel Ralph R. Robinson usmc of Cincpac staff.

[5] Cincpac had no information on Kwajalein later than Feb. 1942 (Halsey's raid). But if it had then been known how quickly the Seabees could transform a coral island into an airfield the only consideration would have been whether a given atoll had an island as much as 6000 yards long.

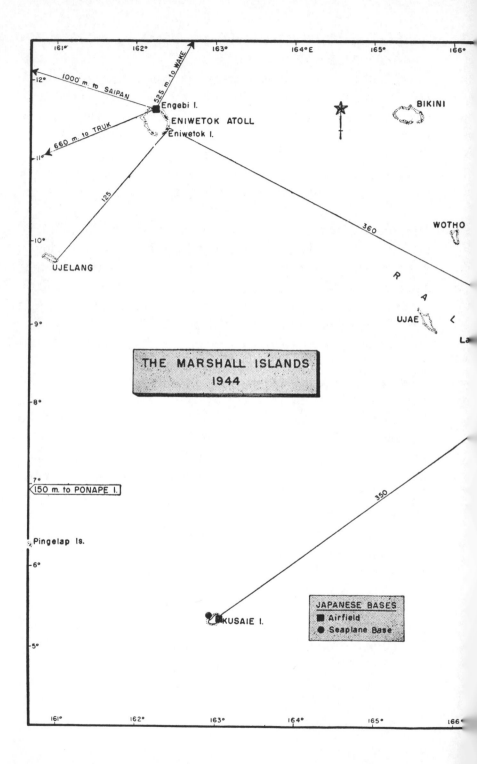

THE MARSHALL ISLANDS
1944

JAPANESE BASES
■ Airfield
● Seaplane Base

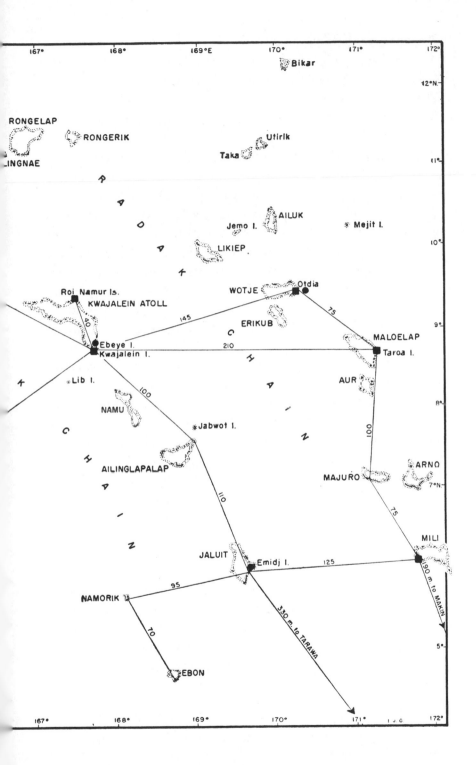

"What do you think of that, Robby?" he asked. "Jesus! This is it!" said Robinson. That photo changed the whole picture.

The final plan, accepted by Admiral Nimitz the very morning after that photo was received, provided that Majuro, an undefended atoll, be taken first, solely because its lagoon would afford anchorage for vessels of the mobile service squadron and a link to the fleet base; that both ends of Kwajalein be assaulted simultaneously the second day; and that the rest of the ground forces be used to take Eniwetok as soon as possible, unless Kwajalein proved unexpectedly tough. That atoll was the hub of the enemy's outer defensive perimeter and the distributing center for his Marshall Islands spider's web. So, in accordance with the leapfrogging strategy already being practised by MacArthur and Wilkinson, it was decided to strike first at the center. Four strongly defended atolls with airfields — Wotje, Maloelap, Mili and Jaluit — were to be skipped.

A bold plan it was, advancing the war by months; but it raised many misgivings. Admirals Spruance and Turner and General Holland M. Smith argued as strongly as they could in favor of taking Wotje and Maloelap first. Admiral Nimitz decided against them. He correctly estimated that undefended Majuro would provide every benefit that Wotje or Maloelap offered, and that the fast carrier forces, together with aircraft based on the Makin-Tarawa-Abemama triangle, could neutralize Japanese air power in the Eastern Marshalls before the Kwajalein operation began.[6] How right he was!

New operation plans now had to be prepared by all echelons. Additional air reconnaissance was necessary, and charts of Kwajalein and Majuro had to be reproduced and distributed. The new Gilbert Islands airfields proved indispensable for photographic reconnaissance. Moreover, the Gilberts triangle enabled Pacific Fleet planes to do what in 1942 would have seemed miraculous — protect a fleet base in Majuro from enemy planes based 100 miles distant on Maloelap and 75 miles distant on Mili.

[6] Isley and Crowl p. 255.

The organization for Operation "Flintlock" was very similar to that for "Galvanic." Vice Admiral Spruance, Commander Fifth Fleet, commanded the expeditionary force from flagship *Indianapolis;* he would assume the tactical command only if the Japanese Fleet came out and challenged. Rear Admiral Richmond K. Turner, O.T.C. until the ground forces were ready to take over, sailed in a specially equipped command and communications ship, *Rocky Mount.* That new type of naval auxiliary (AGC) had been improvised for Admiral Hewitt in the Salerno operation because the network of communications in modern amphibious warfare had become so vast and complicated, and the officers and men necessary to staff amphibious force headquarters so numerous, that no ordinary combatant or auxiliary ship could hold them. Major General Holland M. Smith USMC, commanding the ground forces here as in "Galvanic," accompanied Admiral Turner.

The plan of attack required three attack forces, instead of two as in the Gilberts. The Northern Attack Force, under Rear Admiral Conolly, had the task of taking Roi and Namur Islands in Kwajalein Atoll. Admiral Turner retained for himself command of the Southern Attack Force, whose main objective was Kwajalein Island where the bomber strip was being built. A third amphibious unit, commanded by Rear Admiral Harry W. Hill, was divided into a Reserve Force and a small Majuro Force. The duties of the Reserve Force were to stand by during the assault on Kwajalein, and if not wanted there, to go on and take Eniwetok.

Altogether, the Marshall Islands Joint Expeditionary Force numbered 297 sail of shipping, not counting the fast carrier task groups, or the submarines. The assault troops numbered about 54,000 as compared with 27,800 for the Gilberts.

To aid these men in their undertaking, a vast amount of intelligence material was gathered; mostly by air, but much by submarine. *Spearfish* reconnoitered Jaluit, *Tarpon* covered Mili and Maloelap, and *Seal* was assigned to Kwajalein. The information obtained by *Seal* was found on her return to Pearl Harbor to be inadequate, and *Tarpon* was ordered to finish the job; her report was very valuable.

The simple natives of Funafuti were astonished in January to see two of the largest and newest United States battleships steam through Te Buabua Passage into the lagoon. *Iowa*, which had recently taken President Roosevelt most of the way to Teheran and back, and *New Jersey*, fresh from shakedown, were now incorporated with *Bunker Hill, Monterey* and *Cowpens* in Rear Admiral Frederick C. Sherman's fast carrier task group. There were three other fast carrier groups, Rear Admiral Reeves's (*Enterprise, Yorktown, Belleau Wood* and three new battleships); Rear Admiral Montgomery's (*Essex, Intrepid, Cabot* and three new battleships); and Rear Admiral Ginder's (*Saratoga, Princeton, Langley* and two new heavy cruisers). Rear Admiral Marc A. Mitscher was now Commander Fast Carrier Forces Pacific Fleet, having relieved Rear Admiral Pownall who now became Commander Air Forces Pacific; he in turn relieving Vice Admiral John H. Towers, who became Deputy Cincpac to Admiral Nimitz. This unusually high command for an "air admiral" reflected the vital rôle of carriers in the Pacific Fleet's sweep through Micronesia.

2. *Amphtracs and Logistics*

Amphtracs (LVTs) had saved the day at Tarawa although the small number available and the large number of casualties had been a serious drawback. At the earnest request of every admiral and general concerned in Operation "Galvanic," Washington gave high priority to amphtrac production. Five hundred a month were turned out early in 1944, with double that number anticipated by June, and assault troops in "Flintlock" had not only better amphtracs than their immediate predecessors but three times as many in proportion to the number of troops.

Two models, LVT–1 and LVT–2, each carrying 20 troops and a crew of six, had been used in the Gilberts. The LVT–2 (armed but not armored) and two new models, LVT–A1 and LVT–A2 (both armed and armored), did the job in the Marshalls. In LVT–A2, both driver and passengers were protected by ¼-inch armor plate, two machine guns of .50 caliber and one of .30.[7] LVT–A1 was not a troop carrier but an amphibious vehicle designed to put concentrated fire on the beach immediately before the first wave landed, to protect the flanks of later assault waves and to cover the infantry while disembarking and forming up. It had a turret like those on land tanks, equipped with one 37-mm cannon and one .30-caliber machine gun, co-axially mounted, together with two machine guns abaft the turret. All assault waves employed in the Marshalls were landed in LVT–2s, with LVT–As to protect their flanks. They were organized as amphibious tractor battalions of the Army or the Marine Corps; the boat crews of naval landing craft had nothing to do with them.

In Mediterranean operations and in the assault on the Treasury Islands in October 1943, the experiment had been tried of arming a few LCIs (Landing Craft Infantry) as shoal-draft gunboats to give close-in fire support to a landing force. The "Elsie Item gunboat" was a huge success.[8] No fewer than 24 LCIs were equipped in time for the Marshalls with five .50-caliber machine guns, three 40-mm, two 20-mm guns and six rocket racks with 72 rockets each which were effective at 1100-yard range. This meant doubling the LCIs' crews and giving up their troop-carrying function. Their job was to accompany the amphtrac waves to the beach, two on each flank. For their size, LCI(G)s delivered a terrific fire power and their performance assured them a permanent rôle in the forces closing in on Japan.

A third innovation was the fighter plane armed with rockets for strafing beach defenses. This method of arming planes had been used by the Royal Air Force for two years and by the Atlantic Fleet air arm for six months; Air Force Pacific Fleet now adopted

---

[7] Alternate LVT–A2s were equipped with flame throwers, but these got so wet in the Kwajalein and Eniwetok landings that they did not work.
[8] See Volume VI of this History p. 294.

it since the ineffectiveness of .50-caliber fire for strafing had been demonstrated on the Betio beaches.

The problem of ammunition supply for this operation was a stiff one indeed. Admiral Turner planned to employ at least thrice the volume of naval gunfire as in the Gilberts, but only a few more fire support ships were available, and the distances from ammunition depots at Pearl Harbor, Efate and Espiritu Santo were even greater. Moreover, every capital ship in the task force had to be provided with a quota of armor-piercing ammunition, of little value for shore bombardment, lest Admiral Koga challenge with the Combined Fleet.

The new battleships were loaded at Efate from naval ammunition ships sent there for that purpose. One division of cruisers got theirs at Funafuti. Support ships and escorts for the Southern Attack Force took on their ammunition at San Diego. The majority were loaded at Pearl. An additional supply of 6-inch and 5-inch projectiles was brought up to the Marshalls in transports, LSTs and LSDs, to be drawn on during the assault phase; and some of it was needed. But the battleships and heavy cruisers carried more than enough for their bombardment assignments.

The mobile supply system that had first been tried in the Gilberts was, as we have seen, enlarged and extended in the Marshalls operation.

Particular attention was paid to the quality as well as the amount of shore bombardment by naval vessels. The small island of Kahoolawe in the Hawaiian group was turned over to the Fleet as a mock-up practice target. The Marines there put up pillboxes and other concrete and coconut-log installations, exactly similar to those on Tarawa, and the ships stood off shore and practised the right sort of shooting to pound them down. Rear Admiral James L. Kauffman, Commander Cruisers and Destroyers Pacific Fleet, directed the close support fire for troops that would follow preliminary bombardment, with particular attention to communications between the ships and shore fire control parties composed of Marines and naval officers.

3. *Air and Submarine Preparation* [9]

Air activity against enemy bases in the Marshalls began even before Operation "Galvanic," continued through it and assumed greater weight and intensity with the construction of new Gilbert Islands airfields. Land-based aircraft, now based 750 miles nearer the Marshalls than before, bore the major burden of air preparation for Operation "Flintlock." Between the Nauru strike of 8 December 1943 and the last week of January 1944, all carrier divisions of the Pacific Fleet were given a much needed rest, overhaul and refresher training. Land-based aircraft carried the ball for seven weeks.

Rear Admiral John H. Hoover remained in command of land-based planes, whether Army, Navy or Marine, in the Ellice and Gilbert Islands. His flagship *Curtiss* sailed north from Funafuti to Tarawa Lagoon about the middle of January, when Major General Willis H. Hale, Commander VII Army Air Force, established headquarters on Bairiki Island, Tarawa. This setup, an army air force under an air admiral, was an old story in the South Pacific, where it worked beautifully. Owing (in the writer's opinion) to certain personalities, it did not work well in the Central Pacific.

The old Japanese airstrip on Betio Island, renamed Hawkins Field after a Marine officer who had lost his life at Tarawa, became operational for fighter planes by 1 December and was promptly extended. From mid-December this field was used to stage Army Liberators in their attacks on the Marshalls. Breaking here their long flights from Funafuti and Canton Island, the heavy bombers dropped 601 tons of bombs on the Marshalls in December.[10] On 1 January some of the B–24s were moved up to Hawkins Field and based there. By that time it had two coral runways each

[9] Comairpac Analysis of Air Operations, Jan. 1944; VII A.A.F. Intelligence Bulletin No. 2; Cincpac Monthly Analysis of Operations for Jan. 1944, with supplementary report on carrier operations, 30 Jan.–24 Feb. 1944; Action Reports of each carrier group commander.

[10] VII A.A.F. General Intelligence Bulletin No. 2 (Review of Gilberts and Marshalls campaign).

over a mile long. On Buota Island, Tarawa, a completely new field was constructed and named Mullinnix after the admiral who went down with *Liscome Bay*. A 6000-foot bomber runway completed there before the end of 1943 became the base for a unit comprising 44 Navy fighter planes, 7 Catalinas and 49 bombers. During January the strip was lengthened and facilities were doubled, in preparation for strikes on the Marshalls. Mullinnix Field also became an important stopover on the air route from Oahu to the South Pacific. By 1 January 1944 some 11,500 troops and sailors were based on Tarawa and 57 anti-aircraft guns from .50 caliber to 90-mm had been emplaced.

Although Nauru had been badly battered in the 8 December raid, and no planes had been flown from the field there for some time, one could never tell what the Japanese might be up to. Consequently, Nauru became a practice target for land-based aircraft. There were two big strikes on it from Tarawa on 23 and 28 December 1943. Here is a description of them by a participant: —

The first raid cost us a swell pilot and crew out of the seven planes that went on the mission. We deck-leveled the Japs off the rock that night from 400 feet off the two runways they have there. There were only 200 known anti-aircraft guns firing at us, but we surprised them by coming in fast — about 340 knots — and low over the water. We were only 50 feet off the water just before we ran into the island. Our pilot led the second attack, which was a dive-bombing job more or less, as we came in at about 8000 feet and dove to one thousand feet before we let the bombs loose on the target. We hit an ammunition dump this time, and the other three planes saw it go up in smoke. One plane got shot full of holes but came back with no one hurt. . . .[11]

At Makin there was a false start, an attempt to construct a landing strip in the swampy western end of Butaritari. Finally a section of the "handle" was found where it was possible to build a 7000-foot runway, and over half of this had been completed by the end of the year. Fifty-five Army fighter planes, 26 Douglas Dauntless dive-bombers (A–24s) and two Catalinas were based at Butaritari. Star-

[11] Letter of Aviation Radioman 3rd Class Jack W. Martin USNR of VB–137, 14 Feb. 1944.

mann Field, as the Makin airdrome was named, was of sand, not coral, and so could not accommodate heavy bombers; but the medium bombers based there were within range of Mili and Jaluit. A–24s, escorted by Navy Hellcats at first and by Army Airacobras (P–39s) as they became available, first went into action 21 December and during the next ten days made nine strikes on Mili and one on Jaluit. The airstrip, together with 25,000 feet of taxiways, was completed in January and by the end of the month one squadron of dive-bombers and two of fighter planes were based there, and a seaplane base had been constructed on the lagoon side. By 1 January 1944 about 7000 troops and bluejackets were based on Makin, and defense installations ranged from 155-mm coast defense down to .50-caliber machine guns.

O'Hare Field, Abemama, named after the *Enterprise* group commander who lost his life in the Gilberts operation, was built by the 95th Seabees on the large island that rounds the north end of the atoll. This strip was a "honey." The surface of live coral, kept hard by being sprinkled with salt water, was ready for emergency landings on 10 December and officially opened on the 17th.[12] When completed, the runway, 8000 feet long, was better oriented for big bomber take-offs than any other in the Gilberts. By 1 February 1944 this advanced naval air base comprised over 5000 men and 100 guns from .50 caliber up and 112 planes including a squadron of PB4Ys that conducted daily searches up to Eniwetok, Ujelang and Kusaie. During February O'Hare Field flew 1045 sorties, over 300 of them by 4-engine planes, and fed out 1,182,924 gallons of aviation gasoline. But by 8 March 1944 the armed forces of the United States had moved so far westward that no more searches were flown out of Abemama.

Japanese attempts to harass the Gilberts were rendered futile in daylight by a strong combat air patrol; 34 out of 35 air raids that got through to Makin and Tarawa during December and January

---

[12] War Diary Commander Aircraft Abemama, examined there in June 1944. Abemama had been intended as the place for a pool of carrier planes and for training carrier plane crews, but this purpose was never fulfilled there as Majuro was better situated for it.

were at night. In addition there were three raids on Abemama. The total damage inflicted on all three bases was 33 planes and 2 landing craft destroyed, 9 planes damaged, 5 men killed and a few wounded.

While a carpet to Tokyo was being laid through the Gilberts and Marshalls, its lower end was supposed to be rolled up. Around 1 January 1944, Baker Island airfield was abandoned and only maintenance men were left on Wallis.[13]

By the end of January 1944, Admiral Hoover had at his disposal approximately 350 combat planes. That month's operations and those of February obtained photographic intelligence, destroyed enemy air power in his five important bases, and attacked enemy shipping wherever encountered. Mili, Wotje, Maloelap and Roi-Namur each received about 200 tons of bombs from land-based aircraft during January. After a Tarawa-based strike on Jaluit had mined the channel there on 4 January, most of the Japanese shipping and all but one seaplane were withdrawn. Mili was attacked nearly every day in January. About the middle of the month, two P–39s followed two Japanese 4-engine bombers right up to the airfield there and shot them down as they were attempting to land. That seemed to discourage the enemy, as no more planes were sighted over Mili. Wotje and Maloelap received the most serious treatment. After three B–24s had been shot down by anti-aircraft guns in a midday raid on Maloelap, 2 January, the Liberators were limited to night attacks, and with the equipment that they then carried, night attacks were not accurate.

Photographs taken 9 January showed 10 medium-sized and 14 small vessels anchored in Kwajalein Lagoon. Two days later, ten Navy Liberators (PB4Ys) were sent there to get them. Five bombed Roi; the others swept across the lagoon and sank a 3000-ton converted gunboat, *Ikuta Maru*. "The American attacks are

[13] Funafuti, Nanomea and Nukufetau were still going strong when this writer visited them in early July 1944; but Abemama had seen its best days as an air base. Only transport planes passed through, the garrison was reduced, and the natives, having reclothed themselves and acquired a valuable collection of canned goods and miscellaneous gadgets by working for the U.S. Navy at a shilling a day plus rations, were beginning to move back to their own villages and resume life as lived in the days of R.L.S.

becoming more furious," a Japanese soldier then noted in his diary. "Planes come over day after day. Can we stand up under the strain?" [14] They could and did.

Besides *Ikuta Maru*, only one small merchant vessel was sunk by Admiral Hoover's land-based air forces in January. Only heavy bombers could fly the great distance to the naval base at Kwajalein where most of the shipping lay, and as they had to fly unescorted, their attacks were made mostly at night. The great proportion of air effort in that region was applied to reconnaissance and to the destruction of enemy air power.

Taroa Field on Maloelap was beyond fighter-plane range from Makin, so the Liberators had to attack it by day without escort. The B–24s would come in between 8000 and 12,000 feet altitude, flying in a staggered V. Since Taroa had search radar, the Japanese "Zekes" arose in good time, horsed around while the ack-ack did its worst and then pursued the retiring bombers, attacking at every opportunity. "The Jap dug deep into his bag of tricks and tried every method of attack he could improvise," including the performance of acrobatic tricks by one plane to distract an American pilot's attention from another getting on his tail. This monkey business ceased after 26 January when a squadron of P–40s lay in wait for the Japanese on the retirement course and downed six of them.

Although Admiral Hoover's land-based command performed useful preliminary work, it failed to obtain complete air supremacy over the Marshalls. The Japanese still had about 150 serviceable planes in the Marshalls on 27 January, *but none on D-day, the 31st.* What had happened in the meantime? The big carriers had swung into action.

This was the first time the big carriers really demonstrated what they could do to help an amphibious operation. In the Gilberts, they had been mainly used defensively, to ward off enemy air attack. But the new Commander Fast Carrier Groups Pacific Fleet,

[14] Jicpoa Item No. 5913; also No. 7224.

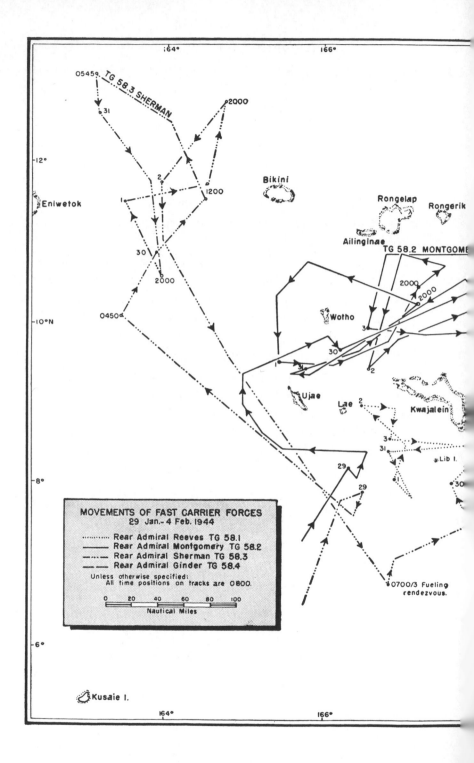

MOVEMENTS OF FAST CARRIER FORCES
29 Jan.- 4 Feb. 1944

··········· Rear Admiral Reeves TG 58.1
————— Rear Admiral Montgomery TG 58.2
—··—··— Rear Admiral Sherman TG 58.3
——— Rear Admiral Ginder TG 58.4

Unless otherwise specified:
All time positions on tracks are 0800.

0   20   40   60   80   100
Nautical Miles

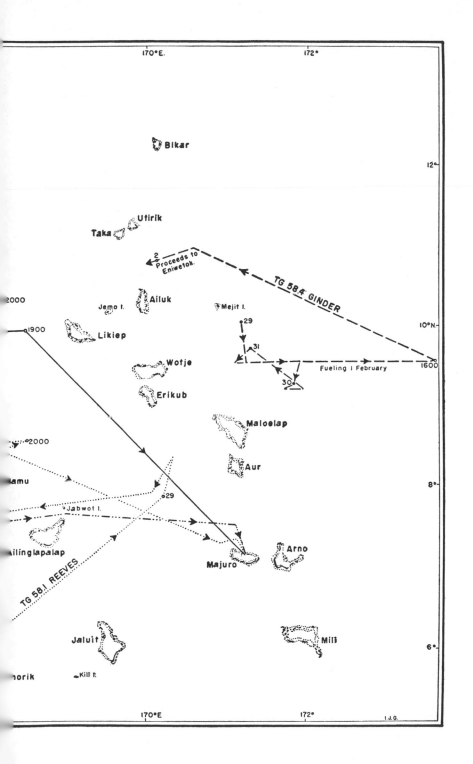

Rear Admiral Marc A. Mitscher, who had "grown up in the air," was eager to develop the offensive function of his beloved flat-tops. Fast carrier operations in the Marshalls campaign were planned to annihilate enemy air power in that theater before D-day. More and more, the responsibility for tactical air support of an amphibious operation (including combat air and anti-submarine patrol at the objective, strafing the landing beaches and affording close air support to troops ashore) was given to the escort carriers included in the amphibious groups.

The timetable of Admiral Mitscher's Fast Carrier Forces can be seen at a glance in the following schedule.[15] It differed in many respects from the Cincpac staff plan, for one of the great advantages of carriers is mobility, rendering a flexible schedule possible. Admirals Spruance and Mitscher were able to bring their concentrated power to bear on widely separated objectives at short notice, as a changing situation and the need of surprise suggested.

PLACES ATTACKED

Date	TG 58.1 Reeves	TG 58.2 Montgomery	TG 58.3 Sherman	TG 58.4 Ginder
29 Jan.	Taroa (Maloelap)	Roi Island	Kwajalein I.	Otdia (Wotje)
30 Jan.	Kwajalein Island	Roi Island	Eniwetok	Otdia and Taroa (Maloelap)
31 Jan.	Kwajalein, in support of landings	Roi, in support of landings	Eniwetok	As above
1 Feb. 2 Feb. 3 Feb.	As above, in support of advancing ground forces.		Eniwetok / Fueling	Fueling / Eniwetok
4 Feb.	En route to Majuro			Eniwetok
5 and 6 Feb.	At anchor, Majuro			Eniwetok

The salient feature of these air operations was the virtually complete destruction of enemy aircraft and shipping in the Marshalls,[16]

[15] This table was compiled from two Action Reports of CTF 58, dated 16 and 19 March 1944, and Comcardiv 3 (who became CTF 58 on 6 Jan.) (War Diary for period covered). For composition of each group see Appendix III.

[16] On 29 Jan. two squadrons of Coronado seaplanes from Midway bombed Wake for the tenth time since it had fallen into Japanese hands, and for the first time since 5 Oct. 1943. Wake, less than 600 miles from Kwajalein, was still a threat.

before the initial landings. These 1944-model strikes were much more scientific than the pass at Kwajalein on 4 December, less than two months earlier. Pilots were now so well trained and provided with such accurate information that revetments could be individually assigned to fighter planes for strafing in preliminary sweeps preceding bomber missions, and air strikes were closely articulated with naval bombardment by accompanying battleships and cruisers.

Almost a hundred planes were based on Roi, center of enemy air power in the Marshalls, on 29 January, when the air assault was opened by Admiral Montgomery's *Essex* group. The high cover, twelve Hellcats, met and engaged a squadron of "Zekes" about two miles over the island and knocked down several. While this fight was going on, other Hellcats came in strafing enemy planes in revetments, then worked over those in open parking areas. Nine "Zekes" jumped them while they were engaged in this pleasant pastime, but seven of the nine were shot down. Fifty SBDs, ordered to bomb anti-aircraft emplacements, silenced or knocked out most of them while Avenger torpedo-bombers dropped fragmentation clusters on the parking areas, aprons and strip areas, and 2000-pound bombs on the runways. Teamwork conquered; the last Japanese fighter plane ever seen in the air over Kwajalein was shot down at 0800 that day, and half an hour later the carriers' combat air patrol destroyed six "Bettys" attempting a getaway. No enemy plane came near the ships. Thus a single carrier-based strike ended Japanese air power at Roi and Namur at the cost of four Hellcats and one TBF. That night the battleships bombarded the shore, and next day Montgomery launched a second carrier strike to clean up.

Kwajalein Island at the southeast corner of the atoll, and Ebeye the seaplane base, were taken care of by Rear Admiral F. C. Sherman's *Bunker Hill* group. Few enemy planes were seen here, but ack-ack was intense and accurate, accounting for one torpedo-bomber. Hence Sherman's planes concentrated on installations.

The big lagoon was empty when the carrier planes arrived, but destroyer *Burns* (Lieutenant Commander D. T. Eller) of Sherman's screen disposed of a merchant convoy that was trying to escape in the small hours of 30 January. She had picked up three *Bunker Hill* aviators who had splashed, had transferred one to *South Dakota* for medical treatment, and was off Ujae Atoll en route to her carrier group when four targets showed up on the radar screen. *Burns* claimed to have sunk them all by radar-controlled gunfire, but the postwar checkup indicates that she got only two of over 500 tons.[17]

The airfield on Otdia Island, Wotje Atoll, was naked of planes when Admiral Ginder's *Saratoga* group attacked on 29 January, but anti-aircraft fire cost him a fighter plane and a torpedo-bomber with their entire crews. Otdia next day was bombarded by a fire support group of Rear Admiral Oldendorf's Northern Attack Force, consisting of one heavy (*Louisville*) and three light cruisers (*Santa Fe, Mobile, Biloxi*) and screen of 6 destroyers. During the initial phase of this bombardment, at 8000 yards, the enemy replied briskly with 5.5-inch guns; and before the group could open range a salvo hit destroyer *Anderson* square on her C.I.C., killing the captain (Commander John G. Tennent), two ensigns and three bluejackets, and wounding 14 more. The enemy paid a high price for his impudence, since this bombardment group, well served by spotting planes, pumped 250 rounds of 8-inch, 1813 rounds of 6-inch and 4567 rounds of 5-inch ammunition into Otdia, rendering the airfield useless.[18]

Taroa Field on Maloelap Atoll, an air base second in importance only to Roi-Namur, was the target of Rear Admiral Reeves's *Enterprise* group. At the time of launching the first pre-dawn strike, 29 January, this group was passing through heavy rain squalls with the result that only 17 out of 31 fighters found the target. Very few planes were found there. Next day this group proceeded to Kwajalein Island while Admiral Ginder divided his attention between Wotje and Taroa. Few targets were left in either place,

[17] *Paran Maru* (562 tons) and *Akibasan Maru* (4600 tons), the latter sinking attributed to air as well as surface craft. Vessels under 500 tons are not noted in JANAC.
[18] CTG 53.5 and *Anderson* Action Reports 6 and 3 Feb.

and two Avengers which collided over Maloelap were lost with all hands.

Engebi Island of Eniwetok, the latest atoll to receive attention as it was the last to be taken, received the largest number of sorties and bomb tonnage. These were delivered by Admiral Ginder's group — grand old "Sara," her faithful light companion *Princeton* and the new *Langley* — while heavy cruisers *Boston* and *Baltimore* contributed 8-inch bombardment. Engebi was more nearly pulverized before the landing than any objective taken by an amphibious force in 1944.

As a result of this series of strikes and those of the land-based planes on Mili and Jaluit, enemy air power in the Marshalls was eliminated before the troops landed; complete control of the air had been gained. Only one air attack of any consequence developed after our ground forces came ashore in the Marshalls, and that came up from Kusaie. And, most marvelous in comparison with earlier campaigns, not one United States naval vessel was attacked by an enemy plane during the entire operation.

The cost was neither slight nor heavy, as may be judged from this table [19] covering the activities of Task Force 58 from 29 January through 11 February 1944: —

	TG 58.1	*TG 58.2*	*TG 58.3*	*TG 58.4*	*Total*
TOTAL SORTIES	1397	1704	1108 *	2023	6232 *
SORTIES OVER TARGET	886	1146	668	1321	4021
TONS BOMBS DROPPED	243.1	274.5	207.9	431.1	1156.6
Air Combat Losses					
AIRCRAFT	7 VF, 2 VT	8 VF	1 VF, 2 VT	1 VF, 1 VT	17 VF, 5 VT
MEN	8 pilots	2 pilots	2 pilots	2 pilots	14 pilots
	4 crew		4 crew	2 crew	10 crew
Air Operational Losses					
AIRCRAFT	1 VF, 3 VT	1 VF, 2 VT	1 VF, 5 VT, 3 VB	7 VF, 4 VT	10 VF, 14 VT, 3 VB
MEN	2 pilots	2 pilots	5 pilots	1 pilot	10 pilots
	4 crew	1 crew	9 crew		14 crew

* Approximate.

[19] CTF 58 Action Report 6 Mar. 1944.

Vice Admiral Lockwood (Comsubpac) assigned six submarines [20] to Operation "Flintlock." The deployment was similar to that in "Galvanic" and based on the same strategic and tactical plan. *Permit, Skipjack* and *Guardfish* were assigned to quadrants around Truk; *Sunfish, Seal* and *Searaven* to stations off Kusaie, Ponape and Eniwetok respectively.

Although the Japanese Combined Fleet ignored the Marshalls invasion, the three boats off Truk found good hunting. On 26 January *Skipjack* sank plane ferry *Okitsu Maru* and destroyer *Suzukaze* and damaged a freighter. *Guardfish*, which had sunk the 10,000-ton tanker *Kenyo Maru* on 14 January before joining the "Flintlock" deployment, put destroyer *Umikaze* down on 1 February. *Permit* spotted but could not attack battleships *Nagato* and *Fuso*, moving from Truk to Palau. *Searaven* conducted a photographic reconnaissance of Eniwetok on 27 and 29 January and then stood by as a lifeguard until 12 February. Neither *Seal* off Ponape nor *Sunfish* off Kusaie sighted a Japanese ship. Those waters, which in 1942–43 had been teeming with *Marus*, picket boats and escorted convoys, were now almost deserted. Japanese afloat were getting out; but those ashore had to stay and fight, or rot.

4. *Enemy Preparations*

The Japanese made almost no attempt to meet this massive onslaught. The Halsey-MacArthur campaign against the Bismarcks Barrier had thrown enemy forces off balance, and that balance they were not to regain until the Pacific Fleet attacked Saipan. The Marshalls were only a "holding" front for the Japanese; Imperial Headquarters had long since decided to let the garrisons fight a delaying action and to concentrate on fortifying the next defensive perimeter, Timor–Western New Guinea–Truk–Marianas.[21] Ad-

[20] See end of Appendix III.
[21] See Vol. VI 25.

miral Koga dared not commit the Combined Fleet against Spruance's Fifth Fleet, because the air groups of his carriers had been
sliced off to defend Rabaul. For the same reason, he could give
his Marshalls bases no air reinforcement after 25 November, when
the 24th Air Flotilla brought in 40 bombers and 30 fighters from
Hokkaido and the Kuriles, and 18 more "Zekes" were sent up
from Rabaul. And the Fourth Fleet, charged with the defense of
the Marshalls, was a mere skeleton.[22]

Imperial Headquarters left Koga to decide how to defend the
Marshalls with what he had. Since he and his staff made the bad
guess that the Americans would attack the nearer Marshalls before
they dared take on Kwajalein, he shifted troops from Kwajalein
to Mili,[23] and the few thousand fresh troops placed at his disposition by Imperial Headquarters were sent to reinforce the garrisons of Wotje and Maloelap. This left a fairly formidable defense
force of about 9000 men on Kwajalein, evenly divided between the
northern and the southern ends of the atoll. The Japanese 82nd
Infantry Division, which American forces expected to encounter
in the Marshalls, was still on its way from Japan to Truk.[24]

A limited deployment of Sixth Fleet submarines was made from
Truk; but the only knowledge we have of them is of the four
boats that American naval forces sank, in positions which sug-
gest that they had been sent to guard the by-passed atolls. *RO–39*
was the first victim, on 1 February 1944, to destroyer *Walker*
(Commander H. E. Townsend) at a point very near Wotje. Next,
destroyer *Charrette* (Commander E. S. Karpe), screening Rear
Admiral Sherman's carrier group on the night of 4–5 February at
a point about 100 miles NW of Jaluit, was directed to investigate
a surface radar contact. She tracked it to 3200 yards and opened
gunfire; the submarine (*I–21*) submerged. A depth-charge attack
followed. Destroyer escort *Fair* (Lieutenant D. S. Crocker USNR)
now joined the chase and was coached in by *Charrette*'s radar to

[22] *Inter. Jap. Off.* pp. 132, 143, 411.
[23] Same, p. 86. Mili had a garrison of over 5100 when the Marshalls campaign opened.
[24] Isley and Crowl *U.S. Marines and Amphibious War* p. 270.

make a hedgehog attack [25] at 0050 February 5. Heavy underwater explosions were heard, and although the two attackers were awarded only a "probable," *I–21* was never heard of again.

Destroyer *Nicholas*, escorting a task unit to Kwajalein, encountered submarine *I–11* at 0300 February 17 at a point 200 miles NE of Maloelap. This was almost on the great-circle course from Johnston Island to Kwajalein, a likely spot for underwater pickings, but it was the sub that got picked off instead. *Nicholas* made radar contact at 24,000 yards, closed, sighted the boat in the act of submerging at 0346 and opened gunfire. *I–11* could not shake off the destroyer, which tracked it relentlessly and delivered three depth-charge attacks between 0600 and 0630. *Nicholas* too was awarded only a "probable," but she had disposed of the submarine.[26]

RO–40, snooping around Kwajalein, fell afoul of a mixed screen protecting a disposition of LSTs, LCIs and oilers. On the bright sunny afternoon of 15 February, in a smooth sea, destroyer *Phelps* made a sound contact followed by a depth-charge attack at 1751. Minesweeper *Sage* then picked up the contact and dropped a pattern. Destroyer *MacDonough*, ordered to maintain contact lest the submarine overtake the convoy, delivered a depth-charge attack of her own. The assessors at Washington coldly evaluated all this as "insufficient evidence of presence of submarine"; but all the same, *RO–40* was sunk.[27]

[25] See Vol. I 211–12.
[26] U.S. Fleet *A/S Bulletin* Apr. 1944 p. 26; Lt. F. K. Zinn (*Nicholas*) Action Report; JANAC p. 9.
[27] Lt. Cdr. D. L. Martineau (*Phelps*) and Cdr. J. W. Ramey (*MacDonough*) Action Reports; JANAC. Submarine *I–40* was also lost about this time in the Marshalls area, for causes unknown.

CHAPTER XIV

Majuro [1]

31 January–8 February 1944

"THE importance of the early seizure and harbor development of Majuro for use as an advanced base in the Marshall Islands operation was realized from the start," wrote Rear Admiral Harry W. Hill.

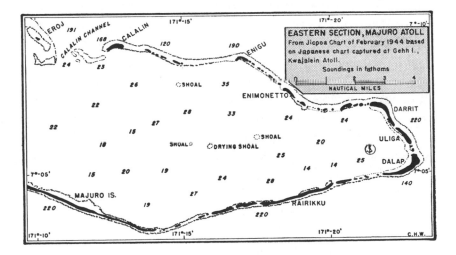

Majuro, lying right in the center of the Jaluit–Maloelap–Mili triangle, was well described by Mrs. Robert Louis Stevenson as "a pearl of an atoll." No less than 56 islets threaded on a single line of reef enclose a lagoon 21 miles long and 6 to 8 wide, "clear and

[1] Rear Admiral Hill's Majuro Action Report 15 Feb. 1944; Lt. Cdr. J. J. Delaney Report to Rear Admiral Cotter 15 Apr. 1944; conversation with Capt. Jones in Apr. 1944 and Jicpoa Information Bulletin No. 58–43 *Lesser Marshalls,* 20 Dec. 1943.

in color like a golden-green chrysoprase."[2] A long, thin island also named Majuro closes the lagoon on the southern side; but the most important islands, Darrit and Dalap, are on the eastern or windward edge. Several maritime nations had contemplated a naval development there. Germany established a small supply base on Darrit and German cruisers used the lagoon in 1914, but Allied sea power made it untenable and Majuro's chief function in World War I was to offer refuge to an occasional raider. Japan neglected the atoll in favor of other places in the Marshalls. Three or four hundred troops were sent there after World War II began, but someone in Tokyo changed his mind and all the men (except three) were moved to Mili by the end of 1942.

Rear Admiral Hill in *Cambria* commanded a small amphibious outfit designated the Majuro Attack Group. The main units, heavy cruiser *Portland*, two escort carriers, two minesweepers, a transport and an APD, departed Pearl Harbor 23 January 1944 in company with the Reserve Force. The assault troops comprised one BLT of the 106th Infantry Regiment 27th Division.

The outward passage was almost as pleasant as a peacetime cruise; all hands were able to indulge in sun bathing topside. But gunnery practice was held and the escort carriers' planes simulated air attacks. The only discomfort came after sundown when the boatswain's mates sang out, "Now hear this! Prepare to darken ship!" When hatches were battened down and portholes closed, the older transports with antiquated equipment became hotboxes. Many men slept topside, taking the chance of sudden showers rather than sweating it out below. The two groups separated 30 January, Admiral Hill proceeding to Majuro while the Reserve Force under Captain Loomis continued to its stand-by area off Kwajalein.

D-day, 31 January 1944, opened warm and partly cloudy with scattered showers. Blessed with fair weather, Admiral Hill prepared to assault the atoll — which, photographic interpretation of the buildings had informed him, might be defended by three to four hundred Japanese. This intelligence was confirmed by natives

[2] *Cruise of the Janet Nicol* p. 151.

on the channel islets, where a scout party of Marines, led by Captain James L. Jones USMCR of Abemama fame, had landed the previous evening.[3] In order to see for themselves, the Marines reëmbarked in APD *Kane* and steamed to the eastern end of the lagoon. Before D-day dawned they had overrun Dalap and Uliga, found nary a Jap, and heard from natives that there were none on Darrit. Captain Jones was unable to convey this information to Admiral Hill in time to stop his scheduled bombardment of Darrit. At 0655, after the shoot had been going on for 18 minutes, he managed to get the word through. The Admiral then ordered his guns to stop talking and his scheduled air strikes to be suspended, pending verification. The Marines crossed over to Darrit and at 0931 Captain Jones reported that island to be vacant.

In the meantime most of the task group had passed through Calalin Channel and anchored in the lagoon. At 0950, Admiral Hill notified Admiral Spruance that Majuro had been secured. Five minutes later the Stars and Stripes were raised on the first Japanese territory — Japanese before the war — to fall into American hands.

When the Japanese abandoned Majuro, in November 1942, they left many finished or nearly completed buildings and barracks, an observation tower, seaplane hangars and good construction equipment and matériel. Fortunately nothing was seriously damaged during the 18-minute bombardment by *Portland* and *Bullard*. Most of the 455 projectiles expended hit coconut palms and detonated harmlessly in the air.

Two LCVPs filled with soldiers were sent ashore to bring Captain Jones on board *Cambria* for a conference. The soldiers, seeing naked Marines swimming and sun bathing, were with some difficulty restrained from taking a crack at them as probable Japanese. The Navy, too, was suspicious, and insisted that the Marines inspect Majuro Island on the south side of the lagoon. There, they actually rounded up three Japanese.

[3] The natives meant that the Japanese had formerly been on the atoll, but the Marines' Gilbertese translator, who did not know Marshallese very well, slipped up. (Conversation with Capt. Jones 24 April 1944. He is brother to Maj. William K. Jones USMC of the Betio battle.)

At first light 1 February, *Cambria* debarked her troops. The largest completed building on Darrit was converted into a base hospital and the barracks were turned over to the garrison. Some 25 structures were used just as they were and 10 others were remodeled.[4] *Oracle* and *Sage*, with the assistance of Lieutenant Commander John C. Tribble of the United States Coast and Geodetic Survey, marked channels and anchorages in the lagoon so smartly that a large-scale anchorage chart, printed on board *Cambria* the night of 1 February, was available for use next day. During the evening of 2 February, battleships *Washington* and *Indiana* limped in, having collided in the darkness when *Indiana* left station to fuel destroyers. By next day, 3 February, there were about 30 ships in the anchorage and 50 more expected. Admiral Hill departed by plane for Kwajalein to confer with Admiral Turner; *Cambria*, with *Oracle* and *Sage* as escorts, followed at best speed.

Majuro Atoll, secured without the loss of a man, was promptly made an advanced naval and air base. The garrison force, 7165 officers and men, arrived a few days later in transports under Commander Carl E. Anderson, who had seen to it that they were properly combat-loaded in Pearl so that the stuff came out "like sand running out of a sleeve." An airstrip was promptly constructed on Dalap, and soon received a number of carrier planes for a nucleus land-based air force. Work on a second airstrip on Darrit was started. This place was a paradise for American soldiers and sailors, compared with atolls taken by assault where the garrison had to camp in tents among the debris of battle, with the stench of death in the air.

Majuro Lagoon served the mobile supply system to perfection.[5] The largest fleet of tankers the Pacific Fleet had ever assembled entered it shortly after the capture, so that most of the scheduled fueling at sea during the Marshalls operation could be called off. Service Squadron 4 was absorbed into Servron 10 under the command of Captain Worrall R. Carter, who became S.O.P.A. Majuro

[4] Lt. Cdr. J. J. Delaney's Report 15 Apr. 1944.
[5] See chap. vi.

on 8 February. Barges were towed up, mobile lighters were constructed of metal pontoon units and giant outboard motors, and in no great time this lagoon was the busiest of naval advanced bases. Enemy air attacks were anticipated, but locally based planes, with the aid of those in the Gilberts, kept pounding away at Mili, Maloelap and Wotje to such good purpose that not a single Japanese plane from these bases ever showed up over Majuro. And the encircling reef afforded complete protection against submarine attack.

On 15 April 1944, when Rear Admiral John F. Shafroth, Inspector General of the Pacific Fleet, visited Majuro, the new 5800-foot airstrip had been completed and there were over 150 ships anchored in the beautiful lagoon. Majuro had become almost a second home to the fast carrier forces between strikes.

CHAPTER XV

Kwajalein

(Operation "Flintlock")

31 January–7 February 1944

1. *The Atoll, the Plan and the Approach*

TWO points on Kwajalein Atoll, Roi-Namur in the north and
Kwajalein Island in the south, were the main objectives of the
Marshall Islands operation. These were the positions by which the
enemy set greatest store in that large group of atolls. If they fell,
all others between them and the Gilberts could be neutralized with
comparative ease.

Kwajalein is the world's largest coral atoll.[1] Shaped roughly like
an old-fashioned horse pistol, with Roi-Namur at the hammer
and Kwajalein Island at the butt, it is 66 miles long in a NW–SE
direction and has a greatest width of 20 miles. No fewer than 97
islands and islets, with a total area of only 6⅓ square miles, are
strung along the reef, surrounding a lagoon that has an area of
839 square miles. The only islands big enough for military installations are Kwajalein and neighboring islets at the southeast end
of the atoll, Roi and Namur at the northern end, and Ebadon at
the western end.

---

[1] Discovered by the Spaniards; named after his ship by Capt. Mertho of the
British merchantman *Ocean* in 1804, with the names of his daughters Lydia, Cath-
erine and Margaret for the northern, western and southern islets. Capt. L. A.
Hagemeister, a Russian shipmaster, called in 1829 and renamed it Menchikof
Island after the then C. in C. of the Imperial Russian Navy. The native name, which
first appears as Quadelen on Kotzebue's chart of his voyage in *Rurik*, 1817, gradually replaced all others and was officially spelled Kwajalein by the Germans. It
is pronounced Kwa-dja-linn, with scarcely any accent. Roi and Namur (I am sat-
isfied after combing through the accounts of all French and Russian voyages to
the Marshalls) are native names, not French.

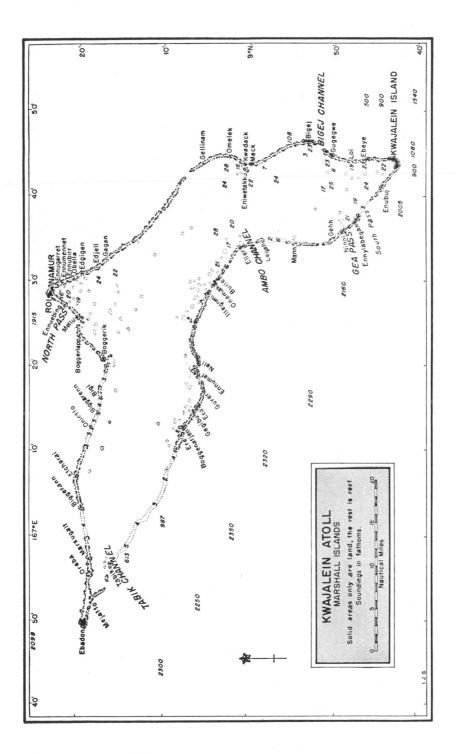

KWAJALEIN ATOLL
MARSHALL ISLANDS

Solid areas only are land, the rest is reef.

Soundings in fathoms.

Nautical Miles

I. J. G.

Owing to the small land area and poor soil, the natives were neither numerous nor enterprising. Like the other Marshallese that our forces encountered, they had been browbeaten by the Japanese and subjected to forced labor drafts; and although naval bombardment could not avoid killing some, the rest greeted the change of régime with enthusiasm.

Roi-Namur was the enemy's principal air base, Kwajalein Island his principal naval, and Ebeye his seaplane base. The two groups were about 44 miles apart, hence Admiral Turner's plan contemplated two separate but simultaneous amphibious assaults. Roi-Namur was allotted to the Northern Attack Force commanded by Rear Admiral Conolly, with the 4th Marine Division as the ground force. Kwajalein Island and Ebeye were the task of the Southern Attack Force commanded by Admiral Turner himself, with the 7th Infantry Division United States Army as the assault troops.

The Northern Attack Force included plenty of veteran combatant ships, but most of the transports were new, with green crews, and the 4th Marine Division, created since the war began, had never been blooded. The Southern Force, on the contrary, consisted of experienced ships and veteran troops.

The Japanese high command had ordered Roi-Namur to be defended to the last man. And the number of defenders there was high for so tiny an area; somewhere between 3500 and 3800 men, under naval Captain Seiho Arima. It would not be easy for a green unit such as the 4th Marine Division then was to rub out a garrison of that strength; even for combat-seasoned troops it would have been a tough assignment.

Rear Admiral Dick Conolly,[2] who had gone from destroyer

[2] Richard L. Conolly, b. Illinois 1892, Annapolis '14, service in *Virginia* and *Vermont* and in *Smith,* one of the World War I DDs based on Brest; won distinction as member salvage party of torpedoed transport *Westbridge.* Helped fit out and served as "exec." of three destroyers in turn; postgraduate course in electrical engineering, taught that subject at Annapolis, in the meantime serving as ass't engineer officer of *New York.* Engineer officer of *Concord* 1927, C.O. *Case* and *Dupont* 1929–30; War College course and staff duty; staff of Com. cruisers Scouting Force 1933, navigator *Tennessee* 1935–36, instructing at Naval Academy 1936–39; Comdesdiv 7 and 6 to April 1942, his division serving as screen for Halsey's carrier force. After duty in Navy Dept. became Com. Landing Craft and Bases NW Africa under Adm. Hewitt and had command of a major task force in the

duty in the Pacific to Admiral King's planning staff, had been raised to flag rank in 1943 in order to lead one of the amphibious groups that pulled off the Sicilian landing. He handled that assignment so brilliantly that Admiral King sent him to the Pacific Fleet, and he took command of the third group of the V Amphibious Force on 23 October 1943. After conferring with Admirals Nimitz and Turner[3] at Pearl Harbor, he set up headquarters at Camp Pendleton near San Diego, where the 4th Marine Division, organized 15 August, was being trained by Major General Harry Schmidt usmc. The story of Tarawa became known late in November, and every effort was made to benefit by this experience. On 1 December when Admiral Conolly hoisted his flag in the new amphibious command ship *Appalachian* at San Diego, neither he nor the General had learned definitely that they were to attack Roi and Namur, nor did they until mid-December. After two weeks' ship-to-shore training with the transports (but not, unfortunately, with the LVTs) a rehearsal was held at San Clemente Island on 2–3 January 1944. Most of the fire support ships and assigned escort carriers were present.

The tractor units, consisting of 15 LSTs carrying amphtracs, escorted by 7 LCIs, 3 minesweepers and 2 destroyers, departed San Diego 5–6 January; the main echelon comprising three transport divisions, five fire-support units commanded by Rear Admiral Jesse B. Oldendorf in *Louisville*, three escort carriers, nine LCI gunboats, several minesweepers and ocean-going tugs, all with suitable screens, left 13 January. All staged through Kauai or Lahina Roads, and *Appalachian* called at Pearl Harbor for a final conference at Cincpac headquarters.

During the passage from the Hawaiian Islands, the only source of anxiety was the escort carriers. On 25 January a plane landing on *Sangamon* went through the barrier and caught fire among the

---

Sicilian campaign. Under the Pacific Fleet he participated in most of the amphibious operations through 1945, became Deputy C.N.O. after the war, Com. U.S. Naval Forces Europe 1946 to Aug. 1950, when he became President of the Naval War College.

[3] At their first meeting Conolly made a few remarks based on Mediterranean experience, to which Turner characteristically replied, "If you stay around here, you and I goin' to fight!" But they respected each other and got on famously.

planes parked on the deck. One officer and seven men were killed, ten seriously injured; four fighter planes and one scout bomber were destroyed. The fire on deck was very serious, but the crew by heroic efforts brought it under control. Later, as the task force was refueling, *Suwannee* on the way to her flying station collided with *Sangamon*. Fortunately, both vessels were slowly backing when they clashed, and only superficial damage to the flight decks resulted.

Rear Admiral Oldendorf's fire support units broke off from Conolly's force at 1200 January 29 to bombard Wotje, and rejoined at 1800 January 30. That day the Northern Attack Force was getting into position for the assault. At 2000 the escort carriers with their screen were detached to render air support. An hour later, two transport divisions with their screen peeled off to reach their debarking area on the lee side of the atoll, about five miles off Ennuebing and Mellu Islets.

A chart of the northern part of Kwajalein Lagoon resembles one of those diagrams of an upper jaw on which a dentist checks the cavities in one's teeth, the islets being arranged on the reef like teeth in the gums — but many teeth are missing. Roi and Namur, the main objectives, represent the front incisors. Connected by an artificial causeway, their total length was a mile and a quarter. Roi was covered with an airfield and Namur with barracks and other installations neatly bestowed under coconut palms, presenting an attractive picture. Stretching southeast from Namur, on the right side of the jaw, are Ennugarret the cuspid, Ennumennet and Ennubirr the bicuspids, with Obella, Edgigen and other molars evenly spaced. The reef is continuous here; there are no entrances to the lagoon on the windward or eastern side. On the other side, however, most of the teeth are missing. Between bicuspids (Ennuebing and a nameless drying reef) is the North Pass into the lagoon, and between two molars (Mellu and Boggerlapp) is the South or Mellu Pass.

This northern bend of Kwajalein Atoll has a peculiar beauty as one approaches it on a bright, gusty winter day such as the last day of January, 1944. Sea and land seem to enhance each other, making their colors unbelievably vivid: the most dazzlingly white white-caps on the deepest of blue seas, reflecting luminous clouds wherever shipping makes a lee or a slick; brightest of green foliage on islets bordered by coral beaches the color of rich cream,

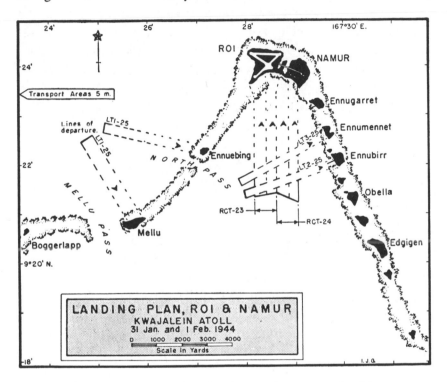

LANDING PLAN, ROI & NAMUR
KWAJALEIN ATOLL
31 Jan. and 1 Feb. 1944

with surf dashing up. Mellu Islet is prettily covered with coconut and pandanus palms, breadfruit trees and thick undergrowth; Boggerlapp from a distance looks like one of those round wooded islands off the coast of Maine.

There were several sharp showers during D-day, blotting out all this brightness for a brief spell and serving to wash some of the salt out of the Marines, who had already been thoroughly soaked in their landing craft. The troops were wearing the standard Marine herringbone twill, steel helmets with spotted camouflage covers, "boondocker" field boots with canvas leggings.

Yet, in spite of Kwajalein's being the principal Japanese air and naval base in the Marshalls, the enemy had placed no coast defense artillery on the islets flanking the lagoon passes either here or in the south; there were no defensive booms or nets and no mines laid in the entire lagoon. Tarawa had been better protected.

The Northern attack plan proposed to take advantage of this weakness by (1) landing troops on Ennuebing and Mellu to secure the North Pass; (2) sending forces across the lagoon to secure Ennumennet and Ennubirr; (3) siting the divisional artillery on these islets; (4) bringing every transport inside the lagoon to land the main assault force on Roi and Namur on D plus one day, 1 February. It was a very ambitious and extremely complicated plan, easily upset by stress of weather or minor failures in timing or execution, of which there were plenty; but it did work by virtue of quick decisions by the Admiral and commanding general, and by the energy of everyone else.

Establishing field artillery bases on islets adjacent to the main targets in order to support the principal assaults was an essential feature here, as in the South. The troops chosen for this mission to Ennumennet and Ennubirr were the three battalion landing teams of the 25th Marine Regiment[4] which, with the attached units, was commanded by Brigadier General James L. Underhill USMC and embarked in transports *Callaway*, *Sumter*, *Warren* and *Biddle*.

2. *Initial Landings in the North, 31 January*

As D-day, 31 January 1944, opened, Admiral Conolly with the initial forces and fire support group was steaming peacefully along at 12½ knots northeast of Roi. At 0130 the fire support units were

---

[4] The 1st, 2nd and 3rd BLTs were commanded by Lt. Cols. C. J. O'Connell, L. C. Hudson and J. M. Chambers respectively, and Col. S. C. Cumming commanded the regiment.

released to enter their assigned areas. By 0511 *Appalachian* with the transports carrying the 25th Regiment had arrived in the designated position about seven miles to leeward of the North Pass, five miles from the line of departure. Twenty minutes later commenced the transfer of assault troops from transports to amphtracs, which had already rolled out of the LSTs of the initial tractor group. All available LCVPs were used to effect this transfer. But there were not enough amphtracs; Landing Team 3 had to wait.

H-hour for the landing on Ennuebing and Mellu had been set for 0900, but conditions and contretemps delayed the schedule. Heavy seas retarded the double process of debarkation and transfer, a force 7 tradewind and westerly set of current prolonged the trip from transfer area to line of departure; Ennuebing and Mellu were not clearly visible until 0630.

Fire support units commenced bombardment of this whole northern bight of the atoll at 0650. Destroyer *Phelps* was to mark the line of departure; six LCI gunboats were to support the landing on Ennuebing and then enter the lagoon to support those on the other islets. Air strikes were delivered by planes from the three escort carriers in Conolly's force and from the three large carriers in Montgomery's group.[5] H-hour was postponed to 0930, but since the amphtracs were 46 minutes late leaving the line of departure it was evident that even that hour could not be kept. So *Intrepid's* planes continued strafing Ennuebing until 0942 in order to cover the first wave, which hit the beach ten minutes later. With close supporting fire from one destroyer, LCI gunboats, planes and LVTs, this initial landing team could hardly have failed to click; it was disappointing to find only 20 to 25 Japanese on Ennuebing. One company secured the islet in half an hour, and the 14th Marine Regiment promptly began siting artillery in order to support the assault on Roi next day.

[5] The baby flattops also performed anti-submarine patrol while the big ones assumed combat air patrol for this northern sector. During D-day and the next, flights of planes were launched on the hour every hour, Admiral Montgomery putting up about two thirds of them, and orbited in readiness for call strikes. These tactics proved indispensable for prompt air support in subsequent amphibious operations.

A simultaneous occupation of Mellu Islet aborted because the LVTs attempted to land on the outer coast through the surf. After one had capsized on the reef, drowning several Marines, the rest entered the pass and landed on the lagoon side at 1034. This island, too, was quickly overrun and the Marine cannoneers landed their 105-mm guns that afternoon.

At 1035, as soon as these two minor landings were completed, minesweepers, LCIs and Fire Support Units 1 and 2 steamed through North Pass and across the lagoon. They drew some fire from the shore but no mines were found and the sweep was completed in two hours. Destroyers *Porterfield* and *Haraden*, lying off Ennubirr and Ennumennet outside the lagoon, raked these islets with high explosives, augmented by carrier-based air bombardment.

Since there were insufficient amphtracs for all hands to be embarked in them initially, it seemed reasonable to use what there were more than once. The LVTs that landed troops on Ennuebing and Mellu were ordered to rendezvous in a designated area to embark other Marines for landings across the lagoon. But there was so much delay and confusion in carrying this out that the hour for the landings on Ennubirr and Ennumennet, originally noon, was postponed to 1500. Destroyer *Phelps* (in which Captain E. R. McLean, organizer and controller of the troop landings, was embarked), could not steam through the North Pass as planned, because it turned out to be much more shallow than the charts indicated. She had to take a longer route by the South Pass, and that confused the LVTs which were to follow her in; they had to be rounded up and sent through the North Pass under control of SC–997 which lacked necessary communications facilities.[6]

Finally the boat waves were formed at 1435 and started in to their afternoon objectives. *Haraden* covered the landing at Ennubirr while *Porterfield* supported that on Ennumennet. Each land-

[6] For shortcomings of LVT and LST crews, see Comtransdiv 26 (Capt. A. D. Blackledge) Action Report 18 Feb. 1944, Isley and Crowl pp. 272–73 and the Wendell monograph (see footnote 8 below). They were less well trained than those in the south, but the LVTs had a much harder assignment — rougher water, greater distances, and more continuous service required.

ing team was preceded by three LCI gunboats and 18 LVT–As, while *Porterfield* and *Haraden* made smoke off Obella Island in order to shield the boats against possible enemy fire on their southern flank. The first wave reached Ennumennet at 1512, followed three minutes later by the first on Ennubirr. Both islets were lightly defended and the Marines established beachheads quickly. Ennubirr was the site of an enemy communications center, but most of the Japanese escaped to Namur; only 34 of them were killed on the two islets. Both were secured by 1630.

As the last afternoon of January waned, the schedule was about four hours late and much remained to be done. Any delay in an operation of this nature throws the whole out of gear. Although howitzers had been preloaded at San Diego in amphtracs and LCMs, carried in LSTs for prompt landing,[7] the gunners to serve them depended on LCVPs to take them ashore. But the failure of many LVTs to show up tied up some of the LCVPs in landing assault waves, and the gunners had to wait two hours more. They had some guns ready to fire before midnight, but only by working all night could they get the necessary ammunition ashore for the preparatory fires on D plus 1 morning; and it was not until 1500 that day that all their guns were ashore.

In the high wind, Kwajalein Lagoon was unexpectedly rough. Two amphtracs turned turtle in the surf while trying to land, drowning four men and losing two 75-mm pieces.

Ennugarret, the canine tooth between the Ennumennet bicuspid and the Namur incisor, was scheduled for occupation D-day afternoon. Captain James G. Headley USMCR, a company commander of BLT 3, observing that time and tide were ripe for this movement and that very little enemy fire was coming from Ennugarret, started his men across without waiting for confirmation. Appropriating three landing craft and a few LVT–As, he ferried his company over the half-mile gap, some on top of the amphtracs. Lieutenant Colonel Justin Chambers USMCR, the landing team com-

---

[7] Each of the three 75-mm battalions was preloaded in 15 LVTs, and the battalion of 105-mms in 13 LCMs.

mander, approving Headley's initiative and observing his success, took the rest of the battalion over the same way.

Thus, at the cost of great agony of mind and to the accompaniment of more profanity than this quiet lagoon had ever heard in its entire history, every foul-up was finally straightened out and every D-day objective was attained shortly after nightfall. North Pass was safe for the passage of ships; Roi and Namur were flanked on both sides; artillery was established ashore. Casualties for 31 January in the 25th RCT, which bore the burden of the day's operations, amounted to only 24 dead and missing and 40 wounded.

3. *Roi and Namur, 31 January–2 February* [8]

Although the Northern Task Force devoted the greater part of its energy on D-day to securing the five flanking islets, Roi and Namur were the real objectives. These two islands, joined by a narrow sandspit and artificial causeway, may be considered as one, for as such they were used by both the Japanese and the Americans.

Kelly Turner was right when he predicted that Roi-Namur would be a tougher nut to crack than Betio. Of even smaller extent, it was more heavily defended with fixed emplacements and had a bigger garrison in proportion. The comparative ease of the assault was due almost entirely to the length and strength of the preliminary bombardment, and to the application of other lessons learned at Tarawa.

When the last week of January began the Japanese had plenty of wherewithal to defend themselves on Roi and Namur: six mobile artillery positions, eight or nine blockhouses, about 65 pillboxes

[8] Admiral Turner's Report on Operation "Flintlock," 25 Feb. 1944; CTF 53 (Rear Admiral Conolly) "Report on Capture of Roi and Namur" 23 Feb. 1944; General Schmidt USMC "Final Report on Marshalls Operation" 17 Mar. 1944; Isley and Crowl *U.S. Marines in Amphibious War* (1951) chap. vii; "The Marshall Islands Operation Prepared by Historical Division U.S. Marine Corps," by Maj. W. G. Wendell USMCR.

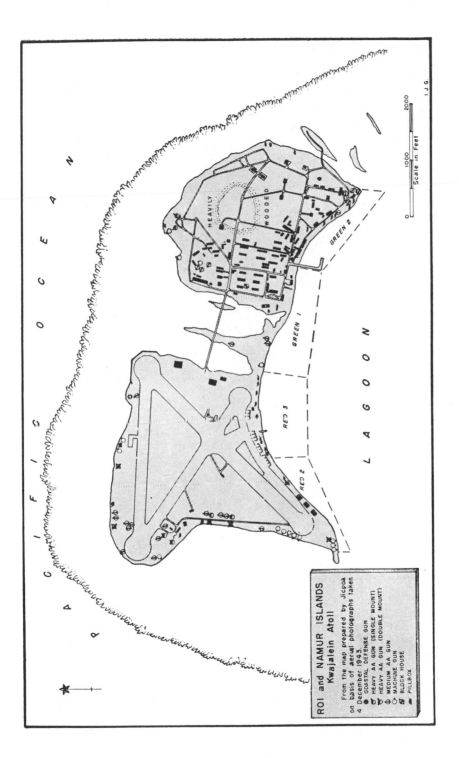

PACIFIC OCEAN

HEAVILY WOODED

GREEN 2
GREEN 1
RED 3
RED 2

LAGOON

Scale in Feet
0   1000   2000

I.J.G.

ROI and NAMUR ISLANDS
Kwajalein Atoll

From the map prepared by Jicpoa
on basis of aerial photographs taken
4 December 1943.

COASTAL DEFENSE GUN
HEAVY AA GUN (SINGLE MOUNT)
HEAVY AA GUN (DOUBLE MOUNT)
MEDIUM AA GUN
MACHINE GUN
BLOCK HOUSE
PILLBOX

and some 200 buildings including two large hangars. But Rear Admiral Montgomery's carrier group, which began bombing and bombarding the islands at daybreak 29 January, destroyed every one of the 83 Japanese planes based on Roi. Consequently this whole operation went through without one single strike by enemy air power. Admiral Reeves's *Enterprise* group joined Montgomery's on the 30th and 31st; Fire Support Units 1 and 2 joined also. Most of the bombs and shells were placed on Namur, because Roi was largely covered by the airfield which the Americans wished to use.

Three days' bombing and bombardment were not enough to pulverize the Roi-Namur rectangle, roughly 2300 yards long and 900 wide. Much of the larger and some of the smaller ordnance had withstood it. The most powerful survivors, five circular concrete pillboxes of German model with four-foot walls, steel embrasure-closure plates and slotted steel observation turrets, were (fortunately for the Marines) sited to meet assault only from the sea, and most of the other defenses had been designed to repel air attack.[9]

On 31 January the 23rd and 24th RCTs of the 4th Marine Division transferred from transports five miles out into LSTs, which cruised off shore during the night, while destroyers *Porterfield*, *Hopewell* and *Ellet* and six LCI gunboats delivered intermittent fire on Roi and Namur and threw up star shell to disclose enemy movements. It is difficult to see how the defenders could have slept a wink for three nights before the landings. And, in contrast to the "tough hombres" the Marines had encountered at Tarawa, the defenders of Roi and Namur were pretty well "pooped out" before any troops landed.

At 0100 February 1, the three destroyers commenced rapid fire on Roi and Namur for a period of three minutes, to cover a bold reconnaissance of the landing beaches then being undertaken in rubber boats by a naval raider unit brought up for that purpose in

---

[9] Col. C. H. M. Roberts USA "Marshall Islands Japanese Defenses and Battle Damage," comments on amphibious operations prepared for the Commanding General Central Pacific Area, 1 Mar. 1944.

APD *Schley*. The raiders reported that landings were practicable on Roi and Namur at any point of the lagoon-side beaches.

Bombardment ceased an hour before dawn and the fire support units moved into their regularly assigned areas. At 0645 bombardment was renewed. Unit 2 (DuBose's cruisers) moved to within 1900 yards of the outer shoreline of Roi, and destroyed some more strong points. Unit 1 (Kingman's battleships), on the eastern side of Namur, closed the range to about 3500 yards but failed to destroy the concrete structures on Namur.[10] Nevertheless, say the Marine Corps historians, "Naval gunfire and air support . . . met the most sanguine expectations, enabling the troops to go ashore standing up." As in the Gilberts, it was proved that naval bombardment, to be effective on definite objects, must be delivered at very short range. Before World War II it had been assumed that battleships would stand about ten miles off shore to deliver a bombardment instead of closing almost until they could "see the whites of their eyes," as in days of sail. The risk of so close a range could not have been accepted without the Navy's having indisputably gained command of the surrounding waters and air.

At Roi-Namur, if the results were not perfect, a vast amount of damage was done and a large proportion of the 3700 defenders were killed. The Marines were so impressed with the results, especially with the sight of battleships bombarding less than a mile off shore, that they nicknamed the Admiral "Close-in Conolly." About 6000 tons of explosives, including aviation bombs but not counting 75-mm projectiles and smaller shells such as rockets, were hurled at Roi and Namur before the assault began, as compared with 2400 tons at Betio. Even "Howling Mad" Smith loved the Navy after this assault — for a few days.[11]

The four Marine artillery battalions, as we have seen, had been laboring all night to get enough pieces and projectiles ashore on the three little islets to permit them to take part in the pounding. Their

[10] CTF 53 Report, Enclosure B.
[11] Isley and Crowl p. 278; H. M. Smith *Coral and Brass* pp. 121, 145. But, adds the General, the Navy never did so well by her amphibious forces again.

guns were registered on targets at dawn. Preparatory fires concentrated on the beach for about three hours before the landing, then shifted inland and continued until they began to endanger the rapidly advancing assault troops. These guns fired over 5000 rounds of 75-mm and 105-mm ammunition on Namur and Roi.

The 23rd and 24th RCTs, already transferred to LSTs the previous afternoon, were now supposed to effect the landing in the LVTs used the previous day. That sounds simple enough, but the amphtrac crews were so wearied and confused by D-day activities that many fell down on the job. Each LVT was supposed to go on board its mother LST for the night to fuel, make necessary repairs and load the Marines. LSDs *Epping Forest* and *Gunston Hall* were also on hand to gas them. But some could not find their way back to the LSTs in the dark. Others ran out of gas and stranded on various islets, and many of their crews were completely exhausted. There had been a heavy chop in the lagoon, everyone was soaked through, and when darkness fell the men became chilled. As some of the amphtracs were groping their way to the LSTs, they hailed *Phelps* and begged to come on board for coffee, food and dry clothes. This could not be denied; the destroyer was warm and comfortable, the sailors were eager for scuttlebutt, and the amphtrac drivers needed little urging to spend the night. At one time there were 12 LVTs tied up astern of *Phelps*, and there they remained until she weighed early next morning to move to the line of departure.

Admiral Conolly decided to send the LSTs inside the lagoon where they might launch amphtracs in slightly more sheltered water. This was not according to plan and some of the LSTs did not know what was expected of them. Owing to the failure of the 24th RCT's amphtracs to turn up, part of the reserve companies which had already embarked in LCVPs had to be used in the first assault wave for Namur. The general reaction of the Marines on whom this honor unexpectedly fell was expressed by shouts of laughter and cries of "Jeez! Whaddya know?" [12]

[12] Report of RN observer, Cdr. Harry Hopkins, p. 10.

Reveille had been sounded in the LSTs carrying the Marines at 0130, and the troops were supposed to land on Roi and Namur at 1000; but at 0900 the LSTs carrying the 23rd RCT were 5½ miles distant from the beach and those of the 24th RCT were 4 miles distant, while the line of departure itself was approximately 5000 yards from the shore. It was still very rough in the lagoon. By 1100, the postponed H-hour, the waves of the 23rd RCT were fairly well lined up, but those of the 24th were not. General Schmidt now ordered the control officer (Captain E. R. McLean) in *Phelps* to launch the attack as soon as possible. He did so at 1108 before the waves were really lined up; for, as the General pointed out, over 500 landing craft were milling about inside the lagoon, and nobody could tell which were ready and which were not.

To investigate beaches Red on Roi and Green on Namur at first light, Lieutenant Commander John T. Koehler USNR [13] had brought up the first of the Navy's underwater demolition teams (the famous UDTs). The drone boats that they used refused to obey remote control and ran amok, one beaching itself and the other almost ramming the control boat, but the swimmers managed to get back somehow. They reported the beaches to be good ones with no reefs to hold up landing craft; LVTs were really not necessary. A long pier stuck out from Namur, surmounted by a power-driven crane which, to the disgust of the landing force, was ruined by a destroyer with her very last salvo.

In spite of the confusion around the line of departure, the boat waves of the 23rd RCT for Roi pulled themselves together and made a fairly orderly landing. The first wave, starting in at 1111, consisted of 18 LVT–A1s, accompanied by LCI gunboats equipped with rockets; the next five waves had an average of 9 troop-carrying LVTs each. *Phelps* hove-to on a median line about two miles out as guide, while destroyers *LaVallette* and *Johnston* delivered support fire on the west point of Roi, where coast defense and anti-aircraft guns had been spotted, and on "Sally Point," the south-

[13] Appointed Assistant Secretary of the Navy 15 Feb. 1949.

eastern promontory of Namur. The day before, carrier planes had made six sorties on these positions with 2000-pound bombs, but many Japanese were still very much alive there.

During the run to the beaches a heavy rain squall made up, drowning out the amphtracs' radios. At 1145 the LVT–A1s opened fire on the Roi shore. A minute later, the personnel amphtracs were seen passing through the LCI gunboats 1000 yards from the beach. At 1150 the air observer dropped parachute flares to indicate that the initial wave was 500 yards outside the beach. Every ship and craft except those in the wave itself ceased fire, and for a few minutes one heard only the drone of motors as a background to the unfamiliar *whoosh* of the gunboats' rockets and the familiar *whoomp* of tank guns. At 1157 the first wave landed Marines of the 23rd RCT on the Red beaches at Roi, and about three minutes later the initial echelon of the 24th hit the Green beaches on Namur.

Very rapid and vigorous was the action on Roi. The island appeared to be completely deserted and utterly devastated, and the first defenders encountered acted punch-drunk. But about 300 resolute Japanese had survived the terrific bombardment and were hidden in wrecked blockhouses and piles of rubble, mostly along the oceanside. The Marines advanced to the O–1 line (the line designated as the objective at the end of D-day) only 20 minutes after stepping ashore; their medium tanks exceeded orders and penetrated to the north coast; but they were ordered back to the O–1 line until that position had been consolidated.

By 1311 the 1st and 2nd Battalions [14] of the 23rd Regiment were in full force on the O–1 line on Roi, and a regimental command post had been set up on the beach. Between 1530 and 1600 the attack was resumed, so successfully that the north coast was reached promptly, and Colonel L. R. Jones sent a company of riflemen and some medium tanks to Namur, where the going was much tougher. The 23rd RCT then concentrated on mopping up around Roi airfield. Japanese who had taken cover in drainage ditches adjacent to

---

[14] Commanded by Lt. Cols. H. O. Hammond and E. J. Dillon respectively.

View in the direction of Roi

Marines displaying souvenirs

After the Battle, Roi-Namur

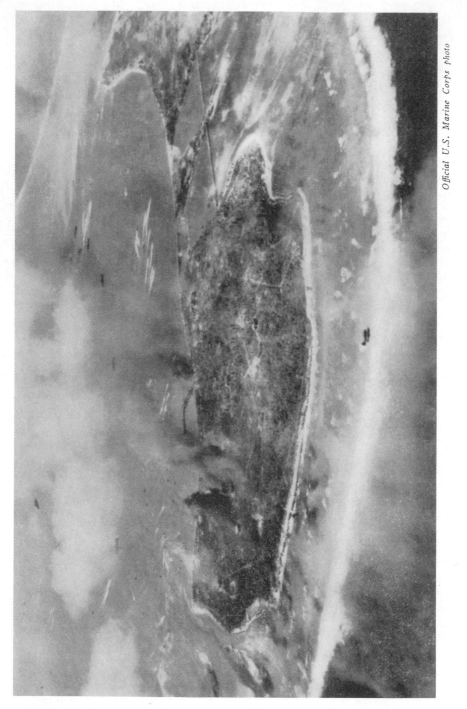

Aerial View of the Landings on Roi-Namur

runways fired upward from the ditches and had to be blown out with bangalore torpedoes or satchel charges.

Thus, enemy opposition at Roi was light, and so were the American casualties; but, as one Marine observed, "It was no walk in the park." By 1735 Roi was secured and equipment was already being landed to repair the Japanese airfield. All that remained to be done as the day closed was to wipe out a small sector of resistance on the north coast and finish mopping up.

Over on Namur the assault of the 24th RCT, Colonel Franklin A. Hart USMC commanding, was ragged. Only 62 of the 110 LVTs assigned to the troop lift could be located, and it was necessary to use some of the reserve companies already boated in LCVPs. Around the line of departure the scene was one of utter confusion. Under normal circumstances, this assault would have been delayed until things straightened out; but Admiral Conolly and General Schmidt, remembering how the enemy had profited by a half-hour delay at Betio, decided to send the Marines in just as they were; most of them had been boated for hours and were mad to go in and have it over. When the control officer in *Phelps,* under the Admiral's orders, signaled the first wave to leave the line of departure at 1111, the 3rd BLT started right in. The other assault BLT, the 2nd, not completely assembled, followed as best it could. To add to this confusion, two companies of LVT–A1s, which had been ordered to precede the assault waves up to 100 yards inland, halted for some undetermined reason before reaching the beach, getting in the way of succeeding waves. Elements of the 24th had to be committed piecemeal as LVTs and LCVPs became available, and units became woefully mixed up. But the enemy derived no benefit from the disorderly nature of this assault and offered no resistance at the water's edge.

An anti-tank ditch extending behind the beach prevented the amphtracs from proceeding inland as at Roi, so the Marines debarked at the water's edge. Only light resistance developed as they pushed rapidly ahead on foot. Rockets from LCI gunboats, which on D-day had fallen short, hit their objectives on 1 February and their violent explosions had a most detrimental effect on the enemy. Within a quarter of an hour the 24th Marines had pushed 200 yards inland, except on the extreme right where "Sally Point" was fiercely resisting. Suddenly, about 1245, the crackle of rifle fire and the rat-tat-tat of machine guns were drowned by a tremendous explosion. Fragments of concrete, steel, wood, shrapnel and even torpedo warheads rained over the surrounding area, killing about 20 Marines and wounding many more. A carrier plane overhead, containing the Marine Corps air observer, Major Charles Duchein, was hoisted about a thousand feet in the air. "Great God Almighty! The whole damn island has blown up!" radioed the Major.[15] A blockhouse filled with torpedoes and heavy ammunition had exploded, whether by American gunfire or by Marines placing satchel charges against the structure, or as a suicide stunt by Japanese inside, will never be known. Two other less violent explosions occurred on Namur within the next half-hour, and these three accounted for over half the casualties suffered by the 2nd Battalion.

The only big fight on either island developed during the attack north of the Namur O–1 line, launched at 1630. The 3rd Battalion on the left jumped off on time, supported by Captain Denig's five light tanks. Owing to the great amount of debris and large number of strong points, the Japanese were able to bring heavy rifle, machine-gun and grenade fire to bear. Light tanks swept across the island in close coördination with the troops, charging through dense undergrowth and fallen timber, shooting at prepared positions. When command tank "Hunter" paused to reconnoiter, she was stealthily boarded by a Japanese from a nearby foxhole. He blasted the interior with a hand grenade, killing the gunner and mortally wounding Captain Denig.[16]

At 1820 Colonel Hart ordered his men to make every effort to secure the north shore of Namur before dark. Medium tanks from Roi arrived by 1830, and shortly afterward attacked along the

[15] Morris Markey in Baltimore *Evening Sun* 10 Feb. 1944.
[16] There is a good illustrated story of this episode by Don Wharton (drawings by T/Sgt. Wexler) in *Look* 19 Sept. 1944. It is based on a story by Sgt. C. R. Vandergrift USMC, a combat correspondent who was there.

perimeter of their sector, preceded by a half-track carrying a 75-mm gun. By 1930 when darkness closed in, the 2nd and 3rd Battalions were about 175 yards north of the O–1 line. Colonel Hart then ordered his men to establish perimeter defense, hold the ground gained and prepare to resume attack in the morning.

During the night of 1–2 February the most serious danger was unnecessary firing by units near the beach, which exposed them to infiltrating Japanese and endangered the Marines holding the front. Green troops almost always do that, and there is nothing one can say that will stop them. Afloat, the night was peaceful enough. Three transport divisions, the LSTs of the Reserve Tractor Group, and Admiral Conolly's flagship *Appalachian* had entered the lagoon during the afternoon and were lying at anchor by 1630. Fire support ships and the three escort carriers and their screens patrolled outside.

During the darkness small groups of Japanese, some without weapons, infiltrated. Shortly after 0700 February 2, they executed a series of small banzai charges for about half an hour, by the end of which they were liquidated. At 0900 the 3rd Battalion resumed its forward movement with three companies attacking, supported by medium tanks. They quickly overran the remainder of their sector and by noon, 2 February, were resting on the ocean shore of Namur.

In the right sector elements of the 1st Battalion mixed with the 2nd, under command of Lieutenant Colonel Aquilla J. Dyess USMC, made an encircling attack assisted by light tanks and half-tracks, which followed the beachline, destroying pillboxes and other installations which were still intact. Dyess led the troops in person, with the utmost intrepidity; while standing on the parapet of an anti-tank ditch directing an attack against the last enemy position he was killed by a burst of machine-gun fire. At noon, the troops, assisted by the half-tracks, reached the northern shore of their sector, subduing the last organized resistance on Namur.

General Schmidt announced at 1418 February 2 that Namur was secured. He had already set up his command post in a Japanese pillbox and the American flag was promptly run up on an improvised flagpole.

Considering that the 4th Marine Division was untried in combat and that the training it had received at San Diego fell short of what was required for a major amphibious operation, it deserves high credit for performing a very difficult and complicated mission in so short a time as 26½ hours. The 4th could now stand up to the 2nd Division, the victors of Tarawa, and say, "We showed we could take it too," to which the obvious and not unfair retort was, "Yeah, we showed you guys how, the hard way; but look at what the Navy gave before you hit the beach — if we'd had half of that, some of our buddies would now be alive." Admiral "Close-in" Conolly had more than justified high expectations, by his ability to cope with exceptional and unexpected difficulties, and General Schmidt had earned a niche in the Marine Corps hall of fame.

Namur was a stinking mess of debris and dead Japanese. Hardly a tree was left alive in what had been a pretty wooded island, and of the hundred or more buildings not one was usable. Roi's appearance was somewhat less repulsive, because so large a part of its surface was taken up by runways; but here too the coconut palms and pandanus that had successfully concealed Japanese planes from carrier raiders were down or stripped of their fronds. A dismal prospect met the garrison group (16th Marine Defense Battalion and Seabees) when it steamed into the lagoon a few days later to relieve the 4th Division. But in two weeks' time the debris was cleared away, bomb craters were filled, Quonset huts were set up, and a row of homemade windmill washing machines merrily clacking on the windward beaches announced that the Marines had come to stay. Planes of Rear Admiral Hoover's land-based air force, flown up from the Gilberts, were already using the Roi airdrome — whence, only two months earlier, aircraft of the Imperial Japanese Air Force had taken off to attack Admiral Pownall's carriers.

4. *The Southern Attack Force* [17]

Admiral Turner's Southern Attack Force, whose mission was to capture Kwajalein Island and the southern islets, matched Admiral Conolly's Northern Attack Force in composition and strength. Turner's ground troops, however, were of the Army, the 7th Infantry Division which had captured Attu and occupied Kiska. From that chilly outpost it had been withdrawn to Oahu in mid-September 1943 for rehabilitation and new equipment. Only late in December did its new commanding general, Charles H. Corlett, know that the 7th would be employed against Kwajalein. "This appeared to be a special operation radically different from anything for which the Division had previously been trained," he wrote. After studying Turner's operation plan and digesting the fact that it called for the capture of 27 islets, 12 of which would probably be defended by the enemy, he realized that the 7th was in for "a campaign rather than a strike against a single island."

It certainly was! General Corlett visited Tarawa shortly after its capture to study the Japanese defenses, and relayed his knowledge to every officer under his command. On the Ewa plain of Oahu, "islands" were taped out corresponding to those to be captured, mock-up pillboxes and other Japanese types of defenses were constructed and the troops practised attacking them with mortars, tanks, flame throwers and supporting artillery. Every such "attack" was thoroughly analyzed and discussed; noncoms and GIs learned

[17] Maj. Gen. Corlett's Report to the Adjutant General of the 7th Division's Participation in Marshalls Operation, 8 Feb. 1944, a very detailed report in 14 vols. or sections, examined by Lt. Salomon at HQ shortly after the operation; Com V 'Phib (Admiral Turner) Report of "Flintlock" Operation, 25 Feb. 1944, and War Diary; articles on land phases by Lt. Col. S. L. A. Marshall USA in *Infantry Journal* LV and LVI (1944–1945) which were later collected in a "Penguin" book, *Island Victory*. We are indebted to Brig. Gen. Archibald V. Arnold USA and officers of his staff for reading and checking the first draft of this account. Gen. Arnold relieved Gen. Corlett as Commanding General 7th Division when it returned to Oahu after the operation, Gen. Corlett going to England to take part in the invasion of Europe.

what they were expected to do, and their interest and enthusiasm were gratifying.

Since the amphibious truck (dukw) and the amphtrac (LVT) were to play an important part, dukw and amphtrac schools were set up at Waianae and Makua, and each battalion landing team had three full days of amphibious exercises on the kind of craft they were to use. The divisional artillery, 105-mm and 155-mm howitzers, trained in dukws and LCMs respectively. Communications schools were established, men trained and equipment readied for Operation "Flintlock." The reconnaissance troop, formerly a cavalry outfit, trained for six days in destroyer transports, and an underwater demolition team, similar to Lieutenant Commander Koehler's UDT at Roi, practised with the tricky drone boats.

Between 12 and 17 January, the Division participated with the 22nd Marine Regiment in a final rehearsal at Maui and Kahoolawe. By the time that the Southern Attack Force sailed from Pearl, the 7th Division was in top form, mentally and materially. It had enjoyed the most intensive training in amphibious warfare of any unit, whether Army or Marine, in the Pacific up to that date.

The two tractor units of the Southern Attack Force departed Pearl 19 January in LSTs; the main part followed three days later, steaming 35 miles ahead of Conolly's Northern Force. Admiral Turner followed his usual practice of exercising every ship in tracking drill and gunnery, emergency day and night maneuvers against simulated submarine and air attack, and battle deployment. Aircraft from escort carriers maintained daylight combat air patrol.

The plan of attack on the southern islands of Kwajalein Atoll was similar to that employed in the north. On D-day, 31 January, Ninni and Gea Islets about 10 miles northwest of Kwajalein Island were to be occupied in order to secure Gea Pass, main entrance to the lagoon, as well as two other islets, Ennylabegan and Enubuj.

5. *Initial Landings in the South,*
31 January–2 February

The general layout of this southern bight of Kwajalein is similar to that of the northern one, reversed. If a chart of the northern part resembles a dentist's diagram of the upper jaw, the southern bend may be compared with an elongated lower jaw. Kwajalein

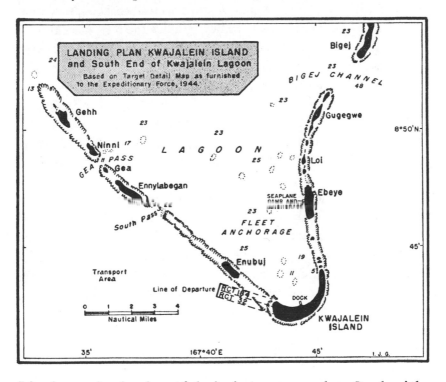

Island occupies the place of the incisors, run together. On the right, after two tiny canines, one comes to a good-sized bicuspid, Ebeye Islet, which was the enemy seaplane base. Next comes a row of molars, of which one, Gugegwe, was well defended; then a gap in the gums, Bigej Channel, on the north side of which is the wisdom tooth, Bigej Islet. On the left of Kwajalein Island the teeth are very irregular. Enubuj will do for a bicuspid, Gea for a molar. Then comes South Pass with two wisdom teeth, Ninni and Gehh, on the other side.

At 2300 January 30, destroyer transports *Overton* and *Manley*, carrying the 7th Division Reconnaissance Troop (Captain Paul B. Gritta USA), steamed ahead and with some difficulty located Gea Pass. At 0341 D-day (31 January) *Overton* commenced lowering rubber landing craft with outboard motors into the rough sea. These, directed with the aid of ship's radar, were to tow rubber boats, in which the horseless cavalrymen were embarked, to within half a mile of Gea and Ninni beaches, whence the men were to row ashore. This was a tough assignment, for the tradewind blew fresh that night, the sea was rough for rubber boats, the moon set early and a current around the passes added to their difficulties. They could never have done it but for the fine amphibious training that men and boat crews had had at Oahu. These troops landed on Gea at break of day, and after a short but spirited fight took the islet at the cost of one killed and one wounded; 22 Japanese were killed and four were taken prisoner.

In the meantime the platoons destined for Ninni had landed on the wrong islet, Gehh, at 0545. This turned out to be a stroke of good luck from the intelligence standpoint, but it then looked like a very bad break. On Gehh were about 125 armed Japanese who had come ashore from a beached tug or patrol vessel. After Captain Gritta's men had killed a few of them, he was ordered by division headquarters to shift over to the right islet, Ninni, to secure the pass. Since all but one of the rubber boats had been punctured on the reef, the transfer took some time; but there were no Japanese on Ninni.

Next day, 1 February, when the troopers were being relieved by an infantry company, the enemy opened fire from Gehh. So a platoon went right over and secured a beachhead. That evening, destroyer *Overton* took Gehh under fire and at 0900 February 2 the rest of the dismounted troopers returned there. This time they knew where they were and what they wanted. "A furious, close-in fight developed. Our machine guns laid down a continuous automatic fire and riflemen and submachine gunners dueled with individual Japanese riflemen. The Japanese machine gun was knocked out with grenades. Dead Japs were actually stacked behind their one machine gun." The final score was 125 dead Japanese at a cost of three troopers killed and 21 wounded.[18]

Now came the intelligence pay-off. The beached vessel from which these doomed Japanese had come ashore was examined and about 75 secret charts of Japanese-held lagoons and harbors were discovered in her chartroom. The value of these for the conquest of Micronesia, and even for later operations, was immense. Advanced units of the Hydrographic Office reproduced the Japanese charts and sent copies to every ship engaged in amphibious operations.

We return to 31 January to find the transports arriving in their area southwest of Kwajalein Island at 0545, before dawn. *Zeilin, Ormsby, Windsor, President Polk, Virgo* and *Ashland* proceeded to the troop transfer area, which extended from five to twelve miles west of Gea Pass. Here they were to meet the LSTs, which, together with LSD *Ashland*, boated the amphtracs in which RCT 17 of the 7th Division was to land on Ennylabegan and Enubuj.

The 1st and 2nd BLTs of the 17th RCT, transferred to four LSTs, went below and climbed into the amphtracs, 17 of which were carried in each LST. These left the transport area at 0810 and moved up to tractor rendezvous off the lines of departure for the two islets, opened bow gates and let the LVTs roll out.

The previous day, battleship *Washington* had pounded Enubuj and Ennylabegan with forty 16-inch high explosive shells and an assortment of 5-inch stuff. Commencing at 0810 D-day, cruiser *New Orleans* threw 141 eight-inch shells into Enubuj. Destroyers *McKee* and *Stevens* rendered close-in fire support for the landing on Enubuj, while *Ringgold* and *Sigsbee* performed a similar service for the troops landing on Ennylabegan. The destroyers continued to fire until H-hour, 0910, dropping over 2000 rounds of 5-inch ammunition on their objectives. Moreover, 51 escort carrier planes

[18] *Overton* Action Report and conversations with Capt. Gritta.

dropped 21 tons of bombs as well as rocket projectiles and expended 50,000 rounds of ammunition of .50 caliber in strafing. It is little wonder that when RCT 17 hit the beach between 0911 and 0917, it was unopposed. By 1050 all eight waves, boating the two BLTs, were ashore.

Ennylabegan, a mile and a half long with an average width of 200 yards, was covered with dense vegetation which had been torn apart by the bombardment. A reef extending only 200 yards and covered by three feet of water, offered no obstacle to the amphtracs. There were no defense installations and only a handful of Japanese who put up light rifle and automatic weapon fire. The islet was secured at 1300 without a single American casualty. The 3rd Battalion then landed and an overhaul base for LVTs and dukws was promptly established.

Action on Enubuj, the canine tooth next to Kwajalein Island, was even more rapid, for the troops had only 1500 yards to march before reaching the other end of the islet. Destroyer *Sigsbee* stood by to render call fire, but none was called for. After very light resistance and the taking of about 20 prisoners at a cost of one man wounded, the islet was secured at noon. Enubuj was immediately put to good use by the divisional artillery commanded by Brigadier General Archibald V. Arnold USA. At 1250 the 105-mm pieces began rolling ashore in dukws out of LSTs and by 1800 all 48 guns were registered [19] on Kwajalein. To make sure that the enemy would really feel the bite of artillery, the landing of the larger guns in LCMs began at 1540 and continued all night. By 0800 next morning, 1 February, all twelve 155-mm guns, in addition to the 105s, were registered on Kwajalein Island.[20] At 1700 January 31 General Corlett and staff left the crowded command ship *Rocky Mount* and set up headquarters on Enubuj, but the

[19] To register artillery is to set it up and then fire tracer shots at one's objective until one has the correct range. In this case, Ebeye was divided into squares with certain guns allocated to certain squares. As the guns fired their tracers, a spotting plane would aid them until they got the range.
[20] The 155-mms were carried in the holds of *Virgo* and *President Polk*, and had to be transferred to LCMs for landing.

corps commander, Major General H. M. Smith USMC, remained afloat. It is said that General Corlett threatened to put him under arrest if he came ashore and interfered!

So far everything had gone "according to plan," a rare occurrence in amphibious operations. Ninni, Gea, Ennylabegan and Enubuj were secured; Gea Pass was under American control and both field and heavy artillery were in position to support the major landings on Kwajalein. The channel and part of the lagoon had been swept by the minecraft, who found no mines but obtained information on suitable anchorages. Consequently the transports from which RCT 17 had landed were ordered inside the lagoon to unload cargo in sheltered waters.

The night of 31 January–1 February passed uneventfully except for ineffective Japanese artillery fire from Kwajalein and Ebeye. *New Mexico* and *Murray* stood on and off during the night to add intermittent fire to that of the shore-based artillery, while destroyer *Hall* harassed Ebeye Islet, which was known to contain several hundred enemy troops. The remaining ships of Admiral Turner's task force put out to sea.

6. *The Assault on Kwajalein Island, 1–6 February*

Before time had marched on to H-hour, the defenders of Kwajalein had begun to feel the cutting edge of the American war machine, plied by the irresistible team of Turner and Corlett. The Admiral, who had been first to admit that Tarawa had not been bombarded long enough or well enough, was determined that Kwajalein should be properly pulverized. To execute this worthy object, he used the five fire support units of his task force, three escort carriers, and Rear Admiral Reeves's carrier group comprising *Enterprise*, *Yorktown*, *Belleau Wood*, three new battleships, one anti-aircraft light cruiser and nine destroyers. Yet carrier planes played a relatively small part in the destruction of Kwajalein, flying only 102 sorties over the island and lagoon on D-day. For Admiral

Turner, because of heavy rains that day, canceled all remaining bombing missions at 1300 and assigned the main task of pounding down the island to naval gunfire. The proper rôle for planes, he believed, was to render the air safe over ships, and to deliver call fire as required. One had to wait for Saipan to see full use of carrier plane bombardment in an amphibious operation.

Bombardment of Kwajalein Island commenced 30 January when battleships *Massachusetts, Indiana* and *Washington* fired about 1000 rounds of 16-inch ammunition. *Pennsylvania* and *Mississippi* took over at 0618 January 31. During the rest of the day these two old battleships, together with *New Mexico* and *Idaho* and heavy cruisers *Minneapolis, San Francisco* and *New Orleans,* intermittently bombarded Kwajalein, with occasional attention to Ebeye, delivering on the bigger island approximately 1340 rounds of 14-inch ammunition, 400 rounds of 8-inch and 5000 rounds of 5-inch.[21] They also located two small cargo ships, an oiler and various small craft in the lagoon and sank them all.

Regimental Combat Teams 184 and 32, three battalions in each, were transferred by landing craft from transports to LSTs during the afternoon of 31 January.[22] These troops found themselves in front-row seats for the bombardment, which they watched with keen interest, knowing that each hit would make their job easier. They bedded down early on the decks of the LSTs.

In the meantime beach reconnaissance parties, consisting of specially selected soldiers and sailors boated in LCVPs and LVTs, examined the reefs and approaches to Beach Red 1 and Beach Red 2, on the western end of Kwajalein Island, at high and low water. They reported surf and reef conditions satisfactory, no underwater obstacles and no evidence of mines.

Kwajalein Island,[23] only 2½ miles long, is shaped like an old-fashioned hunting horn; or, to use a simile more appropriate to the

[21] Turner Report, Enclosure E.
[22] Except two reserve battalions, boated in LCVPs.
[23] Called Dove I. on some of the older charts, a name given by Capt. Moore of the missionary brig *Morning Star* in 1857.

Pacific, an Australian boomerang with one end pointing north and the other to the west. The two Red beaches chosen for the landing were on the square-cut western end, which is about 800 yards wide. Any reader who has followed American armed forces through Micronesia may wonder why a landing on a short beach at the extreme western end of a narrow island, tactics which had been adjudged wrong for Tarawa, were considered right for Kwajalein. But Kwajalein Island is so deeply embayed on the lagoon side that any force landing there would have been exposed to a murderous crossfire from the two ends of the boomerang; much worse than on Beach Red 1 at Betio. Besides, in an end-on attack, beaches and successive defense lines could be plastered by gunfire from ships both outside and inside the lagoon, and, in this case, from the field artillery on Enubuj.

Long before daylight 1 February, reveille sounded on the transports and LSTs, and breakfast was eaten before dawn. The troops were dressed in green coveralls; those of the assault waves in the LSTs blackened their faces to add to the camouflage and attached black-and-white squares to their backs for identification.

By 0558, transports were in their designated area about 7500 yards west of the beaches. Five minutes later, Admiral Turner signaled to Captain Knowles, Commander Southern Transport Group, "Land the landing force and take charge!" Captain Knowles immediately signaled "Boats away!" and in every ship the boatswain's mates piped and bawled out that classic order, which has started every amphibious assault since the days of Julius Caesar. As the assault troops filed below and got into the amphtracs, and the LSTs maneuvered into position to discharge them, and the troops in the big transports clambered down rope nets into landing craft, naval bombardment recommenced. Battleships *Mississippi* and *Pennsylvania* opened fire at 0618. It was still dark; and as the first salvo thundered out, a sailor topside yelled in the direction of the shore, "Reveille, you sons of bitches!"

This bombardment was delivered against guns, obstacles and defenses behind Red beaches 1 and 2 and at a constantly closing range, down to 1800 yards.[24] It continued until 0745, when *Mississippi* shifted her attention to Ebeye Islet while *Pennsylvania*, *New Mexico* and three heavy cruisers concentrated on Kwajalein. At the same time *Ringgold* and *Sigsbee* entered the lagoon to support the landings from the north. An hour before the landing, five heavy bombers which had flown all the way from Mullinnix Field, Tarawa, dropped 2000-pounders on the beach area, which was "what the doctor ordered" for Betio but didn't then get. All surface fire ceased at 0840 to prevent interference with another air strike undertaken by 18 SBDs and 15 torpedo-bombers from the carriers. These were followed by strafing Hellcats. As soon as that strike was over at 0905, the two battleships, a cruiser and three destroyers, now joined by *Idaho*, resumed fire on Kwajalein and continued until H-hour, 0930. Fire was then shifted to targets ahead of the advancing troops.

So much for air and naval bombardment; but the 7th Division artillery on Enubuj got into it, too. The plan called for 161 tons of high explosives from 105- and 155-mm howitzers to be thrown on the two Red beaches, 600 yards long and 250 yards deep, in an hour's time. But, owing to difficulties in unloading the 155-mm ammunition, fire with that caliber did not start until 0920; and the weight of metal delivered by H-hour was much less than planned.

There was neither confusion nor delay in this landing, no needless bouncing about of troops in small boats for hours, no shots falling short in the water, no (well, hardly any) bellowing of angry orders to laggard landing craft. At 0900 the swirl of boats around the line of departure 5000 yards from the beaches reminded Captain Knowles of "traffic on Broadway at rush hour"; but everyone knew his place and every amphtrac was in position and ready to go at 0900 when the Blue Peter was hauled down on the control

[24] CTG 52.8 (Rear Adm. R. C. Giffen) Action Report 22 Feb. 1944. Apparently it was respecting this mission that the following conversation was overheard by an Army officer on the flagship bridge, after Admiral Turner had given orders for the fire support ships to close the range. C.O. of *Pennsylvania*: "I can't take my ship in that close." Turner: "What's your armor for? Get in there!"

craft. Each flank of the first wave, composed of 8 LVT–2s and 8 amphibious tanks for each of the two beaches, was marked by a landing craft control boat which moved into the beach with it, while *SC–1066* and *SC–539* stood by as control vessels on the line, flagging the successive waves off at four-minute intervals. Two hundred yards ahead of the amphtracs three LCI gunboats steamed abreast, for close support fire. At 0917 they opened with 40-mm guns, and four minutes later let off rocket salvos. As soon as the first wave of amphtracs was 200 yards from the beach, the Elsie Items obliqued to the flanks and for a few minutes stood by for call fire.[25] At the same time two destroyers were firing on Red 2 from outside the atoll and two others on Red 1 from inside the lagoon.

A well-executed amphibious assault is as beautiful a military spectacle as one can find in modern warfare, and this one was superbly executed in the glorious setting of deep blue white-capped sea, fluffy tradewind clouds, flashing gunfire and billowing smoke over the target, gaily colored flag hoists at the yardarms of the ships and on the signal halyards of the control craft. One thought of the thundering hoofs and gleaming sabers of a cavalry charge, or

[25] Conversations in 1944 with Lt. Cdr. Theodore Blanchard USNR, Commander LCI Group 8, and with Lts. (jg) G. H. Callahan and Richard W. Poor, skipper and "exec." of *LCI–441*. Summary and timetable of Waves 1–4: —

	Composition	Left Line of Departure	Hit Beach Red 1	Hit Beach Red 2
LVT–2 1st Wave	3 LCI(G)	0859		
	16 LVT–2			
	16 LVT–A1 (tanks)	0900	0930	0931
	2 LCC on flanks			
	2 LCVP in center			
LVT–2 2nd Wave	16 LVT–2			
	2 LCC on flanks	0904	0933	0934
	2 LCVP in center			
LVT–2 3rd Wave	18 LVT–2			
	4 LCVP on flanks and in center	0908	0935	0939
LVT–2 4th Wave	18 LVT–2			
	4 LCVP on flanks and in center	0911	0939	0942

of the chariots and horsemen of Israel. At 0928 all four waves of LVTs were approaching in line abreast and the first was about to land. Every amphtrac was on time, not one of the 84 fell behind more than a couple of boat lengths; all kept up an even 5-knot speed in spite of the swell that heaved around the end of Kwajalein. Their cupped tracks were churning the blue water into curling sheepskins of white foam, their square bows threw spray until everyone on board was drenched, but nobody cared. This was what the 7th Division had come for, to kill more of those (you know what) who had cost them so many buddies on Attu. Elsie Item gunboats were flashing and crackling; battleships off shore were booming and belching huge gobs of orange-tinted smoke, and on the island palm trees and parts of buildings were rising in the air.

The first wave hit the beaches right on the button — Red 1 at 0930; Red 2, which was a trifle farther, at 0931. The amphibious tanks, first to waddle over the reef, kept right on going for 100 yards or more to support the troops as they organized. Inside of twelve minutes, 1200 officers and men had got ashore without a single casualty. So well had the naval, air and field artillery bombardment done its work that enemy resistance was confined to sporadic small-arms fire and the two assault battalions organized on the beach without difficulty. The young officer who wrote the report of the 3rd Battalion, 184th RCT, recorded: —

The behavior of our men at this time was superb. Where was this bugaboo that we had feared, that men coming under fire for the first time are shocked to the extent that they are unable to move forward? Never was anything truer than "as a man trains, so will he fight." The months of training and rehearsing we had put in stood in good stead.

General attitude — "Why, Hell, it's just like a maneuver!" And like a maneuver it was, only better. We did not lose a second. Our boys with flame and explosives proceeded to destroy at once the installations and those Nips that were fortunate (?) enough to survive the bombardment. We lost some men, but we killed a helluva lot of Japs.

"Our leading wave was supported by elements of Company A, 708th Amphibian Tank Battalion, and they really know their stuff.

VII Army Air Force Liberator over Kwajalein Island, October 1944

Wings over Kwajalein

Blockhouse area, 31 January

3 February 1944

Kwajalein Before and After

Without hesitation they moved right in and destroyed some pillboxes by the simple process of sticking the muzzles of their guns in the apertures of the pillboxes and blazing away. This obtained very satisfactory results both here and later on with our land tanks." [26]

A new feature of this operation was the close coördination of immediate supply with troop landings. LSTs selectively loaded with water, ammunition and emergency rations were maintained near the line of departure in order to deliver these essentials to landing craft on call from shore. The LCMs that boated the land tanks could not get over the reef, but the tanks were able to make their own way ashore, as the day and hour of landing had been so chosen that there were not more than 30 inches of water for them to wade through. Neither could the LCVPs carrying the reserves float over the reef, so a shuttle service of LVTs was provided to take the troops off them about 800 yards off shore and run them in. This too worked well.

Never had a landing in force on strongly defended hostile territory been handled as well as this one on Kwajalein Island. And it belied the assertion that the United States Army and Navy could not coöperate. Actually, they got along much better than the Navy and Marines did at Roi and Namur.

The boomerang-shaped Kwajalein Island now lay before the American invaders. It had been heavily wooded, principally with coconut palms, before the battleships opened fire. An area 450 by 5000 feet on the western half of the island had been cleared and graded for that uncompleted airfield, the aërial photograph of which had marked down Kwajalein as an objective. All parts of the island were connected by a network of 20-foot-wide dirt roads to which Army Intelligence assigned names like "Will" and "Nora." Inasmuch as this had been the main supply dump and military stores center for the Marshalls and Gilberts, the Japanese had built a fine L-shaped pier (now called the N.O.B. pier) 30 feet wide and 1600 feet long, extending out across the reef to a good

[26] Report of 7th Division XI, Report of RCT 184 Enclosure V.

depth of water in the lagoon. At the northern end, immediately served by this pier, was a Japanese shore base of more than a hundred buildings, some of them of heavy concrete construction. Here was where the stiffest resistance was encountered. Hospitals and barracks were mostly wooden structures with corrugated iron roofs and concrete cisterns underneath to store rainwater.

The defenses of Kwajalein, as of Tarawa, were concentrated along the beaches, mainly on the ocean side, and consisted of a trench system augmented by about 15 pillboxes, anti-tank traps, blockhouses and air-raid shelters which were useful as defense points.[27] There were no prepared positions in depth. The few covered positions, although of reinforced concrete, proved more vulnerable to naval shelling and artillery fire than the coconut-log and coral-sand pillboxes at Betio. The total garrison numbered somewhat over 4000 officers and men; less than that of Betio, although the area defended was thrice as large. But Rear Admiral Monzo Akiyama, the Marshall Islands commander whose headquarters were there, was not ill-prepared to meet an invasion. Many of his installations were still intact after the bombardment, whose results made it most difficult for the Americans to move tanks and supplies forward. Uprooted palms, shell holes, bomb craters and various wreckage were hazards to men and vehicles alike.

Supporting naval gunfire continued after the troops landed and a creeping barrage from the field artillery on Enubuj preceded them as they advanced.[28] Tanks started coming ashore at 0947. The 7th Division maintained tanks expertly and expended comparatively few, but its use of them was far from effective.

For two hours the invaders had it all their own way, but by 1130 the Japanese were offering determined, well-organized resistance with machine guns and small arms. By 1500 the troops

[27] Col. C. H. M. Roberts "Marshall Islands Japanese Defenses and Battle Damage" 1 Mar. 1944; Jicpoa Bulletin No. 48–44 "Japanese Defenses Kwajalein."
[28] There were only 25 minutes during D-day when the guns on Enubuj were not shooting, and that was during an air strike. (7th Division Report XII, Report of Divisional Artillery.)

had advanced only 950 yards, to the western end of the airfield. The 11,000 men ashore by 1600 might have rushed the enemy lines, but that was not Army technique. In contrast to the Marines, the Army was taught not to advance until all possible fire had been brought to bear on the path ahead of the troops. This took time. During the first six hours of fighting on 1 February, the two regiments lost only 30 killed and 40 wounded. The 2nd Battalion 32nd RCT reduced "Worden" strong point — a nest of machine guns, deep trenches and anti-tank traps — at 1805 and then tied in with the 3rd Battalion 184th RCT to establish perimeter defense for the night. They had a good laugh when the 1st Battalion of the 32nd Regiment in the rear telephoned the following message: "One Jap passed Command Post with pistol and bayonet. . . . Jap is now dead." [29]

The first night ashore was far from peaceful. Harassing fires were maintained by ships and field artillery with periodic star shell and searchlight illumination. Some fire support ships patrolled outside the atoll; others anchored in the lagoon or stood by for call fire.[30] At 2300, in heavy rain, a counterattack by 50 or more Japanese supported by knee-mortar fire developed and had momentary success. Some men were panicked, but Lieutenant W. R. Gauger USA, who directed a line of machine-gun fire across the Japanese flank, stopped the advance. At 0135 February 2, the enemy counterattacked the 184th on the lagoon side where the lines were thin, costing the regiment a machine-gun section and a number of casualties. Small numbers kept infiltrating throughout the hours of darkness, but were liquidated at daylight.

At 0200 February 2, General Corlett issued orders for the day's attack to be launched at 0715. A company of the tank battalion was to push hard on the left to breach fortified positions in an area about 500 yards north of the H-shaped pier (called Center Pier), and then swing northeast to knock out a strongly fortified

---

[29] 7th Division Report IX, Report of RCT 32, Message log.

[30] They were a good deal bothered by near-misses from coastal guns, the exact location of which was never determined; probably they were the guns on Ebeye.

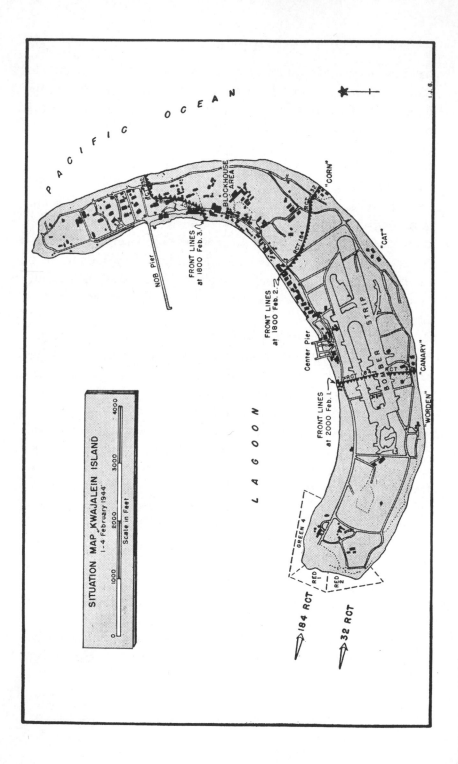

PACIFIC OCEAN

"CORN"

"CAT"

BLOCKHOUSE AREA

NOB Pier

FRONT LINES at 1800 Feb. 3.

FRONT LINES at 1800 Feb. 2.

Center Pier

FRONT LINES at 2000 Feb. 1.

RCT 184

RCT

BOMBER STRIP

"CANARY"

"WORDEN"

LAGOON

GREEN 4

RED 1

RED 2

184 RCT

32 RCT

SITUATION MAP KWAJALEIN ISLAND
1–4 February 1944

Scale in Feet

0   1000   2000   3000   4000

position designated "Corn." By following this route the tanks would circumvent a treacherous tank trap extending halfway across the island just south of "Corn" and at the same time assist the 32nd in its forward move. Commanders were urged to make full use of available naval gunfire and Enubuj-based artillery, for General Corlett knew that his troops were now reaching a really tough spot. Concrete pillboxes, long emplacements, blockhouses, trenches and rifle bays were closely placed both along the lagoon and the seaward beaches, with strong points at intervals in depth. Frequently these defensive works were joined by communications trenches and in some cases by tunnels. Fortunately photographic interpretation had been exceptionally accurate and these obstacles were anticipated.

After preparatory fires from the artillery on Enubuj and their own 4.2-inch mortars, both regiments jumped off at 0715. *Idaho*, *Meade* and *Bailey* furnished call fire at short ranges, while destroyer *Haggard* relieved *Sigsbee* inside the lagoon. Air strikes also were arranged for selected targets in strong points north of the pier.

As the 2nd Battalion 32nd RCT moved forward on the ocean side, it came under fire from enemy dual-purpose guns on the northern part of the island. After advancing 200 yards it called for air support. What happened illustrates the difficulty sometimes experienced by the Navy in helping ground troops. Fifteen dive-bombers took off from a carrier to silence the troublesome guns shortly after the call was initiated. Six of the planes, after some difficulty in locating the guns, dropped 1000-pound bombs on them about 0945, and 13 fighters followed this up with a strafing attack. Before they were through, someone on the regimental staff, fearing lest the bullets hit his men, called the planes off. But at 1005 the battalion commander radioed the air support commander afloat, "Troops were excited. Half misjudged where bullets fell. You did a damn good job!" [31]

The first real nut the 32nd Regiment had to crack on 2 February

[31] Messages log, as above.

was "Cat" strong point, about midway down the ocean shore. Reducing it, with the aid of artillery and tanks, took about three quarters of an hour. By 1020 the 2nd Battalion 32nd was getting ready to assault "Corn." The 3rd Battalion, which had been engaged in mopping-up activities to the rear of the 2nd, now prepared to pass through it and carry the assault forward over the tank trap. In the meantime the 2nd Battalion 184th was pushing up the lagoon side, followed by the 1st. Supported by ten medium tanks, two companies of the 2nd made rapid progress and by 0900 had passed Center Pier. But at 1215 the 2nd Battalion was ordered to wait for a battalion of fresh troops to pass through it. This was the first of many unnecessary delays that afternoon. There were long lulls in naval gunfire and air support, due to the failure of Army headquarters (still suspicious of naval bombardment) to ask for it; troops sat idly waiting for their own artillery to support them; strong point "Corn" held up the advance; and at 1448 the enemy fired white phosphorus shells which disorganized the troops and forced tanks to retire. Finally at 1539 seven tanks crossed the trap that protected "Corn"; the 3rd Battalion 32nd — supported by carrier planes, naval gunfire and Army artillery — moved in on the strong point and captured it. More confusion followed, owing to a misunderstanding by the 32nd Regiment of how far the 184th had advanced on the lagoon side. Hence the night line of defense was irregular and not as strong as it should have been.

The Red beaches were unsuitable for landing supplies, as the reef was an obstacle to all landing craft but LVTs. On February 2 unloading was shifted to Beach Green 4 nearest the western point of the island on the lagoon side, and there it continued during the night from ships that had moved into the lagoon. By the evening of 2 February, *Zeilin*, *Ormsby*, *Ashland* and *Windsor* were 95 to 100 per cent unloaded; *Polk* and *Leedstown* 57 per cent; all others 30 per cent or less.[32] During the day progress was made in clearing and repairing roads, and this helped to maintain a satisfactory flow of supplies to the forward areas.

[32] CTG 52.5 Action Report.

At 2030 February 2, General Corlett sent his two regiments the following message: —

Progress today generally satisfactory. Keep pressure on tonight. Organize vigorous attack 0715 tomorrow. Be alert for counterattack at any time day or night. It is bound to come. Keep some fire power in reserve near front. . . . Finish the job not later than 1300 February 3. The Northern Force has finished its job. Your use of tanks has been noneffective due to failure to give officers, NCO's and drivers specific instructions. You must insure that profitable tank targets are available. . . . Get the tank men pepped up to do their job.

The employment of tanks on Kwajalein left much to be desired, owing to lack of coördination between them and the foot soldiers. It was difficult for tank troops to adapt themselves to atoll warfare, since they had been trained to charge across open spaces; the lessons of Makin and Tarawa in this respect had not been taken to heart. Better communications between infantry and tanks would have helped, but most of the tanks' telephones had been drowned out coming ashore so that the only way an infantry officer could make his wishes known to the men inside was to scramble topside and bang the tank's armor until someone looked out. Fortunately the enemy had no magnetic anti-tank mines. A Japanese would hold a grenade up against a tank and keep it there until it exploded, blowing his arm off but resulting in no damage to the tank. Medium tank "Sad Sack," rumbling up to demolish a pillbox, was attacked by five Japanese officers who beat their long swords against its armor plate. "When the crew recovered from its first astonishment, they gave the Japanese officers the honorable death which they had sought."

It was a wild night for the troops ashore. As one man described it, "I was so scared that I prayed like hell!" [33] Field artillery and naval units continued their harassing fire. Four battleships with a screen of five destroyers patrolled off the atoll; the cruisers and other destroyers remained inside the lagoon. *Schroeder* furnished star-shell illumination which proved very effective in showing up

[33] Richard Wilcox "Kwajalein," *Life* 21 Feb. 1944 p. 10.

infiltrators. "From midnight on the enemy was very active, screaming and yelling in a fanatical manner, and one counterattack after another was attempted until daybreak." [34]

Preceded by a short artillery preparation, the two regiments jumped off for a coördinated attack at 0715 on 3 February.[35] The 32nd Infantry on the ocean side forged ahead more rapidly than the 184th, opening a gap between the two. General Corlett was worried about the slow rate of advance. If the front lines were to be kept straight, the 32nd would have to stand by until the 184th had cleaned out their difficult area, protracting the operation a day or more. Brigadier General Joseph L. Ready usa, the assistant division commander, called a meeting of commanding and operations officers of the two regiments, at which the tactical situation was thrashed out. As a result, General Corlett ordered the 184th to concentrate on liquidating the enmy in the "blockhouse area," freeing the 32nd to push northward and overrun the northeastern end of the island.

The strongest resistance on Kwajalein was encountered this day as the 184th moved into the blockhouse area, heavily defended with concrete blockhouses and bombproof shelters that had been little damaged by naval and air bombardment. The numerous steel, wood and coral buildings among the concrete had, however, been reduced to twisted heaps of rubble which afforded the Japanese excellent shelter so that the infantry had to resort to street-fighting tactics. Indeed, the action this day more resembled the battle for Monte Cassino in Italy, after its pulverization by air bombardment, than anything yet encountered in the Pacific; with the important difference that Japanese seldom surrender and are far more difficult than Germans to defeat. The battle was conducted by small, independent and often isolated groups of infantrymen inching forward, blasting out one knot of Japanese after another from ruins, heaps

[34] 7th Division Report XI, Report RCT 184 Enc. V.
[35] This is the day described by Col. S. L. A. Marshall in "One Day on Kwajalein," *Infantry Journal* Aug. 1944 pp. 12–23.

Dukws and an LVT–1

LVT–1 in center. Waiting to get loaded

LVT Tanks Going Ashore at Eniwetok

of debris and concrete buildings, with rifle and machine-gun fire, grenades, satchel charges and an occasional flame thrower; while the tanks remained "part of the scenery," and were mainly useful as cover for advancing foot soldiers. "The scene was indescribably chaotic; it was like trying to fight one's way across the landscape of a nightmare . . . a fight in which small skirmishes eddied around churches and outhouses, a fight in which Jap snipers sometimes waited shoulder high in the water of a concrete cistern on the chance that an American would pass the eight-inch space which was their field of vision." [36]

Neither naval gunfire nor land artillery could help where friends and foes were so mixed up, but *San Francisco*, led by minesweeper *Requisite*, closed Kwajalein during the afternoon and destroyed pillboxes visible on the northeastern point of the island. She had a busy night firing main battery, supplying 5-inch call fire and furnishing illumination by star shell and searchlight. From time to time, enemy artillery fired back but made no hits.

The troops had another tough night between 3 and 4 February, meeting fierce enemy counteraction — white phosphorus shells from heavy mortars and at least two organized enemy counterattacks which were stopped.

At 0700 February 4, gunfire from Army artillery and destroyer *Schroeder* blasted at the little territory the Japanese still held on Kwajalein. On the left, the 184th encountered determined pockets of enemy resistance, difficult to eliminate. Ten tanks were available for their use, but because the tank radios and telephones were out of commission it was impossible to give them proper instructions. The best use of tank cannon on concrete structures, it appeared, was to blast their sides, which made the Japanese pop out; but even this was ineffective against a very heavy structure which faced the front line of the 184th Infantry. Small groups of men worked up under cover of rifle and machine-gun fire and finally reduced it with individually placed charges. [37] At 1045 a unit

[36] Col. Marshall in *Infantry Journal* Aug. 1944 pp. 14, 19–22.
[37] 7th Division Report XI, Report of RCT 184, Enclosure V.

arrived with public-address system and a Japanese interpreter who broadcast an invitation to surrender. This brought in 35 to 40 of the enemy.

The 32nd Infantry reached the foot of NOB Pier by 0940 and requested the 184th to cease firing in that direction. The second road beyond was attained only at 1410 after a hard battle, but when it was, the enemy could no longer fight back. The remaining 600 yards of Kwajalein were overrun by 1530, when General Corlett announced that organized resistance had ended. Next morning, 5 February, a systematic and thorough mopping-up was done, and the enemy dead, many of whom had been rotting under the sun for several days, were buried. No man who was there will ever forget the smell of decaying bodies intermingled with that of burnt coconut wood.

On 6 February the 32nd and 184th Infantry Regiments' troops reëmbarked in their transports and turned conquered Kwajalein Island over to garrison and defense forces. The Marines might have taken the island in less time, as their friends firmly believe; but no two regiments ever performed an operation in finer spirit than the 32nd and 184th of the 7th Division United States Army. The extreme toughness of the struggle again proved the amazing survival power of Japanese troops and installations under naval gunfire and air bombardment. Although both had been delivered in much greater quantities than at Tarawa, they had not been enough to greatly reduce, much less to eliminate, ground resistance.

7. *Ebeye and Minor Islets, 2–6 February* [38]

There still remained about twenty islets of Kwajalein Atoll to be dealt with, and the staffs of Admirals Conolly and Turner and

[38] General Richardson's *Participation Report;* Report of Commanding General Northern Landing Forces; Report of the 25th RCT, Enclosure F; 7th Division Report VIII, Report of RCT 17; CTG 52.8 (Rear Adm. R. C. Giffen) Action Report.

of Generals Schmidt and Corlett were kept busy organizing individual amphibious assaults to take them.

In the northern sector, as we have seen, the 25th RCT of the 4th Marine Division secured the five islets flanking Roi and Namur on 31 January. Next day two battalions were released to clean up the rest of the islets in that sector. Under Colonel Samuel C. Cumming USMC they worked south from Ennubirr. No Japanese were encountered but 47 natives were picked up and a camp was established for them.[39] Boggerlapp, west of Mellu, also was secured the same day, and on 3 February Boggerik and an unnamed islet in the same direction were occupied.

Operations were now beyond the scope of landing craft, so Colonel Cumming was given two LSTs, two LCIs, six LSMs and destroyer *Hopewell* to float his troops and artillery and clean up the remaining islets. The Colonel shipped 34 amphtracs on board the LSTs and between February 4 and 7 landed on every bit of dry land in the northern part of the atoll. No Japanese, only friendly natives, were encountered. By the night of 7 February Ebadon, the westernmost point of land, had been secured.

In the southern sector, the 7th Division enjoyed no such pleasure cruises as were afforded the Marines; the islets northeast of Kwajalein Island gave plenty of trouble.

Ebeye, 1770 yards long and 200 wide, supported a Japanese seaplane base and a garrison of 400, well dug in. Between 30 January and 3 February, five battleships, three heavy cruisers and six destroyers threw 639 tons of explosive shells into Ebeye, while 87 tons of bombs were dropped by carrier-based aircraft. Destroyer *Franks* brought in an Army reconnaissance party which, helped by the cruisers' float planes, located the main island defenses. Both *Franks* and *San Francisco* were taken under fire by heavy machine guns. These were quickly silenced but not before the cruiser had

---

[39] Relations with the natives were much furthered by the forehandedness of one of the 7th Division chaplains in having learned Marshallese. Good article on fraternization in *New Yorker* 9 Sept. 1944 p. 47.

received several hits. One penetrated the officers' "head" but (as reported by that ship) "appropriately did not explode, there being no officers present." Artillery sited at Enubuj also prepared Ebeye for assault.

The 17th RCT (Colonel Wayne C. Zimmerman), which had taken Ennylabegan and Enubuj, drew the assignment for Ebeye on 3 February. The 1st and 3rd Battalions with their LVTs embarked in four LSTs, and the rest of the assault troops in transport *Zeilin*. Shortly after 0700 the LSTs, LCIs and LCMs with the required control boats left Ennylabegan for the line of departure off a beach on the southern part of Ebeye. A few minutes later, cruisers *San Francisco* and *New Orleans* and destroyers *Stevens* and *McKee* began lashing Ebeye with gunfire, which they kept up until the landing was effected. From 0800 to 0928, two battalions of the artillery on Enubuj inflicted continuous and concentrated fire on the islet. Both artillery and naval fire were checked long enough to allow carrier planes to come in for a dive-bombing attack on the beach and adjacent areas.

This landing was a complete success. The troops moved inland with slight losses, as the southern 200 yards of the island had been neutralized by the preparatory fires; but after that portion had been passed, determined resistance was encountered in the shape of rifle and machine-gun fire coming from pillboxes and air-raid shelters. Rocket launchers, flame throwers, explosives and artillery were used in pushing the attack; but progress was slow. At 1900 February 3, defensive positions were taken for the night on a line about 50 yards south of "Bailey Pier," midway on the lagoon side.

Night was the time when the Japanese flourished and did their best; and that of 3–4 February was as trying for the soldiers on Ebeye as for those on Kwajalein. The enemy made darkness hideous with spasmodic machine-gun and rifle fire; and about 0400 he appeared to be organizing in small groups for a counterattack. Mortar illuminating shells and a destroyer's searchlight lit up the area where he was concentrating, naval gunfire and army mortar fire were directed into it, and that particular counterattack was frustrated; yet the enemy attempted no fewer than three more between dawn and 0730 February 4, when the 17th RCT resumed its advance. Four pillboxes, cleaned out once but reoccupied during the night, were demolished with the aid of 75-mm howitzers and the troops swept forward. Naval aircraft bombing missions were then delivered on targets located by information from prisoners of war. These included an ammunition dump, an anti-aircraft gun position and a bombproof shelter. By 1130 the enemy was completely disorganized, and Ebeye was secured at noon.

Colonel Zimmerman had been directed by General Corlett to seize the islets on each side of Ebeye as soon as the situation there permitted. Those between Kwajalein and Ebeye were taken under fire by destroyer *McKee* during the morning of 3 February while four LCIs subjected them to automatic weapon and rocket fire. Five LVT–A1s rolled in at 1502, and these islets were secured by 1630.

That same afternoon, three LCIs steamed in column, accompanied by *McKee*, firing on the two islets north of Ebeye, the northernmost of which is called Loi. At about 1500, twenty-five natives — men, women and children — appeared on the beach of the islet south of Loi [40] waving white flags, and surrendered to the "Elsie Items," much to the delight of their crews.

Next morning, 4 February, *Minneapolis* took under fire Gugegwe, two miles north of Loi, in order to protect landings on Loi and another islet unnamed. Destroyer *Hall*, three LCI gunboats and the artillery on Enubuj stood by to deliver fire support, but none was needed. Loi had been bombarded with 13 tons of shells on 30 January and 1 February, and the landing there was unopposed. Some 23 unarmed men whom the 17th Infantry first took to be natives turned out to be Japanese laborers. They refused to surrender and had to be clubbed or bayoneted into submission.

[40] Report of Lt. Cdr. Blanchard 10 Mar. 1944, in which he said this incident occurred on Loi, but in conversations with him in 1944 it was established that he was mistaken, and he recommended the writer to make the above change. Also conversations with Lts. (jg) Callahan and Poor of *LCI-441*.

The next objective was a group of three islets north of Loi, the largest of which, adjoining Bigej Channel and the lagoon, was believed to harbor over 100 enemy troops. Gugegwe had been bombarded by the Navy every day but one from 30 January through 5 February. Battleships, cruisers and destroyers had fired 447 tons of projectiles into it while Navy planes had strafed it with machine-gun fire, 56,000 rounds of .50 caliber. For the landing on Gugegwe and its two satellites on 5 February, three battalions of infantry were embarked in six LSTs, each carrying 17 amphtracs; 16 medium tanks and five LVT–A1s were also supplied; cruisers *Minneapolis* and *San Francisco* and destroyers *McCord* and *Trathen* delivered supporting gunfire, commencing at 0720 February 5 and continuing until the troops landed at 0930. Two 105-mm batteries, which had been shifted from Enubuj to Ebeye and Loi, also supported the landings.

Gugegwe landings were easy. The LSTs moved up to the line of departure and discharged their amphtracs with troops embarked. The waves formed up according to the now classic plan and hit Gugegwe, and the first islet adjoining, by 0941. Heavy undergrowth slowed the troops' advance. When a point opposite the pier was reached, they met small-arms fire coming from dugouts. These were demolished with explosives and flame throwers and the advance continued.[41] Gugegwe was secured at 1514; about 200 of the enemy were destroyed at a cost of three Americans killed and ten wounded. Immediately after, the adjacent islets were secured.

On the same morning, 5 February, the 7th Reconnaissance Troop made a pre-dawn landing, in rubber boats from destroyer *Overton*, on Bigej which lies a mile northeast of Gugegwe across the like-named channel. This islet, approximately 3300 yards long and 300 wide, covered by dense vegetation, was defended by about 100 Japanese. Since 30 January, two battleships and three destroyers had thrown 19 tons of projectiles onto it while Navy planes had dropped an additional 16 tons of bombs and strafed the islet with

[41] 7th Division Report XI, Report of RCT 184, Enclosure V.

machine-gun fire, 66,000 rounds of .50 caliber. *Overton* and *Manley* resumed fire on 5 February and supported the operations ashore. This softened up the islet to some extent, but it was still too strong for the reconnaissance troop to handle alone. Part of the 3rd Battalion 184th RCT was sent over from Gugegwe. "Marched on down the island," reported their commander, Captain K. E. Brown USA. "Killed thirteen Japs. The rest very obligingly blew themselves up in front of our advancing troops. We had no casualties. Finished the job about 1700, then back to the LSTs. Next morning we boarded the transport. Wow! Could an old, crowded and hot ship look so good?"

While the three Gugegwes and Bigej were being occupied, the 2nd Battalion 17th Infantry had been split into two reinforced rifle companies; the eastern under Major D. L. Bjork to secure islets north of Bigej, and the western under Captain R. J. Edwards to take those north and west of Gehh across the lagoon. Both left Ennylabegan at 0730 February 4 and saw quick action. Captain Edwards's riflemen had occupied all the islets from Gehh north as far as Eller, at the bottleneck of the lagoon, by 1300. An hour later they landed on Eller unopposed but soon came under enemy machine-gun fire from three stranded merchant ships. Destroyer *Hoel*, which had been standing by for call fire on Bigej, steamed over to shell these ships. Major Bjork's eastern force, which had occupied Mack and Kwadack Islets on the other side of the bottleneck without opposition, also was ordered across the lagoon to help. By 1900 February 5, the occupation of Eller was completed. One Japanese surrendered and 101 were killed, with a loss of one American killed and five wounded.[42]

When darkness fell these two rifle companies reëmbarked in the LSTs, which stood by during the night. Their last objective, an islet with the forbidding name of Ennugenliggelap, was occupied without incident on the 6th. And as air reconnaissance had revealed no trace of Japanese on the entire western arm of the lagoon, the numerous islets in that sector could wait.

[42] 7th Division Report I, Enclosure A; VIII, Report of RCT 17.

8. *Conclusion and Comment*

Thus by 7 February Admiral Turner's Joint Expeditionary Force had completed its mission and the whole of Kwajalein Atoll was in American hands. One of the most complicated amphibious campaigns in all history, involving landings on some 30 different islets, fights on at least ten of them, and prolonged bloody battles on four, had come to a successful conclusion within a week.

The price for this spectacular victory was far less than had been paid for the Gilberts. The Navy suffered a mere handful of casualties, since not one ship was sunk and only a few hits were sustained from coast defense guns. But 372 soldiers and Marines died on this atoll over 2000 miles from Hawaii so that their comrades might continue the march across Micronesia.[43]

	Troops Committed	Killed, Missing and Died of Wounds	Wounded	Casualty Total
Kwajalein (South)	21,342	177	1,037	1,214
Kwajalein (North)	20,104	195	545	740
	41,446	372	1,582	1,954

According to military standards, these losses were light. But the Japanese side of the score sheet told a different story: —

	Estimated Total Enemy Strength	Casualties Counted Killed	Prisoners	
Kwajalein (South)	5,112	4,398	174	(incl. 125 Koreans)
Kwajalein (North)	3,563	3,472	91	(incl. 40 Koreans)
	8,675	7,870	265	

The light American casualties may be attributed to careful planning and preparation in view of lessons learned at Tarawa, to over-

[43] The figures in both tables are from the Report "Marshall Islands Japanese Defenses and Battle Damage," prepared by Col. Roberts. These appear to be the most accurate available. Isley and Crowl follow Gen. Holland Smith's Report Enclosures E and H, 6 Mar. and 22 Feb. 1944; the main differences from the above are 436 wounded in Kwajalein (North) and 4650 enemy dead in Kwajalein (South). Of the troops committed at Kwajalein (South) all but 2288 were of the 7th Division; of those committed at Kwajalein (North) all but 1192 were of the 4th Marine Division.

Major Generals Holland M. Smith USMC *and Charles H. Corlett* USA
On board U.S.S. *Cambria*

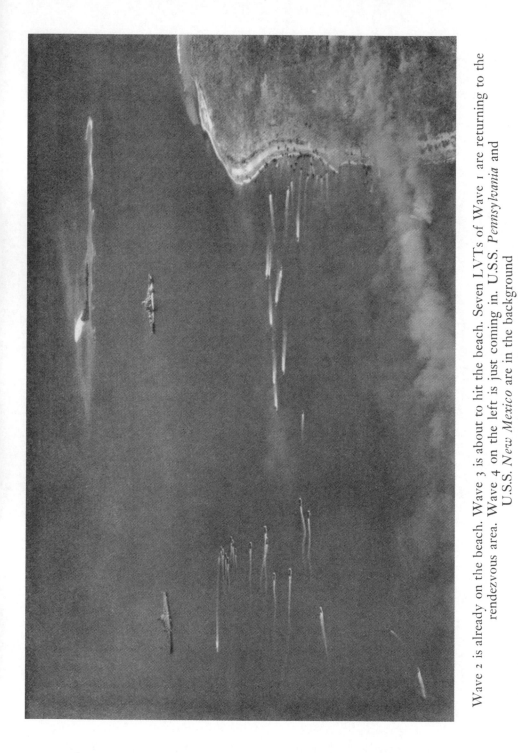

Wave 2 is already on the beach. Wave 3 is about to hit the beach. Seven LVTs of Wave 1 are returning to the rendezvous area. Wave 4 on the left is just coming in. U.S.S. *Pennsylvania* and U.S.S. *New Mexico* are in the background

LVTs Landing at Engebi Island, Eniwetok Atoll

whelming strength in air and sea and a sufficient margin on the ground, and to bad Japanese tactics. As summed up by a member of General Corlett's staff, "No coast defense guns protected the lagoon openings and no underwater obstacles or mines were set to impede the landing. The enemy's defense amounted to a retreat through a maze of previously prepared positions. Only in a few instances, and largely at night, did he leave the shelter of pillboxes and dugouts with their limited field of fire, and attempt to delay the advance by fighting in the open." [44]

The captured Japanese who were interrogated seemed to be imbued with a curious superstition about the Americans. They believed we had a secret weapon which could detect metal after sunset, because anyone who came out of dugouts or hiding places in the evening was almost immediately killed. After the first day they doffed helmets and grounded bayonets after the sun went down. But the American secret weapon was concentrated and accurate fire power delivered from land, sea and air; fire power that was designed to leave as few Japanese alive as possible. It is unlikely that any portion of this globe had ever before received such a concentration of bombs and shellfire.[45] Yet, as we have seen, more of the same was needed. The total bomb tonnage dropped on Kwajalein Island and the southern sector of the atoll was slightly over 300 tons, but naval gunfire on this area amounted to nearly 4000 tons, and that of land-based artillery to about 1300 tons. "The rôle of aviation was to render the air safe for the operation of surface ships, and to furnish local support against enemy personnel or specific installations as required." [46]

Another factor in the Kwajalein victory was improved ship-to-shore technique. The LCI gunboats more than justified the high

[44] 7th Division Report IV, Report of Assistant Chief of Staff, G–2.

[45] Admiral Conolly's Report on Operations in the Northern Sector states that during 8 hours of daylight 31 Jan. his fire support ships fired 23.4 rounds per minute, and during 5 hours of daylight 1 Feb., 40.9 rounds per minute. This does not include the following ammunition expended by his 12 LCIs: .50 caliber 56,285 rnds; 20-mm 23,700 rnds; 40-mm 13,065 rnds; 4½-inch rockets (smoke) 144 rnds; and 4½-inch rockets (TNT) 2541 rnds.

[46] Comairpac "Analysis of Pacific Air Operations" Feb. 1944.

expectation that had been aroused by their previous performances in the South and Southwest Pacific, and won for themselves a permanent place in amphibious warfare. Amphtracs made trouble at Roi and Namur, but in the south, where they were handled by experienced and well-disciplined crews who were used to working under naval command, they demonstrated their worth.[47] The method of ship-to-shore assault used in this operation — amphtracs flanked by LCCs and supported by LCI gunboats — became doctrine for future amphibious operations.

The tactics used at Kwajalein proved a willingness to learn on the part of Army, Navy and Marine high commands. Seldom has military thinking been so agile and open to suggestion, so eager to grasp any new idea which sounded reasonable. How promptly were the hard lessons learned at Tarawa put into practice!

Above all tactical and technical factors in this victory was the coöperation of all branches of the armed services, conspicuous except in the unpleasantness between LST crews and LVT drivers in the north. Officers of the 7th Division who had worked with the Navy at Attu and Kiska and then at Kwajalein felt "almost as if they were Marines." They attributed their success to the "complete understanding that existed throughout between the Army and the Navy." Good feeling and mutual respect between the services never reached a higher pitch than in the Kwajalein operation.[48] General Richardson wrote that Admiral Turner's "sympathetic understanding" of Army problems as well as his "great

[47] The southern group, 708th Amphibious Tank Bn, actually had had no more experience with LVTs than the northern, but had spent two years training with land tanks not radically different in mechanization from LVTs. Maj. J. D. Kooken USA in conversation with the writer attributed the good performance of LVTs in the south largely to the excellent and continuous maintenance rendered by experienced personnel. About 50 out of 276 LVTs of all types were lost during the operation — all but 2 of them in the Northern Sector. (Figures from the Wendell Report on the Marshalls.)

[48] Based on conversations with officers of the 7th Infantry Div'n, Schofield Barracks, Oahu, May 1944. Statements by Lt. Col. C. G. Fredericks USA were of particular interest since his position as assistant operations officer gave him intimate contact with the Navy during the planning and the operation.

experience" were major factors in victory.[49] And General Holland M. Smith USMC, who was not accustomed to toss bouquets, wrote: "The coöperation and coördination of action at Kwajalein was the most satisfactory ever experienced." [49] Laudatory messages from top-ranking Army and Navy officials poured into Admiral Nimitz's headquarters after the operation. Admiral King's was the most succinct and appropriate, with a suggestion of more work ahead: —

"To all hands concerned with the Marshall Islands operation: Well and smartly done. Carry on."

[49] *Participation Report,* "Visit to Marshalls," p. 9. V 'Phib Corps Report, 6 March 1944.

CHAPTER XVI

Eniwetok [1]

(Operation "Catchpole")

31 January–4 March 1944

West Longitude dates, Zone plus 12 time.

1. *Preliminaries*

WITH Kwajalein in the bag, flag officers and generals turned their attention to Eniwetok. This large, round atoll, shaped like a stringy doughnut, lies 326 miles WNW of Roi, and only 1000 miles from the Marianas. The very name Eniwetok, meaning "Land between West and East," suggests its strategic importance. For the primitive Micronesians it had been a place of call and refreshment in their long canoe voyages from west to east; now it would become an important staging point for the United States Army, Navy and Marine Corps in their spectacular progress from east to west.

Eniwetok's circular reef is less frequently studded with islets than that of Kwajalein; there are only 40 in all, with a total area of only two and a quarter square miles. About 25 of the larger

---

[1] Pronounced En-ni-we-tok, all vowels short and practically no accent. Discovered in 1794 by Capt. Thomas Butler of the British trading sloop *Walpole,* it was named Brown's Range after the factor of his firm at Canton. This name appears on Admiralty charts and the Japanese Navy continued to call the atoll "Brown" throughout the war. Main sources: Action Reports of Rear Admiral Hill and of the Commanding General, Brig. Gen. Thomas E. Watson usmc. Jicpoa Bulletins Nos. 3–44 and 89–44, Information Bulletin on Eniwetok and "Japanese Defense of Eniwetok." Lt. (jg) Henry Salomon usnr of the writer's staff took part in the operation on board *Leonard Wood* and obtained from participants many details not to be found in action reports.

ones are provided with native names of strange cacophony, which in the American operation plan were humorously replaced by names of the more fragile and frivolous flowers. All were narrow in extent and poor in soil; the coconut groves were stunted and in 1944 the natives numbered fewer than one hundred. But Eniwetok Lagoon was the second largest in the Marshalls, covering 388 square miles, and most of it was navigable. There was no northern entrance to the lagoon; the only passes suitable for deep-draught vessels were in the southeast quadrant. As at Kwajalein, the enemy had improved islands in the extreme north and the far south. Engebi, a triangular island on the northern bulge, had a coral-surfaced bomber strip 4025 feet long, with the usual defenses. On Eniwetok and Parry Islands in the south there were search radars, coast defense guns and barracks concealed under a heavy cover of coconut and pandanus.

Eniwetok had long been an object of interest to strategists at the Naval War College and elsewhere. Cruiser *Milwaukee* on her maiden voyage had paid the atoll an unwelcome visit in October 1923. Washington knew nothing of what had gone on there since, but expected the worst. The Japanese made no military use of it until November 1942, when about 800 construction workers moved into Engebi Island to build an airfield, but these were transferred to Kwajalein after their work was done. The Engebi air base, which began to function about the end of November 1943, was used only for staging planes between the Marianas and the Carolines and Marshalls, and the few aircraft which happened to be there before the American attack on Kwajalein were disposed of by the bombardments and strikes of Mitscher's fast carrier forces.

Until the Gilberts fell, Japan made no serious preparation to defend Eniwetok, but on 4 January 1944 the 1st Amphibious Brigade of the Imperial Japanese Army, components of which had formerly been stationed in Manchuria, arrived to take charge of the defense. In the five or six weeks' grace that they had they accomplished little in the way of permanent installations, but planned to do much more, as proved by the presence of large

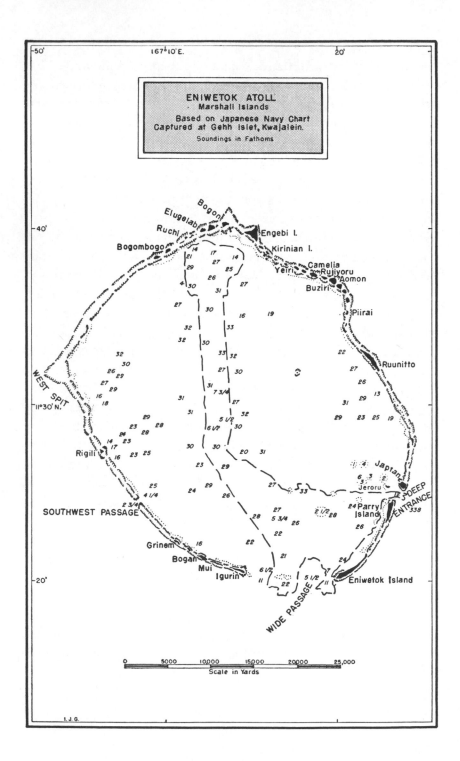

amounts of construction material. Three heavy anti-aircraft guns and twenty-eight 20-mm dual-purpose guns arrived at Engebi just ahead of the Pacific Fleet.[2] Admiral Nimitz chose an opportune moment to order the assault; even a week later it would have been much more costly.

Before "Flintlock" started it was assumed that Eniwetok would have to be postponed for a month or two, because the Joint Chiefs of Staff had ordered an amphibious operation against Kavieng in the Bismarcks which would employ the fast carrier forces, most of the gunfire support and a large part of V 'Phib. Admiral Spruance, before the departure of the Marshalls Expeditionary Force from Pearl, expressed to Admiral Nimitz the hope that he could push on into Eniwetok right after Kwajalein was secured. He had his wish; by 10 February Operation "Catchpole" for the seizure of Eniwetok was on. Fortunately it was not held up for Kavieng, an operation which the J.C.S. canceled on 12 March.[3]

The Reserve Force, Captain D. W. Loomis's nine transports filled with Brigadier General T. E. Watson's 8000 troops who had not been committed at Kwajalein, was on hand ready to be thrown into Eniwetok. This reserve formed part of the third amphibious group commanded by Rear Admiral Harry W. Hill. The LCIs and control vessels used in the capture of Roi and Namur, the dukw drivers and other men of the Kwajalein attack force trained in landing artillery, and the skilled amphtracs of the 7th Division, also were assigned to Admiral Hill for "Catchpole."

Planning began at a conference on board *Rocky Mount* between Admirals Turner and Hill and General Watson, at sea. Harry Hill eagerly assumed the command and called a conference of flag and commanding officers on 14 February. His small staff in *Cambria* began the detailed planning immediately. An innovation in the operation plan which greatly pleased the Marines was giving their

[2] Cominch Report "Amphibious Operations Marshall Islands, Jan.–Feb. 1944" p. 48.
[3] See Volume VI of this History p. 423.

general the command of ground troops as soon as he stepped ashore. In every earlier amphibious operation the admiral had commanded everything until the objective was secured.[4]

Intelligence data about Eniwetok Atoll was very vague. Search planes from the Gilberts had taken some good verticals, and more photographs were obtained by carrier planes of Admiral Sherman's and Admiral Ginder's groups, which started working over the atoll 30 January.[5] But these gave no hint that the southern islands, Parry and Eniwetok, were occupied, because the enemy had been there too short a time to build the sort of thing that catches a camera's eye. The secret Japanese chart of Eniwetok picked up on board the abandoned patrol boat at Gehh Islet was a godsend for hydrographic data, but showed no defense installations. No mine fields were entered on this chart, but Admiral Hill nevertheless decided to sweep the channel and lagoon.

The same distance factor which gave Eniwetok its potential value meant that naval and air interference from Saipan (1017 miles) and Truk (669 miles) must be expected unless they were hit first. Hitting them first took the shape of the biggest carrier and surface raids yet staged by the United States Navy — on Truk, 16–17 February,[6] and on Saipan a week later. D-day for Eniwetok was fixed for the 17th because by that time Admirals Spruance and Mitscher would have neutralized Truk. Without such diversions of the enemy, Admiral Hill might have encountered heavy air opposition.

A bad taste of what the Marshalls operation would have been without air supremacy was experienced by the ground forces at Roi. The large supplies of food, ammunition and construction gear recently landed there were concentrated in one huge dump between the two legs of the airfield because no other space was available. At 0230 February 12, six Japanese 4-engine flying boats from

---

[4] Brig. Gen. O. T. Pfeiffer to Brig. Gen. G. C. Thomas USMC, 23 Feb. 1944, in "Command Folder" at the Corps Historical Division.

[5] U.S. submarine *Searaven* reconnoitered Eniwetok for Admiral Hill but did not get photographs to him in time to be of use.

[6] West long. dates: see chap. xviii below.

Saipan, staged through Ponape, exploded this dump as neatly as if men had gone around with torches touching it off. And it was a high-level bombing attack, too. The enemy planes, none of which were shot down, destroyed 80 per cent of the Marines' supplies, so that for the next two weeks they had to subsist on emergency rations. One LCI and one LCT were burnt out but later salvaged; 25 men were killed and 130 seriously wounded.

Ponape, 573 miles from Kwajalein, lay only 362 miles from Eniwetok. It had to be neutralized before Eniwetok could be invaded, and the VII Army Air Force took care of that. They even got their first strike airborne before the Japanese rapers of Roi returned home. Between 15 and 26 February Liberators based at Hawkins and Mullinnix Fields, Tarawa, made five visits to Ponape, a flight of over 900 miles each way, dropping 118 tons of bombs and over 6000 incendiaries. At the conclusion of these strikes Ponape was out. Like other bombed enemy bases it refused to stay out, but gave no trouble during the Eniwetok operation. Kusaie, the pretty Caroline island which could also have served as a staging field for Japanese planes, lay so near the direct route Tarawa–Ponape that the B–24s gave it an occasional swipe going or coming, and the airfield there never became operative.

The first American air strike on Eniwetok Atoll was delivered on 31 January 1944 by planes of Rear Admiral Sherman's fast carrier group. Eighteen fighters took station over Engebi before dawn to destroy aircraft taking off, orbiting as the bombers dropped bombs and incendiaries on the field. As day broke, the fighters came down to strafe. All 15 "Bettys" present were destroyed and some small shipping in the lagoon was sunk. The same carrier group continued to work over Engebi the first three days of February. It was relieved by Rear Admiral Ginder's group, which continued the good work through the 7th and returned for more on the 11th and 13th. By this time few installations were visible above ground except concrete blockhouses and command posts. Strikes preparatory to the assault began 17 February, with planes

from the *Saratoga* group and from three escort carriers.[7] Naval
gunfire, too, poured at least 2800 tons of projectiles into Engebi
before the landings began; one regrets that no scientific analysis
could have been made of the comparative destruction wrought by
the two types of bombardment.

2. *Engebi, 17–18 February*

Rear Admiral Hill's force, now redesignated the Eniwetok
Expeditionary Group (51.11), sortied from Kwajalein Lagoon in
the afternoon of 15 February and covered the 326 miles to Eniwetok by two different routes. The Admiral's flag was in *Cambria*,
an attack transport with special communication facilities. Captain
D. W. Loomis in *Leonard Wood* commanded the transports: five
carrying the 22nd Marine Regiment, four carrying two battalions
of the 106th RCT 27th Division, LSD *Ashland* big with tanks
and two APDs (*Kane* and *Schley*) carrying the scout detachment.
He had also 9 LSTs, 6 LCIs and 2 SCs. The fire support group,
commanded by Rear Admiral Oldendorf, comprised battleships
Pennsylvania, Colorado and *Tennessee,* heavy cruisers *Indianapolis,
Portland* and *Louisville.* Fifteen destroyers provided the screens
for both. Rear Admiral Ragsdale's escort carrier group, *Sangamon,
Suwannee* and *Chenango,* with four destroyers, a minesweeper
group, two oilers and four tugs, were included in the expeditionary
group.[8] Brigadier General Thomas E. Watson USMC commanded
the landing force. The 22nd Marine Regiment, after eighteen
months' garrison service in Samoa, was now to see action for the
first time in this war. There never was a new outfit more eager to
meet the enemy or better qualified to fight. Including soldiers
of the 27th Division and various attached units, there were just
under 8000 officers and men in the landing force.[9]

---

[7] Comairpac "Analysis of Pacific Air Operations – Supplementary Report on
Carrier Operations 30 Jan.–24 Feb." pp. 10–11.
[8] For detailed organization see Appendix III, the ships marked (E).
[9] Cincpac Analysis Feb. 1944 p. 7 of Annex B.

Rear Admiral Ginder's carrier group supported them by operating north of the atoll from 17 to 28 February, helping the CVEs to maintain a daytime combat air patrol, conducting wide searches and making numerous strikes. An enemy surface or submarine attack in the face of so bold a challenge as this assault had to be anticipated. Admiral Spruance in *New Jersey*, off Truk on the morning of 17 February, was ready to assemble his capital ships to intercept in case that happened. But he had already seen to it that this could not happen. Nary a Japanese ship or plane disputed the invasion of Eniwetok.

The operation plan that Admiral Hill and General Watson concocted in Kwajalein Lagoon closely resembled the one which had just worked so well there. Eniwetok was to be taken in four bites: (1) two islets adjoining Engebi; (2) Engebi itself in the north; (3) Eniwetok and Parry Islands in the south; (4) mopping up remaining islets.

Engebi, the only island with an airfield, was necessarily the main objective; but, unless one made the hazardous attempt to land through the surf on its outer and windward coast, the only way to reach it was through the lagoon, entering either by Wide Passage at the extreme south, which was full of shoal spots, or by Deep Entrance between Parry and Japtan Islets, which one must assume to have been mined. This was where the captured Japanese chart proved a godsend.

D-day, 17 February, opened windy and overcast as Admiral Hill's force approached Eniwetok. Nobody replied to the preliminary bombardment to which cruisers and destroyers subjected Eniwetok Island and the islets flanking Deep Entrance. The Japanese in the south were playing possum. Subsequent interrogation of prisoners disclosed that the local commander had ordered his men on no account to disclose their presence during the entrance of the American force. Both passes were swept by the minesweeper groups, starting shortly after 0700. Deep Entrance was clear; but a mine field, the first to be encountered in Micronesia, was discovered inside Wide Passage. Two hours elapsed before a channel had been swept, and the transports were delayed accordingly, passing into Deep Entrance at 0915. That gallant old battlewagon *Tennessee* preceded them.

Thus, D-day went off to a slow start and the enemy's silence boded no good. General Watson was eager to get his artillery ashore and registered before dark. After the expeditionary group

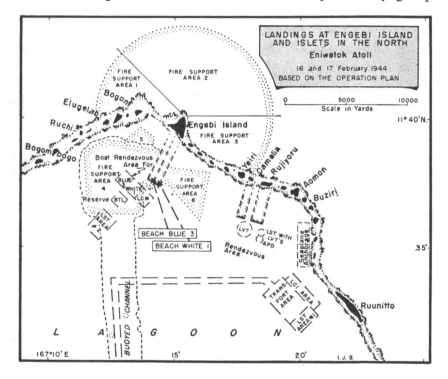

entered the lagoon — and it was not all in until 1034 — the ships still had ten miles to steam before reaching the transport area off Engebi. They negotiated that distance without mishap, for not a mine had escaped the efficient sweepers. Admiral Hill afterwards admitted that this first trip across Eniwetok Lagoon was the most anxious one in his naval career.

The transports arrived in their area at 1230 but in a state of confusion. A subchaser which had taken no part in the rehearsal had been designated convoy guide. *SC–1066,* the one chosen, had a lucky number for an invasion but she took station off the wrong islet. Destroyer transport *Kane*, whose boats were to take supplies ashore from *LST–272*, sent them to the wrong LST, adding to the confusion. This situation was straightened out and at 1338 the reconnaissance party in three amphtracs landed on Rujiyoru Islet unopposed, followed shortly by three more LVTs with a reconnaissance party for "Camelia," which had no native name. Ammunition and artillery were ordered ashore immediately, but the process took two hours.

All these contretemps brought the tempers of commanding officers to boiling point. Admiral Hill, regarding the performance of *SC–1066* as "completely unsatisfactory," relieved the skipper of his command; General Watson fired the commander of his regimental artillery. Captain Loomis received a visual message from Admiral Hill conveying his displeasure with the afternoon's operations in no uncertain terms, and ordering necessary measures taken "to assure more satisfactory performance tomorrow." This was a sad blow to Captain Loomis, who knew as much about amphibious warfare as any older officer in the expeditionary group.

Since no opposition developed, the day's objectives were accomplished in spite of the confusion. The 22nd Marines landed twelve 75-mm pack howitzers, and the 27th Division got twelve 105-mm cannon ashore on Rujiyoru and Camelia by 1530, and all guns were registered before dark. Bogon Islet also was occupied in order to close a possible escape route for the enemy.

The transports now shifted anchorage to the northwest in preparation for the major task of landing on Engebi next morning. But the day's work was still incomplete. To check the accuracy of intelligence data, the V 'Phib reconnaissance company was embarked in small boats at 1700 and sent under the cover of heavy supporting fires to inspect the approaches to the Engebi landing beaches. The scouts, under machine-gun fire, went in to within 50 yards of the beaches, planted buoys indicating boat lanes and shoals and collected valuable information for assault troops and fire support ships.

Sundown brought no respite for the enemy on Engebi. Pinned down, he had to take a simultaneous pounding from sea, air and land-based artillery. American ground forces knew from earlier experience that no possible bombardment would kill all the Japanese, but trusted that survivors would be punch-drunk and deprived of any facilities above ground. They were fortunate to be boated for their ship-to-shore trip by the Army amphtrac outfit [10] which had served the 7th Division so well at Kwajalein.

D plus 1 day, 18 February, opened with showers which were soon swept away by a strong tradewind. At 0700 naval guns and artillery on the islets opened up and kept it up until 0838, with one ten-minute interruption to allow carrier planes to strike. At 0805 the first wave scheduled to land was at the line of departure in amphtracs, and nine minutes later started for the beach.

The 1st and 2nd Battalions 22nd Marines were to land on adjoining beaches, making a front of 800 yards. The first wave on each beach consisted of 20 LVT–A2s, personnel amphtracs both armored and armed, supported by 17 amphibious tanks arranged on the four flanks and preceded by Lieutenant Commander Blanchard's group of six LCIs which had already done a fine job at Kwajalein. As the first two waves hit the beach they could bring to bear on it a total of seventeen 37-mm cannon, forty .50-caliber machine guns and seventy-one .30-caliber machine guns. In addition the troops were supported by gunfire from destroyers, battleships and the land-based artillery.

At 0838 parachute flares were dropped from spotting planes as a signal that wave 1 was 200 yards off the beach. All ships checked gunfire and the wave hit the beach at 0844. Amphtracs of the two first waves advanced inland 100 yards in support of the troops, then retired to the beach to protect the flanks. Those of subsequent waves reëntered the water after unloading and rendezvoused outside the reach of small arms.[11]

[10] The 708th Army Amphibious Tank Battalion, 120 of whose LVTs were attached to the Eniwetok Expeditionary Group.
[11] Field Order No. 2, 708th Amphibious Tank Battalion (USA), prepared in the field, 8 Feb. 1944; conversations with Maj. Kooken, operations officer.

Japanese mortar fire from the southeastern point of Engebi (which the bluejackets called "Skunk Point") hit control vessel *SC–539* eleven minutes after the landing, and wounded three officers. At 0933 a tank-loaded LCM took a lurch when all buttoned up in preparation for landing. The tank smashed open the ramp, pitched overboard and sank in 40 feet of water; only one man of its crew escaped drowning.

The landings on the eastern beach progressed smoothly; within half an hour it was secure. But things did not go so well on the western beach, which lay close to the airstrip around which the enemy had concentrated his defenses; and behind it rose a bank about ten feet high. The reserve battalion, boated in LCVPs from *Leonard Wood*, had to be ordered in to help. With its commitment the entire 22nd Regiment with attached units, 3500 strong, was on Engebi, of which the Japanese garrison, over 1200 strong two days earlier, had been reduced perhaps one third by the preliminary air and naval bombardment.

By 1030 "the situation was well in hand" on both beaches and a few tanks had overrun the island. No longer could the punch-drunk survivors offer organized opposition in the classic use of that term.

A number of very thin, slit-like trenches or foxholes formed pockets of resistance, but in general the Japanese defense was broken down to the point where each soldier fought independently, and about all he could do was to infiltrate the American lines or rise up out of a well-concealed foxhole in the rear of the Marines, forcing them to adopt what someone described as "vertical warfare." Their laborious mopping-up required a sensitive eye, since the only way to detect the slits in the ground was to observe the small shadows cast by their lips. But by 1640 on the day of landing, 18 February, General Watson was able to announce that Engebi was secured.

About a thousand enemy troops lay dead and burned on the charred islet that had become America's newest acquisition by right of conquest. The Marines had lost 85 dead and 166 wounded.

3. *Eniwetok Island, 19–23 February*

Engebi was almost a pushover, but the southern operations against Parry and Eniwetok Islands turned up a number of surprises and proved far tougher than anyone had anticipated. But for one lucky break, the capture of these islands might have exacted casualties comparable to those of Tarawa or Saipan.

The Japanese had neatly fooled the Americans into the belief that Parry and Eniwetok Islands were unoccupied. They had successfully concealed themselves and their weapons from the prying cameras of the carrier planes before D-day, from the hawk-eyed photo interpreters of the Pacific Fleet, and from the binoculars and telescopes of Admiral Hill's lookouts when his ships passed only a biscuit-toss from Parry. What the Japanese expected to gain by playing possum is not clear. Possibly the atoll commander intended to wait until American naval forces had retired, hoping that they would be content to occupy Engebi and that the "Greater East Asia Annihilation Fleet" (that phantom of Tojo's propaganda) would appear and help the commander to reconquer the atoll. In the end, hiding underground while American planes roared overhead and the Fleet steamed close aboard availed him nothing. Intelligence officers, combing through the debris on Engebi, found papers indicating that Eniwetok and Parry Islands were actually defended by 808 and 1347 men respectively. Most of these troops belonged to Major General Nishida's 1st Amphibious Brigade, a veteran unit of the toughest fighters bred in Japan. Ensign D. M. Allen of the Jicpoa intelligence team had the captured material translated by 1400 February 18, and presented General Watson with the bad news.

Faced with this situation, the General revised his plan. Simultaneous landings on Eniwetok and Parry were discarded; all possible strength must be brought to bear upon each island in succession. He decided to throw both battalions of the 106th Regiment into Eniwetok, and to have the Marine reserve battalion which had

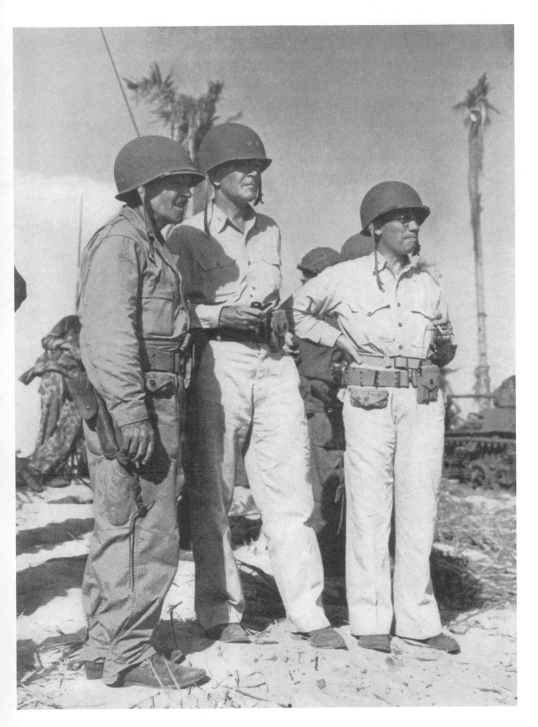

Colonel Ayers, Admiral Hill and General Watson at Eniwetok

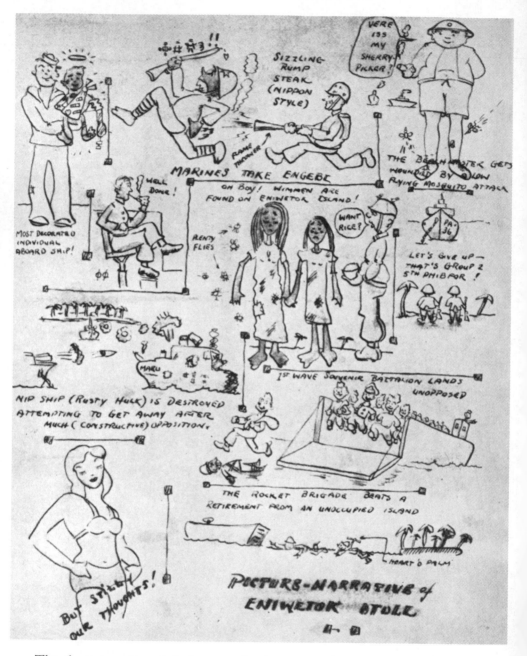

The character upper right is meant for Commander Carl E. Anderson. Native women are wearing prewar "Mother Hubbards"

The Lighter Side of the Eniwetok Landings
By Lieutenant Commander Robert A. MacPherson

helped take Namur boated and available. So the Marines' transport, *Leonard Wood*, steamed across the lagoon and arrived off Eniwetok Island at 0840. The two Army battalions were already there, loaded in amphtracs.

Club-shaped Eniwetok Island, 4700 yards long, 250 yards wide at the western end and tapering down to a point in the north, was all

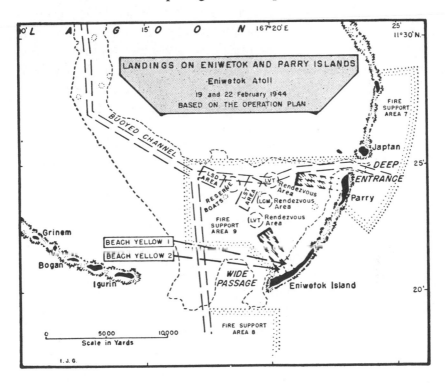

coral sand. The club's bending around the circular curve of the atoll made the lagoon side concave, and so, bad for a landing; but the convex outer shore, with a nasty reef and high surf, was out of the question. Beaches chosen for the landings, designated Yellow 1 and 2, began just south of the Japanese pier. The plan called for one battalion to mop up the bulbous southern sector, where all enemy strong points were supposed to be located, while the other marched up the handle.

Owing to American ignorance that Eniwetok was occupied, it

had received only a token air and naval bombardment, and no attention whatever from land-based artillery. There was now little time to make up for lost opportunities, but the assault waves were encouraged by an improvised bombardment. Heavy cruisers *Portland* and *Indianapolis* and destroyers *Hoel* and *Trathen* were stationed on the flanks of the LCI gunboats, and inside of them were the LVTs. Double the planned number of shells was fired into Eniwetok as soon as it was known that there were plenty of Japanese ashore; but that double was not half enough nor heavy enough. The thick foliage and heavy undergrowth on the island and its 20-foot elevation — a mountain in the Marshalls — called for more ammunition than Admiral Hill's fire support ships had left after their earlier shoots.

Preparatory fires completed, amphtracs started in, accompanied by the Elsie Items. The soldiers were all asking each other the same question: "Are we drawing fire from the beach?" American amphibious forces, whether Army, Navy or Marine Corps, always assumed that if they once got ashore and established a beachhead the rest would be "duck soup." They learned better later; but never during the war did this writer hear one American soldier or sailor doubt the ultimate success of an amphibious operation. That was an important element of his strength.

The first wave landed on the Yellow beaches at 0918, and by 0930 some of the infantry had worked 200 yards inland in their effort to whipsaw the island. Other waves landed in quick succession and met only light sniper fire. Nevertheless, the beach jammed up. Behind it was an embankment, twice as high as the one on Engebi, which stopped the tanks until an avenue could be found through or around. This barrier discouraged the troops, some of whom began digging foxholes on the beach contrary to orders.

By 0947, when the fifth wave of the 1st Battalion had been landed on Beach Yellow 2 and the sixth wave was waiting off the beach, troops and tanks were piling up badly. General Watson at 1015 signaled Colonel R. C. Ayers usa, who commanded the landing force, ordering him to get his troops off the beaches and move in.

This had a tonic effect and by 1045 the beach had been partially cleared; by 1125 boats could be brought in to evacuate casualties.

Yet the movement was slow. Assault troops of the 106th Infantry "did not move forward rapidly from the beaches (thereby causing a serious congestion), did not operate in close coöperation with tanks and failed to realize the capabilities of and to use to the fullest extent naval gunfire and close support aviation." [12] By 1230 they had only managed to cut a corridor across the island and make a small indentation on enemy positions to the south. GI Joe was running into all kinds of unpleasant opposition — machine-gun fire, mortar fire and snipers. The Japanese were all over the place, and he didn't like it, not one bit.

Since 0914 the reserve battalion of Marines had been boated in landing craft, milling around in formation circles, awaiting a call to the line of departure. The northeast tradewind had kicked up a rough sea on the lagoon and the Marines, huddled in LCVPs, soaked by rain squalls and salt spray, puking over each other and exhausted from bouncing around for 3½ hours, were relieved when at 1245 word came for them to land on Beach Yellow 1 at 1330.[13] Five minutes after that, the first wave landed and promptly ran into a strong pocket of enemy resistance on its flank, just north of the pier. At the same time communications, always a tough and complicated problem in amphibious operations, fouled up. An urgent message from the Army at 1344 for medium tanks required almost an hour to get through to *Ashland*.

By 1400 the 3rd Battalion 106th RCT was making slow but good progress toward the northern neck of Eniwetok; the 1st Battalion was pinned down and making no headway southward. The Marines' reserve battalion which had just landed was ordered to cross the island to the ocean side and then push south, abreast of the Army battalion, which could then confine its efforts to the lagoon

[12] Report of Brig. Gen. Watson, who attributed this to their defective amphibious training. Compare action of another regiment of this 27th Div. at Makin.

[13] It gets very rough in big lagoons like Kwajalein and Eniwetok. Mr. Salomon admits he came nearer losing his lunch in Eniwetok Lagoon than at any other point of his naval career, and has only commiseration for seasick troops in landing craft.

side. It was hoped that by reinforcing the GIs' left flank the log jam would be broken and the club end of the island overrun without further delay. At about 1550 it was broken. By the time darkness had settled over Eniwetok, the southern attack was still moving ahead. Everyone secured for the night at 2100; at least, so they thought.

That night, 19–20 February 1944, proved to be as near a Marine's conception of hell as he would care to experience. Warships were shelling the southern end of the island, while Army artillery threw mortar projectiles onto the northern handle. Star shell and naval searchlights dissipated the darkness. GIs and Gyrenes added to each other's discomfort by their differing tactics in land warfare. The Marines consider that an objective should be overrun as quickly as possible; they follow up their assault troops with mop-up squads which take care of any individuals or strong points that have been by-passed or overlooked. Marines dig in at night and attempt never to fire unnecessarily, because night shooting seldom hits anyone but a friend and serves mainly to give one's position away. They allow the enemy to infiltrate — keeping good watch to prevent his accomplishing anything — and, when daylight comes, liquidate the infiltrators. Such tactics require good fire discipline of seasoned troops who have plenty of élan but keep their nerves under control. The Army, in World War II, preferred to take an objective slowly and methodically, using mechanized equipment and artillery barrages to the fullest extent, and advancing only after everything visible in front had been pounded down. Army tactics required enemy infiltrators to be shot at sight. This night, of all times, was the worst for Army and Marine Corps to work together on parallel lines. On the Marines' 400-yard front there was no shooting, but on the adjoining front GIs shot at anything that moved, including Marines. One could never be quite sure whether the man a few feet away was another soldier or a Marine or a Japanese. The general idea seemed to be to take no chances. Fortunately God loves the Marines, and apart from a few wounds the main results were unpleasantness and foul language. When finally "came the dawn," about 40 Japanese staged a banzai raid on the Marine command post. Sergeant C. E. Green USMC distinguished himself by pretending he was dead when shot in the leg, and then mowing down 15 Japanese with his automatic when they came into view. He disposed of seven more, rallied his men and saved the command post, but not until ten officers and men, including Captain Clark the operations officer, had been killed.

Escort carrier planes opened 20 February with a strafing attack on the Japanese in the club handle. This encouraged the 3rd Battalion 106th to advance 300 yards; they then encountered a thin but well dug-in line of Japanese across the narrowest part of the handle. It was too heavy a line of resistance to be cracked right away.

On the club-head, the Army and Marines had their hands full prying each individual Japanese out of the southerly rim of the islet from the sea to the lagoon. Fortunately the enemy had not had time to construct concrete pillboxes and the coconut-log bunkers that had been so fatal on Betio. At 1005 the Marines reported that they were meeting heavy resistance here, and again at 1340, requesting some medium tanks; but only light ones were available.[14] Such tanks as they had were still firing on enemy defenses on the southwest end of Eniwetok at 1430; but the Japanese were at the end of their rope. "We cornered fifty or so . . . on the end of the island, where they attempted a banzai charge," wrote Lieutenant Meyer, "but we cut them down like overripe wheat, and they lay like tired children with their faces in the sand."[15] At 1520 the Marines announced their section of the island secured. The 1st Battalion 106th, parallel to them, still had a pocket of resistance to cope with on the lagoon side, but liquidated that the next day, 21 February.

The troops on the north end were as slow as their fellows of the 27th Division at Makin. Too long they were held up by groups of defenders not one tenth their strength. The men were all right but their training and leadership alike were poor — "If only someone

[14] These operations proved conclusively the superiority of the medium tank over the light tank for this type of warfare.

[15] Lt. Cord Meyer USMCR "On the Beaches," in *Atlantic Monthly* CLXXIV (Oct. 1944) p. 42.

would tell us what to *do!*" said one of them. The earthwork barrier which checked their advance was subjected to heavy naval and air bombardment, but that was not good enough to encourage them to surmount it until one more night had passed. The soldiers started forward again cautiously at 1930 February 21 after carrier planes had inflicted another strafing attack. Enemy resistance then began to break down, and at 1630 Admiral Hill reported Eniwetok Island secured.

Early in the morning of the 21st the Marines, who had done more than their share, were reëmbarked in *Leonard Wood*. They came on board tired and very dirty, but well supplied with souvenirs and trophies of battle. They were badly in need of a rest, but General Watson counted on them to help take Parry next day — since they were in much better shape than the 106th — and they had to spend most of their time on board trying desperately to get their weapons and gear into shape.

4. *Parry, 19–23 February*

Parry Island is shaped like an elongated teardrop. Over 2000 feet wide on the northern end, it tapers off to a point in the south. Like Eniwetok, it was a neglected coconut plantation where tropical undergrowth that no airborne camera could penetrate had grown up under the palms. On 17 February, as the expeditionary group was entering the lagoon, an observation plane flew back and forth over Parry at very low altitude without drawing fire or seeing any sign of life. The first hint of anyone's being there came from the intelligence material discovered at Engebi, and on Eniwetok Island another stroke of good fortune delivered to American hands the Japanese defense plan for Parry. The defenses were shown to be mobile and fluid, revolving around a few strong points. Enemy troops on Parry numbered 1347 as against 808 on Eniwetok, and General Nishida's headquarters of the 1st Amphibious Brigade were supposed to be there. Accordingly, the Navy and Army prepared to give Parry as good a softening-up as limited time permitted. And before they were through with it, this once-verdant coconut grove was a scorched-earth of ruins and blasted tree trunks with a few dying palm fronds clacking miserably in the tradewind.

Japtan Islet, across Deep Entrance from Parry, was seized upon as the ideal place for the Marines to set up their 75-mm pack howitzers. They landed there without opposition, began bombarding Parry at 2000 February 20 and kept it up until the landing on the 22nd. Naval, air and surface units helped out by plastering Parry with every type of projectile they had, day and night, for three days. For the most part it was carried out by battleships *Pennsylvania, Tennessee* and *Colorado*, heavy cruisers *Louisville* and *Indianapolis*, and planes from that trey of veteran escort carriers, *Sangamon, Suwannee* and *Chenango*. The fire support ships operated inside the lagoon in 23 to 28 fathoms of water, while the flat-tops cruised around outside. Air bombardment proved to be more effective than gunfire because all the Japanese installations were underground and the ships fired at such short range that their projectiles had a flat trajectory and did little or no harm to anything below the surface. After the final bombardment, at daybreak 22 February, the entire island appeared to be blowing up; eyewitnesses wondered whether there would be anything left when the smoke cleared. There was plenty left.

The first two battalions of Marines — those that had conquered Engebi — were to land abreast on two beaches just north of a small pier on the lagoon side, about three quarters of a mile from the rounded end. The plan was similar to the one for Eniwetok Island. Both BLTs were to cut across the islet; one would then swing left and overrun the northern and fatter half while the other, with the aid of the 3rd BLT which had taken Eniwetok, would deploy right and secure the long, narrow section. Since the landing place was the enemy's strongest point, once it was knocked out the rest should be easy. Such was the plan, and that was the way it worked out. But before that, there was a regrettable incident afloat.

At 0805, when the LCI gunboats were maneuvering near the line of departure, the Marine attack team requested their commander to support the right flank where the heaviest opposition was expected. Lieutenant Commander Blanchard assigned three LCIs, his "most daring ships," to the right flank and stationed the remaining three on the left flank. At 0845 destroyer *Hailey*, from an area bearing SW from the LCIs, opened fire on assigned targets near the two beaches. At the same moment the LCIs left the line of departure and preceded the first wave of LVTs toward the beach by about 50 yards. Smoke from the shore bombardment blew down on the boat waves, limiting visibility to about 400 yards. The LCIs had just opened fire with their 40-mm guns when they came under "friendly" fire from *Hailey*. A projectile burst over *LCI–442*, killing six men and wounding five. A moment later *LCI–440* was hit twice, sustaining heavy casualties for so small a vessel — 7 killed and 39 wounded. And before a spotting plane could get word to *Hailey* to cease fire, *LCI–365* too had been hit. Admiral Hill, after reviewing the facts, attributed the accident to poor visibility caused by smoke and dust from the close supporting gunfire, cleared *Hailey's* commanding officer of culpability and praised "the gallantry and contemptuous disregard of danger displayed by all LCIs attached to this command." [16]

Landings began at 0908, but the enemy was still full of spirit and fight. His emplacements were so well concealed as to be difficult to spot from even a few feet away. Most of them were underground hideouts large enough for a few men, with no embrasures or firing ports. A typical strong point was arranged like a spider's web. In the center would be an underground shelter for five to ten men, lined and roofed with coconut logs, over which were strips of corrugated iron and then a thick layer of sand. The radiating tunnels were lined with headless gasoline drums placed end to end, big enough for a Japanese to crawl through, and far better concealed than a mole's tunnels in a lawn. Around the periphery of the web

[16] Com LCI Group 8 Flotilla 3 (Lt. Cdr. Blanchard) Action Report and War Diary; "Proceedings of a Board of Investigation Convened on Board *Indianapolis* 22 Feb. 1944," 20 Mar. 1944.

were round foxholes 10 to 15 feet apart, most of them roofed with corrugated iron and interconnected by narrow trenches or tunnels. If his central shelter was discovered the Japanese would crawl to the periphery, pop out and take a shot at one from the rear, and pop in again. The Marines had already encountered similar defenses on Eniwetok Island, but Parry was honeycombed with them, well camouflaged and very hard to find. It reminded one of a prairie-dog town on the Western plains.

The assaulting troops pushed rapidly forward behind tanks, with demolition and flame-thrower parties directly behind to burn or blow up each enemy nest. Combat teams of three or four men were found to be most effective. But the Japanese were prepared for tanks, with anti-tank guns and mines which detonated on 35 pounds' pressure and tore men apart with horrible results, blowing whole sections of their bodies to bits. Dismembered men, mashed up with clothing and blood, looked dead or completely done for when brought on board ship, yet many of them survived, owing to medical skill and their excellent physical condition.

Naval gunfire supported the land action until 1055, when it was checked as it began to reach the American lines. Enemy resistance was still strong and both boat lanes were subjected to mortar fire. Seasoned men of the V 'Phib reconnaissance party were ordered in as reinforcements, and landed at 1313. About that time the situation improved. Tanks and troops reached the rounded north end of Parry at 1330, and, although the enemy persistently held an area 200 yards north of the pier on the lagoon side, the Marines were advancing south behind their tanks on the ocean side of the islet. In skirmish line they pushed on to their final goal, the southern end where the enemy was in the open. "Finally we killed them all," wrote Lieutenant Meyer. "There was not much jubilation. We just sat and stared at the sand, and most of us thought of those who were gone — those whom I shall remember as always young, smiling and graceful, and I shall try to forget how they looked at the end, beyond all recognition." [17]

[17] *Atlantic Monthly* Oct. 1944 p. 43.

At 1930 February 22 the General announced that Parry was secured. Digging the enemy out from the bowels of Parry Island cost twice as many men as taking Eniwetok, but it was even more costly for the enemy.

CASUALTIES IN THE CONQUEST OF ENIWETOK ATOLL [18]

| | American | | Japanese | | |
	Killed and Missing	Wounded	Killed, Burial Count	Prisoners	Total Present
Engebi I.	85	166	934	16	1276
Eniwetok I.	37	94	704	23	808
Parry I.	73	261	1027	25	1347
Other islets	—	—	12	—	?
	195	521	2677	64	3431 +

Eniwetok Atoll was secured. American forces had struck another swift, sudden and hard blow against Japan.

On 24 February Admiral Hill placed the now famous Commander C. E. Anderson USNR in charge of unloading activities at the Eniwetok beaches, where his tireless energy and knack of getting work out of the most unwilling men expedited matters. That day the weary 22nd Marines were reëmbarked; the 10th Marine Defense Battalion became the garrison of Eniwetok Island while a portion of the 106th Infantry moved to Parry. Most of the combatant ships and transports departed that day or next. Escort carrier *Manila Bay* relieved the three CVEs; tender *Chincoteague* arrived together with patrol planes which inaugurated air searches westward. Landing places for LSTs were cleared at Engebi and Eniwetok beaches.

By 4 March the ships that had brought in the garrison and occupation forces with their supplies and equipment had unloaded and departed, and by the end of that month Eniwetok Island was so covered with new buildings that landmarks of the battle were completely erased.

[18] Cincpac Analysis Feb. 1944, Jicpoa item No. 89-44 for last column. Slightly different statistics are given in Isley and Crowl p. 299, and p. 607 footnote 81.

CHAPTER XVII

Marshalls' Mop-up[1]

February–June 1944

1. Development of Bases

AFTER the last week of February, when the principal American conquests in the Marshalls were secured, naval activities in that archipelago fell into three categories: development of advanced naval and air bases; neutralization of enemy-held atolls; securing minor atolls and looking after the welfare of the natives.

Majuro, an unusually pretty atoll, untouched by the ravages of war, became a valuable advanced base for further penetration of the Pacific. A 5800-foot airstrip, constructed on Dalap Island, could be used for emergency landings as early as 12 February 1944; in March it became a staging point for light bombers used to keep down the four enemy-held atolls. The lagoon became an important fleet anchorage, where the fast carrier groups rested briefly between strikes, and to which other ships of the Pacific Fleet returned for fueling and the services of the Mobile Service Squadron. By the end of February about 5000 men were stationed at Majuro.

Captain V. F. Grant, the atoll commander, took a great interest in the natives, whose ranks had been thinned by the enemy's removal of the young and able-bodied of both sexes to Jaluit. His war diary has a Stevensonian touch: "29 February 1944. King Langlan, Queen and Royal Party were entertained at lunch by Captain Grant." He established a trading post where the Majurians could

[1] Cincpac Monthly Analyses for the period; USSBS Naval Analysis Div. *The American Campaign Against Wotje, Maloelap and Jaluit* (1947); W. G. Wendell "The Marshall Islands Operations" sec. x.

obtain gaily printed cotton (for their lava-lavas) and black twist tobacco, in return for pandanus-leaf baskets, mats, model canoes and other products of their skill. Thus the souvenir racket which develops wherever American bluejackets set foot was somewhat regulated. The King and Queen even rated a royal salute from Captain Grant's "Majuro Navy," consisting of four LCIs, ten LSTs, a small minesweeper and tug *Arapaho*.

Kwajalein's strategic importance was signaled by the appointment of Rear Admiral Alva D. Bernhard as atoll commander. Roi and Namur had been stripped of vegetation by the prolonged bombardment; out of hundreds of Japanese installations, only pockmarked concrete blockhouses, a few command posts and the twisted steel of the old hangar remained. Everything else was sheared off by the Seabees' bulldozers and the area, less than 1200 yards square, was improved as an airfield named after the heroic Captain Dyess of the Marine Corps. On Namur a flock of Quonset huts was erected to house the garrison. The lack of fresh water and abundance of sand made these islands rather dreary stations; but the many sail of ships ever present in that northern and protected bight of the great lagoon prevented the garrison from becoming lonely.

Admiral Turner assigned subchasers, LCIs, LSTs and small craft to Admiral Bernhard as local defense forces on 16 February. At the southern end of the lagoon Ebeye Island was developed as a seaplane base, whilst Kwajalein Island became the center of Army air effort in Micronesia. By early March it had two runways 4000 and 6300 feet long, and heavy bombers were moved up there from Abemama. On 1 April over 14,000 men were stationed on Kwajalein Island, 6500 on Roi and Namur, and a few thousand on Ebeye.

Eniwetok, of which Captain E. A. Cruise became atoll commander, was developed like Kwajalein at both ends and in much the same way. Engebi fighter strip became operational by 27 February, an 8200-foot bomber strip was completed in March, and the two were named Wigley Field.[2] This and the new Stickell Field[3]

---

[2] After Lt. Col. Roy C. Wigley, C.O. 531st Fighter Squadron VII A.A.F., lost in an attack on Jaluit 18 Jan. 1944.

[3] Named after Cdr. John H. Stickell of Illinois, a naval aviator and former RAF

on Eniwetok Island became forward bases for air searches and for Liberators and other heavy bombers employed in keeping Truk and other Caroline Islands useless to the Japanese. A small seaplane base was constructed on Parry Island, but not much used. There were 11,200 men stationed on Eniwetok Atoll by 1 April; and three months later, during the interval between the Saipan and Guam operations, one could steam the long diameter of Eniwetok Lagoon from south to north and see at least a hundred fighting ships and auxiliaries at any one time, with others hull down although anchored in the lagoon.

Possession of these bases raised the American horizon, as set by the farthest sweep of search and carrier planes, another two thousand miles. The Marianas and Palau were already in sight.

2. Neutralizing Enemy-held Atolls [4]

Now that Jaluit, Mili, Maloelap, Wotje and Nauru had been "leapfrogged," the only interest that the Pacific Fleet had in them was the negative one of neutralization. Not wanted for military purposes, they were not worth the American lives that would be expended in taking them. These atolls were like tough characters who have been knocked down but who have to be kicked every so often so that they will stay down. Island bases are useful only so long as striking forces can operate from them. When cut off through loss of sea command, they are a liability. And an airfield from which planes cannot operate is as harmless as a tennis court.

During February 1944 the VII Army Air Force flew about 1000 sorties against the four by-passed Marshall Islands, so that the Abemama-Mili-Taroa route became known as the "milk run." [5]

---

pilot, a master tactician in air combat, who was wounded in a strike on Jaluit 12 Dec. 1943 and died after reaching Funafuti.

[4] USSBS Naval Analysis Division *The American Campaign Against Wotje, Maloelap, Mille and Jaluit* (1947).

[5] Exact figures are difficult to arrive at. "Operations of the VII A.A.F. 1 Feb.–2 Mar. 1944" gives 1073 sorties; the Feb. "Analysis of Pacific Air Operations" issued by Comairpac, p. 11, lists 878, to Mili, Jaluit, Wotje and Maloelap. One says 176, the other 237, to Ponape and Kusaie.

Not a single flight was intercepted by enemy planes, but Japanese anti-aircraft fire was becoming more accurate. Instead of throwing up a curtain of ack-ack around their airfields, as the Japanese gunners did when plenty of ammunition was at hand, they concentrated on shooting down individual bombers, tactics which cost the VII Army Air Force 7 bombers and 2 fighters in February. After every strike on Taroa (Maloelap) or Otdia (Wotje) the Japanese garrison would work feverishly repairing at least one airstrip, apparently to receive Rising Sun planes that never arrived. The Mili field became inoperable for bombers 4 February, but was good for staging fighter planes three weeks longer. As Imperial Headquarters had kept its island garrisons supplied with six months' to a year's provisions and ammunition, there was no great privation until the second half of 1944.[6] No supply ships called after the fall of Kwajalein. Two submarines brought about 60 tons of provisions and ammunition to Mili in March 1944, but in the same month *I–32*, in trying to supply Wotje, was sunk by the combined efforts of destroyer escort *Manlove* and *PC–1135*. Towards the end of May the Japanese tried again. Submarine *I–184* successfully transported food and ammunition from Yokosuka to Mili. Subsequently she was ordered to patrol to the eastward of Guam where she was sunk on 19 June by a plane from *Suwannee*.

When the Liberators were moved up to Kwajalein and Eniwetok, medium bombers such as SBDs and fighter planes armed with bombs were substituted for the heavies in striking the by-passed atolls. These, it turned out after the war, were far more effective than the B–24s which (as a Japanese officer at Mili reported) "invariably missed the runway."[7] They would take off from Abemama, Tarawa or Makin, bomb one of the enemy-held airfields, alight at Majuro for refueling and arming, and hit another atoll before returning to the Gilberts.

Mili showed an unexpected row of teeth when Rear Admiral

---

[6] By July 1944 the daily rice ration, normally 720 grams, had been reduced to an average of 300 gr. in the 4 by-passed atolls, and by Jan. 1945 it was only 70 gr.
[7] *Inter. Jap. Off.* pp. 87–88.

Willis A. Lee led in battleships against it on 18 March 1944. *Iowa* and *New Jersey* with destroyers *Hull* and *Dewey* bombarded gun emplacements, buildings and other installations for almost three hours in the morning, and again for two hours in the afternoon. Between these bombardments and after the second, carrier *Lexington* launched air strikes. Mili did not take this lying down; the shore batteries repeatedly straddled ships of the mission and even subjected mighty *Iowa* to the indignity of two 6-inch hits. Similarly, on 4 April, shore batteries at Wotje scored three hits, one a dud, on destroyer *Hull* as she was picking up a Marine flier shot down in an air raid the previous day.

Occasionally a reconnaissance party from some naval vessel landed on an islet of Wotje, Mili or Maloelap to get in touch with the natives and find out what went on. They usually found that the Japanese garrisons had no intention of surrendering, and were not downhearted. A Gilbertese cook to the Mili garrison, who escaped from there in May, reported that the enemy still enjoyed three "squares" per day and had plenty of ammunition and a radio, radar, electric power and coast defense guns. This information, verified in part by photographic reconnaissance, was not at all pleasing to the aviators who had subjected the atoll to four months' intensive bombing, at a cost of 26 planes. In truth, the Japanese were far from happy. Those at Mili worked hard on building defenses until mid-1944, after which they were mainly concerned with fishing, growing gardens and hunting rats for food. Out of a total of 4700 officers and men at Mili on 1 February 1944, about 1600 died before the surrender from disease, starvation and eating poisonous fish, and 900 more as a result of air raids; most of these would have recovered but for lack of medical supplies and proper food.[8]

In the summer of 1944 the Army bomber groups which so far had carried the burden of the air offensive moved up from the Gilbert and Ellice bases to the Marianas and other forward areas. The Fourth Marine Aircraft Wing, greatly to its disgust, was then given the Marshalls assignment. Since these atolls were no longer

---

[8] *Inter. Jap. Off.* pp. 87–89; statistics corrected by *American Campaign* p. 208.

of any use to Japan, and not wanted by the Americans, there was no sense in taking them by assault; and in Japanese hands, ever fewer and more feeble, they remained until the surrender.[9]

3. *Occupation of Minor Atolls*

Apart from the four atolls held by the Japanese in some strength, and those captured by the United States in February, there were 28 to 30 atolls or islands in the Radak and Ralik (windward and leeward) chains of the Marshalls. Arno, very near Majuro, was occupied peacefully by a reconnaissance party on 12 February; the occupation of the others was effected by a series of armed reconnaissances from Kwajalein. These afforded much gratification to junior naval officers who had the pleasure of reading Admiral Nimitz's proclamation and assuming a paternal and benevolent sway over the Micronesians, while the Marines who formed the "expeditionary forces" found virgin fields for souvenir collecting. The natives were uniformly friendly, joyfully assisting the Marines in hunting down stray Japanese and in providing souvenirs.

The first armed reconnaissance, of Wotho Atoll, took off from Kwajalein 7 March. Major Crawford B. Lawton USMC commanded two companies of the 1st Battalion 22nd Marines; he was accompanied by a civil affairs officer (Lieutenant L. C. Bergquist USNR), medicos, Japanese and Marshallese interpreters, and a few Kwajalein natives who had relatives or friends in the islands to be visited. LVTs and jeeps were brought along in two LCIs and one LST, escorted by destroyer *Callaghan* and minesweeper *Requisite*. Lieutenant Commander Robert Eikel, commodore of this "Naval Force," as he calls it in his report, entered the pass to Wotho

[9] In Sept. 1944, learning that the natives of Wotje would like to get out, the Navy sent two small craft into the nearby Erikub Atoll and sent native scouts into Wotje; and 700 men, women and children, together with poultry and pigs, sailed over by night to Erikub, whence they were taken to another atoll under American control. In Mar. 1945 a similar evacuation of 452 natives was made from Wotje Atoll, by an LCI commanded by Lt. H. B. Wilson USNR. (Navy Dept. releases of 2 Oct. 1944 and 31 Mar. 1945.)

Marines Bartering with Micronesian Natives

Truk Lagoon, Taken by a Plane from U.S.S. Intrepid, 17 February 1944

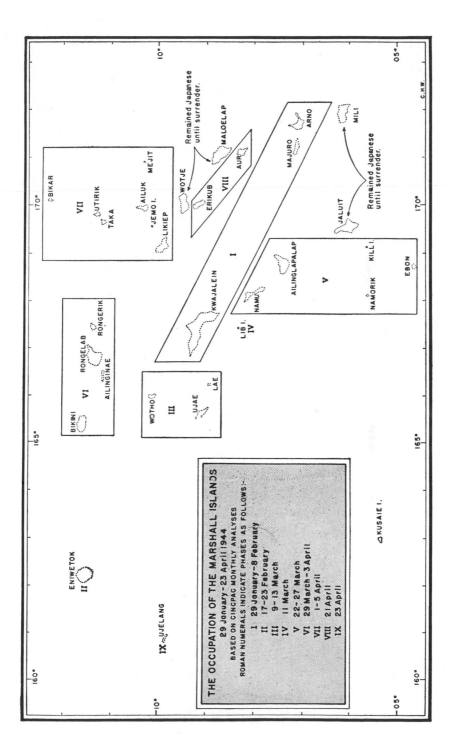

THE OCCUPATION OF THE MARSHALL ISLANDS
29 January – 23 April 1944
BASED ON CINCPAC MONTHLY ANALYSES
ROMAN NUMERALS INDICATE PHASES AS FOLLOWS:-

I   29 January –8 February
II   17–23 February
III 9 – 13 March
IV   11 March
V   22–27 March
VI   29 March –3 April
VII 1–5 April
VIII 2 April
IX   23 April

Remained Japanese until surrender.

Remained Japanese until surrender.

Lagoon on 8 March. No signs of human life could be discovered, but toward midnight an LCI with native scouts on board returned with news that there were twelve Japanese on one of the islets, the crew of a plane that had made a forced landing. The Marines went ashore next day, but upon their approach the Japanese committed suicide.

The native population of Wotho, reported to be "well nourished, clean and intelligent," rallied around as the American flag was raised and accepted largesse in the shape of salvaged Japanese rice, canned salmon, laundry soap and black twist tobacco. The women were disappointed that no cloth had been brought, but the Marines did not appear to mind. Lelet, the atoll chief, sometime skipper of a missionary schooner out of Hawaii, had his authority confirmed by Lieutenant Commander Eikel, who then formed up his "Naval Force" and departed for fresh fields of insular conquest.

Ujae came next. One of the scouts on board had relatives ashore who informed him that six Japanese were present, in charge of a weather station. Ensign S. E. Ballinger USNR, a graduate of the Navy's Japanese Language School, drafted a note demanding their surrender, which was delivered by a native. The enemy, however, did not seem to appreciate his Boulder (Colorado) Japanese. One of the LCIs next morning received rifle fire and retaliated with machine guns, but nobody on either side was hurt. After this bloodless Battle of Ujae, the Marines landed. Again the Japanese disappointed them by committing suicide; all but one, who performed a mere token hara-kiri and was taken prisoner. The flag was duly raised, the naval force departed. It went through the same procedure on Lae, where there were no Japanese, and returned to Kwajalein gorged with glory, good spirits and souvenirs.[10]

This expedition is a sample of several others which visited or occupied 20 more Marshall atolls by the end of April. A party that undertook during 22–27 March to cover those SE of Kwajalein — Namu, Ailinglapalap, Namorik, Ebon and Kili — ran into a little more trouble. Ailinglapalap was the seat of a royal family that had

[10] Atoll Commander Kwajalein to Commander Forward Area 28 Mar. 1944.

ruled the whole Ralik chain under the Germans and the Japanese. Two enemy barges had grounded there after being bombed by American planes, and some 46 of their passengers and crew were still at large. A party of Marines landed from *LST–23*, chased the Japanese around the island, killed 37 and took 9 prisoners at a cost of 5 Marines wounded. King Jamata, whose royal residence had been destroyed by gunfire during the cleanup, was appeased by presents of tinned salmon, tobacco and soap, and cheerfully swore allegiance to the United States as doubtless he had done to the Emperor of Japan.

The party then proceeded to Namu, where the only Japanese were a policeman and a schoolteacher with his wife and three children. The Marine major in command of this detachment took himself very seriously. "The Japanese inhabitants were on the beach with a white flag," he wrote. "Information concerning their number was correct with the addition of one (1) child. There is no information to account for this discrepancy." At Ebon Atoll, southernmost of the Marshalls, 5 Japanese soldiers and 20 civilians showed fight, killing 2 and wounding 8 Marines before they were disposed of on 24 March. On Namorik, reached two days later, there was but one Japanese, a charcoal burner who took to his woods; the solemn young major "decided that his capture would be insignificant so far as the war effort was concerned and this insignificance did not justify the expenditure of more time in searching for him." [11]

In early April another reconnaissance party visited the Radak or windward chain, calling at seven atolls, on only two of which were any Japanese found. On Ailuk the natives requested permission through an interpreter to "start praying again." Permission granted! God had returned to the Marshalls, with globe and anchor insignia.

[11] Bikini ("Fanned by Palms," subsequently fanned by something more powerful) was taken 30 March after the garrison of 5 men had committed suicide. At Rongelap on 1 Apr. an observation tower was shelled by a DE and fuel dumps and food stores were destroyed, but, according to strict military punctilio, the flag was not raised because the garrison of 11 Japanese reported by the natives successfully concealed itself in the bush. At Utirik there was a sharp fight with 14 Japanese who were killed at no cost to the Marines, and there the flag was raised. (Wendell "Marshall Islands Operations" p. 53; Report by Lt. L. C. Bergquist USNR, chief of Civil Affairs Section.)

As the United States Army clamored to be let in on these picnics, it was given the honor of cleaning up Ujelang, westernmost of the Marshalls and right on the Eniwetok–Ponape route. Ten officers and 150 men of the 11th Infantry Regiment USA landed there 21 April and exterminated the 18 Japanese occupants without loss to themselves.

In mid-April a regular fortnightly series of inspections of the lesser Marshalls was organized, in three units, each consisting of a platoon of infantry, a civil affairs party and a doctor, embarked in an Elsie Item. The naval surgeons showed great energy and skill in restoring the health of the natives, and the civil affairs officers set up the old tribal organizations and encouraged the inhabitants to govern themselves.

Thus within three months the "impregnable" Marshall Archipelago had become an American possession — always excepting stubbornly held Wotje, Maloelap, Mili and Jaluit.

CHAPTER XVIII

First Strike on Truk[1]

(Operation "Hailstone")

17–18 February 1944

East Longitude dates, Zone minus 10 time.[2]

A S SOON AS the principal Marshall Islands were secured, preparations began for the next major amphibious operation in the conquest of Micronesia. What this step should be — Truk, the Marianas or the Central Carolines[3] — was not yet decided; but the mounting of an operation so deep in enemy waters created many logistic and shipping problems; the minimum time required for preparation was not less than four months.

In the meantime the Pacific Fleet employed its great and growing carrier strength in a series of massive raids on Japanese strongholds, such as Truk, Saipan, Yap and the Palaus. And on one memorable occasion the fast carrier forces swept down on Hollandia, New Guinea, to assist and support General MacArthur's Army and Admiral Kinkaid's Seventh Fleet.

Carrier warfare had now come of age. Beginning with this strike

---

[1] CTF 50 (Vice Adm. Spruance), CTF 58 (Rear Adm. Mitscher), TG commanders' and individual ships' Action Reports; and, for the Japanese side, USSBS "Truk Report" (see Volume IV of this History p. 5 for full title) and USSBS Naval Analysis Division *The Reduction of Truk* (1947), a mine of information about Truk under Japanese rule; Cdr. C. Nakajima of Combined Fleet staff, *Inter. Jap. Off.* p. 144; Diary of Gen. Kimihara at Rabaul, Cincpac-Cincpoa *Weekly Intelligence* I No. 17 (3 Nov. 1944).

[2] West Longitude dates are used in the Action Reports, as for Eniwetok, but both dates and times have here been transposed to the local ones.

[3] According to the C.C.S. Directive of 24 Aug. 1943 (see chap. v) Ponape should have been taken before Truk, but by Feb. 1944 the J.C.S. had agreed to let Ponape be by-passed because it had too much rainfall for a major air base and in general was not worth the effort.

on Truk, it assumed the pattern that it was to follow until Japan surrendered. In the various strikes coördinated with the Marshalls operation, as we have seen, Fast Carrier Forces Pacific Fleet sealed off certain enemy-held atolls that the Americans intended to occupy, and interdicted others to the enemy, so that amphibious forces encountered no interference from outside the immediate target. One more step remained to be taken in this tactical evolution: to beat down a major enemy base without the aid of land-based air power and without any follow-up by amphibious forces. Hence the significance of the Truk strike of 17–18 February 1944.

This strike was closely articulated with the capture of Eniwetok and the encirclement of Rabaul. It was intended to cover the one, pull the strings on the other, and clean out of Truk the Japanese Fleet which was waiting for a chance to pounce on General MacArthur. For Truk lies almost equidistant from Eniwetok (669 miles) and Rabaul (696 miles). It was a vital staging point for sea and air communications between Japan and the Bismarcks "fish weir." Now that Kwajalein had fallen and the big L of Micronesia had been clipped back to long. 165° E, the anchor of the Japanese outer defense system lay in Truk Lagoon.

For Truk, capital of the Carolines under German and Japanese rule, is situated almost in the geographical center of Micronesia. Possessing the best fleet anchorage anywhere in the Mandates, it was very valuable to Japan during the first two years of the war. Indeed, the main motive of Imperial Headquarters in taking Rabaul, Lae and Salamaua early in the war was to protect Truk from Allied air attack and reconnaissance.[4] Important as it was to the Japanese, Americans were inclined to overemphasize its strength, as is evident by such deceptive phrases as "Japanese Pearl Harbor," and "Gibraltar of the Pacific." The combined area of all the islands is not equal to that of Oahu; the largest town, Dublon, never had more than 1200 buildings or facilities for more than temporary repairs to naval vessels. But the Combined Fleet was based on Truk

[4] Capt. T. Ohmae in *U.S. Naval Institute Proceedings* Jan. 1951 pp. 57–59.

Lagoon from July 1942, and its flagship, super-battleship *Musashi*, was generally stationed there. Commander Sixth Fleet (submarines) kept his headquarters on Dublon Island during the same period. In addition, Truk was an important air base and staging point for planes between Japan and the South Pacific. Fortifications were started as early as 1940, and all defensive works were speeded up in January 1944; but Truk was weakly defended, by American standards. Some 7500 Army troops and 3000 to 4000 sailors and aviation personnel were stationed there in mid-February 1944; but there were only 40 anti-aircraft guns in the archipelago, and all fire control radar had been lost when the ship bringing it thither was sunk by a United States submarine.

Geographically, Truk resembled nothing that American forces had yet encountered; it was a drowned mountain range inside a coral ring. Take a coral atoll of the type already familiar in the Marshalls, the reef shaped like a rounded equilateral triangle with 35-mile legs; dump into the lagoon a dozen volcanic islands rising to 1500 feet above sea level; scatter about the lagoon 30 or more islets; and you have Truk. The Japanese named the islands after the four seasons, trees, and the days of the week.

These wooded islands, standing out prominently and easy to identify, may be approached by any one of four passes through the reef, all of which were defended by coast defense guns on their flanking islets. The Northeast Pass, nearest entrance (10 miles) to Dublon and to the Eten airfield, also had been mined. Any surface attack on Truk, therefore, would first have to break a passage through one of these strongly defended passes and then assault high, well fortified positions inside, island by island. The Japanese atoll commander, Rear Admiral Chuichi Hara, remarked after the war that when hearing American radio broadcasts refer to his bailiwick as "The Gibraltar of the Pacific" he only feared lest the Americans discover how weak it was. Its essential strength was given by nature. Naval gunfire from outside the reef could reach neither the islands nor the fleet anchorage in the lagoon. But air power could.

THE LARGER ISLANDS OF TRUK LAGOON, WITH INSTALLATIONS
AND FACILITIES AS OF 17 FEBRUARY 1944

Native Name	Japanese Name	Meaning	Military Installations
Moen	Haru Shima	Spring	Bomber strip 3340 ft., combined seaplane base and fighter strip, with 68 planes, coast defense and anti-aircraft guns, radar, torpedo storage, torpedo boat base.
Dublon	Natsu Shima	Summer	Main town and docks, main seaplane base with 27 planes, submarine base, naval HQ, 2500-ton floating drydock, oil and torpedo storage, magazines, coast defense and anti-aircraft guns, aviation repair and supply station.
Fefan	Aki Shima	Autumn	The supply center, with pier, warehouses, ammunition dumps, search radar, two 5-inch dual-purpose guns.
Uman	Fuyu Shima	Winter	Search radar, torpedo boat base.
Eten	Take Jima	Bamboo	Airstrip 3340 × 270 ft., revetments, 20 planes fully equipped; 180 planes awaiting pilots or repairs.
Param	Kaide Jima	Maple	Airstrip 3900 × 335 ft. with 40 planes, eight 5-inch, four 80-mm dual-purpose, 3 medium anti-aircraft guns.
Ulalu	Nichiyo To	Sunday	Radio Direction Finder station.
Udot	Getsuyo To	Monday	Three 8-inch dual-purpose guns.
Tol	Suiyo To	Wednesday [5]	Four 6-inch coast defense guns and a battery of anti-aircraft guns, radar, torpedo boat base.

There were two schools of thought about Truk in the American high command. Certain higher officers urged that an all-out attempt be made to capture it before proceeding farther on the road to Tokyo. They pointed out that no place short of Palau offered sufficient anchorage and land for a combined air-naval base. The Marianas had plenty of land but no good harbor; Eniwetok had a perfect harbor but a minimum of land. On the other hand, several American strategists believed that Truk was almost impregnable to direct assault and argued that a protracted siege operation would pin down several divisions of troops and hundreds of ships. They

[5] The two western peninsulas of Tol, biggest of the islands, are called Thursday and Friday. Fala Beguets Island was Tuesday, and Onamue, Saturday.

Destroyer Akikaze *under Attack off Truk*

TBF over Destroyer Tachikaze

Rescue by OS2U in Truk Lagoon

Lieutenant (jg) Denver F. Baxter's Kingfisher being hoisted on board U.S.S. *Baltimore* after
rescuing Lieutenant George M. Blair. Crewman Reuben F. Hickman standing on wing

advocated neutralization as soon as the United States could bring sufficient air power to bear on the atoll. The Joint Chiefs of Staff, after a conference at Washington with Admiral Nimitz and Lieutenant General R. K. Sutherland (MacArthur's chief of staff), decided against the Truk-takers in favor of the Truk-neutralizers on 12 March 1944. But at the date of the big strike nobody knew whether or not it would pave the way for an assault.

Plans for the strike called for employment of three out of the four fast carrier groups that had taken part in the Marshalls operation, leaving Admiral Ginder's to cover the capture of Eniwetok.[6] The first photographic reconnaissance was made 4 February 1944 by a Marine Corps Liberator of the Airsols command, based at Torokina, Bougainville. Owing to the length of its flight — about 850 miles — and to cloudiness over the atoll, complete coverage was not obtained; but the photographs were accurate enough as to installations and revealed tempting targets at anchor in the shape of one battleship, two carriers, five or six heavy and four light cruisers, twenty destroyers and twelve submarines, together with a large number of *Marus.* This was the Combined Fleet of Admiral Koga, less *Nagato, Fuso* and other ships which had already departed for Palau. Now tipped off by the reconnaissance, Admiral Koga sent most of the other combatant ships to Palau while he himself in *Musashi* returned to Japan. Light cruiser *Agano,* as unlucky a ship as there ever was, did not repair the damage inflicted by *Scamp* the previous November in time to sortie with the rest. Departing Truk 16 February, she encountered *Skate* (Lieutenant Commander William P. Gruner), one of ten submarines sent by Cincpac to prowl around Truk and knock off fleeing vessels. *Skate* (who had hit mammoth *Yamato* on Christmas Day)[7] made three torpedo hits and *Agano* went down after transferring her crew and the Emperor's portrait to destroyer *Oite.*[8] So, by 17 February, all com-

[6] See Appendix IV for Task Organization.
[7] See Vol. VI 71, 411.
[8] The only other submarine of these 10 (see Appendix IV for names) to get anything was *Tang,* which sank the 6800-ton transport *Gyoten Maru* bound for Truk.

batant ships had departed Truk except two light cruisers and eight destroyers. Spruance and Mitscher found plenty of targets, however. About 50 merchant ships and auxiliaries, which had been delayed in fueling or unloading by several days of rough weather, were still anchored in Truk Lagoon; and during the previous ten days many more planes en route to Rabaul landed on Eten Field and were detained there for want of ferry pilots.

The three fast carrier groups, after completing their several missions in Operation "Flintlock," retired to Majuro for rest and fueling. Thence they sortied 12/13 February and made their approach to the north of Eniwetok, where two days later they rendezvoused with five fleet tankers. (This circuitous approach was made to evade enemy snoopers.) From the fueling point they made the final run-in at high speed, undetected by Japanese plane searches, and reached their initial launching point, about 90 miles ENE of Dublon Island, before dawn 17 February. That day opened fair with high visibility, scattered clouds that afforded good temporary cover, and wind 10 to 11 knots from the ENE.

The object of the initial strike, comprising 72 fighter planes launched before dawn from five different carriers, was to knock out enemy air power in and over the atoll. This new technique, devised by Admiral Mitscher, proved very effective. Some 45 Japanese fighters attempted to intercept and almost as many more took off before the Americans struck, at sunrise (0610), but over 30 of them were shot down. The Hellcats, much elated, proceeded to strafe planes on the Moen, Eten and Param Fields, where they destroyed about 40 more. All but four of the American fighters returned safely to their ships. Immediately following this strike, 18 Avengers loaded with fragmentation clusters and incendiaries showered the plane dispersal areas on Moen, Eten and Param. Mitscher's objective was more than attained. Of 365 aircraft at Truk when the raid began, fewer than 100 remained unscathed; and when a pre-dawn sweep was pulled off next day not one Japanese plane rose to contest it.

Next came the turn of Japanese shipping. At 0443 the five

light carriers, from a position about 80 miles ENE of Dublon Island, began launching full deckloads (half their available planes) of fighters, dive-bombers and torpedo-bombers, so staggered as to provide a continuous flow. Altogether they carried 369 thousand-pound and 498 five-hundred-pound bombs, and about 70 torpedoes. Small-scale enemy interception continued intermittently throughout the day, and the island batteries threw up plenty of ack-ack; but the bombers had a merry day of it, hitting ships in the anchorages or those which were trying to escape from the lagoon. The power of this bombing attack may be gauged roughly by the fact that there were 30 strikes in all, each stronger than either of the two Japanese strikes that had done all the damage at Pearl Harbor.

At 1900, when Mitscher was maneuvering east of Truk and his three carrier groups were within 10 to 20 miles of each other, the enemy launched from Param Field his first and only counterattack. Only six or seven "Kate" torpedo planes took part in it, but they were equipped with radar so that evasive maneuvering was of no avail to the ships. Ack-ack from the screen kept them at a safe distance for about two hours, but an attempt to down one of them with a night fighter proved ineffective. This night fighter, catapulted from *Yorktown* about 2120, was vectored out with the aid of radar bearings to a torpedo plane that was approaching Admiral Montgomery's group. Unfortunately the two did not connect and the torpedo-bomber made a hit on *Intrepid* at 2211 February 17. The torpedo struck her on the starboard quarter, killed or blew overboard 11 men, wounded 17, flooded several compartments and jammed the rudder. Accompanied by *Cabot*, two cruisers and four destroyers, *Intrepid* retired to Eniwetok at 20 knots, steering by her engines. Several months elapsed before she was in condition to rejoin the Fleet.[9]

Between midnight and dawn Mitscher launched the first night bombing attack on shipping in the history of United States carrier

[9] She suffered several mishaps during her repairs which, in addition to the Truk hit, earned her the unhappy nickname of "The Evil I."

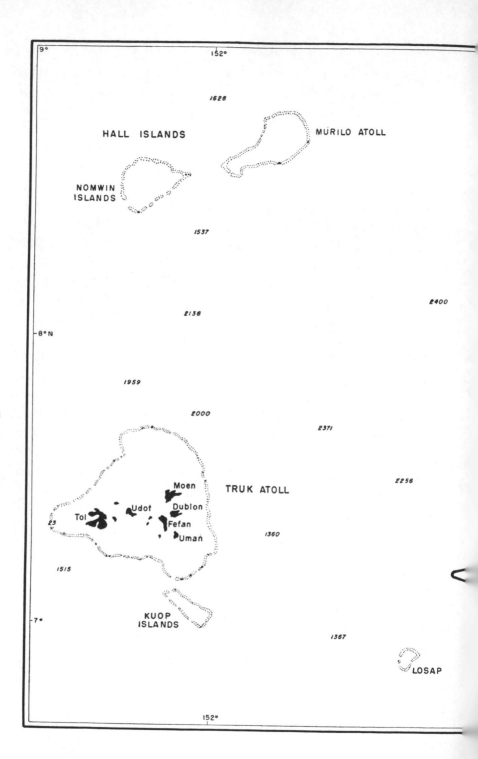

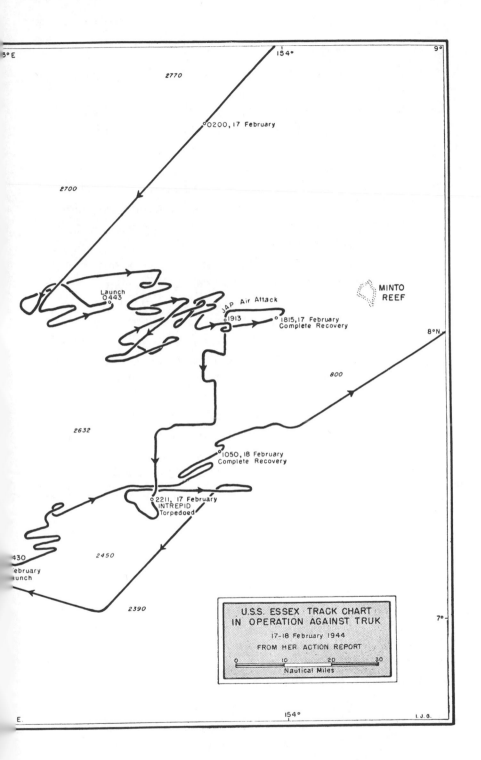

153°E   154°   9°

2770

○0200, 17 February

2700

Launch
0443 ○   JAP Air Attack   ○ 1815, 17 February
                                  ○ 1913   Complete Recovery

                                                                                    MINTO
                                                                                    REEF

                                                                                    8°N

                                              800

2632

                          ○ 1050, 18 February
                          Complete Recovery

                ○ 2211, 17 February
                  INTREPID
                  Torpedoed

430
ebruary
aunch   2450

              2390

                                                                                    7°

E.   154°   I. J. G.

operations. Almost two years of intensive practice and preparation were behind this attack.

Lieutenant Henry Loomis USNR, a young radio expert who had opened the radar school at Pearl Harbor, and Lieutenant William L. Martin who, since graduation from Annapolis, had specialized in night instrument flying, first discussed this technique with fellow members of Bomber Squadron 10, on board *Enterprise*, at the time of the Battle of Santa Cruz. Around the turn of the year, during a lull in carrier operations, they borrowed torpedo planes and spent many nights experimentally bombing islands and reefs around Espiritu Santo on radar contact. They found that by careful instrument flying with radar one could safely approach within a hundred yards of a beach on the darkest night. Loomis returned to the radar school as executive officer, and, as a result of his efforts and representations, Torpedo Squadron 10 was given specially equipped Avengers (TBF–1C) for night bombing attacks. By the time of the Truk strike Martin had become the squadron commander,[10] while Loomis was taking a busman's holiday on board the "Big E."

The attack group consisted of 12 TBF–1Cs, each armed with four 500-pound general-purpose bombs. Planes were catapulted at 0200 when *Enterprise* lay 100 miles east of Truk. The moon had just turned last quarter; the sky was less than half overcast. Rendezvous being effected with the aid of aldis lamps and running lights, the Avengers blacked out. Two initial points were established whence planes departed at one-minute intervals to attack shipping in the Dublon and Eten anchorages. They were detected flying over the reef, as indicated by a Japanese hospital ship's switching on her lights, but the dozen Avengers remained over the lagoon for 20 to 30 minutes searching the assigned areas, locating ships by radar and making repeated deliberate runs on them at masthead height at a speed of 180 knots. Ack-ack increased but never became accurate except when planes' exhausts were sighted. Twenty-five runs were made, resulting in 13 direct hits, 7 near-

[10] Owing to an accident to Lieutenant Martin, the strike was actually commanded by Lieutenant Van V. Eason USNR.

misses and 2 hits on islets mistaken for ships. This night bombing run resulted in about one third of the total damage to shipping effected by the entire carrier force.

So emphatic a demonstration of the value of night low-altitude bombing eventually had a great influence on carrier tactics, but not for several months. After the Battle of the Philippine Sea had proved the need for specialized night bombing, *Enterprise* and two CVLs were designated night carriers and began intensive training in offensive night work.[11]

Full-scale operations were resumed by *Enterprise, Yorktown, Essex* and *Bunker Hill* at dawn 18 February. As the lagoon was now almost clear of live targets, special attention was paid to airfields, hangars, storage tanks and ammunition dumps. When Admiral Mitscher gave the order for retirement at noon, 1250 combat sorties had been flown, 400 tons of bombs and torpedoes had been used on shipping, and 94 tons dropped on airfields and shore installations.

The results of this two-day strike were distinctly worth while. Inside the lagoon, carrier planes had destroyed auxiliary cruisers *Aikoku Maru* and *Kiyosumi Maru*, destroyer *Fumizuki*, submarine tenders *Rio de Janeiro Maru* and *Heian Maru*, aircraft ferry *Fujikawa Maru*, six tankers, and 17 more *Marus;* the total tonnage being about 200,000.[12] This was a sad blow to the Japanese mer-

[11] Lt. Cdr. Loomis letter to Cincpac 23 Mar. 1944; conversations with him and Admiral Towers; Comairpac Monthly Analysis Pacific Air Operations Feb. 1944 p. 8; *N.Y. Times* 12 Apr. 1944. These night bombers must not be confused with the "Black Cats," "Black Widows" etc. which were defensive in character and developed independently; see Vols. V and VI of this History. Loomis in the letter above mentioned observed, "The present policy of combined day and night operations from one carrier imposes unreasonable hardships on both the carrier and the air group. . . . At present the United States Fleet has overwhelming air superiority during daylight, but at night it is almost totally lacking in both hitting power and effective defense." He pointed out that night minimum-altitude bombing requires high skill and constant practice in instrument flying, highly trained and intelligent plane radar operators, training as a team, an exacting upkeep of radar and all flight instruments, and a minimum of day work for flight and deck crews.

[12] JANAC pp. 9–10, 49–51. Some of these were left burning or beached, but were total losses. Others, including "an impressive-looking yacht at anchor," suspected to be the flagship of the atoll commander, were hit.

chant marine; but the carrier sailors thought they should have done better, considering the amount of ammunition expended.[13] The truth seems to be that the pilots of this task force had so long been trained to intercept enemy planes and to deliver close support of amphibious operations that for months they had had little or no practice at bombing ships; and their leaders occasionally showed bad judgment in target selection. For instance, six aërial torpedoes and twelve half-ton bombs were expended on one fast-stepping destroyer without making a hit, while other and better targets were allowed to escape. But five Avengers from *Enterprise*, led by Lieutenant Grady Owens, made a neat coördinated attack on destroyer *Fumizuki* steaming at 27 knots, which finished her in 90 seconds, although but one torpedo hit. Destroyer *Oite* was tagged by bombs and sunk as she was entering North Pass. She took down with her not only her own crew, but 523 of *Agano's*.

Much of the disappointment over the results of the carrier strikes was derived from the notion that aviators were supermen — a supposition that they did not altogether discourage — and therefore should have excelled in every sort of air combat. Actually, like destroyer crews, anti-aircraft gun crews and any other sailors, naval aviators need special training and quickly lose efficiency if afforded no "live" practice.

Admiral Spruance conducted a round-the-atoll cruise on the first day, 17 February, to catch escaping vessels. The group that made this sweep (TG 50.9), consisting of the two biggest battleships (*New Jersey* and *Iowa*), two heavy cruisers (*Minneapolis* and *New Orleans*) and destroyers *Izard*, *Charrette*, *Burns* and *Bradford*, was formed northeast of Truk at 0923. Carrier *Cowpens* furnished combat air patrol.

As Spruance's group steamed in the direction of reported enemy ships, mighty *Iowa* at 1118 was attacked by a bold "Zeke." It made a near-miss alongside the wing of the bridge where Admiral

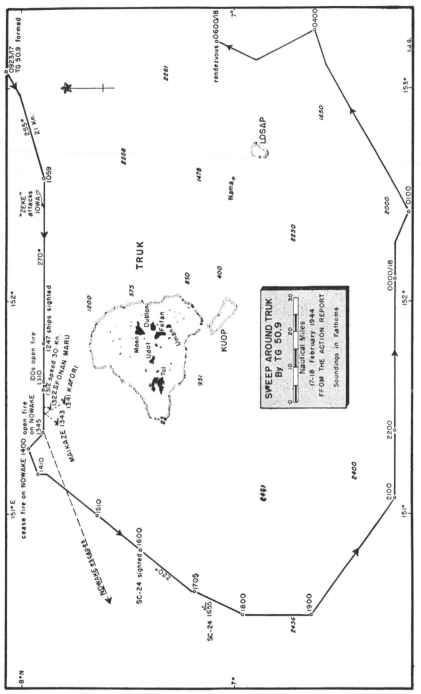

SWEEP AROUND TRUK
By TG 50.9

17-18 February 1944
FFROM THE ACTION REPORT
Soundings in Fathoms

Nautical Miles
0 10 20 30

Hustvedt was eating his lunch. "That was *my* bomb," said the Admiral, and went on eating. The "Zeke" got away.

At 1247 — when the formation was due north of North Pass — *New Jersey's* spotter plane reported enemy ships dead ahead, distant 25 miles. These were light cruiser *Katori* and two destroyers (*Maikaze* and *Nowake*) that were being bombed by American planes as they endeavored to get away,[14] and trawler *No. 15 Shonan Maru* that was approaching Truk from the north. Destroyers opened fire on this small vessel at 1310 and *New Jersey* sank her with 5-inch gunfire at 1327. Admiral Spruance then ordered *Minneapolis, New Orleans* and two destroyers to "close and sink" *Katori,* which had already been worked over by carrier planes and was almost dead in the water. They sheered out of line to port. *Bradford* and *Burns* first engaged the light cruiser at 17,400 yards; *Minneapolis* and *New Orleans* commenced firing at 19,000 yards, closing to 14,000. *Katori* gamely returned fire as long as her guns were above water, made some near-misses, and launched all her torpedoes. Her after mount of 5.5-inch guns was still being served as she rolled over, exposing gaping holes in her bottom; *Minneapolis* then gave her a final salvo "just to make sure," and down she went, stern-first, at 1341.

In the meantime the American battleships and two destroyers were firing at destroyer *Maikaze,* but she was still floating after they tore by at 30 knots, and the cruisers finished her. *Maikaze* accepted a terrific amount of punishment and continued firing to the last, but burst into flame, broke in two and sank at 1343. She too launched several torpedoes; and it was only because of advance warning from combat air patrol, and by brisk maneuvering, that the American ships escaped hits.

---

[14] Owing to a reprehensible failure in communications, carrier planes were not informed of the movements of Admiral Spruance's group and came within an ace of attacking his ships. Nor was the flagship informed of the planes' movements; Spruance's group opened fire on *Intrepid's* planes returning from a strike on shipping west of Truk. The flight leader, in an SBD, with his IFF turned on, was trying to drop a message on *Iowa's* deck in order to inform her of the position of some cripples. The machine-gun officer directed "Friendly plane; track, do not fire," but gun crews in one sector received the order "Stations" from the officer in

During the half hour of this unequal battle, destroyer *Nowake* made good her escape westward. *New Jersey* and *Iowa* turned right to unmask main batteries, fired at ranges from 34,000 to 39,000 yards and straddled her, even at these tremendous ranges, but made no hits; as a Parthian shot *Nowake* fired a spread of torpedoes, one of which crossed *New Jersey's* bow.

At 1410 Admiral Spruance shaped his course southwesterly. Nothing more happened until 1600, when a small Japanese vessel was sighted hull-down on the starboard bow. Destroyer *Burns* at 1028 was detached to deal with *SC–24*, which this vessel turned out to be. She had the temerity to open fire on the destroyer, and even straddled her, but the contest was one-sided. *SC–24* went down at 1655 with guns defiantly blazing, and of 60 survivors observed to be floating only 6 allowed themselves to be rescued. The intrepid and desperate manner in which the Japanese sailors fought gained the respect and admiration of the Fifth Fleet, whose first surface action this was.[15]

Spruance's task group completed the circuit of Truk without further incident, and at 0600 February 18 rendezvoused with the rest of the striking force. Four hours later, after planes of the early morning strike had been recovered, the entire task force, excepting the small group which had already departed with *Intrepid*, retired toward a fueling rendezvous. On the 21st the force entered Kwajalein Lagoon for a short rest and fueling before going out again to hit the Marianas.

In retrospect this strike on Truk was one of the most successful carrier operations of the war. It reduced by as much as 75 per cent the amount of supplies on hand; it deprived the Japanese Navy of 2 light cruisers, 4 destroyers, 3 auxiliary cruisers, 2 submarine tenders, 2 subchasers, an armed trawler and a plane ferry; and the

charge, misunderstood the word *friendly* as *enemy*, and opened fire without orders at very close range. The SBD was shot down and all hands were lost.

[15] See especially the tribute by Capt. R. W. Bates in *Minneapolis* Action Report (the best on this battle) 24 Feb. 1944, Part V.

merchant marine of 24 *Marus* (5 of them tankers) totaling 137,091 tons.[16] And the 250 to 275 planes destroyed or damaged made a big dent on the Japanese air force. The capture of Eniwetok could now proceed without interference by a single enemy plane, and Airsols fighters over Rabaul, on 18 February, for the first time encountered not one plane airborne over that former hive of aviation activity.

American losses in men and planes were light,[17] but they would have been heavier without smart rescue work by submarines and seaplanes. *Searaven*, stationed about 30 miles NE of the reef, under the route most used by the striking planes, picked up the entire crew of a torpedo bomber from *Yorktown*. A neat rescue of an *Essex* pilot, Lieutenant George M. Blair USNR, shot down inside the lagoon on the dawn fighter sweep 18 February, was effected by other planes. Blair's flight leader broadcast the location and requested a relief patrol; cruiser *Baltimore* catapulted a Kingfisher for the actual rescue. Nine planes circled over the swimming pilot, strafing and driving away destroyer *Fumizuki*, which tried to muscle in. The Kingfisher pilot, Lieutenant (jg) D. F. Baxter, located Blair, picked him up and brought him safely on board ship with just one pint of gasoline left in his plane; for he had gone out short of fuel to allow for another man's weight. Seaplanes from *Massachusetts* also made a good rescue when summoned to pick up a pilot from *Cowpens* whose plane had crashed 70 miles from the formation. Eight other fighters stood by, circling to keep track of their comrade in his tiny raft; they guided the OS2U to the spot, and all landed safely after dark.[18]

The Truk strike seems to have hit Japanese morale harder than any previous blow in the Gilberts and Marshalls. For it was the first dent on the next defensive perimeter. Before it was over, Radio

[16] There were also a few ships under 500 tons sunk. The *Marus* which we have counted as naval vessels, being auxiliaries, totaled 54,617 tons.

[17] U.S. losses as given in Cincpac Monthly Analysis for Feb. 1944 p. 40 are 29 pilots and crewmen killed or missing — all but 3 in combat; casualties in *Intrepid* 11 killed, 17 injured. Plane losses: 12 fighters, 7 torpedo-bombers, 6 dive-bombers. Of these, 4, 1 and 3 were operational, the rest in combat.

[18] CTG 58.3 (Rear Admiral Sherman) Action Report 3 Mar. 1944.

Tokyo declared that the United States had attempted to land troops (in order to claim that they had been repulsed); but on 18 February it made the significant admission:

A powerful American task force suddenly advanced to our Caroline Islands Wednesday morning and repeatedly attacked our important strategic base, Truk, with a great number of ship-based planes. The enemy is constantly repeating powerfully persistent raids with several hundred fighters and bombers, attacking us intermittently. The war situation has increased with unprecedented seriousness — nay, furiousness. The tempo of enemy operations indicates that the attacking force is already pressing upon our mainland.

Truk was still usable for planes; the buildings on Dublon were not badly damaged until after a second carrier raid in April. But its usefulness as a fleet anchorage and advanced naval base was gone after 18 February 1944. And the myth of Truk the Impregnable was shattered. Never again did the eight-rayed flag of Commander in Chief Combined Fleet meet the rising sun in Truk Lagoon.

The spectacular success of the two Marshalls operations did not merely happen. It was brought about by careful planning and other factors that were foreseen. Successful landings were due to sound planning, close gunfire support, an adequate number of amphtracs to take assault waves over the reefs, and split-second timing. Rapid advances on shore with moderate loss were made possible by prolonged bombing and bombardment before the landings and by the effective support of artillery and of naval vessels in delivering call fire as needed. The diversionary strikes on Japanese airfields by Mitscher's fast carrier forces, culminating in the mid-February one on Truk, and the continuous pressure on Rabaul by the South Pacific Force and General MacArthur's command, rendered the Japanese powerless to offer surface or air opposition. There is nothing quite so vulnerable as the huge concentration of shipping at the scene of a major amphibious landing, in the open sea and immobilized by the nature of the task. Yet not once, in the Marshalls, did vessels have to interrupt unloading or other operations to maneuver to avoid air or submarine attack. How different from the state of things in the Solomons a year earlier!

Looking back on the Marshalls after a lapse of seven years, Admiral Dick Conolly said to the writer, "The Marshalls really cracked the Japanese shell. It broke the crust of their defenses on a scale that could be exploited at once. It gave them no time adequately to fortify their inner defensive line that ran through the Marianas." And it advanced the American schedule in the Pacific by at least four months.

The Marshalls campaign did more than any other since Pearl Harbor, more even than the operations for breaking the Bismarcks Barrier, to restore the people's confidence in the United States Navy. Courage and determination the Navy had shown from the first, but in the Marshalls it demonstrated mastery of the art of amphibious warfare; of combining air, surface, submarine and ground forces in order to project fighting power irresistibly across the seas. The strike on Truk demonstrated a virtual revolution in naval warfare; the aircraft carrier emerged as the capital ship of the future, with unlimited potentialities.

What a contrast from the fumbling, often comic and sometimes costly operations in the Aleutians! Only six months had elapsed since Kiska, but the weapons of victory had been discovered; the converging sea lanes to victory had been charted, the American nation had found the material means to future power and security.

Forces Engaged in the Capture of Attu

11–29 May 1943

(Operation "Landcrab")

NORTH PACIFIC FORCE
Rear Admiral Thomas C. Kinkaid

TASK FORCE 16, Rear Admiral Kinkaid

TG 16.1 SHORE-BASED AIR GROUP
Major General Wm. O. Butler USA (XI A.A.F.)
TU 16.1.1 Air Striking Unit, Major General Butler

Bombardment: 28th Composite Group, 8 B–24s (Liberators), 24 B–25s (Mitchells) Lt. Col. R. W. Rodieck USA; 404th Bombardment Squadron, 8 B–24s Maj. Robert C. Orth USA; 21st Bombardment Squadron, 8 B–24s Maj. F. R. Ramputi USA; 406th Bombardment Squadron, 6 B–25s Maj. H. D. Courtney USA.

Fighters: 343rd Fighter Group, 50 P–38s (Lightnings), 50 P–40s (Warhawks) * Lt. Col. J. R. Watt USA; No. 111 R.C.A.F. Fighter Squadron, 16 P–40s (Kittyhawks) Squad. Ldr. K. A. Boomer RCAF; No. 14 R.C.A.F. Fighter Squadron, 12 P–40s Squad. Ldr. B. R. Walker RCAF.

TU 16.1.2 Air Search Unit, Captain Leslie E. Gehres

Units of VB–135; 12 PV–1s (Venturas), at Amchitka, Lt. Cdr. P. C. Williams USNR; VB–136: 12 PV–1s, at Adak, Lt. Cdr. N. S. Haines; VP–43: 10 PBY–5As (Catalinas), at Adak, Lt. Cdr. J. L. Crittenden; VP–62: 10 PBY–5As, at Adak, Lt. Cdr. F. R. Jones; VP–61: 10 PBY–5As, at Amchitka, Lt. Cdr. F. Bruner.

Tenders CASCO Cdr. W. E. Cleaves, GILLIS Lt. Cdr. W. M. Fitts, TEAL Lt. Robert Jacobson, AVOCET Lt. (jg) G. F. Keene, HULBERT Lt. R. B. Crowell.

TG 16.2 ALASKA SECTOR ESCORT & SUPPLY GROUP
Rear Admiral John W. Reeves

Destroyer KING Lt. R. H. Hopkins USNR; minesweeper LAMBERTON Lt. Cdr. B. M. McKay; minelayer RAMSAY Lt. Cdr. R. H. Holmes; corvettes H.M.C.S. DAWSON Lt. A. H. G. Storrs RCNR; H.M.C.S. VANCOUVER Lt. P. F. M. De Freitas

* Lost in this operation.

RCNR; gunboat CHARLESTON Cdr. G. B. Sherwood; minesweepers ORIOLE Lt. Cdr. M. M. Lindsay, TATNUCK Lt. W. B. Coats, ANNOY Lt. J. A. Parrish; fleet ocean tug UTE Lt. W. F. Lewis; netlayers BUCKEYE Lt. Cdr. Elias Johnson USNR, EUCALYPTUS Lt. Cdr. A. S. Einmo USNR; Coast Guard Vessels; Patrol Craft and Harbor Mine-sweepers; LSTs *450, 451, 461, 477;* LCT(5)s *353–358, 394, 395.*

TG 16.3 MOTOR TORPEDO BOAT GROUP, Lt. Cdr. James B. Denny

Squadron 13: PTs *79, 74, 75, 76, 73, 80, 82, 77, 81, 83, 84.*

TG 16.5 SUBMARINE GROUP, Commander Charles W. Gray

Submarines NARWHAL Lt. Cdr. F. D. Latta, NAUTILUS Lt. Cdr. W. H. Brockman; Subdiv 41, Cdr. B. G. Lake: *S–18, S–23, S–28, S–34, S–35, S–38;* Subdiv 52, Cdr. Gray: *S–30, S–32, S–33, S–40, S–41.*

TG 16.6 SOUTHERN COVERING GROUP
Rear Admiral Charles H. McMorris

Light cruisers RALEIGH Capt. A. T. Sprague, DETROIT Capt. E. H. Geiselman, RICHMOND Capt. T. M. Waldschmidt, SANTA FE Capt. R. S. Berkey; destroyers BANCROFT Cdr. J. L. Melgaard, CALDWELL Lt. Cdr. H. A. Lincoln, COGHLAN Cdr. B. F. Tompkins, FRAZIER Lt. Cdr. Frank Virden, GANSEVOORT Lt. Cdr. M. L. McCullough.

TG 16.7 NORTHERN COVERING GROUP
Rear Admiral Robert C. Giffen

Heavy cruisers WICHITA Capt J. J. Mahoney, SAN FRANCISCO Capt. A. F. France, LOUISVILLE Capt. C. T. Joy; destroyers BALCH Cdr. H. H. Tiemroth, HUGHES Lt. Cdr. H. H. Marable, MUSTIN Lt. Cdr. E. T. Schreiber, MORRIS Lt. Cdr. E. S. Burns.

TG 16.8 ATTU REËNFORCEMENT GROUP, Captain Charles L. Hutton
Carrying 32nd Infantry Regiment, less one battalion

Transports U.S. GRANT Capt. Hutton. S.S. DAVID W. BRANCH, PRESIDENT FILLMORE Master J. D. Ryan, CHIRIKOF, RICHARD MARCH HOE Master George Torgersen, JOSEPH HENRY Master August Ekholm, KENNETH A. J. MACKENZIE Master E. Joost, DAVID W. FIELD Master J. R. Hayes.

TG 16.9 TANKER AND SERVICE GROUP (operating independently)

Oilers BRAZOS Cdr. R. P. Glass, CUYAMA Capt. P. R. Coloney, PLATTE Cdr. Harry Keeler, TIPPECANOE Cdr. R. O. Myers, GUADALUPE Cdr. H. A. Anderson, NECHES Cdr. C. D. Emory; destroyer tenders MARKAB Capt. A. D. Brown, BLACK HAWK Cdr. E. H. McMenemy.

TG 16.10 SHEMYA OCCUPATION GROUP, Brig. Gen. John E. Copeland USA
Carrying 4th Infantry and 18th Engineer Regiments

Transport SAINT MIHIEL Cdr. E. B. Rogers, S.S. WILLIAM L. THOMPSON Master H. J. Hasset; small coastal transports NORTH COAST, ALASKA Master O. C. Anderson, YUKON Master Henry Burns; cargo ship FRANKLIN MACVEAGH Master K. Johannessen.

TASK FORCE 51 (ASSAULT FORCE)
Rear Admiral Francis W. Rockwell

TG 51.1 SUPPORT GROUP, Rear Admiral Howard F. Kingman

Battleships NEVADA Capt. W. A. Kitts, PENNSYLVANIA Capt. W. A. Corn, IDAHO Capt. H. D. Clarke; escort carrier NASSAU Capt. A. K. Doyle (26 F4F–4 [Wildcats],

3 F4F–3P [photographic], 1 SOC–3A [Seagull] Lt. Cdr. L. K. Greenamyer);[1] seaplane tender WILLIAMSON Lt. J. A. Pridmore. Desron 1, Capt. R. E. Libby:[2] PHELPS Lt. Cdr. J. E. Edwards. Desdiv 2, Cdr. G. R. Cooper: FARRAGUT Cdr. H. D. Rozendal, HULL Lt. Cdr. A. L. Young, MACDONOUGH Lt. Cdr. E. V. E. Dennett, MEADE Cdr. R. S. Lamb, EDWARDS Lt. Cdr. P. G. Osler, ABNER READ Cdr. Thomas Burrowes, AMMEN Lt. Cdr. Henry Williams.

TG 51.2 TRANSPORT GROUP, Captain Pat Buchanan

Attack transports HARRIS Cdr. A. M. Van Eaton, ZEILIN Cdr. T. B. Fitzpatrick, HEYWOOD Capt. H. B. Knowles, J. FRANKLIN BELL Cdr. J. B. McGovern; destroyer transport KANE Lt. Cdr. F. D. Miller; S.S. PERIDA; destroyers DEWEY Lt. Cdr. J. P. Canty, DALE Lt. Cdr. C. W. Aldrich, MONAGHAN Lt. Cdr. P. H. Horn, AYLWIN Lt. Cdr. R. E. Malpass; minelayers SICARD Lt. Cdr. W. J. Richter, PRUITT Lt. Cdr. R. C. Williams.

TG 51.3 MINESWEEPER GROUP, Lt. Cdr. B. A. Fuetsch

PERRY Lt. Cdr. Fuetsch, ELLIOT Lt. Cdr. Henry Mullins, CHANDLER Lt. Cdr. H. L. Thompson, LONG Lt. Cdr. P. F. Heerbrandt.

TG 51.4 LANDING FORCE, Maj. General A. E. Brown USA

17th Infantry reinforced; one battalion 32nd Infantry, reinforced; 78th Coast Artillery AA; one battalion 50th Engineers; Scout Company and Reconnaissance Troop, 7th Division U.S. Army.

[1] Including also a detachment of VMO–155, Maj. J. P. Haines USMC.
[2] Also Commander Screening Group.

Forces Engaged in Gilbert Islands Operation

(Operation "Galvanic")

10 November–10 December 1943

PACIFIC FLEET
Admiral Chester W. Nimitz, at Pearl Harbor

FIFTH FLEET
Vice Admiral Raymond A. Spruance in *Indianapolis*

ASSAULT FORCE
Rear Admiral R. K. Turner in *Pennsylvania*

TF 52 NORTHERN ATTACK FORCE, Rear Admiral Turner

TG 52.1 TRANSPORT GROUP, Capt. D. W. Loomis
carrying 165th RCT and 105th Battalion Landing Teams 27th Division U.S. Army, Major General Ralph C. Smith USA.

Attack transports: LEONARD WOOD Capt. M. O'Neil USCG, NEVILLE Cdr. O. R. Swigart, PIERCE Cdr. A. R. Ponto, CALVERT Cdr. E. J. Sweeney USNR; attack cargo ship ALCYONE Cdr. J. B. McVey, landing ship dock BELLE GROVE Lt. Cdr. M. Seavey USNR, carrying LVTs and 193rd Tank Battalion U.S. Army.

Destroyer Screen

MUSTIN Cdr. M. M. Riker, KIMBERLY Lt. Cdr. Harry Smith, BURNS Lt. Cdr. D. T. Eller, DALE Lt. Cdr. C. W. Aldrich.

TG 52.2 FIRE SUPPORT GROUP
Rear Admiral Robert M. Griffin in *New Mexico*

Unit 1: Battleships NEW MEXICO Capt. E. M. Zacharias, PENNSYLVANIA Capt. W. A. Corn. Crudiv 6, Rear Admiral Robert C. Giffen: Heavy cruisers MINNEAPOLIS Capt. R. W. Bates, SAN FRANCISCO Capt. A. F. France. Destroyers DEWEY Lt. Cdr. J. P. Canty, HULL Lt. Cdr. A. L. Young. Unit 2: Battleships IDAHO Capt.

H. D. Clarke, MISSISSIPPI Capt. L. L. Hunter. Heavy cruisers NEW ORLEANS Capt. S. R. Shumaker, BALTIMORE Capt. W. C. Calhoun. Destroyers MAURY Lt. Cdr. J. W. Koenig, GRIDLEY Lt. Cdr. J. H. Motes. Unit 3: Destroyers PHELPS Lt. Cdr. J. E. Edwards, MACDONOUGH Lt. Cdr. J. W. Ramey.

TG 52.3 AIR SUPPORT GROUP, *Rear Admiral H. M. Mullinnix

Escort carriers *LISCOME BAY *Capt. I. D. Wiltsie (16 FM-1, 12 TBM-1 [1] Lt. Cdr. M. U. Beebe), CORAL SEA Capt. H. W. Taylor (16 FM-1, 12 TBF-1 Lt. Cdr. J. J. Lynch), CORREGIDOR Capt R. L. Bowman (16 FM-1, 12 TBF-1 Lt. Cdr. G. M. Clifford).

Destroyer Screen, Cdr. E. A. Solomons

MORRIS Cdr. F. T. Williamson, HOEL Cdr. W. D. Thomas, FRANKS Cdr. N. A. Lidstone, HUGHES Lt. Cdr. E. B. Rittenhouse. Minesweeper REVENGE Cdr. F. F. Sima USNR.

TG 54.4 MAKIN LST GROUP NO. 1, Cdr. A. M. Hurst

LSTs *31, 78, 178,* each carrying an LCT. Destroyer DALE Lt. Cdr. C. W. Aldrich.

TF 53 SOUTHERN ATTACK FORCE
Rear Admiral H. W. Hill in *Maryland*

TG 53.1 TRANSPORT GROUP, Capt. H. B. Knowles in *Monrovia*
Carrying 2nd Division U.S. Marine Corps, reinforced,
Maj. Gen. Julian C. Smith USMC

Transdiv 4, Capt. J. B. McGovern: [2] Attack transports ZEILIN Cdr. T. B. Fitzpatrick, HARRY LEE Cdr. J. G. Pomeroy, WILLIAM P. BIDDLE Cdr. L. F. Brown USNR, ARTHUR MIDDLETON Cdr. P. K. Perry USCG, HEYWOOD Cdr. P. F. Dugan.

Transdiv 6, Capt. T. B. Brittain: HARRIS Cdr. A. M. Van Eaton, J. FRANKLIN BELL Capt. O. H. Ritchie USNR, ORMSBY Cdr. L. Frisco USNR, FELAND Cdr. C. A. Mission.

Transdiv 18, Capt. Knowles: MONROVIA Cdr. J. D. Kelsey, DOYEN Cdr. J. G. McClaughry, SHERIDAN Cdr. J. J. Mockrish USNR; attack cargo ships THUBAN Cdr. J. C. Campbell USNR, BELLATRIX Cdr. C. A. Jones, VIRGO Cdr. C. H. McLaughlin USNR; landing ship dock ASHLAND Cdr. C. L. C. Atkeson; transport LA SALLE Cdr. F. C. Fleugel USNR.

Destroyer Screen, Capt. E. M. Thompson

JOHN RODGERS Cdr. H. O. Parish, SIGSBEE Cdr. B. V. M. Russell, HEERMANN Cdr. D. M. Agnew, HAZELWOOD Cdr. H. Wood, HARRISON Lt. Cdr. C. M. Dalton, MCKEE Cdr. J. J. Greytak, MURRAY Cdr. P. R. Anderson.

TG 53.2 MINESWEEPER GROUP, Lt. Cdr. H. R. Peirce USNR

REQUISITE Lt. Cdr. Peirce, PURSUIT Lt. R. F. Good USNR.

TG 53.4 FIRE SUPPORT GROUP, Rear Admiral H. F. Kingman

Section 1: Battleship TENNESSEE Capt. R. S. Haggart; light cruiser MOBILE Capt. C. J. Wheeler. Desdiv 27, Capt. W. Craig: Destroyers BAILEY Lt. Cdr. M. T. Munger, FRAZIER Lt. Cdr. E. M. Brown.

Section 2, Rear Admiral L. T. DuBose: Light cruiser SANTA FE Capt. R. S.

---

* Lost or killed in this operation.

[1] An Avenger torpedo-bomber made by General Motors.
[2] Also Commander Attack Transports.

Berkey; battleship MARYLAND Capt. C. H. Jones; destroyers GANSEVOORT Lt. Cdr. M. L. McCullough, MEADE Lt. Cdr. J. Munholland.

Section 3: Battleship COLORADO Capt. W. Granat; heavy cruiser PORTLAND Capt. A. D. Burhans; destroyers ANDERSON Lt. Cdr. J. G. Tennent, RUSSELL Lt. Cdr. W. H. McClain.

Section 4, Cdr. H. Crommelin: Destroyers RINGGOLD Cdr. T. F. Conley, DASHIELL Cdr. J. B. McLean.

Section 5: Heavy cruiser INDIANAPOLIS Capt. E. R. Johnson; destroyer SCHROEDER Lt. Cdr. J. T. Bowers.

TG 53.6 AIR SUPPORT GROUP, Rear Admiral V. H. Ragsdale

Escort carriers SANGAMON Capt. E. P. Moore (9 TBF-1, 9 SBD-5 Lt. Cdr. B. E. Day; 12 F6F-3 Lt. Cdr. F. L. Bates), SUWANNEE Capt. F. W. McMahon (9 SBD-5, 9 TBF-1 Lt. Cdr. A. C. Edmands; 12 F6F-3 Lt. Cdr. H. O. Harvey), CHENANGO Capt. D. Ketcham (9 SBD-5, 9 TBF-1 Lt. Cdr. R. L. Flint USNR; 12 F6F-3 Lt. Cdr. S. Mandarich), BARNES Capt. G. A. Dussault (22 F6F-3 Lt. Cdr. B. M. Strean), NASSAU Capt. S. J. Michael (22 F6F-3 Lt. Cdr. Strean).[1]

Destroyer Screen, Cdr. Ira H. Nunn

AYLWIN Cdr. R. O. Strange, FARRAGUT Lt. Cdr. E. F. Ferguson, MONAGHAN Lt. Cdr. P. H. Horn, COTTEN Lt. Cdr. F. T. Sloat, COWELL Cdr. C. W. Parker.

TG 54.5 TARAWA LST GROUP NO. 1, Lt. Cdr. R. M. Pitts

LSTs *34, 242, 243,* each carrying an LCT. Destroyer BANCROFT Lt. Cdr. Pitts.

TF 50 CARRIER FORCE, Rear Admiral C. A. Pownall in *Yorktown*

TG 50.1 CARRIER INTERCEPTOR GROUP, Rear Admiral Pownall

CV 10	YORKTOWN	Capt. J. J. Clark

Air Group 5: 1 F6F-3, Lt. Cdr. C. L. Crommelin

VF-5	36 F6F-3	Lt. Cdr. E. M. Owen
VB-5	36 SBD-5	Lt. Cdr. E. E. Stebbins
VT-5	18 TBF-1	Lt. Cdr. R. Upson USNR

CV 16	LEXINGTON	Capt. F. B. Stump

Air Group 16: 1 F6F-3, Lt. Cdr. E. M. Snowden

VB-16	36 SBD-5	Lt. Cdr. Snowden
VF-16	36 F6F-3	Lt. Cdr. P. D. Buie
VT-16	18 TBF-1	Lt. Cdr. R. H. Isely

CVL 25	COWPENS	Capt. R. P. McConnell

Air Group 25: Lt. R. H. Price

VF-25	24 F6F-3	Lt. Price
VF-6	12 F6F-3	Lt. G. C. Bullard
VC-25	10 TBF-1	Lt. Cdr. M. A. Grant

Batdiv 6, Rear Admiral E. W. Hanson

SOUTH DAKOTA Capt. A. E. Smith, WASHINGTON Capt. J. E. Maher.

Destroyer Screen, Lt. Cdr. A. J. Hill

NICHOLAS Cdr. R. T. S. Keith, TAYLOR Lt. Cdr. B. Katz, LA VALLETTE Lt. Cdr. R. L. Taylor, IZARD Lt. Cdr. E. K. Van Swearingen, CHARRETTE Cdr. E. S. Karpe, CONNER Cdr. W. E. Kaitner.

[1] The planes of *Barnes* and *Nassau* were of Squadron VF-1 (Lt. Cdr. Strean), and constituted the air garrison for Tarawa.

TG 50.2 NORTHERN CARRIER GROUP, Rear Admiral A. W. Radford

CV 6   ENTERPRISE   Capt. S. P. Ginder

Air Group 6: 1 TBF–1, *Lt. Cdr. E. H. O'Hare

VB–6	36 SBD–5	Lt. Cdr. I. M. Hampton
VT–6	18 TBF–1	Lt. Cdr. J. L. Phillips
VF–2	36 F6F–3	Lt. Cdr. W. A. Dean

CVL 24   BELLEAU WOOD   Capt. A. M. Pride

Air Group 24: Cdr. R. H. Dale

VF–24	26 F6F–3	Cdr. Dale
VF–6	12 F6F–3	Lt. P. C. Rooney
VC–22B	9 TBF–1	Lt. R. M. Swenson

CVL 26   MONTEREY   Capt. L. T. Hundt

Air Group 30: Lt. Cdr. J. G. Sliney USNR

VF–30	24 F6F–3	Lt. Cdr. Sliney
VC–30	9 TBF–1	Lt. Cdr. J. D. Black

Batdiv 6, Rear Admiral G. B. Davis

MASSACHUSETTS Capt. T. D. Ruddock, NORTH CAROLINA Capt. F. P. Thomas, INDIANA Capt. W. M. Fechteler.

Destroyer Screen, Cdr. H. F. Miller

BOYD Lt. Cdr. U. S. G. Sharp, BRADFORD Lt. Cdr. R. L. Morris, BROWN Lt. Cdr. T. H. Copeman, FLETCHER Lt. Cdr. R. D. McGinnis (with Desdiv 42 Cdr. H. O. Larson on board), RADFORD Cdr. G. E. Griggs, JENKINS Lt. Cdr. M. Hall.

TG 50.3 SOUTHERN CARRIER GROUP, Rear Admiral A. E. Montgomery

CV 9   ESSEX   Capt. D. B. Duncan

Air Group 9: 1 F6F–3, Cdr. J. Raby

VF–9	36 F6F–3	Lt. Cdr. P. H. Torrey
VB–9	36 SBD–5	Lt. Cdr. A. T. Decker
VT–9	18 TBF–1	Lt. Cdr. P. E. Emrick

CV 17   BUNKER HILL   Capt. J. J. Ballentine

Air Group 17: 1 TBF–1, Cdr. M. P. Bagdanovitch

VB–17	32 SB2C–1 (Helldiver)	Lt. Cdr. J. E. Vose
VF–18	36 F6F–3	Lt. Cdr. S. L. Silber USNR

CVL 22   INDEPENDENCE   Capt. R. L. Johnson

Air Group 22: Cdr. J. M. Peters

VF–22	16 F6F–3	Lt. L. L. Johnson USNR
VF–6	12 F6F–3	Lt. Cdr. H. W. Harrison USNR
VC–22	9 TBF–1	Cdr. Peters

Crudiv 5, Rear Admiral E. G. Small

Heavy cruisers CHESTER Capt. F. T. Spellman, PENSACOLA Capt. R. E. Dees, SALT LAKE CITY Capt. L. W. Busbey; light cruiser OAKLAND Capt. W. K. Phillips.

Destroyer Screen, Capt. J. T. Bottom

ERBEN Cdr. J. H. Nevins, HALE Cdr. K. F. Poehlman; Desdiv 96, Cdr. C. E. Carroll: BULLARD Lt. Cdr. B. W. Freund, KIDD Lt. Cdr. A. B. Roby, CHAUNCEY Lt. Cdr. L. C. Conwell.

* Killed in this operation.

TG 50.4 RELIEF CARRIER GROUP, Rear Admiral F. C. Sherman

CV–3 SARATOGA Capt. J. H. Cassady

Air Group 12: 1 TBF–1, Cdr. H. H. Caldwell

VF–12	37 F6F–3	Cdr. J. C. Clifton
VB–12	24 SBD–5	Lt. Cdr. J. H. Newell
VT–12	18 TBF–1	Lt. Cdr. R. F. Farrington

CVL 23 PRINCETON Capt. G. R. Henderson

Air Group 23: Lt. Cdr. H. L. Miller

| VF–23 | 24 F6F–3 | Lt. Cdr. Miller |
| VT–23 | 9 TBF–1 | Lt. Cdr. M. T. Hatcher |

Crudiv 2, Rear Admiral L. J. Wiltse

Light cruisers SAN DIEGO Capt. L. J. Hudson, SAN JUAN Capt. G. W. Clark.

Destroyer Screen, Cdr. C. J. Stuart

STACK Lt. Cdr. P. K. Sherman, STERETT Lt. Cdr. F. G. Gould, WILSON Lt. Cdr. C. K. Duncan, EDWARDS Lt. Cdr. P. G. Osler.

TF 57 DEFENSE FORCES AND LAND–BASED AIR
Rear Admiral J. H. Hoover

At Nanomea, Nukufetau and Funafuti

Seaplane tenders CURTISS Capt. S. E. Peck, MACKINAC Cdr. F. D. Stroop, SWAN Lt. (jg) C. E. Napier.

TG 57.2 STRIKING GROUP, Major General W. H. Hale USA

90 B–24s of VII Army Air Force

TG 57.3 SEARCH AND RECONNAISSANCE GROUP

VP–53 Lt. Cdr. C. Ingram: 12 PBY–5A (Catalina).
VP–72 Lt. Cdr. S. J. Lawrence: 12 PBY–5.
VB–108 Cdr. E. C. Renfro: 12 PB4Y (Liberator).
VB–137 Cdr. E. R. Sanders: 12 PV–1 (Ventura).
VB–142 Lt. Cdr. C. L. Miller: 12 PV–1.
Photo Squadron VP–3 Cdr. R. J. Stroh: 6 PB4Y (F–7).

TG 57.4 ELLICE ISLANDS DEFENSE AND UTILITY GROUP

Brig. Gen. L. G. Merritt USMC

4th Marine Base Air Defense Wing: 90 Fighters, 72 Scout Bombers
Inshore Patrol Squadrons 51, 65, 66: 24 Observation Planes
Air Transport Squadron 353: 12 Transport Planes

SERVICE GROUPS, Vice Admiral W. L. Calhoun, at Pearl Harbor

SERVICE SQUADRON 8, Capt. A. H. Gray at Pearl Harbor [1]

Oilers: SCHUYLKILL Cdr. F. A. Hardesty, SUAMICO Cdr. R. E. Butterfield, NECHES Lt. Cdr. H. G. Hansen USNR, NESHANIC Cdr. A. C. Allen USNR, PLATTE Cdr. C. H.

[1] From Service Force Pacific Fleet records, giving composition about 15 Nov. 1943. Capt. E. E. Paré, chief of staff to Capt. Gray, commanded the group at sea in early 1944.

Sigel USNR, TALLULAH Cdr. J. B. Goode, NEOSHO Cdr. D. G. McMillan, CIMARRON Capt. J. P. Cady, TAPPAHANNOCK Cdr. C. A. Swafford, PECOS Cdr. P. M. Gunnell, SABINE Cdr. A. F. Junker, GUADALUPE Cdr. H. A. Anderson, LACKAWANNA Cdr. A. L. Toney.

Cortdiv 26, Cdr. T. C. Thomas: Destroyer escorts WINTLE Lt. Cdr. L. S. Bailey USNR, CABANA Lt. Cdr. R. L. Bence USNR, DEMPSEY Lt. Cdr. H. A. Barnard, DUFFY Cdr. G. A. Parkinson USNR.

Cortdiv 28, Cdr. W. S. Howard: GREINER Lt. Cdr. F. S. Dowd USNR, STRADTFELD Lt. Cdr. S. Hansen USNR, DIONNE Lt. R. S. Paret USNR.

Hospital Ships: RELIEF Cdr. J. B. Bliss, SOLACE Cdr. C. L. Waters.

Mobile Service Squadron 4, Capt. H. M. Scull

Destroyer tender CASCADE Cdr. S. B. Ogden; oiler SEPULGA Cdr. V. B. Tate; repair ships VESTAL Cdr. W. T. Singer, PHAON Lt. G. F. Watson; survey ship SUMNER Cdr. I. W. Truitt; salvage vessel CLAMP Lt. Cdr. L. H. Curtis USNR; fleet tugs ONTARIO Lt. (jg) R. C. Schulke USNR, KINGFISHER Lt. (jg) J. T. Moritz USNR, ARAPAHO Lt. C. B. Lee, TAWASA Lt. F. C. Clark; rescue tug *ATR-44* Lt. M. L. Wright; motor tug *YMT-205;* minesweepers *YMS-287* Lt. (jg) H. Hoppock USNR, *YMS-290* Lt. (jg) A. K. Mosely USNR; net tender ELDER Lt. Cdr. D. H. Morse USNR; subchasers *SC-1317* Lt. F. C. Cary USNR, *SC-994* Lt. (jg) J. H. Carter USNR, *SC-990* Lt. T. E. Olsen USNR, *SC-1316* Lt. (jg) R. L. Ferguson USNR, *SC-1270* Ens. K. S. Nelms USNR; coastal transports *APc-108* Lt. (jg) K. L. Davey USNR, *APc-109* Lt. J. S. Horton USNR.

GARRISON GROUPS

TG 54.6 MAKIN LST GROUP II, Cdr. H. A. Lincoln

LSTs *476, 477, 480, 481* and *482,* carrying 2 LCTs, Destroyer CALDWELL Cdr. Lincoln.

TG 54.8 MAKIN GARRISON GROUP, Capt. P. P. Blackburn

S.S. YOUNG AMERICA, ISLAND MAIL, CAPE CONSTANTINE, CAPE SAN MARTIN; destroyer escorts WHITMAN Lt. Cdr. C. E. Bull USNR, WILEMAN Lt. Cdr. A. F. Beyer USNR, carrying 7th Garrison Force U.S. Army.

TG 54.7 TARAWA LST GROUP, Lt. Cdr. B. B. Cheatham

LSTs *478, 20, 23, 69, 84, 169, 205, 218, 484,* carrying 2 LCTs. Destroyer COGHLAN Lt. Cdr. Cheatham.

TG 54.9 TARAWA GARRISON GROUP, Capt. H. O. Roesch

S.S. CAPE FEAR, DASHING WAVE; transport PRESIDENT POLK; cargo ship JUPITER; destroyer escorts LEHARDY Lt. Cdr. J. H. Prause USNR, WILLIAM C. MILLER Lt. F. G. Storey USNR.

TG 54.10 ABEMAMA GARRISON GROUP I, Cdr. Carl E. Anderson USNR

S.S. ROBIN WENTLEY, CAPE STEVENS, CAPE ISABEL; transport PRESIDENT MONROE; destroyer escorts CHARLES R. GREER Lt. Cdr. W. T. Denton USNR, HAROLD C. THOMAS Lt. V. H. Craig USNR.

TG 54.11 ABEMAMA GARRISON GROUP II, Lt. Cdr. P. A. Walker USNR

S.S. JANE ADDAMS; destroyer escort BURDEN R. HASTINGS Lt. Cdr. Walker; LSTs *19, 29, 241* and *244,* carrying 3 LCTs.

PATROL SUBMARINES, Vice Admiral Charles A. Lockwood

Truk Patrol: THRESHER Cdr. Harry Hull, *CORVINA *Cdr. R. S. Rooney, APOGON Cdr. W. P. Schoeni.

North and South of Oroluk: *SCULPIN *Cdr. Fred Connaway (Commander wolf-pack, *Capt. J. P. Cromwell on board), SEARAVEN Lt. Cdr. M. H. Dry.

Kwajalein Patrol: SEAL Cdr. H. B. Dodge.

Jaluit Patrol: SPEARFISH Lt. Cdr. J. W. Williams.

Wotje-Mili Patrol (lifeguarding): PLUNGER Cdr. R. H. Bass.

Nauru Patrol (weather station): PADDLE Cdr. R. H. Rice.

Tarawa Patrol: NAUTILUS Cdr. W. D. Irvin, carrying Abemama occupation force.

* Lost or killed in this operation.

Forces Engaged in Marshall Islands Operations

29 January–23 February 1944

("Flintlock" and "Catchpole")

Note that the organization as here set up is for "Flintlock" (Majuro and both ends of Kwajalein) only.

Groups, units and individual ships that also participated in "Catchpole" (Eniwetok) are marked E.

Names of C.O.'s, if the same as in "Galvanic," will be found in Appendix II.

PACIFIC FLEET
Admiral Chester W. Nimitz, at Pearl Harbor

FIFTH FLEET
Vice Admiral Raymond A. Spruance in *Indianapolis*

TF 51 JOINT EXPEDITIONARY FORCE
Rear Admiral Richmond K. Turner in *Rocky Mount*

Also in *Rocky Mount* (Capt. S. F. Patten) were commander Expeditionary Troops, Major General H. M. Smith usmc, and Headquarters Support Aircraft, Captain H. B. Sallada.

TF 52 SOUTHERN ATTACK FORCE, Rear Admiral Turner

SOUTHERN LANDING FORCE
Major General C. H. Corlett usa, 7th Infantry Division
Destroyer Transport Group, Lt. Cdr. D. K. O'Connor usnr
overton Lt. Cdr. O'Connor   manley Lt. R. T. Newell usnr
Advance Transport Unit, Captain J. B. McGovern

Attack transports ZEILIN, ORMSBY, PRESIDENT POLK Cdr. C. J. Ballreich, WINDSOR Cdr. D. C. Woodward USNR.

Attack cargo transport VIRGO, landing ship dock ASHLAND (also E).

Tractor Unit 1, Cdr. R. C. Webb (also E)

LSTs *242, 224, 272, 243, 246, 78, 34, 226*, carrying 708th Amphibious Tank Corps, U.S. Army (LVTs). (At Eniwetok LSTs *29, 127, 218, 240* were substituted for *34, 78, 226, 243.*)

TG 52.5 SOUTHERN TRANSPORT GROUP, Captain H. B. Knowles

Transdiv 6, Capt. T. B. Brittain: Attack transports HARRIS, FAYETTE Cdr. J. C. Lester, HARRY LEE, LEEDSTOWN Cdr. H. Bye; attack cargo ships CENTAURUS Capt. G. E. McCable; landing ship dock LINDENWALD Capt. W. H. Weaver USNR.

Transdiv 18, Captain Knowles: Attack transports MONROVIA, J. FRANKLIN BELL, PIERCE, FELAND Cdr. G. M. Jones USNR; attack cargo ship THUBAN Cdr. J. C. Campbell USNR; landing ship dock BELLE GROVE Lt. Cdr. M. Seavey USNR.

Tractor Unit 2, Cdr. A. M. Hurst: LSTs *31*, (E)*29, 41*, (E)*218*, (E)*127*, (E)*240*, (E)*273, 481* (Corps Reserve).

TG 52.6 CONTROL GROUP, Commander J. W. Coleman USNR

SCs *1066, 999, 539;* LCCs *36* (from VIRGO), *38* (from CENTAURUS).

TG 52.7 Destroyer Screen, Captain E. M. Thompson

JOHN RODGERS, (E) HAZELWOOD Cdr. V. P. Douw, (E) HAGGARD Cdr. D. A. Harris (with Comdesdiv 94, Cdr. J. H. Nevins), (E) FRANKS, SCHROEDER Cdr. J. T. Bowers, (E) HAILEY Cdr. P. H. Brady, destroyer minesweepers (E) ZANE Lt. Cdr. W. T. Powell, PERRY Lt. I. G. Stubbart.

TG 52.8 FIRE SUPPORT GROUP
Rear Admiral Robert C. Giffen in *Minneapolis*

Unit 1, Cdr. J. J. Greytak: Destroyers MCKEE Cdr. Greytak, STEVENS Lt. Cdr. W. M. Rakow. Unit 2, Rear Admiral Giffen: Heavy cruisers MINNEAPOLIS, NEW ORLEANS; battleships IDAHO, (E) PENNSYLVANIA; destroyers BAILEY, FRAZIER, HALL, MEADE. Unit 3, Rear Admiral Robert M. Griffin: Battleships NEW MEXICO, MISSISSIPPI; heavy cruiser SAN FRANCISCO Capt. H. E. Overesch; destroyers COLAHAN Cdr. D. T. Wilber, MURRAY Cdr. P. R. Anderson, HARRISON Cdr. C. M. Dalton. Unit 4, Cdr. Henry Crommelin: Destroyers RINGGOLD, SIGSBEE Cdr. B. V. M. Russell.

LCI(L) Unit, Lt. Cdr. T. Blanchard USNR

LCI(L) Div 15, Lt. Cdr. Blanchard: LCI(L)s *365, 438, 439, 440, 441, 442*, also served at Eniwetok.

LCI(L) Div 13, Lt. Cdr. J. L. Harlan: LCI(L)s *77, 78, 79, 80, 366, 437.*

TG 52.9 CARRIER SUPPORT GROUP
Rear Admiral R. E. Davison (Cardiv 24)

CVE 61   MANILA BAY   Capt. B. L. Braun

VC–7: 9 TBF–1 (Avenger), 3 TBF–1C, 16 FM–2 (Wildcat) Lt. Cdr. W. R. Bartlett

CVE 57   CORAL SEA   Capt. H. W. Taylor

VC–33: 6 TBF–1C, 4 TBF–1, 2 TBM–1 (Avenger), 5 FM–1, 9 F4F–4 (Wildcat) Lt. Cdr. J. J. Lynch

CVE 58   CORREGIDOR   Capt. R. L. Bowman

VC–44: 8 TBM–1, 3 TBF–1C, 3 F4F–4, 6 FM–1 Lt. Cdr. G. M. Clifford

Destroyer Screen
BANCROFT Cdr. R. M. Pitts, COGHLAN Lt. Cdr. B. B. Cheatham, CALDWELL Lt. Cdr.
G. Wendelburg, HALLIGAN Cdr. C. E. Cortner.

TG 52.10 MINESWEEPING AND HYDROGRAPHIC GROUP
Cdr. F. F. Sima USNR

Unit 1: Minesweepers REVENGE Cdr. Sima, PURSUIT Lt. R. F. Good USNR,
REQUISITE Lt. Cdr. H. R. Peirce USNR, LCC-39 (from ORMSBY). Unit 2: YMSs 90,
91, 383, 388, LCC-37 (from THUBAN).

TG 52.11 SOUTHERN SALVAGE UNIT, Lt. Cdr. L. H. Curtis USNR

Ocean tugs TEKESTA Lt. J. O. Strickland, TAWASA Lt. F. C. Clark, ARAPAHOE
Lt. C. B. Lee.

TG 51.3 SOUTHERN DEFENSE GROUP, Cdr. W. J. Whiteside

Destroyer escort DUFFY, Lt. E. P. Lyons USNR; LSTs 23, 227, 244, 484.
Carrying detachment of 3rd and 4th Army Defense Battalions plus attached
units, assigned elements of service units (from Expeditionary Troops).

TG 51.4 SOUTHERN GARRISON GROUP, Capt. H. O. Roesch

S.S. ISLAND MAIL, CAPE STEVENS, CAPE ISABEL, CAPE FEAR, MONARCH OF THE SEAS.
Carrying assigned elements of 3rd and 4th Army Defense Battalions and service
units (from Expeditionary Troops).
Destroyer escorts BURDEN R. HASTINGS Lt. E. B. Fay USNR, LEHARDY Lt. Cdr. E. L.
Holtz USNR.

TF 53 NORTHERN ATTACK FORCE

Rear Admiral R. L. Conolly in *Appalachian*
(Capt. J. M. Fernald)

TG 53.9 INITIAL TRANSPORT GROUP, Capt. A. D. Blackledge (Transdiv 26)

Attack transports SUMTER Capt. Blackledge, CALLAWAY Capt. D. C. McNeil
USCG, WARREN Cdr. W. A. McHale USNR, WILLIAM P. BIDDLE Cdr. L. F. Brown
USNR; attack cargo transport ALMAACK Cdr. J. Y. Dannenberg; landing ship dock
EPPING FOREST Lt. Cdr. L. Martin USNR.

Raider Unit, Lt. Cdr. E. T. Farley USNR

Destroyer transport SCHLEY Lt. Cdr. Farley.
Transport Screen, Capt. J. G. Coward: Destroyers REMEY Cdr. R. P. Fiala,
(E) MACDONOUGH Lt. Cdr. J. W. Ramey, minesweeper HOGAN Lt. Cdr. W. H.
Sublette.
LST Unit 1, Capt. A. J. Robertson: LSTs 222, 38, 122, 221, 270, 271 (with LCTs
aboard), 43, 45, 121; SCs 1012, 670; destroyer LAVALLETTE Cdr. R. L. Taylor.

TG 53.3 MINESWEEPER GROUP, Cdr. W. R. Loud

Minesweepers PALMER Lt. Cdr. R. H. Thomas USNR, CHIEF Lt. Cdr. J. M.
Wyckoff USNR, HEED Lt. M. Dent USNR, MOTIVE Lt. Cdr. G. W. Lundgren USNR;
motor minesweepers 262, 263, 283, 320.

TG 53.4 NORTHERN LANDING FORCE, Major General Harry Schmidt USMC

Preliminary Landing Group, Brig. Gen. J. L. Underhill USMC; Combat Team 25
(reinforced); SC-997 (Inshore headquarters ship); Combat Teams 23 and 24.

TG 53.5 NORTHERN SUPPORT GROUP
Rear Admiral J. B. Oldendorf in *Louisville*

Fire Support Unit 1, Rear Admiral H. F. Kingman: Battleships (E) TENNESSEE Capt. R. S. Haggart, (E) COLORADO Capt. W. Granat, heavy cruiser (E) LOUISVILLE Capt. S. H. Hurt, light cruiser MOBILE Capt. C. J. Wheeler, destroyers MORRIS Cdr. G. L. Caswell, ANDERSON *Cdr. J. G. Tennent. Unit 2, Rear Admiral L. T. Du Bose: Light cruiser SANTE FE Capt. J. Wright; battleship MARYLAND Capt. H. J. Ray; heavy cruiser (E) INDIANAPOLIS Capt. E. R. Johnson; light cruiser BILOXI Capt. D. M. McGurl; destroyers MUSTIN Cdr. M. M. Riker, RUSSELL Lt. Cdr. L. R. Miller. Unit 3, Cdr. J. C. Woelfel: destroyers PORTERFIELD Cdr. Woelfel, HARADEN Cdr. H. C. Allan; LCIs 455, 82, 345. Unit 4, Cdr. C. C. Shute: Destroyers HOPEWELL Cdr. Shute, (E) JOHNSTON Cdr. E. E. Evans. Unit 5, Capt. E. R. McLean: Destroyer (E) PHELPS Lt. Cdr. D. L. Martineau, LCIs 457, 449, 450, 451, 452, 453, Cdr. M. J. Malanaphy.

TG 53.6 CARRIER GROUP
Rear Admiral Van H. Ragsdale (Cardiv 22)
(also in Eniwetok Expeditionary Group)

CVE 26   (E) SANGAMON   Capt. E. P. Moore

Air Group 37: Lt. Cdr. F. L. Bates

VF–37	12 F6F–3 (Hellcat)	Lt. Cdr. Bates
VC–37	9 SBD–5 (Dauntless) 4 TBM–1C, 6 TBF–1	Lt. Cdr. B. E. Day

CVE 27   (E) SUWANNEE   Capt. W. D. Johnson

Air Group 60: Lt. Cdr. H. O. Feilbach USNR

VF–60	12 F6F–3	Lt. Cdr. Feilbach
VC–60	9 SBD–5, 7 TBM–1C, 2 TBF–1	Lt. W. C. Vincent USNR

CVE 28   (E) CHENANGO   Capt. D. Ketcham

Air Group 35: Lt. Cdr. S. Mandarich

VF–35	12 F6F–3	Lt. E. T. Moore
VC–35	4 TBF–1, 5 TBM–1C, 9 SBD–5	Lt. T. Carr USNR

Carrier Screen, Cdr. I. H. Nunn

Destroyers FARRAGUT Lt. Cdr. E. F. Ferguson, MONAGHAN Lt. Cdr. W. F. Wendt, DALE Lt. Cdr. C. W. Aldrich.

(The three DDs above were in Fire Support at Eniwetok, where MORRIS, HUGHES, MUSTIN and ELLET were substituted as CVE screen.)

TG 53.10 MAIN ATTACK DETACHMENT, Capt. Pat Buchanan (Transdiv 24)

Attack transports DUPAGE Capt. G. M. Wauchope USNR, WAYNE Cdr. T. V. Cooper, ELMORE Cdr. D. Harrison, DOYEN Cdr. J. G. McGlaughry; attack cargo transport AQUARIUS Capt. R. V. Marron USCG.

Transdiv 28, Capt. H. C. Flanagan: Attack transports BOLIVAR Cdr. R. P. Wadell, SHERIDAN Cdr. J. J. Mockrish USNR, CALVERT Cdr. E. J. Sweeney USNR, LA SALLE Cdr. F. C. Fluegel USNR; attack cargo ship ALCYONE Cdr. J. B. McVey, landing ship dock GUNSTON HALL Cdr. D. E. Collins USNR. Transport Screen, Lt. Cdr. R. D. McGinnis, destroyers FLETCHER Lt. Cdr. J. L. Foster, HUGHES Lt. Cdr. E. B. Rittenhouse, ELLET Lt. Cdr. E. C. Rider, minesweepers STANSBURY Lt. Cdr. D. M. Granstrom USNR, HAMILTON Cdr. R. R. Sampson. LST Unit 2, Capt. J. S. Lillard,

---

* Killed 30 Jan. 1944, succeeded by Lt. Cdr. J. F. Murdock.

LSTs *119, 126, 223, 274, 42, 128*, SCs *1028, 1031*, destroyer AYLWIN Cdr. R. O. Strange.

TG 53.12 NORTHERN SALVAGE GROUP, Lt. Cdr. H. O. Foss

Ocean tugs MATACO Lt. Cdr. W. G. Baker, CHICKASAW Lt. (jg) G. W. McClead, MOLALA Lt. R. L. Ward.

TG 51.5 NORTHERN DEFENSE GROUP, Lt. Cdr. R. V. Wheeler

LSTs *241, 268, 476, 477, 479*; minesweeper LONG Lt. Cdr. Wheeler.
Carrying detachment of 15th Marine Defense Battalion plus attached units; assigned elements of service units (from Expeditionary Troops).

TG 51.6 NORTHERN GARRISON GROUP 1, Capt. P. P. Blackburn

S.S. YOUNG AMERICA, ROBIN WENTLEY, CAPE SAN MARTIN, CAPE GEORGIA.
Carrying assigned elements of 15th Marine Defense Battalion and service units.
Destroyer escorts H. C. THOMAS Lt. Cdr. E. J. Haddon USNR, WILEMAN Lt. R. M. Tanner USNR.

TG 51.7 NORTHERN GARRISON GROUP 2, Cdr. J. D. McKinney

S.S. TYPHOON, TITAN; destroyer escort SEDERSTROM Lt. Cdr. L. M. King USNR.
Carrying elements of service units (from Expeditionary Troops).

TG 51.1 RESERVE FORCE, Capt. D. W. Loomis
(Later this became TG 51.11, ENIWETOK EXPEDITIONARY GROUP)

Attack transports LEONARD WOOD Capt. M. O'Neil USCG, HEYWOOD Capt. P. F. Dugan, ARTHUR MIDDLETON Capt. S. A. Olsen USCG, PRESIDENT MONROE Capt. G. D. Morrison, attack cargo ELECTRA Cdr. C. S. Beightler.
Carrying 22nd Marine Regiment reinforced, the Reserve Landing Force, Brig. Gen. T. E. Watson USMC.
Transdiv 30, Capt. C. A. Misson, attack transports NEVILLE Capt. B. Bartlett, CUSTER Capt. R. E. Hanson, WHARTON Capt. J. J. Fallon, attack cargo ship MERCURY Cdr. G. W. Graber USNR. Carrying 1st and 3rd Battalions 106th Infantry Regiment reinforced.
Reserve Transport Screen, Capt. A. G. Cook: destroyers MCCORD Cdr. W. T. Kenny, TRATHEN Cdr. F. L. Tedder, HEERMANN Cdr. D. M. Agnew, HOEL Lt. Cdr. W. D. Thomas, STEMBEL Cdr. W. L. Tagg, DEWEY Lt. Cdr. R. G. Copeland, HULL Lt. Cdr. C. W. Consolvo.
(In the Eniwetok operation also participated destroyers HAZELWOOD, FRANKS, AYLWIN, DALE, MONAGHAN, FARRAGUT, HAGGARD, HAILEY, JOHNSTON, minesweepers CHANDLER and ZANE; last two a minesweeper unit under Lt. Cdr. H. L. Thompson.)
A Control Unit, Lt. Cdr. J. R. Fels USNR (minesweepers ORACLE, SAGE, YMSs *262, 383*) and a Service Group, Cdr. A. H. Kooistra (ocean tugs CHICKASAW, MOLALA and oilers GAZELLE, GEMSBOK) were part of Eniwetok Expeditionary Group.

TG 51.2 MAJURO ATTACK GROUP, Rear Admiral Harry W. Hill in *Cambria*

Attack transport (E) CAMBRIA Capt. C. W. Dean USCG (carrying 2nd Battalion 106th Inf., Lt. Col. F. H. Sheldon USA; HQ Majuro Garrison Force, Capt. E. A. Cruise), destroyer transports (E) KANE Lt. F. M. Christiansen USNR, (E) SCHLEY Lt. Cdr. E. T. Farley USNR, carrying V 'Phib Reconnaissance Party. *LST-482*, heavy cruiser (E) PORTLAND Capt. T. G. W. Settle.

CVE 16	NASSAU	Capt. S. J. Michael
VC-66	14 FM-1, 5 TBM-1C, 4 TBM-1	Lt. H. K. Bragg

CVE 62   NATOMA BAY   Capt. H. L. Meadow
VC–63   6 TBM–1, 6 TBM–1C, 12 FM–1   Lt. S. S. Searcy

(For these two CVEs, Rear Admiral Ragsdale's Group, SANGAMON, SUWANNEE and CHENANGO, were substituted for Eniwetok.)

Attack Group Screen, Cdr. C. E. Carroll

Destroyers BULLARD Cdr. B. W. Freund, BLACK Cdr. J. Maginnis, KIDD Cdr. A. B. Roby, CHAUNCEY Lt. Cdr. L. C. Conwell, minesweeper (E) CHANDLER Lt. Cdr. H. L. Thompson.

TG 51.8 DEFENSE GROUP, Lt. Cdr. S. A. Lief USNR

Destroyer escort WINTLE Lt. Cdr. L. S. Bailey USNR, LSTs *480, 276, 277, 84* (with LCTs aboard).

TG 51.9 GARRISON GROUP, Capt. G. B. Carter

Cargo ships CAELUM Lt. Cdr. E. Johnson USNR, ALKES Cdr. W. H. Wight USNR, RUTILICUS Lt. Cdr. H. O. Matthiesen USNR, KENMORE Lt. Cdr. O. H. Pitts USNR, LIVINGSTON Lt. Cdr. L. J. Alexanderson USNR, DE GRASSE Lt. Cdr. W. Jordan USNR, destroyer escorts CHARLES R. GREER Lt. Cdr. W. T. Denton USNR, DEEDE Lt. M. M. Maxwell USNR, DEMPSEY Lt. J. A. Weber USNR. Assigned elements of Defense Battalion and Service Units.

TF 58, FAST CARRIER FORCE, Rear Admiral Marc A. Mitscher

TG 58.1 CARRIER TASK GROUP 1, Rear Admiral John W. Reeves

CV 6   ENTERPRISE   Capt. M. B. Gardner
Air Group 10: Lt. Cdr. W. R. Kane

VB–10	30 SBD–5	Lt. Cdr. R. L. Poor
VF–10	32 F6F–3	Lt. R. W. Schumann
VT–10	16 TBF–1C	Lt. Cdr. W. I. Martin

CV 10   YORKTOWN   Capt. J. J. Clark
Air Group 5: Lt. Cdr. E. E. Stebbins

VB–5	1 F6F–3, 36 SBD–5	Lt. Cdr. Stebbins
VF–5	36 F6F–3	Lt. Cdr. E. M. Owen
VT–5	16 TBF–1, 2 TBF–1C	Lt. Cdr. R. Upson USNR

CVL 24   BELLEAU WOOD   Capt. A. M. Pride
Air Group 24: Lt. Cdr. E. M. Link

VF–24	24 F6F–3	Lt. Cdr. Link
VT–24	6 TBF–1, 2 TBC–1C	Lt. R. M. Swensson

Battleships WASHINGTON Capt. J. E. Maher (Rear Admiral W. A. Lee on board), MASSACHUSETTS Capt. T. D. Ruddock, INDIANA Capt. J. M. Steele (Combatdiv 8, Rear Admiral G. B. Davis on board), light cruiser OAKLAND Capt. W. K. Phillips.

Screen

(Desron 50, Capt. Sherman R. Clark): Destroyers C. K. BRONSON Lt. Cdr. J. C. McGoughran, COTTEN Cdr. F. T. Sloat, DORTCH Cdr. R. C. Young, GATLING Cdr. A. F. Richardson, HEALY Cdr. J. C. Atkeson, COGSWELL Cdr. H. T. Deutermann (Desdiv 100, Cdr. C. F. Chillingworth on board), CAPERTON Cdr. W. J. Miller, INGERSOLL Cdr. A. C. Veasey, KNAPP Cdr. F. Virden.

TG 58.2 CARRIER TASK GROUP 2, Rear Admiral A. E. Montgomery

CV 9   ESSEX   Capt. R. A. Ofstie
Air Group 9: Lt. Cdr. P. H. Torrey

VB-9	1 F6F-3, 34 SBD-5	Lt. Cdr. A. T. Decker
VF-9	35 F6F-3	Lt. Cdr. H. N. Houck USNR
VT-9	15 TBF-1, 2 TBF-1C, 2 TBM-1C	Lt. Cdr. D. M. White

CV 11   INTREPID   Capt. T. L. Sprague
Air Group 6: Lt. Cdr. D. B. Ingerslew

VB-6	36 SBD-5	Lt. Cdr. Ingerslew
VF-6	37 F6F-3	Lt. Cdr. H. W. Harrison USNR
VT-6	7 TBF-1, 7 TBF-1C, 5 TBM-1C	Lt. Cdr. W. G. Privette USNR

CVL 28   CABOT   Capt. M. F. Schoeffel
Air Group 31: Lt. Cdr. R. A. Winston

VF-31	24 F6F-3	Lt. Cdr. Winston
VT-31	8 TBM-1C, 1 TBF-1C	Lt. E. E. Wood USNR

Battleships SOUTH DAKOTA Capt. A. E. Smith (Batdiv 9, Rear Admiral E. W. Hanson on board), ALABAMA Capt. F. D. Kirtland, NORTH CAROLINA Capt. F. P. Thomas; light cruiser SAN DIEGO Capt. L. J. Hudson (with Commander Screen, Rear Admiral L. J. Wiltse, on board); destroyers OWEN Cdr. R. W. Wood (Desron 52, Capt. G. R. Cooper on board), MILLER Cdr. T. H. Kobey, THE SULLIVANS Cdr. K. M. Gentry, STEPHAN POTTER Cdr. C. H. Crichton, ICKOK Cdr. W. M. Sweetser, HUNT Cdr. H. A. Knoertzer, LEWIS HANCOCK Cdr. C. H. Lyman, STERETT Lt. Cdr. F. J. Blouin, STACK Lt. Cdr. R. E. Wheeler.

TG 58.3 CARRIER TASK GROUP 3, Rear Admiral F. C. Sherman

CV 17   BUNKER HILL   Capt. J. J. Ballentine
Air Group 17: Cdr. R. H. Dale

VB-17	1 F6F-3, 31 SB2C-1 (Helldiver)	Lt. Cdr. G. P. Norman
VF-18	37 F6F-3	Lt. Cdr. S. L. Silber USNR
VT-17	18 TBF-1C, 1 TBF-1, 1 TBM-1C	* Lt. Cdr. F. M. Whitaker

CVL 26   MONTEREY   Capt. L. T. Hundt
Air Group 30: Lt. Cdr. J. G. Sliney USNR

VF-30	25 F6F-3	Lt. Cdr. Sliney
VT-30	3 TBF-1C, 2 TBF-1, 4 TBM-1C	Lt. F. C. Tothill USNR

CVL 25   COWPENS   Capt. R. P. McConnell
Air Group 25: Lt. R. H. Price

VF-25	24 F6F-3	Lt. Price
VT-25	9 TBF-1C	Lt. R. B. Cottingham USNR

Battleships IOWA Capt. J. L. McCrea (Batdiv 7, Rear Admiral O. M. Hustvedt on board), NEW JERSEY Capt. C. F. Holden, heavy cruiser WICHITA Capt. J. J. Mahoney, destroyers IZARD Cdr. E. K. Swearingen (Desron 46, Capt. C. F. Espe on board), CHARRETTE Cdr. E. S. Karpe, CONNER Cdr. W. E. Kaitner, BELL Cdr. L. C. Petross, BURNS Lt. Cdr. D. T. Eller, BRADFORD Cdr. R. L. Morris, BROWN Cdr. T. H. Copeman, COWELL Cdr. C. W. Parker, WILSON Lt. Cdr. C. K. Duncan.

* Lt. Cdr. Whitaker and war correspondent Raymond Clapper were killed when their Avenger collided with another Avenger over Eniwetok Lagoon, 2 Feb. 1944.

TG 58.4 CARRIER TASK GROUP 4, Rear Admiral S. P. Ginder
(Also covered Eniwetok Operation)

CV 3   SARATOGA   Capt. J. H. Cassady

Air Group 12: Cdr. J. C. Clifton

VB–12	24 SBD–5	Lt. Cdr. V. L. Hathorn
VF–12	36 F6F–3	Cdr. R. G. Dose USNR
VT–12	18 TBM–1C	Lt. W. E. Rowbotham

CVL 23   PRINCETON   Capt. G. R. Henderson

Air Group 23: Lt. Cdr. H. L. Miller

VF–23	24 F6F–3	Lt. Cdr. H. L. Miller
VT–23	8 TBF–1, 1 TBM–1C	Lt. Cdr. M. T. Hatcher

CVL 27   LANGLEY   Capt. W. M. Dillon

Air Group 32: Cdr. E. G. Konrad

VF–32	22 F6F–3	Lt. Cdr. E. C. Outlaw
VT–32	9 TBF–1C	Cdr. Konrad

Heavy cruisers BOSTON Capt. J. H. Carson (Crudiv 10, Rear Admiral L. H. Thebaud on board), BALTIMORE Capt. W. C. Calhoun; light cruiser SAN JUAN Capt. G. W. Clark; destroyers MAURY Lt. Cdr. J. W. Koenig (Commander Screen, Capt. J. M. Higgins on board), CRAVEN Lt. Cdr. R. L. Fulton, GRIDLEY Cdr. J. H. Motes, MCCALL Cdr. E. L. Foster, DUNLAP Cdr. C. Iverson, FANNING Lt. Cdr. J. C. Bentley, CASE Cdr. C. M. Howe, CUMMINGS Cdr. P. D. Williams.

TG 50.15 NEUTRALIZATION GROUP, Rear Admiral E. G. Small
Heavy cruisers CHESTER Capt. F. T. Spellman, PENSACOLA Capt. R. E. Dees, SALT LAKE CITY Capt. L. W. Busbey, destroyers ERBEN Lt. Cdr. M. Slayton (Desron 48, Capt. J. T. Bottom on board), WALKER Cdr. H. E. Townsend, HALE Cdr. K. F. Poehlmann, ABBOT Cdr. M. E. Dornin; minelayers PREBLE Lt. Cdr. F. S. Steinke, RAMSAY Lt. Cdr. R. H. Holmes.

TF 57 DEFENSE FORCES AND LAND–BASED AIR
Rear Admiral J. H. Hoover

Aircraft tenders CURTISS Capt. S. E. Peck, MACKINAC Cdr. G. R. Dyson, CASCO Cdr. E. R. DeLong.

TG 57.2 STRIKE COMMAND, Maj. General W. H. Hale USA
Six 4-engine Bomber Squadrons (11th and 30th Groups) 72 B–24; four 2-engine Bomber Squadrons (41st Group) 64 B–25; Fighter-Bomber Squadron 531, 24 A–24 (Dauntless); 45th, 46th and 72nd Fighter Squadrons, 75 P–39 and P–40.

TG 57.3 SEARCH AND PATROL GROUP, Brig. Gen. L. G. Merritt USMC
Navy Patrol Squadrons VP–53: 12 PBY–5A; VP–72: 12 PBY–5; VP–202: 12 PBM–3D (Mariner); Bomber Squadrons VB–108 and VB–109: 24 PB4Y–1; VB–137 and VB–142: 24 PV–1 (Ventura); Photo Squadron VD–3: 6 PB4Y–1; Scout Squadrons VS–51, VS–65 and VS–66: 18 SBD–5. Marine Squadrons VMSB–151 and VMSB–331: 36 SBD–5.

PATROL SUBMARINES, Vice Admiral C. A. Lockwood

Truk Patrol: PERMIT Lt. Cdr. C. L. Bennett, SKIPJACK Lt. Cdr. G. G. Molumphy, GUARDFISH Lt. Cdr. N. G. Ward.
Ponape Patrol: SEAL Cdr. H. B. Dodge.
Kusaie Patrol: SUNFISH Lt. Cdr. E. E. Shelby.
Eniwetok Patrol: SEARAVEN Lt. Cdr. M. H. Dry.

Summary of Troops of Joint Expeditionary Force [1]

| | Assault Troops | | Garrison Troops [2] | | | |
	Army	Marine	Army	Marine	Navy [3]	Total
Southern Attack Force	21,768					21,768
Northern Attack Force		20,778				20,778
Majuro Attack Force	1,459	136				1,595
Corps Reserve	3,701	5,624				9,325
Eniwetok Attack Force	4,509	5,760				10,269
	(4,509)	(5,760)	8,558			
Southern Garrison Force				1,832	2,936	13,326
			(4,554)	(1,154)		(5,708)
Northern Garrison Force			7,710		3,175	10,885
			(4,124)			(4,124)
Majuro Garrison Force			1,459	1,978	3,728	7,165
			(1,459)			(1,459)
Eniwetok Garrison Force			5,990	3,212	5,439	14,641
			(3,777)			(3,777)
Force Aggregates	31,437	32,298	16,007	14,732	15,278	109,752
Total duplications	(4,509)	(5,760)	(9,790)	(5,278)		(25,337)
Net total troops employed	26,928	26,538	6,217	9,454	15,278	84,415

[1] Figures shown in parentheses represent duplication resulting from the reëmployment of certain troops for successive missions. For example, some assault troops were reëmployed for garrisons, and all troops used for the Eniwetok attack had been used before. These duplications are deducted at the end to show Net Total Troops Employed.

[2] Not including garrisons sent up later; only echelons assigned to TF 51.

[3] Not including crews of ships, only men temporarily or regularly assigned to shore duty.

Forces Engaged in Strike on Truk

17–18 February 1944

TF 50 TRUK STRIKING FORCE
Vice Admiral R. A. Spruance in *New Jersey*

TF 58 FAST CARRIER FORCE
Rear Admiral M. A. Mitscher in *Yorktown*

TG 58.1 Carrier Group 1, Rear Admiral John W. Reeves

ENTERPRISE   Capt. M. B. Gardner

Air Group 10: Same as in Marshalls Operation (Appendix III), plus: —
VF(N)–101 (detachment A): 4 F4U–2 (Corsair) Lt. Cdr. R. E. Harmer.

YORKTOWN   Capt. R. E. Jennings

Air Group 5: Same as in Marshalls, plus: —
VF(N)–76 (det. B): 4 F6F–3N (Hellcat) Lt. R. L. Reiserer.

BELLEAU WOOD   Capt. A. M. Pride

Air Group 24: Same as in Marshalls.

Crudiv 13, Rear Admiral L. T. DuBose
Light cruisers SANTA FE Capt. J. Wright, MOBILE Capt. C. J. Wheeler, BILOXI Capt.
D. M. McGurl, OAKLAND Capt. W. K. Phillips.

Screen
Desron 50, same as in Marshalls, Capt. Sherman R. Clark.

TG 58.2 CARRIER GROUP 2, Rear Admiral A. E. Montgomery

ESSEX   Capt. R. A. Ofstie

Air Group 9: Same as in Marshalls.

INTREPID   Capt. T. L. Sprague

Air Group 6: Same as in Marshalls, plus: —
VF(N)–101 (det. B): 4 F4U–2 Lt. C. L. Kullberg, except that Lt. Cdr. Ingerslew
is also Commander Air Group.

CABOT   Capt. M. F. Schoeffel

Air Group 31: Same as in Marshalls.

Cruisers, Rear Admiral L. J. Wiltse
SAN DIEGO, SAN FRANCISCO, WICHITA, BALTIMORE

Screen

Desron 52 as in Marshalls, less STERETT, plus STEMBEL.

TG 58.3 CARRIER GROUP 3, Rear Admiral F. C. Sherman

BUNKER HILL   Capt. T. B. Jeter

Air Group 17: Same as in Marshalls, plus: —
VF(N)–76 (det. A): 4 F6F–3N Lt. Cdr. E. P. Aurand, except that Lt. G. N. Owens is Squadron Cdr. VT–17.

MONTEREY   Capt. L. T. Hundt

Air Group 30: Same as in Marshalls.

COWPENS   Capt. R. P. McConnell

Air Group 25: Same as in Marshalls.

Battleships, Rear Admiral Willis A. Lee[1]

NORTH CAROLINA, IOWA, NEW JERSEY, MASSACHUSETTS, SOUTH DAKOTA, ALABAMA

Cruisers, Rear Admiral R. C. Giffen

MINNEAPOLIS, NEW ORLEANS

Screen

Desron 46, Capt. C. F. Espe. Same as in Marshalls, plus STERETT with Comdesdiv 15, Cdr. J. L. Melgaard on board, and LANG Cdr. H. Payson.

TF 17, PATROL SUBMARINES, Vice Admiral C. A. Lockwood

SEARAVEN Lt. Cdr. M. H. Dry, SEAL Cdr. H. B. Dodge, SUNFISH Lt. Cdr. E. E. Shelby, SKATE Lt. Cdr. W. P. Gruner, TANG Lt. Cdr. R. H. O'Kane, ASPRO Cdr. W. A. Stevenson, BURRFISH Cdr. W. B. Perkins,

TF 72, Commodore James Fife Jr.

DARTER Cdr. W. S. Stovall, DACE Lt. Cdr. B. D. Claggett.
For Truk Strike: GATO Cdr. R. J. Foley.

[1] Rear Admirals Hustvedt, G. B. Davis and Hanson were on board *Iowa, Massachusetts* and *South Dakota* respectively.

Index

Index

Names of Combatant Ships in SMALL CAPITALS

Names of Merchant Ships, lettered Combatant Ships like I-boats and PTs, and all Japanese *Marus,* in *Italics*

Task Organizations in the Appendices have not been indexed.

A

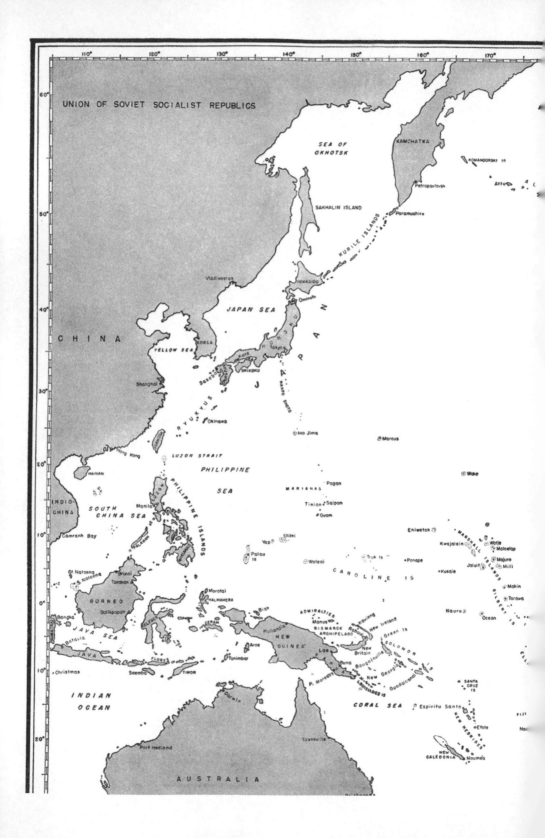

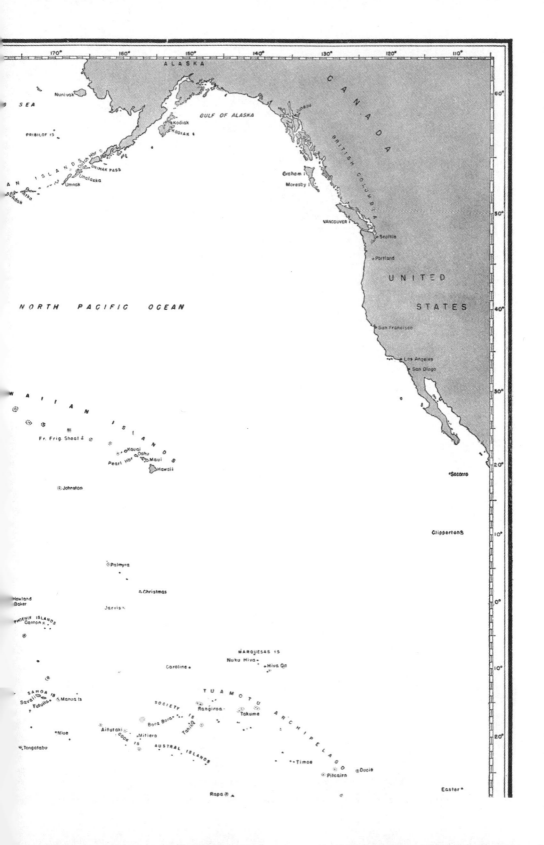

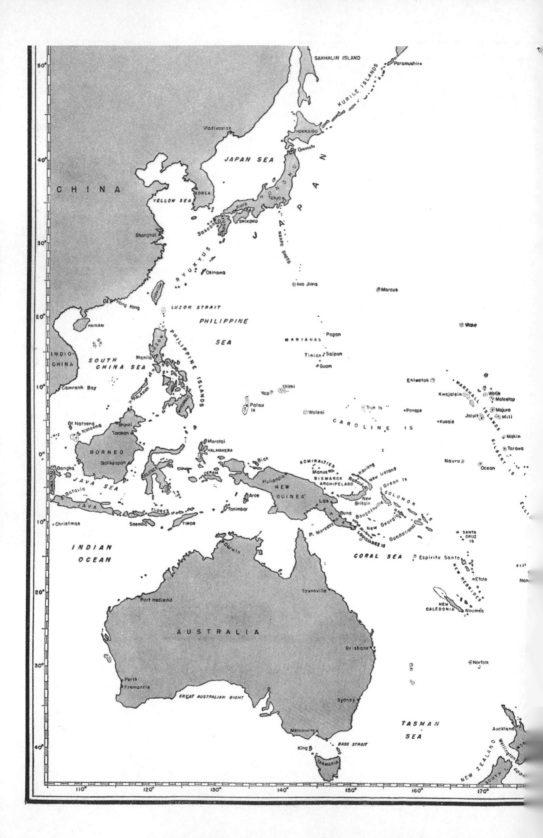

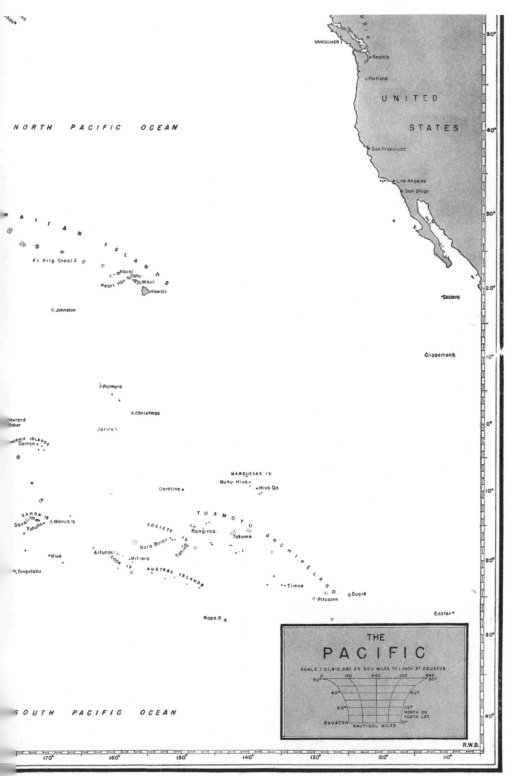

NORTH PACIFIC OCEAN

VANCOUVER I.

Seattle

Portland

UNITED

STATES

San Francisco

Los Angeles
San Diego

50°

40°

30°

HAWAIIAN ISLANDS

Fr. Frig. Shoal

Kauai
Oahu
Pearl Hbr. Maui
Hawaii

Socorro

20°

Johnston

Clipperton

10°

Palmyra

Christmas

Howland
Baker

Jarvis

0°

PHOENIX ISLANDS
Canton

Caroline

MARQUESAS IS
Nuku Hiva
Hiva Oa

10°

SAMOA IS
Savaii
Tutuila Manua Is

SOCIETY IS

Niue

Aitutaki
COOK
Mitiero
IS

Bora Bora
Tahiti

Rangiroa
Takume

TUAMOTU

ARCHIPELAGO

AUSTRAL ISLANDS

20°

Tongatabu

Timoe
Pitcairn

Ducia

Rapa

Easter

30°

THE
PACIFIC

SCALE 1:21,912,092 OR 300 MILES TO 1 INCH AT EQUATOR

0   120   240   360   480
60°   60°

40°   40°

20°   20°
                          NORTH OR
                          SOUTH LAT.
EQUATOR NAUTICAL MILES

SOUTH PACIFIC OCEAN

40°

R.W.B.

170°   160°   150°   140°   130°   120°   110°